Teaching Middle School Mathematics

Teaching Middle School Mathematics

Douglas K. Brumbaugh
University of Central Florida

Enrique Ortiz
University of Central Florida

Gina Gresham
University of Central Florida

LEA

LAWRENCE ERLBAUM ASSOCIATES, PUBLISHERS
2006   Mahwah, New Jersey   London

Senior Acquisitions Editor: Naomi Silverman
Assistant Editor: Erica Kica
Cover Design: Kathryn Houghtaling-Lacey
Full-Service Composition: TechBooks

This book was typeset in 12/14 pt. Helvetica, Bold, Italic and Bold Italic.
The heads were typeset in Futura Medium and Helvetica.

Lawrence Erlbaum Associates, Inc., Publishers
10 Industrial Avenue
Mahwah, New Jersey 07430
www.erlbaum.com

Library of Congress Cataloging-in-Publication Data

Brumbaugh, Douglas K., 1939–
    Teaching middle school mathematics / Douglas K. Brumbaugh, Enrique Ortiz, Gina Gresham.
        p. cm.
    Includes bibliographical references and index.
    ISBN 0-8058-5404-5 (pbk. : acid-free paper)
    1. Mathematics—Study and teaching (Middle school)   I. Ortiz, Enrique, 1955–
II. Gresham, Gina.   III. Title.
    QA11.2.B85 2006
    510.71′273—dc22   2006007717

Printed in the United States of America
10 9 8 7 6 5 4 3 2 1

In loving memory of
Pat and Web Brumbaugh
Ramón and Juana Scott
Ana Celia Reccy-Castro
Enrique Ortiz, Sr.
Laura Norton Harwood

To
Shawn, Mike, Jennifer, and Laura, Doug's kids
Linda Brumbaugh, simply the best
Rosalina Scott, Enrique's mother for her unconditional love
Castro-Reccy for unselfish support
Castro-Mojica for unselfish support
Rivera-Scott for unselfish support
The Daytona Beach extended families for unselfish support
To Enrique Gabriel, Samuel Enrique, and Natalie Marie, Enrique's kids
To Diana Ortiz, patience, perseverance, and kindness are your gifts
Ray Gresham, my beloved husband
Gina's "diddy", Ronnie Harwood, and Mom, Glenda Knowles
My loving, supportive family, Randy, Crispy, Justin, Chloe, Cort, Kevin, Heather, Holly, Chase,
and my god-daughter Madison, whom I adore
Very special friends Brian and the crew for their loving friendship and for believing in me

To all our teachers
To students: past, present, and future

Contents

CONTENTS

Preface

This book is designed to make you, a future teacher of middle school mathematics, think. We have used an informal writing style to dialogue with you. We assume you will think about and do the problems, questions, and activities as you read. Our intent is to have you begin thinking about your future classroom now. We do not expect you to accept all of our ideas, but we do anticipate that you will reflect about them, react to them, blend them with the thoughts of your teacher and peers in this course, blend them with your experiences, and, in the process, begin formulating your own teaching style. We trust you will make informed decisions about how you will approach your teaching career.

We assume you will have had general learning theory and educational methods. This text builds on those, coupled with experiences, specializations, and preferences of your teacher. We provide a collection of examples in a variety of environments to furnish a broad base of ideas that will stimulate the formative development of thoughts and models you will employ in your classroom.

You will see several Your Turn sections that ask you to work with middle school students. We assume that your program offers you the opportunity to do a variety of observations or do internships. If you are not in a setting that has you in a school on a regular, formal basis when you are taking the class using this text, we encourage you to take the time to make a connection on your own and respond to the exercises we present. They are designed to help you think about becoming a professional teacher of mathematics and help you grow in that direction.

You are the major theme of this book. We talk with you. We do not know all the answers. The dialogue between you, your teacher, and us will aid your transition into a teacher of middle school mathematics. We want to motivate you to become a practicing professional who is a lifelong learner. We use technology, reflective-thought questions, mathematical challenges, student life-based applications, games, tricks, and group discussions to stimulate your thinking. These approaches, coupled with the teaching styles you have seen, study and readings in other classes, the interactions in and around the class using this text, and life in general, will all contribute to making you into the teacher you want to become.

ACKNOWLEDGMENTS

All of our teachers, colleagues, and students have helped form us into who we are as professionals. We owe a special thanks to Marie Causey, Michael Minardi, and Peggy Moch, who have taught us so much about the ideas surrounding Data Analysis and Probability. Their influence on chapter 10 of this text cannot be overstated.

Several mathematics education professionals reviewed this manuscript. They provided useful comments, direction, and assistance. We are grateful to Douglas L. Jones, Appalachian State University and Charles E. Lamb, Texas A & M University for their time and effort.

Our editor, Naomi Silverman, was an invaluable motivator. She had the drive and vision to get the whole project started. Without her this book would not exist. Once again, THANKS Naomi.

Erica Kica has proved to be quite useful throughout the entire process. When we had questions, Erica was a fountain of knowledge. Thanks Erica.

People help mold us and what we become. Each person listed here is special. Our family and loved ones are obviously connected to us and have had a tremendous impact on us. Beyond that are all those we have met in the classroom, too countless to name, and yet each has exerted some level of influence on us. To all of you, we say—THANX!

About the Authors

DOUGLAS K. BRUMBAUGH

Depending on how you count, I have been teaching over 45 years. I taught in college, in-service, or K-20 almost daily. I received my BS from Adrian College, and my master's and doctorate in mathematics education from the University of Georgia. Students change, classroom environments change, the curriculum changes, I change. The thoughts and examples in this text are based on my teaching experiences over the years. Classroom-tested success stories from all levels prompted the ideas, materials, and situations you will read about and do. I want these exercises and activities to stretch you while providing a beginning collection of classroom ideas. Learn, expand your horizons, and teach. It is the only way to go!

ENRIQUE ORTIZ

I was born in Raleigh, North Carolina, but grew up in Santurce, Puerto Rico. I traveled to the United States, earning my doctorate at the Louisiana State University in 1987. I now reside in Florida with my wife, two sons, and daughter. From 1976 to 1987, I worked as a middle school teacher of mathematics, curriculum specialist, instructor, and supervisor in Puerto Rico and in the United States. I was an assistant professor for the University of New Orleans from 1987 to 1989. Since 1989, I have been an elementary and middle school mathematics education professor for the University of Central Florida. I am active in the educational community by presenting papers and in-service workshops locally and nationally, developing curriculum materials, writing professional books and articles, teaching methods courses, supervising preservice teachers, advising students in their academic pursuits, doing action research, thesis and dissertation development, and conducting research grants and studies in mathematics education. My major research interests include algebraic thinking, instructional games, professional development, problem solving, and technology. I am certain that the ideas presented in this book will inspire and challenge you to become a star middle school mathematics teacher.

GINA GRESHAM

Wow! How blessed I am! I have been touched by so many people throughout my teaching career: my parents, family, loved ones, friends, students...what an endless list. Many very special people have entered into my life. Many of you know who you are, but one I must particularly thank is my friend, my guide, my supporter, my inspiration, my mentor, "Cap'n" Dougie Brumbaugh. I am so thankful and forever grateful to you! If only I can become half the person you are.

Since 1988, I have been in education. I earned my undergraduate degree from

Jacksonville State University in Gadsden, Alabama. I received my master's, Educational Specialist, and Ph. D. from the University of Alabama in Tuscaloosa. I adopted a motto at a young age and have always had it somewhere, on my wall at home, in my office, in my classroom. It is: "If you believe in yourself and have dedication and pride, you'll be a winner. The price of victory is high, but so are the rewards" (Paul "Bear" Bryant). I hope you can take this motto, combine it with this book, and know and appreciate the rewards of teaching. The job is demanding, but the rewards are priceless. Take this text to heart and challenge each of those you teach with the same desire. Good luck to each of you in your academic endeavors. I will remain with you, Partners in Education!

Teaching Middle School Mathematics

1
Introduction

FOCAL POINTS

- Teaching what mathematics is
- Working at teaching mathematics
- Planning your lessons
- Technology
- Role of mathematics in the world
- Expand concepts or definitions
- Analyze a problem in more than one way
- Use an idea in more than one setting
- Conclusion
- Sticky questions
- TAG (tricks, activities, and games)
- References

Many studies have been conducted to identify the qualities that all good teachers possess. The only two that are consistently identified are warmth and a sense of humor. There is agreement on a need to know the mathematics being taught if one is to be an effective teacher of mathematics. Not all agree that there is a necessity to know about how to teach the mathematics known. Some hold the opinion that if one knows mathematics, one can teach it. This book will focus on the idea that knowing the mathematics is not sufficient to teach it. An effective teacher of mathematics must know the mathematics being taught AND how to present that knowledge in dynamic, interesting, understandable, motivational, and appropriate terms.

If you are not competent and confident with the subject matter, you will struggle to create positive mathematical experiences best suited for students. To that end, you must have the desire to learn mathematics, how to educate the students, and how to supply the optimum mathematics environment for each student. As you continue to investigate new mathematical knowledge and effective teaching strategies, you can stimulate students to follow your lead to new knowledge, each at their respective level and pace. A true teacher is always willing to learn new methods and strategies for introducing concepts to students.

As stated in the National Council of Teachers of Mathematics (NCTM) *Curriculum and Evaluation Standards for School Mathematics* (NCTM, 1989), an effective teacher of mathematics will be able to motivate *all* students to learn mathematics. Similar ideas are raised in NCTM's *Principles and Standards for School Mathematics* (NCTM, 2000). Mathematics opens doors to careers, enables informed decisions, and helps us compete as a nation (Mathematical Sciences Education Board [MSEB], 1989). The only constant today's students will face in their working lives will be change. It is predicted that today's K-12 student will change careers—not jobs—as many as five times, which implies major reeducation. Students must learn to absorb new ideas, adapt to change, cope with ambiguity, perceive patterns, and solve unconventional problems (MSEB, 1989). Without these abilities, today's students will have a difficult time in their working future.

A large segment of our society is willing to make statements like "I hated math in school," "math, yuk," and "I did not do well in math." If someone said, "I cannot read," countless individuals would express sorrow, perhaps pity, and then skirmish to find ways to help that person learn to read. Why is there not such a cry for the one who confesses an inability to do mathematics? It is our commission to set the wheels in motion that will change this attitude.

TEACHING WHAT MATHEMATICS IS

What is mathematics? If we are going to be concerned about teaching mathematics to others, we need some idea of what it is we are teaching. Check the definition of mathematics in a dictionary. Are you comfortable explaining the definition to others? An eminent mathematician once said that he would not be "satisfied with his knowledge of mathematical theory until he could explain it to the next man he met on the street" (Newman, 1956, p. 4). As teachers of mathematics, we are responsible for explaining complex concepts that incorporate real-life mathematical activities, while putting things in words students can relate to and understand. The effective teacher must also emphasize student-centered instruction. The learning environment (social, cognitive, affective, and physical) should be conducive to the optimal learning of each individual.

The preceding paragraph describes a constructivist's approach to teaching mathematics. For the constructivist, students must become active participants in the learning environment. If either the teacher or the student falls short of their responsibility, the net result will be a less-than-satisfactory learning environment. Students need steps of learning that allow for consolidation and success. Students can then practice these steps in groups or alone, with the teacher or other experienced individuals nearby to assist as needed.

No longer can we accept the idea that mathematics is only for the best and brightest. Too many basic mathematical concepts are an integral part of our daily lives. As teachers of mathematics, we must be able to motivate all students to learn. It is our responsibility to create an appropriate atmosphere so that can happen for each and every student. Without such a goal, we, as a nation, risk widening the gap that exists in our society between those who can and cannot do mathematics.

Some say mathematics is a way of thinking. That becomes evident to us as we do proofs, examine patterns, or organize our approaches to new and different problems. Others say mathematics is a language. We can understand that statement as we talk in our special language of Xs and Ys, graphs, and patterns. But, if that language is one spoken only by a select few, what good is it? If we accept that all students are capable of learning mathematics, it is imperative that we include all of them in our inner circle of basic mathematical language. If we reject the premise that all students can learn mathematics, what do we do with those who do not learn the fundamentals of our subject? How do we prepare them to become productive members of our society?

Mathematics is an organized structure of knowledge. If you understand the structure, survival in the world of mathematics is possible. Without the structural understanding, failure, as far as being able to function mathematically, is imminent. Too many students are willing to accept being unable to function mathematically. Did you experience applications of mathematics in real-world settings that were appropriate for your age and interests as you progressed through school? Remember, as you ponder that last question, that you are mathematically oriented. Individuals like those in your class who did not see the applications and understandings are the ones you will be trying to entice into becoming interested in learning mathematics. Far too many students assume there will be no need for mathematics in their future world. How foolish that statement is. Yet, how common it is. If we look through the eyes of students, maybe that statement makes sense. It is our task to get students where they see a need for the power of mathematics in their daily lives. Some instructional strategies to motivate students and prevent math anxiety include the following (partially from Martinez & Martinez, 1996):

Creating an anxiety-free mathematics classroom, which could include different seating arrangements like circles and small groups, where the teacher takes the role of facilitator of learning to help students construct their own knowledge.

Matching instruction to students' cognitive learning level (concrete, pictorial, and abstract).

Planning instruction that connects mathematics to familiar situations in students' everyday lives (context relevant activities).

Incorporating games, humor, and puzzles into mathematics instruction.

Teaching mathematics through reading and writing.

Empowering students by using technology and collaborative or cooperative teaching/learning procedures.

Using peer tutoring as a means of enhancing student learning.

Establishing mentors within the classroom environment to help new students, those who need additional motivation, and so on.

Modeling mathematical thinking and learning by teachers and students.

Incorporating the use of manipulatives into instruction that broaches a new topic.

Mathematics abounds with examples of the study of patterns. It seems natural and useful to those of us who are in the field. How do we communicate that value to our students? For example, the Fibonacci (Leonardo of Pisa, 1175–1230) sequence is 1, 1, 2, 3, 5, 8,..., where each new term is found by listing the sum of the two preceding terms; it supposedly grew out of the study of rabbit reproduction starting with two mature adults, one of each gender. This sequence of numbers appears in a variety of settings. For example, if the clockwise and counterclockwise spirals of a sunflower are counted, the results will always be two successive terms in the Fibonacci sequence. Although Fig. 1.1 is only a partial picture of the center of a Sago Palm, the spirals should be visible to you. Can you see the spirals in the pinecone? There are several Internet sites that show pictures of the spirals. One is http://www.pims.math.ca/education/2000/bus00/sunflower.

A Lucas sequence begins with any two numbers, not one and one, and is built like a Fibonacci sequence. A student writes a 10-term sequence for the class, that the teacher cannot see. The class needs to ensure the addition is correct. When the 10

	Numeric Example	Algebraic Example
	9	x
	4	y
	13	$x + y$
	17	$x + 2y$
	30	$2x + 3y$
	47	$3x + 5y$
	77	$5x + 8y$
	124	$8x + 13y$
	201	$13x + 21y$
	325	$21x + 34y$
Sum	847	$55x + 88y$

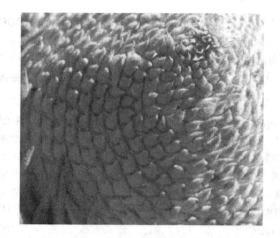

FIG 1.1. Courtesy of Linda S. Brumbaugh

terms are listed, the teacher looks at them and announces the sum of all 10 terms.

This example can be used in several places in the curriculum. Addition practice is not out of the question to be sure the trick worked (Note the beginning of a need for proof.) A more formal proof is in the algebraic approach. The $55x + 88y$ can be expressed as $11(5x + 8y)$. The fourth term from the end in the 10-term sequence is $(5x + 8y)$. Note the distributive property of multiplication over addition on the set of real numbers. Notice how arithmetic, algebra, number properties, and proof are linked in this example. It is important for the mathematical development of your students that you become aware of these connections.

Your Turn

1.1. Determine how the answer to any 10-term Lucas sequence problem can be found quickly.

1.2. Locate some specific applications in nature of the Fibonacci sequence.

1.3. Is there any quick way to find the sum of the first 20 terms of a Lucas sequence? Defend your response.

1.4. If the first two terms of a Lucas sequence are 9 and 4, will the same sum be derived from a sequence starting with a 4, followed by a 9? Why or why not? Develop a series of questions you would use to assist a student in learning this result.

1.5. Is there any set of numbers that could not be used as terms for a Lucas sequence? Defend your answer.

WORKING AT TEACHING MATHEMATICS

How do we work at becoming good teachers of mathematics? There is no definitive list of things that guarantees becoming an effective teacher of mathematics. Attitude and enthusiasm must be considered. If you are not excited about learning and doing mathematics, how can you expect your students to be? If you do not believe that all students can learn mathematics, how do you develop meaningful activities for all students?

Your competency in mathematics is critical. This sounds simple and yet there is not agreement on how many mathematics courses must be taken to provide an adequate background for teaching the subject. Is a collection of mathematical content courses enough? Some programs require a bachelor's degree in mathematics with education courses as a part of a graduate program. Others offer certification as a part of an undergraduate degree program in mathematics education. NCTM and the National Council for Accreditation of Teacher Education (NCATE) have provided guidelines for minimum standards for teacher certification in mathematics. Agree or disagree, but the guidelines are in place.

Effective teachers of middle school mathematics must understand the nature of the students. Investigate their interests and motivations. Knowing how students operate, it becomes your responsibility to use that information to construct lessons that attract their attention and stimulate them to learn. Specific examples are provided throughout this text.

As you consider the nature of the students, it is imperative that you understand how they perceive the world of mathematics. Seeing the world of mathematics through your eyes will not suffice here. You must look at mathematics as your students recognize and experience it. Have you ever heard, or said, something like, "If I had only listened to what my teacher was talking about (<u>you fill in the blank here</u>) when I was in school"? That is the point we are making here. You need to be the bridge or mediator and help students overcome the gap between the more sophisticated mathematical world you know and the mathematical world your students see, which probably consists of procedures, enumerations, and algorithms.

Professionalism cannot be overlooked as you work at being an effective teacher of mathematics. Minimally, you should be a member of NCTM (www.nctm.org), your state mathematics organization (Florida Council of Teachers of Mathematics, FCTM—http://uwf.edu/fctm—for each of the authors of this text), and your local mathematics organization. Membership is not enough. You need to be an active member, attending and presenting at conferences, and subscribing to and reading professional journals. This will stimulate your thinking. It is your responsibility to continue to grow as a professional teacher of mathematics.

An effective teacher of mathematics shows sensitivity to students. This cannot be superficial. You read your teachers when you were in school. Similarly, your students will be able to gauge your sensitivity and sincerity levels.

Part of being sensitive to students relates to readiness, or knowing how ready a student is to complete a learning task. Mowbray and Salisbury (1975) define readiness as "the level of total development that enables a child to learn a behavior, comprehend a concept, or perform a given way with ease" (p. 83). This definition implies that readiness occurs on a continuum and involves students' individual differences influenced strongly by biological development and environmental experiences (Ashlock, Johnson, Wilson, & Jones, 1983). The following is an elaboration of readiness levels. We encourage you to research the topic more extensively.

Content readiness involves students' ability to work with ease on a specific mathematics area. For example, a student who counts objects meaningfully and accurately, effectively demonstrates "take-away" subtraction situation with cubes, knows all or most of the 100 subtraction facts, and understands place value for numbers 9 through 999 has a high degree of content readiness for learning subtraction computation involving two- and three-digit numbers.

Pedagogical readiness considers students' understanding and appropriate use of materials, including objects, pictures, representations of objects, symbols, models, manipulatives, technology, and other instructional materials used to facilitate students' learning of mathematics. For example, in using an algebraic equation to generalize a numerical pattern, some children may not understand the generalization represented by the equation and may not be pedagogically ready for this type of abstraction. They may also need to work with the pattern involving other types of pedagogical materials.

Maturational readiness considers students' natural developmental and cognitive stages and mental ability. For example, it is not appropriate to assume that all sixth-grade students are ready to begin division at the same time. As teachers, we might expect students to know certain mathematical or algebraic concepts and skills, but all students do not have the same level of maturational readiness. In some cases, students might need concrete objects to think with and about.

Affective readiness considers the students' mathematical disposition or motivation, and attitudes toward mathematics. Affective readiness influences the students' success in learning and using mathematics.

Contextual readiness refers to students' awareness of the ways mathematics is used or applied in real-life problem solving, and realization of the importance of mathematics. This aspect of readiness also involves paying close attention to students' backgrounds and interests and incorporating these elements into the teaching/learning activities (Kennedy, Tipps, & Johnson, 2004; Underhill, 1978).

Assuming readiness, if a lesson does not succeed, the first thing you should do is look in the mirror. Did you strive to make the lesson interesting? Was the presentation clear? Were the examples appropriate? Were the students involved in the lesson as it unfolded? Did the students have ample opportunity to seek clarification of the points presented? These questions (and their analysis) will help you construct a more effective learning environment for all students.

Students often perceive the teacher as an answer machine, because they give a direct yes-or-no–type answer to questions. As an alternative, steer inquiries so that students can determine their own answers.

More than likely you have gone home from your mathematics class and tried the homework only to say to yourself that you do not see why you cannot do it. You understood when the teacher discussed it in class. More than likely, the teacher did a problem type and after each step asked you if that procedure made sense. You probably said yes for each step all the way through the problem. But, look at what happened. You followed the teacher through the chosen route, saying yes to each point made by the teacher. How much better would it have been for you to have led the teacher through the process? You would have had more ownership of the process, responsibility for your own leaning, excitement and delight about the discovery and success, and maybe even an "AHA!" or "YES!" exclamation as the light bulb goes on, along with a better chance of remembering and making connections with new ideas. While it may not have been a new discovery for others, if it was for you, excitement abounded! Your students should have opportunities to experience and value those same feelings of ownership, excitement, delight, accomplishment, and success as they learn mathematics.

The message to you is that, as you teach, have the students tell you what to do next in a process rather than you telling them. That way, the students are active rather than passive participants in the learning environment. Refer to the Lucas sequence discussion developed earlier. Would you have investigated why it worked if the algebraic approach had not been given? Would you have connected the factored sum with the seventh term down? Did you expect the answer in the upcoming text? Do you know how to apply Trachtenberg's (Cutler, 1960) multiplication by 11 rule? If self-motivated, lifelong learners are to be generated in your classroom, you have to apply those same principles to your own teaching practice.

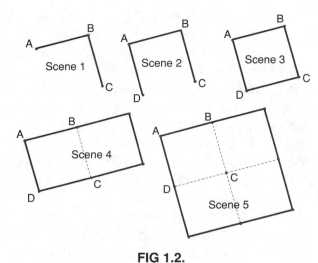

FIG 1.2.

The time to start doing that is now! If you do not walk the walk, how do you justify the talk?

Sample Lesson Idea

Suppose a student is to discover the relation between a squares area and that of a new square after the length of the side of a square is altered. Typically, teachers tell the student that when the side length of a square is doubled, the area is quadrupled; if the side length is tripled, the area is increased by a factor of nine; and so forth.

Use an interactive geometry program.

Draw segment $\overline{AB}$.

Mark endpoint B of the segment as rotation center.

Rotate segment $\overline{AB}$ 90° (scene 1 of Fig. 1.2).

Mark vector BA.

Translate $\overline{BC}$ along vector BA, naming the new endpoint D (scene 2 of Fig. 1.2).

Construct segment $\overline{CD}$ (scene 3 of Fig. 1.2).

(In the following dialogue, T refers to *teacher* and S to *student*.)

T: How can the side length of the square be doubled?

S: Duplicate the square beside itself.

T: How can that be accomplished?

S: Use one side of the square as the mirror and then reflect the rest of the square over it (scene 4 of Fig. 1.2).

T: Is that adequate?

S: No. You need to double the other side too.

T: Why?

S: To make a new square.

T: How can I do that?

S: Mark one long side of the rectangle as the mirror. Then reflect the two squares over it (scene 5 of Fig. 1.2).

T: What has doubling the side of the square done to the original area?

S: The new area is four times that of the original.

T: How do you know that?

This lesson could be extended to tripling the length of the side of the square, or even more as needed. The advantage is that the students can see what is being discussed. Creating a mental image here will help them formulate responses (conjectures and generalizations) to similar future problems.

Your Turn

1.6. If the length of one side of a rectangle is doubled and the other tripled, what is the impact on the area of the rectangle? Does it matter if the roles are reversed as to which side is doubled and which is tripled? Why or why not?

1.7. If the base of a triangle is doubled and the height is quadrupled, what factor is the area multiplied by?

1.8. In a triangle, what factors can be used with the base and height as multiples and still keep the area the same? State a generalization for this situation.

1.9. Given a trapezoid with height h, upper base b_1, and lower base b_2, what is the impact on the area if only the height is doubled? What is the impact on the area if only the length of b_2 is halved? Write a generalization about changing only one of the dimensions of a trapezoid. Don't forget the slant height.

Much mathematics teaching is done via direct instruction, where the teacher is responsible for selecting and directing the learning tasks. Lectures can make a positive contribution to the mathematics classroom if they are dynamic, well planned, and organized. Lecture cannot be the only method of instruction in the classroom. It is the most efficient way for the teacher, but the focus should be on student learning, not convenience for the teacher.

Indirect instruction (guided-discovery or hands-on learning) promotes an increase in critical thinking and problem-solving skills. Students are encouraged to explore and discover information through the use of open-ended questions, group discussions and activities, experiments, and hands-on exercises. Indirect instruction has been shown to improve attitudes toward subject matter, especially for those students with a low success rate with direct instruction. You may never use this approach 100% of the time, but start slowly, maybe with 25% of the time and as you learn increase it to 50% or even 75%. It is worth the time and effort for your students.

Sample Lesson Idea

Why it is necessary to know how to solve an equation like $2x = 6$ for x by showing

$$2x = 6$$
$$\frac{2x}{2} = \frac{6}{2}$$
$$\frac{\overset{1}{\cancel{2}}x}{\cancel{2}} = \frac{\overset{3}{\cancel{6}}}{\cancel{2}}$$
$$\phantom{\frac{1}{1}}_{1}_{1}$$
$$x = 3?$$

Most students will say that the answer is 3, probably based on the knowledge of multiplication facts. The immediate thought might be that there is no application of this process in the real world and, thus, students question the need for learning the process, particularly when the answer seems so obvious. Teachers counter that students need to learn the process to solve more difficult problems. Still, students ask for an application.

Actually, the equation is a variation of $d = rt$, which is used regularly by law enforcement agencies to clock the speed of vehicles. A distance is known, a time is measured, and a rate (speed) is computed. Also, in drag racing, a speed trap is established at the end of the track and $d = rt$ is used to compute the average speed of the car at the end of the quarter- (or eighth-) mile run. In track and field competitions, $d = rt$ is used to determine the average pace of a distance runner. In each of these applications, the distance is known, as is the time required to cover it. Thus, there is a need to compute r, which equals $\frac{d}{t}$. The process is the same as that used to solve $2x = 6$ for x, but the numbers are not so convenient, which mandates a basic understanding of the process to achieve a solution. We used a basic idea to show some appealing applications of mathematics in the real world. Although the applications might be appealing to us, as adults, it is imperative that they appeal to the students.

Your Turn

1.10. Describe at least two different real-world applications that involve the mathematics covered in the middle school curriculum.

1.11. Use a source like Newman's *The World of Mathematics* (1956), the *VNR Concise Encyclopedia of Mathematics* (Geliert, Kustner, Hellwich, & Kastner,

1977), or Eves' *History of Mathematics* (1967) to investigate a mathematical topic found in the middle school setting. You are to learn a new way of working with the topic. Present your conclusions in written form, giving appropriate bibliographic credit.

The sample lesson ideas we have presented so far have been informal ideas. They are a start, but there is a need for a more formal approach to planning, particularly at the beginning of your career. The concept of detailed planning will be developed in the Communication chapter of this book.

TECHNOLOGY

Wherever we start with technology, by the time you read this, it will be outdated because things are changing so fast. Let us start with some assumptions:

You are familiar with, and use regularly, a word processor.

You have an email account.

You can use a spreadsheet.

You have learned how to use presentation software.

You are able to create and manipulate databases.

We will focus on more mathematically specific applications, which you will see us use throughout this text. We will deal with dynamic, interactive software and avoid canned programs or games that perform a specific task or are aimed at a particular objective. Please do not take this avoidance as a judgment on our part about any software that is not listed here. We have opted to focus only on dynamic programs because they are more universal in their applicability and do not become outdated as fast.

Geometry Software

There are several examples of interactive geometry software on the market, which can be used to create intuitive feelings for what eventually will become proofs. For example, suppose the midpoints of the sides of any quadrilateral are joined in order by line segments. What will the resultant quadrilateral be? Figure 1.3 shows how interactive geometry software can be used to establish an informal idea of the answer. The figure made up of the thick segments looks like a parallelogram, which is confirmed by the measurements of the lengths of the opposite sides. Although middle schoolers may not know about slopes yet, those in algebra might and so we also show the slopes. A more formal proof can be established by considering $\triangle$ EFG: $\overline{AB}$ is half as long as $\overline{EG}$ because A and B are midpoints of sides $\overline{EF}$ and $\overline{FG}$, respectively. A geometry theorem states, "if a segment is formed by joining the midpoints of two sides of a triangle, that segment is half as long as the third side, and parallel to it." Because it must be the case that $\overline{CD}$ is also half as long as $\overline{EG}$, it must be the case that $\overline{AB}$ and $\overline{CD}$ are the same length. Similar logic will get $\overline{AD}$ and $\overline{BC}$ to be the same length. It is known that a quadrilateral with opposite sides of the same length is a parallelogram.

It could be shown that the segments parallel to the side of the triangle functioning as a diagonal of the quadrilateral have the same slope, again creating a parallelogram. Or, one pair of sides can be shown to be congruent and parallel to each other, again establishing a parallelogram. Any of these approaches are stimulated by the measures shown in Fig. 1.3. So, the intuitive backgrounds lead to a formal proof.

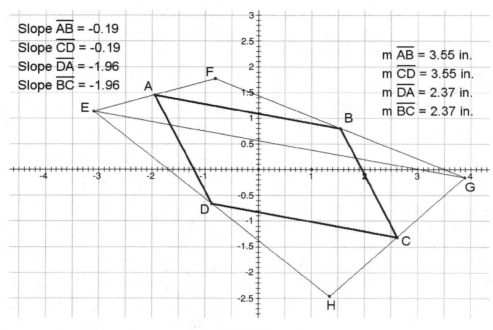

Slope $\overline{AB}$ = -0.19
Slope $\overline{CD}$ = -0.19
Slope $\overline{DA}$ = -1.96
Slope $\overline{BC}$ = -1.96

m $\overline{AB}$ = 3.55 in.
m $\overline{CD}$ = 3.55 in.
m $\overline{DA}$ = 2.37 in.
m $\overline{BC}$ = 2.37 in.

FIG 1.3.

Your Turn

1.12. Duplicate Fig. 1.3 using interactive geometry software. Move the vertices and sides. Move vertex F so that $\overline{AB}$ appears to coincide with $\overline{CD}$. Do you think this could be another way to informally establish that ABCD is a parallelogram? Why or why not?

1.13. Create a situation using interactive geometry software that includes animation to establish the idea for students that respective alternate interior, alternate exterior, and corresponding angles are congruent.

Algebra Software

As with the geometry software, there are several dynamic algebra systems available. Prices range from free to hundreds of dollars and capabilities vary from quite limited to limitless. You should consider a piece that will graph and also show the steps as an answer to a problem is generated. Although we will discuss calculators in a separate section, there is one calculator, Casio FX 2.0 that will graph and show steps for a solution (http://www.casio.com). Texas Instrument's Voyage 200 (http://education.ti.com/us/product/graphing.html) will also function like some algebra software, but since it has a QWERTY keyboard, some argue about it being called a calculator. Graphing calculators will do algebra-type things but typically do not show steps for the solution.

Considering graphing, the dynamic algebra software used for Fig. 1.4 can be used to introduce topics students have not seen before. In the process, rather than being passive, the student becomes an active participant in the learning environment. Suppose the students are not familiar with the impact of the coefficient of x in an equation like y = mx + 2. Two equations could be graphed: y = 3x + 2 and y = 4x + 2. The discussion would first focus on the similarities and differences between the two graphed lines, which should lead to the idea that one is steeper than the other. Then the discussion could be shifted discussing similarities and differences between the two equations, which should

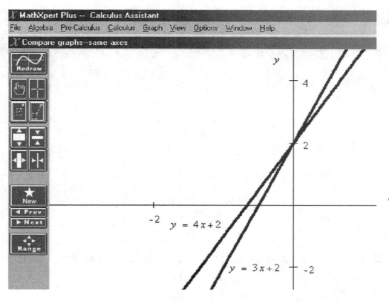

FIG 1.4.

to lead to the idea that the number in front of the x is the only thing that is changed. Add more equations, one at a time to get Fig. 1.5, with a recycling of the discussion about the graphs and equations similarities and differences until someone concludes that the coefficient of x indicates the steep-ness of the graph. At this point, the discussion needs to be finalized and slope would be introduced as the word that is commonly used to describe what has been concluded.

Suppose your students have no idea how to solve equations of the form:

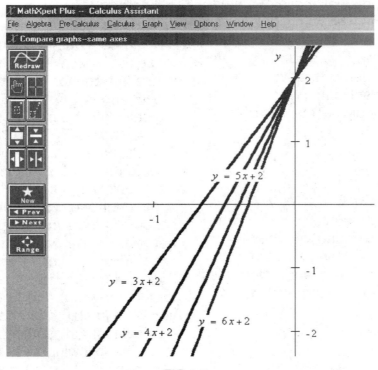

FIG 1.5.

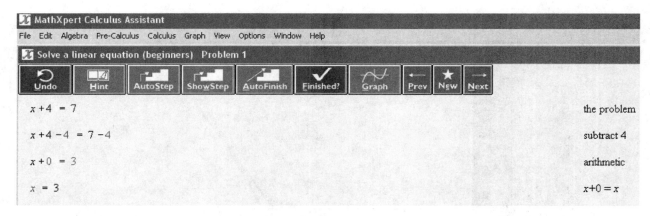

FIG 1.6.

x + 4 = 9. Although there are several ways to approach this, one way could be through technology that shows each step. After doing several examples, the student could be asked for conclusions. In the process of summarizing, they could uncover the ideas teachers have traditionally told students about how to do these problems. Again, the student is an active participant as opposed to being passive in the learning environment. Notice in Fig. 1.6 that, for each step made, a reason is given. Observe that things are done one small move at a time, thus helping anyone who wants to learn to see how to work the problem. The number of examples needed to provide adequate information for students to develop rules that will help them solve this type problem will vary, but you should get the idea of what needs to be done.

Your Turn

1.14. The problem x + 4 = 7 can be done using online sources. One example is algebra.help found at http://www.algebrahelp.com. Click on calculators under the Students heading and select the Equation Calculator. Using it, you will see the following:

Equation as entered:

$$x + 4 = 7$$

Subtract 4 from each side:

$$
\begin{aligned}
+\,x + 4 &= +7 \\
-4 & -4 \\
x &= 3 \\
1x &= 3
\end{aligned}
$$

Use this online source to develop a lesson that would use the technology to lead students to generalize a set of rules for solving equations like 5x + 9 = 17.

Calculators

Although there are several calculators on the market, we will focus on two types: those that work with fractions and give answers in terms of fractions (like the Casio FX-65 and the TI-15 Explorer) and graphing calculators aimed at middle schoolers (like the Casio FX7400 G PLUS and the TI-73). Ultimately students will need to graduate to the more complex graphing calculators on the market.

Although we would love to say middle school students are adept at working with fractions, we know that is not always the case. Suppose your class needs to learn how to add fractions (something that is far too common) and further assume that you want to start at a nonconcrete point in the development, settling on using calculators. The following sequence of problems can lead to some surprising conclusions and, in the process, the students should learn how to add fractions. It is understood that some of the students will have mastered the skills being discussed here, but for the sake of conversation we will assume they are not involved in this development. We will present options for dealing with them at other points throughout this text.

Starting with unit fractions (numerator must be 1) and focusing on denominators that are relatively prime (only common factor is 1), give the students several fractions to add on the calculator. Each fraction problem and its sum should be recorded, after working them on the calculator. Each student's paper should look something like

$$\frac{1}{3} + \frac{1}{4} = \frac{7}{12}$$

$$\frac{1}{3} + \frac{1}{5} = \frac{8}{15}$$

$$\frac{1}{2} + \frac{1}{3} = \frac{5}{6}$$

$$\frac{1}{4} + \frac{1}{5} = \frac{9}{20}$$

After doing a sufficient number, ask the students if they notice any patterns. They should report that the product of the denominators in each example gives the denominator for the sum. Next comes the surprised-toned statement that if the denominators of the addends are added, the result is the numerator in the sum. After that comes a discussion that culminates with the statement that the process does not always work. Yet, with a slight alteration along with some well-placed questions and comments from you, they will discover a surprising disclosure.

Again, have the students do a select set of problems on the calculator, keeping the denominators relatively prime. This time though, use one unit fraction and one nonunit fraction. Although the students would do and record several problems like that in the preceding discussion, here we focus on one example to help clarify the situation. Consider $\frac{1}{4} + \frac{2}{3}$, which according to the calculator is $\frac{11}{12}$. The students will conclude that all the rules developed with unit fractions do not work, but that the product of the denominators of the addends is still the denominator in the sum. Ask how they got the numerator before. Then ask if there is a way to get to 11 by adding combinations of 3 and 4. We know $3 + 4$ does not work. We see that $3 + 3 + 4$ does not work. However, $4 + 4 + 3$ gives a sum of 11. Another way of saying that is that two 4s and a 3 works. But that could be stated as $2(4) + 3 = 11$. Look again at $\frac{1}{4} \ast \frac{2}{3}$, this time concentrating on the segments joining the digits and you see $(2)(4) + (1)(3)$. Some people teach this routine as a method for determining the numerator of the sum of two fractions with relatively prime denominators, but without any of the explanation you have seen grow out of the calculator example.

Although we still have not done all fraction examples, you should see how a calculator that operates with fractions could be used as a tool to teach this information. Once again, the emphasis is on having the student be an active rather than a passive learner. In the process developed here, light is shed on why the rule that has been used works.

Most graphing calculators have built-in statistics capabilities, something we will assume for this activity. Your pulse rate measures the number of beats your heart makes per minute. To take a pulse, one could count for 6 seconds and multiply by 10 but that could insert considerable error into the results. One could count for 60 seconds but that takes more time. Generally the beats are counted for 15 seconds and that result is multiplied by four. This is

TABLE 1.1

	Pulse taken by girl	Pulse taken by boy
1		
2		
3		
Average		

TABLE 1.3

Name	Height in inches	Wrist in inches
Curly	60	6.1
Goofy	66	6.8
Larry	63	6.2
Mo	70	7.3
Schmo	63	6.3

a happy medium between efficiency and accuracy.

Each person should have their pulse taken by three people of the same gender and three people of the opposite gender. Each student should record results using something like Table 1.1.

Extend by examining a graph of the results, but with some additional activity. For this, you might elect to use a few volunteers as sources of data. Repeat this activity of having the pulse recorded while the volunteer is at rest, after the volunteer has walked slowly, after the volunteer has walked briskly, and after the volunteer has trotted. Results should be recorded for a participant in something similar to Table 1.2. All students could insert the data from the table into their graphing calculators and show different representations of the information.

Your Turn

1.15. Develop a lesson, similar to the one for adding unit fractions, for subtracting unit fractions using a calculator that operates with fractions, giving results as a fraction.

1.16. Develop a lesson that would have students show results of some collection

of data as a histogram on a graphing calculator.

Statistics Software

Although the correlation will not be exact, it is reasonable to expect that we could be able to predict height given wrist size. Suppose the information in Table 1.3 is known.

Figure 1.7 shows this table along with a related scatter plot.

A moveable line can be inserted onto the graph and its equation will show. As it is moved, the equation changes in real time. The line can be moved, as shown in Fig. 1.8, until one assumes it is representative of the data. At that point, one would have an approximate formula for predicting height from wrist circumference or vice versa.

We believe what NCTM says in *Standards 2000* about data analysis and probability needing to become a strand of emphasis throughout the curriculum. Given that, you need to think of ways to create opportunities for your students to investigate this new and exciting area of mathematical emphasis. Interactive statistics software provides an avenue for you to do that. You must take the time to learn it (and all the other technological venues available to

TABLE 1.2

	Student 1	Student 2	Student 3	Student 4
Rest				
Walk				
Brisk Walk				
Trot				

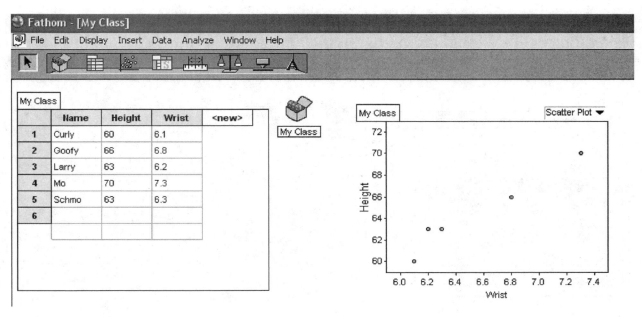

FIG 1.7.

you). One nice thing you might investigate is that, as you change values in a table, the associated graph changes accordingly, in real time. Similarly, Fig. 1.9 shows a data point moved from where it was in Fig. 1.7, and the resultant change in the table, again in real time. Notice how the rightmost point has been dragged down and to the left of where it was initially. Notice also that Mo's height and wrist size have changed to reflect the move. The proposed line of best fit would now need to be changed too, giving a different equation.

The bottom line is that you need to learn to use technology as a teaching/learning tool. The only way that is going to happen is for you to make a commitment to acquire the necessary tools and also to take the time to learn them. You may not feel comfortable with your technology knowledge and thus resist using it with a class. The members of the author team for this text were teaching before technology beyond the overhead projector was known. We have learned. You can do it. It is your professional responsibility. A great way to start is to do each of the examples and exercises in this section of this text. As you go through this book, you will see many more examples and sketches created with technology. Work through them. By the end of this semester, you will be operating like a technological pro. Have fun!

Your Turn

1.17. Measure the height and wrist size of the members of your class in centimeters. Record the information in a table in interactive statistics software and graph it.

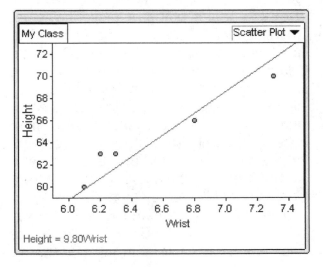

FIG 1.8.

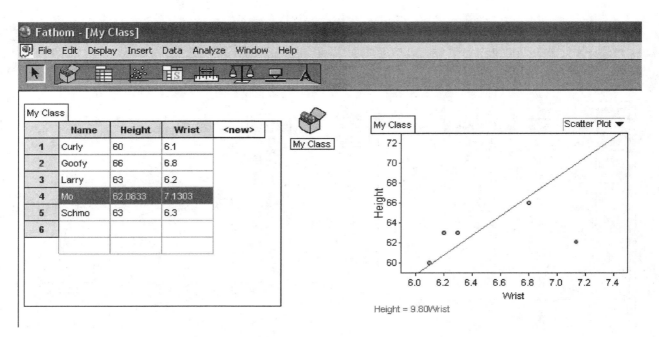

FIG 1.9.

What is the equation generated to predict height from wrist circumference or vice versa? Would the results be different if the measurements were taken in inches?

ROLE OF MATHEMATICS IN THE WORLD

Students often struggle to see real-world applications. For some, mathematics is a dead subject that has not changed over the years. Many of them see mathematics as something chipped onto stone tablets and handed down from a mountain. Far too often students perceive that mathematics is understandable only by the very brightest individuals. We must change these impressions.

Students want to know where the things they are learning are used. That is not an unreasonable expectation, and it is something the NCTM *Standards* repeatedly call for. Granted, we cannot provide a real-world example for each daily topic, but the more we do it, the more credibility mathematics has in the eyes of the students.

Where can one look for real-world application ideas? We all have interests, hobbies, experiences, and imaginations. Combine those and you start to see applications of mathematics. Look carefully at student interests to find applications that could be used in the classroom.

For example, students who play or follow sports could be asked to explain how to calculate certain statistics and their meaning, or keep various statistics on games: a batting average, an earned run average, a quarterback's rating, a player's 3-point shooting percentage, scoring in bowling, lap times in track, and so on. Students could survey people for preferences on soft drinks, junk food, healthy food, music, TV viewing habits, favorite course at school, most desirable skateboard, most recent CD purchased, and so on. Problems or class projects could be developed and solved based on the data from the different sources or collected by students.

The history of mathematics shows a variety of applications. Sometimes the application itself is useful in the classroom.

Sometimes the story of the individuals involved could be used to attract student attention to mathematics and how it developed over the years. That development could lead to additional applications. Many historic topics could be inserted into the middle school curriculum. Examples such as the following might appeal to middle schoolers.

Sonja Kovalevsky was born January 15, 1850, and at the age of 11 was introduced to the study of advanced mathematics because her bedroom was wallpapered with pages of her father's calculus notes. She was the most distinguished female mathematician prior to the 20th century. Barred from pursuing advanced studies in a Russian university because she was female, Kovalevsky contracted a nominal marriage to be free of parental objection to studying abroad. She arrived in Berlin in 1870 but found the university adamant in its exclusion of female students. She accordingly approached Weierstrass directly, who, upon receiving a strong recommendation from Konigsberger, accepted her as a private student. She soon became Weierstrass' favorite pupil. In 1874, she was awarded the degree of Doctor of Philosophy by Gottingen University. From 1884, until her death (February 10, 1891), she served as a professor of higher mathematics at Stockholm University. Her motto was, "Say what you know, do what you must, come what may."

What famous American statesman, diplomat, author, scientist, and printer, was interested in magic squares and magic circles? Benjamin Franklin.

What was the pseudonym that brought the mathematician Charles Lutwidge Dodgson to fame? Although he was a professor of mathematics at Oxford University, the world knows him better as Lewis Carroll, the author of his Alice books.

What mathematician's mother probably saved his life by licking his wounded head for days? Twelve-year-old Nicolo Tartaglia was seriously wounded when the French sacked Brecia on February 19, 1512. The boy suffered several saber cuts that split his skull in 3 places and cleft his jaws and palate. He was left for dead but his mother found him and managed to carry him off. Recalling that a dog, when wounded, licks the injured place, she licked the boy's head for days. He ultimately recovered but the injury to his palate left him with a speech impediment, and it was from this that he received his nickname of Tartaglia, the stammerer. The "g" in Tartaglia is silent so his name also appears as Tartalea.

Writing February 20, 2002, in European style (day, month, year) and using a 24-hour clock yields a rare result. Two minutes past the 20th hour on the 20th would be written 20:02 20/02 2002 or 200220022002. This palindrome is rare, but not unique. A similar situation happened in 1111 A.D. and will happen again in 2112 A.D.

What is arithmetically special about leap years? In the Gregorian calendar every year that is divisible by four is a leap year. However, there is an exception. A multiple of four is a leap year unless it is divisible by 100. The exception is extended to 400; if the year is divisible by 400, it is a leap year. So, 2000 was a leap year. If you live to see 2100, it will not be a leap year because, although 2100 is divisible by 100, 2100 is not divisible by 400.

Which president of the United States was the most mathematically inclined? Thomas Jefferson. He did much to encourage the teaching of higher mathematics in the United States, and during his two terms of office he repeatedly sponsored government support of science. Around 1790, before France adopted the newly created metric systems, he proposed a uniform system of measurement for the United States. He also exhibited mathematical knowledge as an architect in the designing of his home at Montecello and of much of the University of Virginia, an institution of higher learning founded by him.

James Abram Garfield, the country's 20th president, developed a keen interest and fair ability in elementary mathematics. It was in 1876, while he was a member of the House of Representatives and five years before he became President of the United States, that he independently discovered a very pretty proof of the Pythagorean theorem. It should be noted that there are over 370 different ways to show the Pythagorean theorem.

How are π and Albert Einstein related? Einstein was born on March 14, or 3.14, which is one approximation commonly used for π. Einstein has been the most popular mathematical scientist of modern times. He was born in Ulm, Germany, but became a citizen of the United States in 1940. It should be noted that Howard Eves (the source of all of these historical comments) and Einstein were friends. Eves has published a collection of his Einstein stories: Eves, Howard. *Mathematical Reminiscences.* Washington, DC. The Mathematical Association of America, 2001 (ISBN 0-88385-535-6).

All of the preceding historical vignettes were from a personal conversation between Howard Eves and Doug Brumbaugh in Oviedo Florida on January 10, 2002. Professor Eves was born on January 10 and died June 6, 2004, in his beloved Maine.

Your Turn

1.18. Describe mathematical applications or extensions related to a hobby or personal interest you have.

1.19. Select something from the history of mathematics and describe how mathematics was created or refined to meet a need. Your description should be in a form that could be used to attract the attention of a middle school student.

EXPAND CONCEPTS OR DEFINITIONS

Reduce is a common term in discussions about fractions, particularly in the early grades. When a fraction is reduced, common factors are being divided out of both the numerator and denominator. You know that the two fractions are equivalent. How much verbiage and conceptualization can be expected of students? The answer to that question has to influence decisions on when to introduce concepts or expand them.

A student would not be expected to rationalize an algebraic expression without prior exposure to fractions and many other prerequisite skills. That is clear. By the same token, it is fairly clear that you would not expect a student to do standard long division problems without abilities in estimation, place value, multiplication, and subtraction.

In some areas the decision is not as clear. Data analysis and probability are being inserted into the K-12 curriculum. When topics are inserted, prerequisite skills must be defined. Elementary students are capable of arranging numbers in increasing or decreasing order. Does that mean it is appropriate to insert the concept of median into the elementary school curriculum? After learning to divide, students are asked to average their grades. Is it appropriate at that time to enter into discussions about mean? If you say no to those questions for elementary students, would you agree to their insertion into the middle school curriculum? Figure 1.10 shows

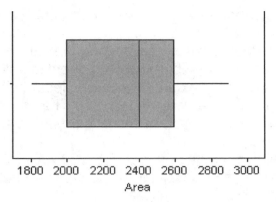

FIG 1.10.

a box and whisker plot. Is this an appropriate topic for the middle school curriculum?

ANALYZE A PROBLEM IN MORE THAN ONE WAY

Consider the classical way of having a class deal with learning a new concept. The formula is given and a few examples are done. Then practice problems are assigned. The problems are all essentially the same; they just use different counting numbers, fractions, decimals, or a combination of elements of the real numbers. How much better it would be if, rather than assigning 20 similar problems, only 5 were given, with the expectation that they be solved more than one way. For example, suppose one third of an individual's income is spent on housing, another third is spent on transportation and education, and 25% is spent on food and entertainment. The individual has $200 left for saving, giving, investing, and shopping. How much does the individual make a month? Algebraically, a solution could be determined through the equation

$$\frac{x}{3} + \frac{x}{3} + \frac{x}{4} = x - \$200$$

where x represents the monthly income. Solving, $\$200 = \frac{x}{12}$, which gives that $x = \$2400$.

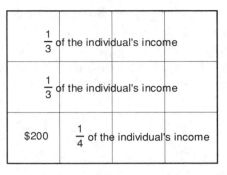

FIG 1.11.

Figure 1.11 shows how that same problem could be done geometrically. The total income (big rectangle) is divided into thirds horizontally and into fourths vertically. The net result is a total of 12 congruent squares, 4 of which represent a third and 3 of which represent a fourth. There is one square left after the fourth and both thirds are represented. But, we know that the leftover money is $200. Because there are 12 congruent squares, the total income must be 12 × $200 = $2400. The problem is solved a second way and the versatility of the student should be enhanced.

Consider another problem to be done more than one way. Nine playing cards are arranged as shown in Fig. 1.12 so five are side by side with the longer edge vertical and four are side by side with the longer edge horizontal. The large rectangle, formed by the nine cards, has an area of 180 square units. What are the dimensions of the cards, assuming they are all congruent?

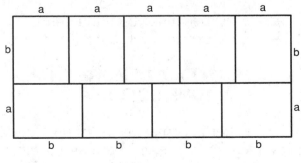

FIG 1.12.

The rectangle is 5a long and $(a + b)$ high. The area is $5a(a + b)$. So, it must be the case that $5a(a + b) = 180$ square units. But, it is also true that $5a = 4b$ from the two long horizontal dimensions, giving $b = \frac{5a}{4}$.

Substituting in $5a(a + b)$ gives $5a\left(a + \frac{5a}{4}\right) = 5a\left(\frac{9a}{4}\right)$. So, $180 = \frac{45a^2}{4}$, which yields $a = \pm 4$ units. Because a card side cannot be negative, the width of the card is 4 units. Substituting in $b = \frac{5a}{4}$, $b = 5$ units, the length of the card.

This same problem could be solved by initially dividing 180 by 9 because it is known that the cards are congruent. The area has to be 20 square units $= ab$. The ratio of length to width would still be $b = \frac{5a}{4}$, and the rest of the solution would be the same.

In both examples, one problem is solved two different ways. Having students do the same routine over and over can create narrow, nonflexible thinking. Conversely, asking students to solve a problem more than one way helps create divergent thinkers. More than likely you have encountered an impasse point on some problem you were trying to solve. When you backed up and started over, you probably ended up at the same impasse point again and again. If you had done problems more than one way in your developmental stages, it could be that, when you started over, your attack on the problem would have been different. Perhaps you would have solved it with the second try, because you had been stimulated to become a divergent thinker.

USE AN IDEA IN MORE THAN ONE SETTING

A computer is sometimes described as a collection of light switches that are either on or off. This leads to a description of how base 2 is involved in computer development.

Base 2 is also an integral part of an interesting number trick. A student is asked to select a counting number less than a given value (we will use 32). The student is then shown a series of cards, one at a time, each of which will have some, but not all, of the values less than 32 on it. The student is to say yes if the selected number is on the card, and no if it is not. After a response is given for each card in the set, you can tell the student the selected number.

Card A	Card B	Card C	Card D	Card E
16	8	4	2	1
17	9	5	3	3
18	10	6	6	5
19	11	7	7	7
20	12	12	10	9
21	13	13	11	11
22	14	14	14	13
23	15	15	15	15
24	24	20	18	17
25	25	21	19	19
26	26	22	22	21
27	27	23	23	23
28	28	28	26	25
29	29	29	27	27
30	30	30	30	29
31	31	31	31	31

If the student selects 31, the answers for cards A, B, C, D, and E would be yes, yes, yes, yes, and yes, respectively. The cards do not have to be shown in any given order, but all cards must be shown. The top value on each card is added if yes is the response. Those values are each whole number powers of 2. Thirty-one is written in base 2 notation as

$$2^4\ 2^3\ 2^2\ 2^1\ 2^0$$
$$31\ \ \ 1\ \ 1\ \ 1\ \ 1\ \ 1$$

Notice there is a 1 in the respective column of the base 2 representation of 31, and 31 appears on each card. Suppose the selected number was 26 which would be written in base 2 as

$$
\begin{array}{cccccc}
 & 2^4 & 2^3 & 2^2 & 2^1 & 2^0 \\
26 & 1 & 1 & 0 & 1 & 0
\end{array}
$$

In this case, for cards A, B, C, D, and E the responses would be yes, yes, no, yes, and no, respectively, indicating the selected number is $A + B + D$ or $16 + 8 + 2 = 26$. Thus, the generalization would be that if there is a 1 in a base 2 representation of the selected number, that number would appear on the card designating that column.

This same base 2 trick can be done with cards configured a different way. The values that go on each respective card are the same, but each card is a square. In addition, each card will have at least one rectangular (remember, squares are rectangles) hole in it. Each card will have yes (Y) or no (N) written on it once. The cards are arranged vertically in a stack with the Y or N facing the ceiling as the students respond (assuming they all know the same secret number). After the final card is placed, the back of the entire stack is shown to the student. The selected number will be the only one showing through a square hole.

The cards are shown in Fig. 1.13, and it should be noted that the last card has values on both sides and no holes in it. For each of cards 1 through 4, the shaded region indicates a hole in the card. For cards 1 through 5, the Y and N indicate how the card is to be oriented in the stack as the students respond Yes or No to whether the secret number is on the card shown. If 19 is the selected value, then card 1, card 2, and card 4 would have the Y oriented toward the ceiling in the stack and card 3 and card 5 would have the N oriented toward the ceiling. When the cards are configured, card 5 must be closest to you as you hold them all so the class can see the bottom of the stack.

Your Turn

1.20. Make a set of cards like those described for the values less than 32, but make your set for all values less than 64.

1.21. Make a set of "hole" cards for values less than 32 and demonstrate the trick to a middle school class. Write a summary of the class reaction.

CONCLUSION

What must an effective teacher of mathematics know and do? The list of items is much longer than what is here, but the following collection of things should help you pursue your goal of becoming the best teacher of mathematics you can be. You should:

Know more than the subject you are teaching.

Motivate your students to want to learn the subject at hand.

Communicate your knowledge to students in words they can understand and that are meaningful to them in their world.

Guide your students to new heights of thinking.

Show your students paths that will lead them to greater insights in mathematics.

Know what to teach when.

Perceive when and why students are having difficulties.

Determine how to make concepts meaningful.

Decide when and how to practice skills.

Figure out how to stimulate productive thinking.

Read mathematics literature and insert it into class instruction.

Do more than just teach the subject.

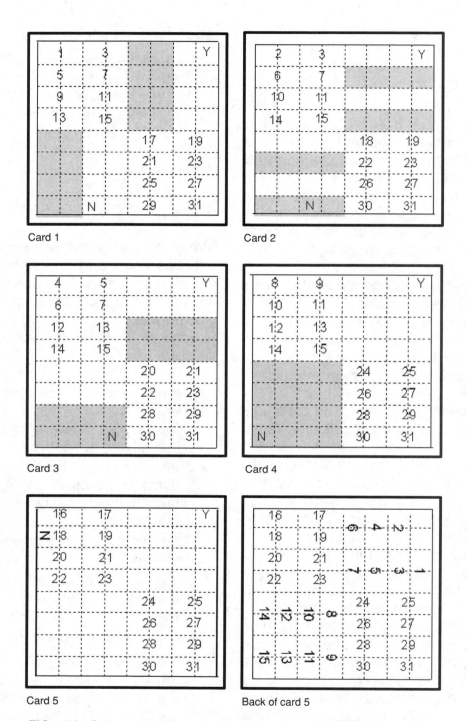

FIG 1.13. Orient top edge of card 5 so 16 from the back is at top-left corner. If you maintain the orientation of card 5 and its back as shown here and glue them together, the alignment will be correct.

Select appropriate goals.

Stimulate the learning of mathematics.

Develop desirable attitudes and mathematics appreciation in yourself.

Develop desirable attitudes and mathematics appreciation in your students.

Develop the ability to solve mathematical problems.

Develop the ability to solve mathematical problems in your students.

Build understanding, accuracy, and efficiency.

Provide opportunities for students at all development levels in your classes.

Evaluate new curriculum proposals.

Get, evaluate, and use audiovisual aids.

Get, evaluate, and use the latest technology as a teaching and learning tool.

Diagnose.

That is only a beginning. This text provides you with ideas you can add to that list and solutions to many of the questions you generate about teaching mathematics at the middle school level.

STICKY QUESTIONS

1.1. Will you further your education if your school does not foot the bill?

1.2. Will you attend professional conferences if your school does not pay your expenses?

1.3. What will you do if your administration does not support the use of technology in the mathematics classroom (calculator or computer)?

1.4. What is the maximum number of students you can effectively teach in a middle school mathematics classroom?

1.5. How can you become better versed in the use of technology as a teaching/learning tool?

TAG (TRICKS ACTIVITIES GAMES)

1.1. What symbol comes next in the sequence?

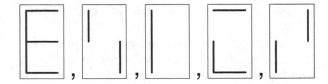

1.2. How do you multiply any two numbers whose ones digits sum to 10 and the rest of the digits are the same in both factors (143×147, 52×58) the fast way (excluding calculators)?

1.3. How do you square a number ending in 3 fast (excluding calculator)?

1.4. Place the first 10 counting numbers, one each on a card. Arrange the cards so that when you start with the top card and spell the number word "one," moving a card to the bottom of the stack for each letter said, after the card for "e" is moved to the bottom of the stack the numeral 1 is showing. Remove the 1. Spell "two," and after the third card is placed on the bottom of the stack the numeral card 2 is showing. Remove it. Continue through all 10 counting numbers, spelling each and removing the card associated with the word spelled. What is the original sequence of cards that makes this work?

1.5. How can the following be done? From 6 take away 9; from 9 take away 10; from 40 take away 50 and when you are done, have 6 left.

1.6. Why does a piece of bread with peanut butter and jelly on one side land bread side up when it slides off a kitchen counter?

1.7. When does $10 + 4 = 2$?

REFERENCES

Ashlock, R. B., Johnson, M. L., Wilson, J. W., & Jones, W. L. (1983). *Guiding each child's learning of mathematics: A diagnostic approach to instruction.* Columbus, OH: Charles E. Merrill.

Crouse, R. J., & Sloyer, C. W. (1977). *Mathematical questions from the classroom.* Boston: Prindie, Webber & Schmidt.

Cutler, A. (1960). *The Trachtenbergspeed system of basic mathematics.* Garden City, NY: Doubleday.

Eves, H. (1967). *An introduction to the history of mathematics* (Rev. ed.). New York: Holt, Reinhart, and Winston.

Geliert, W., Kustner, H., Hellwich, M., & Kastner, H. (1977). *VNR concise encyclopedia of mathematics.* New York: Van Nostrand Reinhold.

Kennedy, L. M., Tipps, S., & Johnson, A. (2004). *Guiding children's learning of mathematics* (10th ed.), Belmont, CA: Wadsworth.

Martinez, J. G. R., & Martinez, N. C. (1969). *Math without fear.* Needham Heights, MA: Allyn and Bacon.

Mathematical Sciences Education Board. (1989). *Everybody counts.* Washington, DC: National Academy Press.

Mowbray, J. K., & Salisbury, H. (1975). *Diagnosing individual needs for early childhood education.* Columbus, OH: Charles E. Merrill.

National Council of Teachers of Mathematics (2000). *Principles and Standards for School Mathematics.* Reston, VA: Author

National Council of Teachers of Mathematics. (1989). *Curriculum and evaluation standards for school mathematics.* Reston, VA: Author.

Newman, J. R. (1956). *The world of mathematics* (Vol. 1). New York: Simon and Schuster.

Underhill, R. B. (1978). Classroom diagnosis. In J. I. Higgins & J. W. Heddens (Eds.). *Remedial mathematics: Diagnostic and prescriptive approaches.* Columbus: SMEAC-ERIC Center.

2
NCTM Principles for School Mathematics

The National Council of Teachers of Mathematics (NCTM) has held a leadership role in our profession for many years. In 1989, NCTM published the *Curriculum and Evaluation Standards for School Mathematics* in which they described what needed to be done to help all students learn more, and better, mathematics. That publication was a bit controversial in that some felt it was too prescriptive and interpreted it as a set of rules that were to be adhered to, and others felt it did not go far enough in terms of providing guidelines for change. The intent was to have these 1989 Standards serve as a guideline for changes to the mathematics curriculum.

In 1991, NCTM published the *Professional Standards for Teaching Mathematics*, which was, along with the *Curriculum and Evaluation Standards for School Mathematics*, designed to guide reform in the teaching of mathematics for the foresee-

able future. Again, the *Professional Standards* were not prescriptive but rather provided a set of ideal guidelines and goals. This publication was aimed at teachers of mathematics and what was felt they needed to know to be effective in their classrooms. It also dealt with teacher evaluation issues aimed at improving classroom performance. The ultimate goal, again, was to provide a sound mathematical education for all students; the *Curriculum Standards* document provides the "what" and the *Professional Standards* document provides the "how."

In 1995, NCTM produced the *Assessment Standards for School Mathematics*, which addresses what should be valued as mathematics is assessed. The focus was not only on improving assessment but also on learning how to teach mathematics better and help students learn additional mathematics more effectively. It made sense to have this third document, because changes in the curriculum need changes in the assessment procedures. It is like having a coin, one side for curriculum and the other for assessment.

The latest in the series of standards published by NCTM, *Principles and Standards for School Mathematics*, came out in 2000. The spotlight here is on how mathematics evolves, and what part of the field all students need to know and be able to use. *Standards 2000* reflects the latest thinking in mathematics education and includes ideas about new mathematics, how mathematics should be taught, assessed, applied, and learned, and the overarching impact of this thinking on the school curriculum made available to all students. Learners need to be able to relate their mathematical learning to thinking and problem solving encountered outside the school environment, often needing it to handle implications rising out of new situations. As should be expected, assessment continues to occupy a section on the center stage of thinking. As we teach, and as students learn in the changing and shifting world of school mathematics, it is imperative that we regularly check to see that what is being done is relevant to us, to mathematics, to the students, and to the world in which we all live and function.

Six strands through all mathematical teaching and learning that are stressed in *Standards 2000* are

> **Equity.** Excellence in mathematics education requires equity—high expectations and strong support for all students.
> **Curriculum.** A curriculum is more than a collection of activities: it must be coherent, focused on important mathematics, and well articulated across the grades.
> **Teaching.** Effective mathematics teaching requires understanding what students know and need to learn and then challenging and supporting them to learn it well.
> **Learning.** Students must learn mathematics with understanding, actively building new knowledge from experience and prior knowledge.
> **Assessment.** Assessment should support the learning of important mathematics and furnish useful information to both teachers and students.
> **Technology.** Technology is essential in teaching and learning mathematics; it influences the mathematics that is taught and enhances students' learning. (pp. 15–16).

Although we provide a brief elaboration of each of these strands, you should study the entire original document.

EQUITY

Equity is elusive. It is said that all students need to have the opportunity to access the same education. There are so many variables that are dealt with: teachers and all our strengths and shortcomings; students and their abilities, backgrounds, and desire to learn mathematics; what is meant by useful mathematics; the meaning of real-world mathematics; what mathematics is applicable; when and how technology should be used; and so on. As individuals apply these variables in differing degrees, what is equitable for that person changes. Granted, all students need to know a basic framework of mathematics, but exactly what is that?

Consider addition, for example. It is accepted that all students need to know the addition facts. Furthermore, all students need to be able to effectively add sets of numbers, using a computation algorithm of choice. Where it becomes practical to shift from adding by hand (for example, using a paper-and-pencil computation algorithm) to using technology is a source of debate though. The continuum from addition facts to the ability to arrive at a correct sum of five 10-digit addends involves multiple skills. Most agree that technology (a lot of calculators will not handle 10-digit addends) is reasonably used at some point along the addition continuum. However, when that technology should be used is open for debate. Another issue that is raised by detractors is that not all students (remember equity) have access to appropriate technology. Now what do we do? We could mandate that no technology be used so there is an equitable situation. We could decree that everyone be given the same technology. You know and we know that neither of those is a reasonable position to adopt. So, what do we do to provide an equitable situation for all students? Like we said, equity is hard to pin down. A working definition of equity could be: set *all* your students up to succeed.

Your Turn

2.1. Explain when and how technology should be inserted into the addition continuum, or should it?

2.2. Describe an equitable solution to the dilemma posed about no technology or the same technology for all that is mentioned in the preceding paragraph.

So, what exactly does equitable mathematics education mean? It starts with opportunity. All students need comparable opportunities to learn meaningful mathematics at their developmental level. With that accessibility comes financial, emotional, and all related support for the teachers and students. This provision does not prescribe a one-size-fits-all curriculum. It does mean that each student should have access to an appropriate mathematics-learning environment. All students deserve a challenging mathematical curriculum, delivered by well-qualified and well-supported teachers of mathematics.

You have seen statements that encourage qualified teachers, interested students, and supportive schools, parents, and communities. These are high expectations, and yet, if our students are to become functional citizens of the 21st century, this is a must. You, the future teacher of mathematics, are a key element in this whole scenario. The education you are receiving now is only a part of the picture. It is imperative that you become involved in professional organizations, which should include NCTM as well as your state and local council of teachers of mathematics. You will need to continue your education through in-service opportunities and additional class work. You need to know what you know and believe now, and it is imperative that you maintain an awareness of that information as it changes through your professional years. That knowledge and effort will help you provide an equitable education for all your students.

CURRICULUM

Realistically, the textbook being used often defines curriculum. An equitable and effective curriculum designed to prepare students for life in the 21st century is much more than following even a well-written textbook through the pages. Today's mathematics curriculum needs to channel students along a path of ever-broadening understanding of the world of mathematics. This world is more than a collection of topics taught in isolation or cubby holes, as has been done for so long. You undoubtedly experienced this in high school and may be seeing it now in your college classes as you learn advanced mathematics and yet fail to make integrated connections between the different topics.

What goes into the curriculum? As noted earlier, number facts, skill in performing algorithmic operations, understandings, and technology play a part. In addition, what we ask the students to do and learn needs to be worth their attention and effort. Granted, some of the things students are asked to learn are background information for future work. Still, we need to carefully show applications that are meaningful to them along the way. If we consistently say, "You are going to need this for what we are going to do next week," the students are quickly going to assume there is no value to learning mathematics. That attitude is unacceptable and it is our responsibility, as teachers of mathematics, to combat it. That leaves a nagging question: How do we decide or tell which are the important ideas worth focusing on?

Curriculum needs to be in a state of flux, changing with the demands of the time and readiness skills of the students. Yet, the curriculum cannot be so open-ended that there appears to be no direction. Teachers need to know what the students have had in prior mathematics classes to plan lessons. At the same time, teachers need to know future expectations so that adequate background can be built into a class. Covering topics in the same or similar manners is a tremendous waste of time. How many times did you learn how to add fractions? With each encounter of a topic, a quick review might be in order, but then the exposure should provide new skills, knowledge, depth, and connections.

Your Turn

2.3. Textbooks will be a part of your world from now on. You need to be familiar with the things done in them. Select one topic and see how the publisher presented it in a series (like pre-Algebra and Algebra I or seventh and eighth grade). The texts should be published about the same time. How are the presentations the same (for example, some series have actually used the same pictures in three different sequential texts)? How are the presentations different? When the topic is treated the second (or third) time, what is done to stimulate new interest?

TEACHING

Teachers deal with the world's most important commodity every day—our kids, who are our future. In the mathematics classroom, it will be your responsibility to increase each student's mathematical horizons. You will need to get some to like the subject. You will need to encourage some to specialize in mathematics as a career. You will need to show them how mathematics shows up in their daily lives. You will need to help them develop their mathemat-

ical problem-solving powers and help them understand how critical these are both in academic and daily life. What all of that says is that effective teaching of mathematics is critical.

That is easily said, and yet there is a deficiency of qualified teachers of mathematics in the classroom today. How do we provide effective teaching of mathematics when we struggle to even get bodies in the classroom? The impact of nonqualified teachers of mathematics is far-reaching within the mathematics curriculum because a qualified teacher who follows a nonqualified or weak teacher of mathematics is going to have to spend time away from the defined curriculum to cover the concepts that the students lack because of poor mathematics teaching in their background.

We are getting a handle on what good teaching of mathematics involves, thanks to research efforts. We know teaching is not simply standing in front of a group and telling them how to do things. Teaching is not merely having students read information out of a book. Teaching mathematics is more than checking tests or homework. Becoming an effective teacher of mathematics involves much more. Teaching is not easy; it takes time, energy, dedication, and resilience. You need to:

- Discuss where the information will be used.
- Motivate the students to want to learn.
- Encourage students to collaborate and learn from each other.
- Patiently elaborate for those who did not get it.
- Deal with multiple learning modalities, capabilities, and needs.
- Discipline with care, compassion, and fairness.
- Assess on-going progress (both yours and the students').

- Grow personally and professionally.
- Be enthusiastic.
- Keep up with, research, and use new technology.
- Employ best practices.
- Master new strategies to effectively teach mathematics.
- Network and share with other professionals.

Teaching is selling. What would you think of a Ford salesperson who drove a Chevrolet? The teacher of mathematics must be an advocate of the field. Belief, excitement, and enthusiasm about what is being presented are mandatory. If YOU do not seem interested in what is going on in class, why should the students be interested?

Three axioms a teacher of mathematics should possess are (Joby M. Anthony, personal communication, May 26, 2004) to know the content being presented, to know more than the content being presented, and to teach from the overflow of knowledge. Knowing the content, and more, and teaching from the overflow of knowledge implies flexibility and adaptability as well as careful planning (more on that in the Communications chapter) and organization. It is imperative that the topics to be discussed in class be carefully contemplated and organized well in advance to allow time for the ideas to germinate and blend in your subconscious. The advanced planning also provides the opportunity to connect topics from different lessons throughout the course. Doesn't all of that sound wonderful? It will not happen unless you commit to making it happen. The flexibility and adaptability words are easily said. The ability to be flexible and adapt to different situations in the classroom comes out of careful planning and knowledge of pedagogy and content. Then you begin teaching from the overflow. Things will happen in class and you will need to make changes on the fly. If you are not organized, knowledgeable, and pliant in your thinking and approach to teaching, you will struggle.

We have said and you will hear that students need to see real-world applications of the material they are learning. That is easier said than done. Real-world to adults, or what adults think is the students' world, may not be anything like what is real-world to them. Getting a connection here is not easily accomplished. That too is a major responsibility of becoming an effective teacher of mathematics. Have you noticed we say teacher of mathematics rather than mathematics teacher? That is done on purpose. We are putting the emphasis on teaching. We see you as being a teacher and happening to deal with mathematics as opposed to you being a mathematician who happens to be teaching. There is a difference! Focus on teaching and you will help all of your students become self-motivated, life-long learners.

LEARNING

For years students have been expected to understand mathematics. What that was perceived as mathematics has changed? In the 19th century, the emphasis was on having students be good arithmeticers. Most of the 20th century states the same goal. Starting with World War II, it became apparent that the arithmetic nature of mathematical learning was not sufficient. The need for more elaborate skills, knowledge, applications, problem-solving capabilities, and reasoning abilities became apparent and those, along with other stimuli, spawned the "Modern Math" movement. Programs like School Mathematics Study Group, University of Illinois Committee on School Mathematics, Ball State Program, Madison Project, and Greater Cleveland Project all had successes.

Still, the drive to teach arithmetic survived. The National Science Foundation pumped piles of money into Academic Year Institutes as a means of encouraging teachers of mathematics and science to further their knowledge. Several organizations and NCTM began calling for changes in the curriculum. Still arithmetic prevailed as the dominant force in most classrooms. It seems as if too many people fail to understand that arithmetic, while an essential piece of the mathematical picture, is only a small part. Problem solving, applications, and the ability to create new ideas based on prior knowledge must be placed in the forefront if students are to effectively learn mathematics. Even today, after the extensive effort put forth by mathematics educators and organizations to stem the tide, arithmetic holds center stage in many classrooms.

A goal of modern mathematical learning is to have students develop an understanding of the content along with abilities to apply what they learn. If students are functional only at the knowledge level (thinking in terms of Bloom's taxonomy), they are going to be uncertain of how to use what they do comprehend. As what they learn makes sense, students gain confidence in their own ability to learn more, apply their new knowledge in exciting ways, and solve new problems they encounter. You, the teacher to be, become a major force in making all of that happen. How you engage them in the learning environment is critical. You must get them to be active participants in their mathematical learning. We cannot afford to have passive learners. The students have to discover how to take the lead and responsibility for their own learning. They have to develop conjectures, assess their own thinking (and that of their peers), interact with peers, and become aware of the power they have to impact their own futures.

Your Turn

2.4. We said in the text "Even today, after the extensive effort put forth by mathematics educators and organizations to stem the tide, arithmetic holds center stage in many classrooms." Assuming that is a true statement, rationalize why that is the case.

ASSESSMENT

Assessment is "the process of gathering evidence about a student's knowledge of, ability to use and disposition toward mathematics, and of making inferences from that evidence for a variety of purposes" (NCTM, 1995, p. 3). "Assessment should support the learning of important mathematics and furnish useful information to both teachers and students" (NCTM, 2000, p. 11). Appraisal should be more than just a score on a test. It should involve a more holistic view of each student's understanding, skills, readiness, and attitudes about mathematics. Evaluation should communicate what we, as teachers, believe is important for students to know and be able to do (Cathcart, Pothier, Vance, & Bezuk, 2003). Evaluation tasks should match student's prior knowledge, the mathematics curriculum, and instructional strategies in use. Teachers should not teach one way and assess another.

The idea that someone is going to assess you conjures up the idea that your work is going to viewed critically. That can generate immediate angst and, yet, that is not the only way to look at it. As you assess what you yourself do in the classroom you can experience fabulous professional growth. Often people will say the objectives are not met because the students are not interested. That is a convenient means of placing the blame, but it is not the first assessment test that a professional applies. One of the most important aspects of assessment involves a mirror. Consider a lesson you have prepared that has objectives, correlates with the standards, considers all special-needs students (ESOL, mainstreamed, gifted, those who need more), wonderful examples, upper-level questions, thorough presentation notes, and even assessment. Alas, that lesson, even though thoroughly planned, is a flop. The easy answer is to say that the kids were not attentive, they did not have the background you thought they did, and so on. The realistic answer is that you need to take a look in a mirror and be sure that you were not to blame. Did you check their readiness for what you were covering? Was your plan as clear as you though it was? Should you have provided more examples? Should the examples have been more staged from easy to difficult? Were your questions too obtuse? Did you do a good job of doing what your plan said you would do? The list could go on, but you get the point. How did YOU do? If you pass that test, then you begin to look at the students for reasons.

One thing you need to realize is that it is impractical for you to assess every piece of work each student does. That position will meet with objections from the students, saying that if you are not going to grade it, why should they do it. Your rationale that they need to build background for future work, they need to learn to do things for their own good, or because I said so, will fall on deaf ears. Before being too critical of students for resisting doing work that is not going to help their grade, consider your own situation. How many things in life do you do totally and absolutely free? You are not looking to score points with anyone; you do not get paid; you are doing it solely out of the goodness of your heart.

As you look beyond the mirror, students are certainly a potential source for things not going well. Whereas motivation, readi- ness, interest, applicability, and reason- ableness are all potential factors, assess- ment could also be a reason. Test anxi- ety is a common phrase, but maybe the students suffer from assessment anxiety. They know when you are watching (as- sessing). It is important to help them re- alize that assessment is done *for* them, not *to* them. At first that could sound like double-speak but, if students can be con- vinced that assessment of their work is done to help them grow and is not to be taken personally, huge strides could be made for all concerned. How that is accom- plished is the challenge. You, in this class, are concerned about your grade. Undoubt- edly, you become somewhat anxious when you have a quiz, test, or a paper due. Poor performance on your part could result in an unflattering assessment from your profes- sor. All it takes to defeat that fear is to pre- pare properly, invest your time in your work and future, do your best, and see assess- ment as part of an ongoing and continuous learning process. The same can be said of your future students. Now, you merely need to figure out how to convey that mes- sage to them. As a teacher, you can work on providing a safe and nurturing learning community in your classroom, where er- rors are part of the leaning process and everybody is valued and respected.

As you enter the teaching profession, you need to develop an assessment plan. Different types of assessment may be used in isolation or in combination with each other. Some types of assessment are as follows (Underhill, Uprichard, & Heddens, 1980):

• Objective assessment refers to testing that requires the selection of one item from a list of choices provided with the ques- tion. This type of assessment includes true/false responses, yes/no answers, and questions with multiple-choice options.

• Alternative assessment refers to non-traditional options. With this, the teacher is not basing student progress only on the results of a single test or set of evidence. This group would include portfolios, journals, notebooks, projects, presentations, tests, quizzes, reports, group work, creative efforts, valuing statements, conversations, interviews, observations, and student descriptions of their own ideas.

• Authentic assessment incorporates real-life functions and applications.

• Performance assessment (often used interchangeably with authentic or alternative assessment) requires the completion of a task, project, or investigation, communicating information, or constructing a response that demonstrates knowledge or understanding of a skill or concept.

• Naturalistic assessment involves evaluation focusing on the natural setting of the classroom and includes observation of student's performance and behavior in an informal context.

• Achievement test battery is composed of subtests of mathematics concepts and skills and usually includes technical aspects of mathematics.

• Standardized tests include content areas and provide useful information about students' mathematical skills. Their validity and reliability depends on three basic assumptions: students have been equally exposed to the test content in an instructional program, students know the language of the test directions and the test responses, and students just like those taking the test have been included in the standardization samples to establish norms and make inferences. The standardized test results could help identify general problem areas.

• Diagnostic tests are used within the model of teaching that consists of diagnosis, prescription, instruction, and ongoing assessment. The diagnostic test results could help identify specific problem areas.

How you react to what you see from students is most important. Visualize getting a paper back that is red with comments. That has to come as a shock on first sight. What do you do first in that situation (besides assume the grade is not good)? You look for the grade. What would you think if the grade was A? After giving a huge sigh of relief, maybe you would realize that the teacher cared enough to look carefully at your work. That is the message you need to send about any assessment of student work. If you ask them to do whatever it is, then you owe it to each of them to look closely at what they provide as evidence of their thoughts and knowledge. Otherwise they will quickly assume that their effort is not valued and might stop trying.

All of the assessment pieces are part of a giant picture called the mathematics curriculum you are dealing with. Focusing too much on only one part (like test results) could lead to false interpretation. Suppose the scores on a particular test are not good. After determining that the test did in fact cover what had been taught (the mirror test), in a manner similar to how it had been taught (mirror test), you need to establish if the assessment being used allowed all students to express their understandings. Furthermore, it could be appropriate to assess the same material in multiple ways to allow for a well-rounded picture of each student's strength and misconceptions.

Varied assessment, as discussed here, is an important part of the teaching/learning environment. An effective assessment plan is essential to your understanding of how students are dealing with the mathematics in their lives. How many teachers do this, particularly those who are nonprepared and filling space? What impact does a poor assessment plan have on your teaching and on the entire mathematical community?

Also, *Assessment Standards for School Mathematics* (NCTM, 1995) includes six standards for special focus: mathematics, learning, equity, openness, inferences, and coherence. These standards should be used to evaluate the quality of the assessment used in the classroom:

1. The mathematics standard states "assessment should reflect the mathematics that all students need to know and be able to do" (NCTM, 1995, p. 11). This implies that you, as a teacher, should align your assessment of students in areas currently recommended by educators and agencies like NCTM.

2. The learning standard states "assessment should enhance mathematics learning" (NCTM, 1995, p. 13). The assessment process not only appraises students' understanding but also encourages and supports further growth in that understanding (Cathcart, Pothier, Vance, & Bezuk, 2003). As stated by NCTM, "assessment should be a means of fostering growth toward high expectations. To do otherwise represents a waste of human potential" (1995, p. 1).

3. The equity standard states "assessment should promote equity" (NCTM, 1995, p. 15). Equity in this context means that all students should have the opportunity to succeed in mathematics. This implies that you should take differences among students into consideration to support the learning of all students. This could be accomplished by providing appropriate accommodations for students' needs in different assessment and other learning situations.

4. The openness standard states "assessment should be an open process" (NCTM, 1995, p. 17). This includes the responsibility to inform the public about the assessment process, involve teaching professionals in the process, and accept review and change along the way.

5. The inferences standard states "assessment should promote valid inferences about mathematics learning" (NCTM, 1995, p. 19). This involves the use of valid and reliable assessment measures and making valid inferences from the data collected. The inference you make from the results of the assessment should stand up to scrutiny (be valid) and should not (within reason) depend on how, where, when, or to whom it was given (be reliable). Different types of assessment and evaluative techniques should be considered and selected according to the situation at hand. One assessment might be appropriate for a given situation and not for another. Also, the student should be considered as a whole. Teachers should always be aware of the students' backgrounds. For example, a student may know the concept but not the words.

6. The coherence standard states "assessment should be a coherent process" (NCTM, 1995, p. 21). This implies that the assessment process must be complete and sensible, match the purposes for which it is being conducted, and be consistent with curriculum and instruction that have been implemented (Cathcart, Pothier, Vance, & Bezuk, 2003). You need to make sure that all parts fit together.

Certainly this is not an exhaustive discussion of assessment. The variety of aspects to assessment is why most schools provide an independent course on the subject. The bottom line is that this is an integral part of the entire education landscape.

Your Turn

2.5. Describe how you will convince your students that assessment is done *for* them, not *to* them.

TECHNOLOGY

How many times have you heard that when someone could not get the VCR to work, they asked some kid from the neighborhood and it was done? Today's students live in a multimedia environment. No longer can you be the sage on the stage, dictating procedures, doing a set of problems and then expecting the students to duplicate your efforts. Technology has changed all of that.

Please understand that we are not saying there is not place for lecture in the mathematics classroom. We are saying that it can no longer be the only, or even primary, mode of instruction. Technology can do so much to enhance your teaching. Consider a calculus class where the goal is to find the area under $y = x^2$ between 0 and 1. We can talk about it. We can show pictures of it, using a few different widths for the rectangular slices, showing that the approximation to the area improves as the slices get thinner. Still, that is static and limited. How much better if dynamic software that permits the rapid changing of the number of slices taken is used. The students see the concept being discussed. Figure 2.1 shows three scenes from a dynamic graphing program.

Making those changes in Fig. 2.1 before the eyes of the students is theatrical. And, the slices could be taken above the curve rather than below, or the software can be set to allow the midpoint of the top side of the rectangle to be on the curve. If only the above and below configurations are used, the concept of limits leaps out as the area

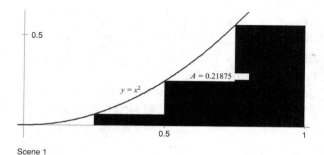

Scene 1

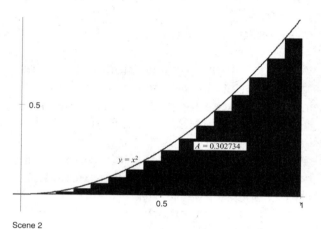

Scene 2

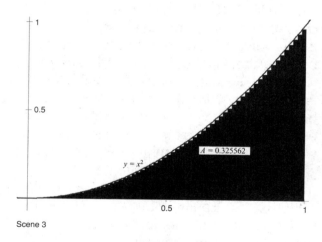

Scene 3

FIG 2.1.

is approached from above and below. Let us see you do that with a board and chalk!

Are we saying that all teaching must use technology? Certainly not. However, we are saying that it is imperative that you become conversant with interactive algebra software, interactive geometry software, interactive statistics software, graphing calculators, fraction calculators, scientific calculators, video cameras, digital cameras, movies, the Internet, overhead projectors, and so on. Conversant carries an implication with it, as we see things. Interactive software and calculators are tools of the trade when it comes to learning and teaching mathematics. Thus, you should own them and integrate them into your teaching and learning. More than likely you have already done half of that last statement, right?

You do know that you will be expected to use technology for providing information relating to events in your classroom that will include clerical tasks, communicating, reporting, and documenting, right? Furthermore, you will be looking for information on the Internet that could provide lesson plans or ideas for supplementing plans. There are online journals that should not be overlooked, like NCTM's ON-Math, which can be found at http://my.nctm.org/eresources/journal_home.asp?journal_id=6.

Read this carefully—technology is not a universal fix-it that will cure all ills. It is another tool in your teaching arsenal. Use it to enhance your delivery. Use it to stimulate your students. Use it to engage them. Use it to WOW them and get their attention. Use it to help you to better understand what they have learned. Use it to complement and support the use of other modes of instruction (such as manipulative materials). Use it to explore new topics on your own. Do you get the point? Use technology!

Technology will not replace the teacher of mathematics, and it provides its own availability and pedagogical challenges. The teacher does have to do things differently than what was done before, without technology. Topics can become available to students earlier. For example, consider an elementary student with a calculator who enters 5–7. The answer of negative 2 potentially opens an entire new arena. Assuming readiness, a quick interaction be-tween the teacher and student could have the student embarking on a wondrous path of independent study. There is a possible downside to that trip though. Later in the curriculum, when integers are encountered in subtraction, the teacher will need to be astute enough to realize that this student is perhaps beyond the others in the class and needs another topic of independent work, perhaps enhancing what is known about integers rather than dealing with a future curricular topic.

Your Turn

2.6. Realizing that we are spending your money, rationalize why it is or is not appropriate for each future teacher to own interactive software and calculators.

2.7. Understanding the magnitude of this statement, we strongly recommend that you read, summarize, and discuss all four of NCTM's basic *Standards* books:

Curriculum and Evaluation Standards
Professional Standards
Assessment Standards
Principles and Standards

CONCLUSION

We could not possibly discuss the impact of NCTM on the middle school mathematics curriculum. Not everyone agrees with NCTM's positions on some matters, and that is good because it stimulates discussion. It is imperative, for the good of our profession, that you examine the standards placed before you, be they national, state, regional, or local. Know your subject. Know how to teach it. Know your students. Know their mathematical needs both present and future. THINK about what goes on in your classroom, make informed decisions, and just DO IT!

STICKY QUESTIONS

2.1. It has been said that individuals should not be permitted to teach until they are at least 28 years old. That way, they will have world experiences that will enable them to provide realistic responses to questions like, "Why do I have to learn this stuff?" Provide a rationale on why you agree or disagree with the need to be 28 years old before beginning a teaching career.

2.2. You will be encouraged to join NCTM, your state council of teachers of mathematics, and your local or district council of teachers of mathematics. Realizing that teachers do not get stinky rich, rationalize why this is (or is not) a wise investment.

2.3. You have read summaries of positions put forward by NCTM on equity, curriculum, teaching, learning, assessment, and technology. Are these reasonable positions to adopt for your classroom? Why or why not?

2.4. According to the Triangle Coalition and NCTM, results of the 2003 Program for International Student Assessment (PISA) reinforce the importance of ensuring that students learn with real understanding so that they can use their knowledge in real-life situations, and highlight the urgent need to address the achievement gap among groups of students. PISA results show that 15-year-olds in the United States performed lower on average than their counterparts in the participating countries in both math literacy and problem solving. Describe how you would resolve this issue.

"PISA Results from the U.S. Perspective" can be found at http://nces.ed.gov/surveys/pisa. A copy of the full 2003 PISA report is available at http://www.pisa.oecd.org.

TAG

2.1. Use three 9s and one minus sign to make 1.

2.2. A customer at a 7-11 store selected four items to buy, and was told that the cost was $7.11. He was curious that the cost was the same as the store name, so he inquired as to how the figure was derived. The clerk said that he had simply multiplied the prices of the four individual items. The customer protested that the four prices should have been ADDED, not MULTIPLIED. The clerk said that that was OK with him, but the result was still the same: $7.11. What were the exact prices of the four items (no rounding or using mils)?

2.3. How do you show 15 minutes with only two hourglasses, one that goes for 7 minutes and one that goes for 11 minutes?

2.4. Do the following and see what you get: From 6 take away 9; from 9 take away 10; from 40 take away 50 and when you are done, have 6 left.

2.5. Take ace through king of any suit from a bridge deck of cards. Stack the cards so that when you spell "ACE" by taking a card and without looking at it say the letter "A," a second card saying "C," and a third saying "E," the next card will be the ace. Then do the same thing spelling "two," and so on. As a card is viewed, it is removed from the stack. Continue until all cards are shown and the resultant removal stack is in the proper order.

2.6. Did you know that 86,400 equals 1,440 and that 1,440 equals 24 and that 24 equals 1? How is this possible?

2.7. A fish had to swim 1,010 feet to reach the other fish. Every 5 minutes the fish swam 30 feet upstream, but then in the next 2 minutes, the rushing current pushed the fish back 10 feet downstream. The fish continued swimming for 5 minutes, then resting for 2 minutes until reaching its destination. How long did it take the fish to swim the entire 1,010 feet?

2.8. Madison injured her leg surfboarding and, while absent from school, received 31 get-well cards from her friends. There were 5 more cards from girls than boys. She got a card from each classmate and 6 other cards from girls in other classes. How many boys and how many girls are there in Madison's class?

REFERENCES

Cathcart, G. W., Pothier, Y. M., Vance, J. H., & Bezuk, N. S. (2003). *Learning mathematics in elementary and middle schools* (3rd ed.). Upper Saddle River, NJ: Pearson Education.

National Council of Teachers of Mathematics. (1989). *Curriculum and evaluation standards for school mathematics.* Reston, VA: Author.

National Council of Teachers of Mathematics. (1991). *Professional standards for teaching mathematics.* Reston, VA: Author.

National Council of Teachers of Mathematics. (1995). *Assessment standards for school mathematics.* Reston, VA: Author.

National Council of Teachers of Mathematics. (2000). *Principles and standards for school mathematics.* Reston, VA: Author.

Undershill, R. B., Uprichard, E., & Heddens, J. (1980). *Diagnosing mathematical difficulties.* Columbus, OH: Charles E. Merrill.

3
Representation

FOCAL POINTS

- Different ways of saying the same thing
- Representation in the middle grades
- Conclusion
- Sticky questions
- TAG
- References

My name is Gina Gresham and I am one of the authors of this book. My refrigerator is covered with pictures my goddaughter Madison has drawn for me. She enjoys drawing pictures of items she sees. I try to visualize her thoughts in these pictures as she draws line segments or curves, squiggles, and shapes to represent the beach, sand, a house, her name, and other things. They are creations of colors and illustrations often indecipherable by those who see them. However, when you ask her what they are, she can tell you in full detail what each one represents. Figure 3.1 with its two rows of shapes shows Madison's representation of her name, done when she was three years old. It appears as if she has begun to establish a feel for her name (and what it represents for her in her mind) by attempting to draw rectangular shapes with one shape representing each letter of her name, or one-to-one correspondence. Her style is unique. When asked what the drawing is, she says, "Oh, that's my name," and points to each shape and spells her name—M, a, d, i, s, o, n—obviously annoyed that I could not see this through her illustrations. However, it is clear she

does not know how to write the actual letters. Madison's pictures truly are "re-presentation." Madison uses the pictures not just to stand for something, but also to re-present it. It is in this new presentation that that which is presented gains a new meaning and, perhaps, a new life.

DIFFERENT WAYS OF SAYING THE SAME THING

Representations are something like Madison's illustration of her name. Her drawings show she is developing and deepening her understanding for ways to model, communicate, and interpret ideas in her physical and social world. Consider what representation means to you and what the interpretation of representation means to others.

The term *representation* refers both to process (in Madison's case, drawing rectangles representing each letter of her name) and product (Madison's name) and is central to the study of mathematics—in other words, to the act of capturing a concept or relation in some form (process) and connecting it to the final mathematical model (product). Moreover, the term applies to processes and products. Some are observable externally (such as manipulating cubes to represent a specific quantity or Madison's attempts to represent her name). Some occur in the minds of people creating the image (making abstractions or connections to new learning). All

FIG 3.1.

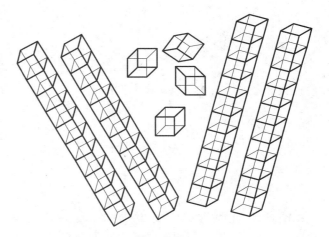

FIG 3.3.

of these meanings of representation are important to consider in school mathematics (National Council of Teachers of Mathematics [NCTM] 2000, p. 67).

Representations should be treated as essential elements in supporting students' understanding of mathematical concepts and relations; in communicating approaches, arguments, and understandings to one's self and to others; in recognizing connections among related concepts; and in applying mathematics to realistic problem situations through modeling.

Mathematical concepts can be shown using different learning levels (concrete, pictorial or representational, and abstract) and related modes of representation: real-word situations (concrete level), manipu-

lative models (concrete level), pictures of manipulative models (pictorial or representational level), oral language (abstract level), and written symbols (abstract level; Behr, Lesh, Post, & Silver, 1983). Figure 3.2 illustrates these modes of representation and possible interconnections. A student can represent the concept of "five" with five fingers (real-world application), with five cubes (manipulative model), with five flowers (pictures), by saying the word (oral), and by writing the word "five" or the numeral "5" (written symbols).

As mentioned earlier, modes of representation can take on many forms. The following interpretations (see Figs. 3.3, 3.4,

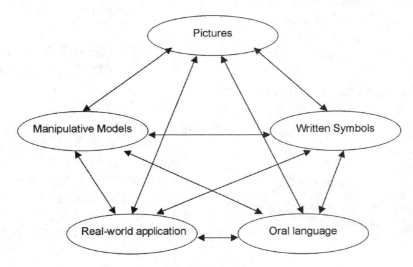

FIG 3.2.

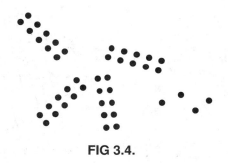

FIG 3.4.

and 3.5) show how students modeled their understanding of 44 using different representations.

Group 1 illustrated their understanding by using base 10 blocks at the concrete level. They used longs and units to show four groups of ten and four ones (see Fig. 3.3).

The interpretation of Group 2 shows their understanding by using dot arrays at the pictorial or representational level (see Fig. 3.4).

Group 3 modeled their understanding using dots and segments, also at the representational level (see Fig. 3.5).

Research shows that student understanding is enhanced when they are encouraged to make translations between modes of representation and learning levels. Heibert (1990) stated, "meaning or understanding in mathematics comes from building or recognizing relations either between representations or within representations" (p. 32).

Student understanding of mathematics comes from (Cathcart, Pothier, Vance, &

Bezuk, 2003; Hiebert, 1990):

- Building or recognizing relationships between representations: a student listens (spoken language) to a teacher describing a problem, represents and manipulates the problem with blocks (concrete objects), and then writes a response or solution to the problem (written symbols).
- Building or recognizing relationships within representations: a student recognizes patterns while using base 10 blocks by noticing the corresponding decreasing size of the blocks (looking at the cubes, longs, flats, and units).
- Transforming an idea from one form and representing it in another: a student restates ideas in other words, constructs a graph, and draws a diagram to illustrate a concept.
- Translating an idea from one mode to another: a student is asked to represent a concept in more than one mode (this is indicated by the arrows in Fig. 3.6), such as when the teacher asks a student to show five fingers, draw a picture with five objects, and form a group of five cubes. This same figure also presents other possible combinations of teacher and student moves.

REPRESENTATION IN THE MIDDLE GRADES

Representations encourage students to organize their thinking and help them make mathematical ideas more available for reflection. Through the middle grades, student mathematical representations usually are about objects and actions from their experience. They begin to create, compare, and use mathematical representations for more abstract ideas, to solve problems, or to portray, clarify, or extend a mathematical

FIG 3.5.

Teacher Moves

		Concrete	Pictorial	Symbolic	Verbal
Child's Response	**Concrete**	**C →C** Teacher shows concrete representation; student manipulates concrete objects	**P →C** Teacher shows picture; student manipulates concrete objects	**P →S** Teacher writes; student manipulates concrete objects	**P →V** Teacher talks; student manipulates concrete objects
	Pictorial	**C →P** Teacher shows concrete representation; student chooses or draws picture	**P →P**	**S →P**	**V →P**
	Symbolic	**C →S** Teacher shows concrete representation; student writes symbol	**P →S**	**S→S**	**V →S**
	Verbal	**C →V** Teacher shows concrete representation; student discusses/talks	**P →V**	**S →V**	**V →V**

FIG 3.6.

concept. They begin to communicate their thinking through the use of physical objects, drawings, charts, graphs, and symbols.

For example, consider this problem: The surf shop sells black, red, and blue surfboards. The black surfboards are sold 4 times as often as the red ones. During the time in which 3 red surfboards sell, 5 blue surfboards sell. How could the potential surfboard sales situations be shown?

Students can use a variety of approaches to represent and solve this problem. Figure 3.7 shows a discrete model

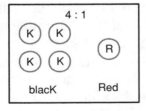

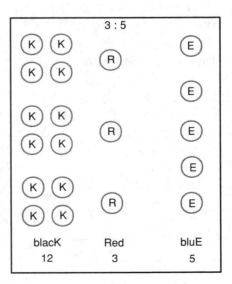

FIG 3.7.

that could be used. It is a merging of the information from the two ratios in the problem statement.

Your Turn

3.1. Make your own representation to illustrate what ratio of the surfboard sales are black.

3.2. Make a model to show what percent of the surfboard sales are blue.

3.3. If 60 black surfboards were sold in a month, what is the total number of red and blue surfboards sold in that month, assuming the described ratios hold? Make a representation to show this number.

3.4. Write the descriptions in the empty cells in Fig. 3.6.

The representation for the surfboard sales combines visual and numerical information, which can be appreciated in solving many problems involving ratios, proportions, and percents. Consider another problem. Several students go to the local pizza parlor for dinner. They have $60 to spend. If the tax and tip is 25% more than the food prices shown on the menu, how much can they spend on the food so that the total cost will be $60? Figure 3.8 illustrates one way to solve this problem. Four sections represent the price of the food and one section represents the tax and tip. Because there are five equal parts and the total is $60, each part must be $12. Therefore, the total price allowed for food is $48 (Bennett, Maier, & Nelson, 1988).

This particular representation (Fig. 3.8) could also help students understand that,

when one quantity is 125% of a second quantity, then the second is 80% of the first. Furthermore, this same figure can help students understand that a situation like this can be interpreted more than one way. Either one segment (the shaded part of Fig. 3.8) is 80% of the whole, or the whole is 125% of the shaded segment.

We realize that this food problem has limitations. Many students would react to it by saying it is a silly problem. Assuming the students are sensitive to tipping, it is likely that someone would solve it saying that the food should total about $50, add tax to that, and the difference between that sum and $60 is the tip. Still, problems such as this are quite common. We encourage you to be judicious as you select problems for examples, assign problems to be worked, or create problems. The desirable setting would be for the students to work with problems that they find intriguing, interesting, and challenging.

It is important to note that there are alternate methods for solving this problem. Guess and check, for example, could be seen when the students say spend about $50 for food. A tremendous follow-up question to the student would be, "How do you know?" Here, the request is for evidence to support the response. This enhances communication, mathematical and representational connections, and discussion.

Representations are also used to convey numbers and operations. When you begin to use sentences like $a + b = c$, the level of abstractness increases. Not only can you represent specific numbers and operations, but you can also represent and preserve relationships (Troutman & Lichtenberg, 2003). To think algebraically, we must know how the symbols of representation are combined. Figure 3.9 shows how to reflect the combination of using the power of representation, number sentences, and operations by grouping the set

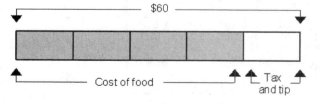

FIG 3.8.

This shows 13 tiles will make
4 groups with 3 and 1 more.

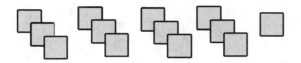

Mathematically, we represent
this grouping like this:
(4 x 3) + 1 = 13

Example 1

This shows 13 tiles will make
2 groups with 6 and 1 more.

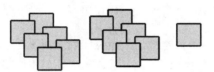

Mathematically, we represent
this grouping like this:
(2 x 6) + 1 = 13

Example 2

This shows 16 tiles will make
4 groups with 3 and 1 more.

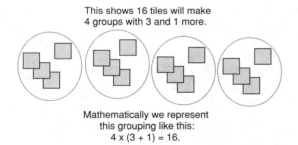

Mathematically we represent
this grouping like this:
4 x (3 + 1) = 16.

Example 3

FIG 3.9.

of 13 tiles two different ways. Example 1 in Fig. 3.9 shows how four groups of three and one more could be expressed. Example 2 depicts how two groups of six and one more show a total of 13. Finally, Example 3 illustrates how four groups of three and one more can represent 16.

Your Turn

3.5. Make a mathematical representation for as many groupings of 18 as you

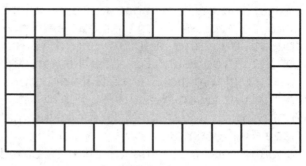

FIG 3.10.

can. Examples could include 17 + 1, 16 + 2, 16 + 1 + 1.

3.6. Figure 3.10 represents a pool with a one-ceramic-tile-wide border (Ferrini-Mindy, Lappan, & Phillips, 1997). Explain in words, with numbers or tables, visually, and with symbols the number of tiles that will be needed for pools of various lengths and widths (NCTM, 2000).

Students will be better able to solve problems if they can easily move from one type of representation to another. Middle grade mathematics often begins with tables of numerical data to establish a pattern underlying a linear function. Students should learn to represent those data in the form of a graph or equation when they wish to characterize the generalized linear relationship (NCTM, 2000). Flexibility can emerge as students gain experience with multiple ways of representing a contextualized problem.

CONCLUSION

Reys, Lindquist, Lambdin, Smith, and Suydam (2001) noted the importance for middle grade students to have repeated opportunities, both to invent their own ways of recording and communicating mathematical ideas and to work with conventional representations. Mathematical ideas can often be represented in very different ways, and each of those representations may be appropriate for very different purposes. You may elect to use a variety of these representations to illustrate the same mathematical ideas. Different representations for an idea can lead us to different ways of understanding and using that idea. Representations are ways of thinking about ideas. Mathematics offers a broad selection of representations that are helpful in problem solving and communicating. One of the goals of mathematics instruction is to help students build bridges from their own ways of thinking so that they come to understand, value, and use the mathematical tools available to them. This is the power of representation.

STICKY QUESTIONS

3.1. How would you define a "normal" seventh grader?

3.2. Assuming situations like the food problem associated with Fig. 3.8 are silly, how do we avoid similar presentations?

3.3. "Representation" as used by NCTM presents one idea. How would you define representation in terms that a middle school student could understand the verbiage?

TAG

3.1. A person likes 225 but not 224; 900 but not 800; 144 but not 145. Which would be preferred; 1600 or 1700? Why?

3.2. Take any number. Subtract the sum of the digits. That missing addend will always be a multiple of nine. Example: $736 - 16 = 720$.

3.3. Place digits 1 through 6 in the circles so the value inside the triangle is the sum of the digits at its vertices (see Fig. 3.11).

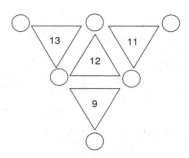

FIG 3.11.

3.4. Arrange three 6s in a configuration that equals 20.

3.5. How many pennies can you arrange so each penny touches every other penny?

3.6. Arrange six pennies in the form of a cross (see Fig. 3.12). Move the coins and form two straight rows with four pennies in each.

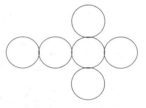

FIG 3.12.

3.7. In the pattern O T T F F S S, what comes next?

REFERENCES

Behr, M. J., Lesh, R., Post, T. R., & Silver, E. A. (1983). Rational number concepts. In R. Lesh & M. Landau (Eds.), *Acquisition of mathematical concepts and processes*. New York: Academy Press.

Bennett, A., Maier, E., & Nelson, T. (1988). *Math and the mind's eye*. Oregon. The Math Learning Center.

Cathcart, G. W., Pothier, Y. M., Vance, J. H., & Bezuk, N. S. (2003). *Learning mathematics in elementary and middle schools* (3rd ed.). Upper Saddle River, NJ: Pearson Education.

Ferrini-Mindy, J., Lappan, G., & Phillips, E. (1997). Experiences with patterning. *Teaching Children Mathematics, 3*, 282–288.

Hiebert, J. (1990). The role of routine procedures in the development of mathematical competence. In T. J. Cooney & C. R. Hirsch (Eds.), *Teaching and learning mathematics in the 1990s (1990 Yearbook)*. Reston, VA: NCTM.

National Council of Teachers of Mathematics (2000). P*rinciples and standards for school mathematics.* Reston, VA: Author.

Reys, R., Lindquist, M., Lambdin, D., Smith, N., & Suydam, N. (2001). *Helping children learn mathematics.* Wiley and Sons. Hoboken, NJ.

Troutman, A., & Lichtenberg, B. (2003). *Mathematics: A good beginning.* CA: Wadsworth/Thomson Learning. Stamford, CT.

4
Connections

The mathematics students learn is valuable information. We know that. Convincing them of that is sometimes a challenge. Why is that? One common response is that students wonder where what they are learning is used, voiced with something like, "When am I going to use this stuff?" While not easily answered, the question is important and cries for a reasonable response, in terms the students understand. What is an appropriate comeback? *Standards 2000* lists the following overview for the Connections Standard, which is perceived as a fundamental standard for the entire mathematical curriculum. Instructional programs from prekindergarten through grade 12 should enable all students to:

- Recognize and use connections among mathematical ideas.
- Understand how mathematical ideas interconnect and build on one another to produce a coherent whole.
- Recognize and apply mathematics in contexts outside of mathematics (NCTM, 2000, p. 64).

It makes sense that, if students realize the mathematics they learn is not compartmentalized or in cubby holes but rather is interconnected, then what they learn is going to be much more understandable. Both Howard Eves and Peter Hilton have said that without geometry you would have a lot of algebra questions that were not asked and without algebra you would have a lot of geometry questions not answered (D. K. Brumbaugh, personal communication with Howard Eves and Peter Hilton, Orlando, FL, 1995). There you have two mathematicians of some renown talking about the interconnectedness of mathematics.

CONNECTIONS WITHIN MATHEMATICS

Eves and Hilton made a prophetic statement. As we look at the world of mathematics, starting with the primary grades, much work is preparation for future work. Can you envision asking a typical first grader to do long division problems? You probably chuckled at that last statement, thinking about the necessary skills that typically would not have been established: estimation, rounding, placement, multiplication, subtraction, and unusual placement. For example, consider $35\overline{)23485}$. After the estimation, the multiplication, which typically would have looked like $\begin{array}{r} 35 \\ \times 6 \end{array}$, now looks like $\begin{array}{r} 6 \\ \times 35\overline{)23485} \\ \underline{210} \end{array}$, which is very unusual even if the multiplication process has been mastered. That alone opens a plethora of different considerations. Without ample understanding of the multiplication process, long division will pose a significant hurdle for students.

Similarly, mastery of addition, subtraction, multiplication, and division of whole numbers is expanded to include fractions, decimals, and integers; further interconnectedness within mathematics. All of the operational work with different sets of numbers is background for algebra as well as for measurement and related geometric applications. Algebra is background for trigonometry, which is needed for precalculus, which comes before calculus, and so on. Eliminate one of the topics in the string presented in the last sentence, and you have a gap in mathematical knowledge that becomes an impasse, preventing any student owning it from moving on, not only in mathematics, but also in many other areas.

All the way through the curriculum, connections play a critical role. They help students frame the work they do in learning concepts and skills. How often have you encountered a request for "real-world problems" as a part of your preparation for becoming a teacher of middle school mathematics? Connections help students see the need for learning the mathematics we go through with them. Connections: they are important!

CONNECTIONS WITH OTHER AREAS

Can you imagine doing chemistry without mathematics? It is often said that physics is just applied mathematics. Think of the many careers that involve significant study of mathematics as foundational work, like engineering, for example.

Within the academic world, they are easy to find.

What about mathematics outside the academic world? Ask a tradesperson (carpenter, plumber, mason, mechanic) if they see a need for mathematical skills in their work world and you will more than likely hear something like, "If I had only known how much I would be using mathematics, I would have paid more attention to my teachers." One of the authors of this text was involved in laying out a rectangular concrete slab for a church. Trigonometry was used, along with surveying instruments. A person who does concrete work for a living came up with an easier way, noting that the diagonals of a rectangle have to be the same length. A string was stretched across one diagonal, marked and then put on the other diagonal, which was about a foot shorter than the first, indicating that the form was not a rectangle. Experience and subliminal mathematical skills told the worker how to move things to get a rectangle. It was trivially obvious to that one person; the rest of us simply marveled at the applied mathematics.

Think of sports. Can you see any mathematics there? How do they measure the distance a snow ski jumper travels from the end of the jump to the touchdown point on the hillside? How are batting averages computed in baseball and softball? Lance Armstrong won a record-setting sixth consecutive Tour de France in July of 2004. His times were reported as hours and minutes required to traverse the given distances—mathematics again. Is there any mathematics involved in constructing skateboard ramps?

How about hobbies? Is there any mathematics in sewing? Have you ever seen a dressage event? Check it out and see the mathematics. Have you wondered about the average speed as you skate, bike, jog, trot, walk, or run for 15 minutes? Do artists use mathematics? Is there mathematics in music?

What would happen if we had a mathless day? You could not tell time because that is measurement. You could not drive because how would you tell if you are speeding? As a matter of fact, your car engine could not function because the cylinders fire in a specific order, over and over again. You could not read because the page size, font size, page numbering, and so on could not be used. What could you do on a mathless day?

Your Turn

4.1. List at least three careers requiring mathematics beyond the courses taken by a college-bound high school graduate.

CONCLUSION

Mathematical connections abound, both within the field and in most of the things we do each day. It is difficult to imagine life without mathematics when you think about it, which brings out a very important matter. As a future teacher of mathematics, you will need to convince your students of the value of learning mathematics. Perhaps that seems trivially obvious to you because you saw the need, but you probably liked studying mathematics, found it to be interesting and not overly difficult, and could see where it would be useful in your future. At the same time, many students who were in school with you saw you as being strange, because they could see little or no value to learning mathematics. Your challenge, as a future teacher of mathematics, is to figure out how to stimulate all students to understand the vital role mathematics plays in our lives. Making connections is not automatic. It is your responsibility to provide real-world experi-

ences in which mathematical connections are made. It is not an easy challenge, but it can be done. Good luck.

STICKY QUESTIONS

4.1. Is there any part of mathematics that can be taught as a disconnected section from the rest of the curriculum? If you say yes, describe what that material would be and rationalize why it can stand alone. If you say no, rationalize why there are no unrelated areas within mathematics.

4.2. Is it reasonable to expect you to be able to provide a broad variety of applications of mathematics from the real world? Rationalize your response.

4.3. Are the things that interested you when you were 12 to 14 years old still of interest to that age group today? Rationalize how you can incorporate real-world situations that are relevant to middle school students into the curriculum. Discuss how you can become aware of what those topics might be.

TAG

4.1. 1729 is the smallest number that can be expressed two different ways as the sum of two cubes. What are the two ways? The story behind this problem relates that the mathematician G. H. Hardy arrived in a taxi numbered 1729 when visiting the mathematician Srinivasa Ramanvjan and the question was posed.

4.2. Sum the consecutive counting numbers from 1 through N. This is a great place to relate the Gauss story about discovering how to do this.

4.3. Divide the following 4 × 4 grid into two congruent shapes, each resulting in the same sum when the elements in the cells are added:

5	5	1	25
5	25	10	10
1	5	5	10
10	10	25	10

4.4. If you have 142 Hatfields and 154 McCoys fighting for 69 oil wells over 5 years, who won? Type 14215469 × 5 on your calculator. Turn it upside down to read the answer.

4.5. A person likes 225 but not 224; 900 but not 800; 144 but not 145. Which would be preferred, 1600 or 1700? Why?

4.6. You are given a choice of two payment options: (1) one cent on the first day, two cents on the second day, and double your salary every day thereafter for the thirty days; or (2) exactly $1,000,000. (That's one million dollars!) It should be noted that this problem is posed in many forms, one of which is connected to the legend that this kind of payment arose from an ancient king of the Middle East. The king promised to pay a poor and unworthy suitor of the king's daughter to go away. The agreement was that the king would pay 1 grain of rice on the first square of a chessboard, 2 on the second, 4 on the third, and so on for all 64 squares. Alas, the king became the pauper and the suitor possessed all of the wealth. The suitor and the daughter married and lived happily ever after. What is the better option to take? Why?

4.7. If you add 9 and 9 you get 18, and if you multiply 9 by 9 you get 81 (the reverse of 18). There are two more pairs of numbers with the same characteristics and where the result is two digits: $24 + 3 = 27$ and $24 \times 3 = 72$ and $47 + 2 = 49$ and $47 \times 2 = 94$. However, there is only one pair of numbers with a triple digit result and its reverse. What are the numbers?

4.8. Arrange four nine's to equal 100.

REFERENCE

National Council of Teachers of Mathematics. (2000). *Principles and standards for school mathematics.* Reston, VA: Author.

5
Communication

You know what I mean, right? How often have you heard that as a part of a discussion? When you heard it, did you know what was meant? If you did not, did you admit your confusion, or did you let it slide to avoid nonflattering appearances about your ability to understand?

Any questions? The teacher just said that to your class. The implied question could be something along the line of, "Did you understand my wonderfully clear explanation of the situation?" Certainly teachers do not use that phraseology, but many times the veiled statement is there. Dare you speak up? Or, do you remain silent, indicating that you do understand and hoping that you will figure it out later?

The National Council of Teachers of Mathematics (NCTM) speaks to communication from the students' vantage point, saying:

Instructional programs from prekindergarten through grade 12 should enable all students to—organize and consolidate their mathematical thinking through communication; communicate their mathematical thinking coherently and clearly to peers, teachers, and others; analyze and evaluate the mathematical thinking and strategies of others; use the language of mathematics to express mathematical ideas precisely. (NCTM, 2000, p. 60)

Like so many things, that is a lot easier said than done. Yet, it is your responsibility to create an atmosphere in which students grow, thrive, and discuss mathematics in meaningful terms. Conversations about mathematical concepts are essential in the classroom. Exemplary instruction mandates promoting communication. As a teacher of middle school mathematics, it is your professional duty to help students understand the need to communicate both with, and about, mathematics. Without that ability, how handicapped will their futures be?

CLARITY OF THOUGHT

Communication is a key. It also relies on being able to easily and purposefully teach from both the student perspective and the mathematical community perspective. Communication is a two-way street. In the classroom, it is imperative that the explanations you give are understandable. We assume that the following will not happen in your classroom, but, regretfully, it happens in some way, shape, or form all too often. The teacher explains something to the class and the following interaction occurs:

Student: I don't get it.

The teacher carefully and patiently explains it again, almost word for word. It could have been that the student was not paying attention during the first coverage.

Student: I don't get it.

The teacher sighs and explains it again, again, almost word for word.

Student: I still don't get it.

The teacher (a very patient individual) explains it again, almost a carbon copy of the first coverage. This time, there are clipped words with staccato timing. It is clear that the patience is wearing thin.

Student: Sorry, but I still don't get it.

The teacher loses patience and asks, "What is wrong with you?" The teacher continues, "I have gone over this four times now!" Although the teacher would never react like that (we hope), there is a certain mentality that is presented that is far too common.

Do you see a communication gap in that last vignette? Granted, a second explanation could parallel the first because the student might not have been paying attention. After that allowance, however, well-prepared teachers take a different approach to bridge this gap. It is the teacher's responsibility to take the knowledge of students, mathematics, teaching, and group dynamics to get things into words student can understand.

You know what you know. It is your responsibility to organize and provide clear, logical, coherent, and interesting lessons for your students. That is not an easy task. It is communication. That is what clarity of thought is all about!

WAYS OF EXPRESSING WHAT YOU KNOW

As you attempt to stimulate student learning, you need to use a variety of approaches, many of which are discussed throughout this text. We assume you have heard about things like lecture, group work, individualizations, portfolios, learning logs, and so on in your education foundations classes. We further assume that you will be able to adapt those general ideas to the specific examples and discussions we provide. The teacher is responsible for directing, shaping, and designing students' activities so the students grow intellectually in mathematics. Communication must take multiple forms. Discussions, written work, diagrams, drawings, spreadsheets, graphs, journaling, special projects, student-written problems, and quick-writes are all communicative formats that can be effective and beneficial. The difference between this book and your foundations texts is that we will give examples that relate to the middle school mathematics curriculum.

This text contains a chapter on problem solving. There, we elaborate on the advantage of solving a problem more than one way, a process that is far too uncommon. Think about it though—if you are able to solve a problem only one way, how flexible is your thinking? On the other hand, if you solve a problem more than one way, you are developing the ability to look at a situation from multiple vantage points. This will be a handy skill when you encounter a situation that is not transparent as far as solving it is concerned. After a failed attempt, you can examine the setting from a different perspective.

Shortly you will read a discussion on how to do the same problem more than one way. With this flexibility in your repertoire, you should be able to clearly communicate a solution to all students or understand student solutions because you will be beyond thinking of a problem from only one vantage point. Surely one of those ways will make sense to each student. Does this mean you should do the same problem all these different ways? Not necessarily, although it could be a wonderful means of demonstrating flexibility of thought. Rather, these different ways provide you the opportunity to reach a student who does not understand your primary coverage or explanation, or to find meaning in a student's solution of a problem. It is your responsibility to take the information you and your students communicate and use it to clarify, encourage, and facilitate communication. Students need the opportunity to probe different approaches to problems to see the beauty and interconnections in mathematics. This is communication!

Suppose there are 205 teams in a single-elimination (you lose, you are out) tournament. How many games must be played to determine a winner? Students typically solve this problem by saying:

One team gets a bye (meaning they do not play in the first set of games).
204 teams will mean 102 games, and 102 winners.
The bye team is inserted and another team gets a bye.
102 teams means 51 games and 51 winners.
The bye team is inserted.
52 teams means 26 games and 26 winners.

26 teams means 13 games and 13 winners.
One team gets a bye.
12 teams means 6 games and 6 winners.
The bye team is inserted and another team gets a bye.
6 teams means 3 games and 3 winners.
The bye team is inserted.
4 teams means 2 games and 2 winners.
2 teams means 1 game and 1 winner, the champion.

Then $102+51+26+13+6+3+2+1=204$, the number of games played. There is nothing wrong with solving the problem in this manner, but there is another, much faster way.

Mathematicians often do a simpler problem as a means of solving a situation that may appear complex. Ironically, this procedure seems to be difficult for many students to acclimate to, perhaps because it is not used often in approaches they have seen. In this instance, starting with a smaller number of teams could prove beneficial:

2 teams means 1 game.
3 teams means 2 games.
4 teams means 3 games.

A pattern appears, and there is one less game than the number of teams. Thus, with 205 teams, there would be 204 games.

There is still another way to solve this problem. If there are 205 teams and it is a single-elimination tournament, then there must be 204 losers. But each loser comes from a game, so there are 204 games.

Any one of these solutions is no better than the other. They are just different. If you are stressing logic in the class at the time of this lesson, the idea of 204

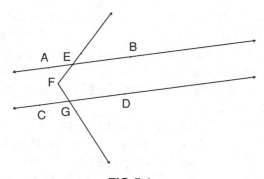

FIG 5.1.

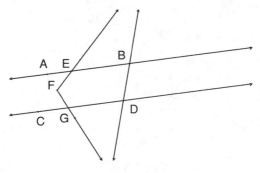

FIG 5.3.

losers might be the primary explanation. If, on the other hand, patterning is the focus of the lesson, the idea of looking at the problem from that perspective could prove advantageous. Either way, did you notice the connection between this and a representation of mathematics in the real world?

The single-elimination tournament discussion is an example of communicating with mathematics. Here is one that would be an example of communicating about mathematics. Suppose you have Fig. 5.1, $\overleftrightarrow{AB}$ knowing that is parallel to $\overleftrightarrow{CD}$, and you want to know the sum of the measures of ∠BEF, ∠EFG, and ∠FGD.

One way to solve the problem would be to draw $\overleftrightarrow{FH}$ parallel to $\overleftrightarrow{AB}$ and $\overleftrightarrow{CD}$, as shown in Fig. 5.2. You now know that ∠BEF + ∠EFH = 180°   (corresponding interior angles of parallel lines are supplementary) and that ∠HFG + ∠FGD = 180°. Adding   the   two   equations   gives

∠BEF + ∠EFH + ∠HFG + ∠FGD = 360°. However, ∠EFH + ∠HFG = ∠EFG, making ∠BEF + ∠EFG + ∠FGD = 360°.

Another solution would be to draw $\overleftrightarrow{BD}$, making pentagon BDGFE, as shown in Fig. 5.3. It can be determined that the sum of the measures of the interior angles of a convex pentagon is 540°. It must be the case that ∠EBD + ∠BDG = 180° (corresponding interior angles of parallel lines are supplementary). That leaves ∠BEF +∠EFG +∠FGD = 360°. Did you think of that solution?

How about this one? Establish J as the intersection of $\overleftrightarrow{EF}$ and $\overleftrightarrow{CD}$, as shown in Fig. 5.4. With that, you can ascertain the following:

$$∠BEF = 180° - ∠FJG$$
$$∠EFG = 180° - ∠JFG$$
$$∠FGD = 180° - ∠FGJ.$$

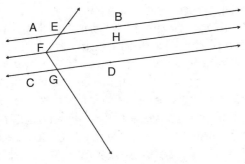

FIG 5.2.

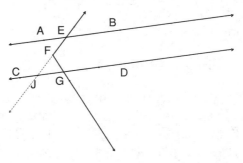

FIG 5.4.

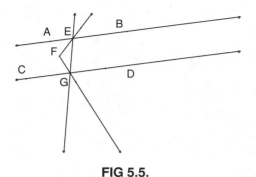

FIG 5.5.

Adding those three gives

$$\angle BEF + \angle EFG + \angle FGD$$

$$= 540° - \angle FJG + \angle JFG + \angle FGJ.$$

But, $\angle FJG + \angle JFG + \angle FGJ = 180°$ since they form a triangle. Thus,
$\angle BEF + \angle EFG + \angle FGD = 360°$.

Just for fun, Fig 5.5. gives one more way to show $\angle BEF + \angle EFG + \angle FGD = 360°$. Here $\overleftrightarrow{EG}$ is established. With that, the following is known:

$\angle BEG + \angle EGD = 180°$ (corresponding

interior angles of parallel lines)

$\angle EFG + \angle FGE + \angle GEF = 180°$ (triangle).

Adding those two gives
$\angle BEG + \angle EGD + \angle EFG + \angle FGE + \angle GEF = 360°$.
But,

$$\angle BEG + \angle EFG = \angle BEF$$

and

$$\angle FGE + \angle EGD = \angle FGD,$$

leaving

$$\angle BEF + \angle EFG + \angle FGD = 360°.$$

Are you surprised that we came up with five different ways to show that $\angle BEF + \angle EFG + \angle FGD = 360°$? That shows a variety of ways to communicate the knowledge in our heads to students

or understand students' communication efforts. The one selected first is influenced by multiple factors: teacher's favorite, background knowledge of students, whether or not students need a more challenging approach, and so on.

Another way of having students communicate their understanding is through writing. Written communication provides a way to listen to students. It gives you the opportunity to obtain a sense of the depth of a student's understanding of the concept being taught. Writing in mathematics will help you assess how students feel about investigating the concepts at hand, their ability and success as mathematics students, and their perceptions of their development in the subject (Huetinck & Munshin, 2004). Writing helps students reflect on their learning and experiences. It helps clarify understanding and enables them to sift thought patterns to incorporate previously gained knowledge to make connections. For example, for the 205 teams in the single-elimination tournament, have students write and explain this problem or have them answer questions such as: "I became confused when," "I do understand how to...", or "I do not understand...." Writing is a unique mode of learning. It challenges students to use intellectual skills and go beyond memorization.

Consider any concept you feel you understand. There are levels you go through as you learn that concept. First, you work with it through assignments, your reading, your thinking, and your reflections. As you do that you begin to understand it. Then, as the understanding begins to take form, you are able to speak about it. Finally, after you have spoken (which could include discussions and more thought and reflection), you are able to write about what you know. This ability to write about the concept is a high-order representation of what you know. Even at that, the writing will probably go through multiple revisions before it is ready for public consumption. This layered learning becomes an assessment of your own growth and development. As you consider assessment of students, do not forget that their growth is a work in progress. They too need to realize the value of assessing and reflecting on their own work.

It is imperative that you have adequate command of the content, your students, pedagogical processes, and your abilities to be able to take the knowledge you have and put it in words the students can relate to. Furthermore, it is important to help guide students to write their own thought processes into words for even greater understanding. That is communication.

IMPORTANCE OF PLANNING MATHEMATICS LESSONS

Are you asking, "How do we communicate in a variety of ways and do this effectively?" The answer to that begins with good lesson planning. Teaching mathematics is not simply standing in front of a group of students and telling them how to add and subtract. It is more than grading homework, papers, tests, or telling which page to read and what problems to do for homework. One important aspect of becoming an effective teacher of mathematics is taking the necessary time to plan the lesson that conveys the mathematical ideas and information your students need to learn. That is, communicate what you want them to learn and give them a variety of approaches in which to do so!

Teaching is not easy. It requires tremendous time, energy, dedication, and resilience. You need to:

- Motivate the students to want to learn.
- Create appropriate learning environments.

- Patiently explain the material.
- Provide activities that focus on and integrate mathematical ideas.
- Deal with a variety of learning modalities and capabilities.
- Establish classroom management skills.
- Assess progress (both yours and the students).
- Grow personally.
- Be enthusiastic.
- And so much more!

Teaching is selling. You must be an advocate of mathematics. Belief, excitement, and enthusiasm about the learning of mathematics are a necessity. If you do not seem interested in what is going on in class, why should your students? Good classes do not just happen. They are carefully planned and orchestrated. Certainly there are deviations from the plan, depending on happenings during the class, but the framework is laid out well ahead of time.

Prior to teaching, it is imperative that the covered topics be carefully contemplated and organized. Planning also provides the opportunity to connect topics from different lessons and subject areas throughout the course.

What Should Be Planned?

This is not a simple question. Teachers generally have little input into the curriculum for a given course. The broad course objectives may be dictated at the federal, state, district, school, and even department levels. Some schools and districts mandate that a given course be covered in lock-step fashion. All classes are given the same objective to be completed within a given time frame. Even with constraints such as these, there is opportunity for individualization by the teacher. Variation of presentation styles, relating the subject matter to background material, calling upon student strengths established earlier in the curriculum, and use of technology can all provide extra time that permits some flexibility for teaching.

Teachers can vary their curriculum in a manner that will best meet the needs of all students as long as objectives are met. Thus, the effective teacher looks at the full year and establishes an outline that covers the topics, builds needed readiness, determines a sequence in which the concepts will be covered, and defines an assessment plan. At this level, the goals and statements will be broad and general, but they provide a basic skeleton from which to work. Often times this framework is dictated by the textbook, which is written to meet the needs of a wide variety of students. You may need to alter the topic sequence to meet the needs of your students. There is nothing wrong with that, as long as appropriate readiness and background is considered.

As a new teacher, you might get little guidance with planning your yearly objectives. Initially you will need to rely on the resources and material you have learned in your mathematics education program to help navigate the curriculum your students need. Your colleagues can provide helpful insight into the year's objectives and goals. By your second or third year of teaching you will have a better feel for those concepts that are more difficult for your students.

Once the long-range plan has been established, consideration should be given to smaller, but still sizeable, chunks of information. Chapter headings in a textbook may determine those topics. You need to reserve the right to delay sections of a chapter, or a whole chapter, until it is more suitable for your class. You may need to alter and perhaps supplement the information in the text with material from the other resources. Certainly, each daily lesson must be carefully prepared and set forth.

Pressures or time constraints often hinder the development of well-planned lessons. Suppose the specific objective is to cover how to add two fractions with unlike denominators. Consider a teacher who did not plan, but skimmed the text for a few seconds prior to class thinking, "OK, I know how to do that." Class begins and the teacher says something like, "Today we are going to add fractions; you know, something like $\frac{1}{4} + \frac{3}{8}$," writing the two fractions on the board while talking. Then there is a short pause and the teacher asks a series of questions such as the following, with the class providing appropriate responses before going on to do the next question.

What is a fraction?
   Define numerator.
   The denominator of a fraction tells...?
   In $\frac{1}{4}$, the numerator is...?
   And the denominator is...?
   When we add things, basically what do we do?
   And so on.

What is the teacher doing? These answers are all things the class should know. If they do not, how can the teacher justify dealing with the topic at hand? Ask a class of students what the teacher is doing and they will tell you the teacher is stalling. The teacher, for whatever reason, momentarily forgot how to add fractions with unlike denominators. While each of those mundane questions was being asked, the teacher was probing memory banks, trying to recall how to do the problem, how to organize thoughts, and attempting to devise a coherent explanation. Most of us are very quick to say that would never happen to us. Many of us would say that we would not draw a blank on something as simple as that. Maybe or maybe not. The real issue is not whether or not it *will* happen. The question is *when*? The solution to the dilemma is so simple. **PLAN!** Thoughtful planning can help create an overflow situation for you and for your students; so **PLAN!**

Lesson Plans

A good rule of thumb for planning is to formulate ideas weeks before delivery time, look the plan over a few times between development and delivery, and take time to review it the day before it happens. This procedure enhances the connections between different plans, stimulates thoughts, and amplifies needed changes. Yes, this takes time, but it is a part of being a professional. Even with all that, there will still be many times when changes will be made right before or during the class. It is also part of the process of building the background that becomes overflow. Over the years, you will probably need less time to effectively plan your lessons because of your experience and knowledge of student development.

Remember that certain factors may impact your plans, including students, ability levels, administrative decisions, departmental procedures, personal bias, standards, textbook, homework policies, testing practices, and available class time. This list will continue to grow throughout your career. You will have authority over some of the items on the list but others will be beyond your control.

Planning and Textbooks

It is common to rely heavily on textbooks in day-to-day teaching. Typically this is even more common with mathematics classes. Most decisions about what to teach, how to teach, when to teach, and the associated exercises are based largely on what is in the textbook. Some people are concerned about the quality of textbooks, the way they

are written, and the tremendous influence they have. Prior to the academic year, carefully read through your teacher's edition of the mathematics text. Many times, it provides helpful ideas for planning. Also, there may be suggestions about common student errors and areas that typically need reinforcement when teaching that particular concept. The teacher's edition can be a wonderful resource and guide, but it is not your only resource.

American education utilizes a spiral curriculum approach. It is not uncommon for a topic to be encountered more than once in a textbook. If subsequent coverage adds nothing new to the knowledge base, why bother with it? **IF**, and note that is a big if, the material is learned the first time, there should be no need for repetition (excluding practice of the skill, of course). If these subsequent encounters with a topic do add to the knowledge base, how much time is necessary to review the prior material? Again, IF the material was learned the first time, there is no need for the review, with the possible exception of a few minutes to relate the new topic to the earlier work and orient the students. Still, it is rather common for the text to provide more review than is necessary. Blindly following the text without consideration for the development and needs of students can lead to excessive repetition. This constant repetition can lead to bored students who become disenchanted with mathematics.

Be very careful as you think about what you just read. Covering a concept can have multiple meanings. Something is covered because it is in the text, the curriculum, the defined standards, and many other reasons. At times, the covered is best interpreted as covering up. The topic at hand is presented, but there is no enlightenment for the students; thus, it is covered up. We as teachers of mathematics should strive to help students uncover the mathematics they are learning. It is somewhat like peeling an onion. We want to open the layers, one at a time so each student grows and understands the essentials of mathematics, as they are uncovered in their curriculum. This layering is an amplification of what the curriculum is all about. Topics are revisited not simply to review. They are amplified, grown, and nurtured. Furthermore, the opportunity for additional representation, connection, and communication about the topic becomes more evident to all involved.

Your Turn

5.1. Should your lessons follow the structure of the text? Why or why not?

5.2. Should two teachers in the same grade, with students of the same ability, in the same school, follow the same lesson plans? Why or why not?

5.3. If you can't finish the curriculum, how do you decide what to sacrifice?

5.4. What are the ramifications of eliminating some topics in the curriculum? Is there a way this dilemma can be resolved?

CONTENTS OF MATHEMATICS LESSON PLANS

We provided some informal lesson plan samples earlier. Now we take a more formal approach. There is an adage that should be considered: "Anything worth doing is worth doing *poorly*—until you learn to do it well." Detailed planning is a form of communication between teacher and students and is a significant part of learning to teach mathematics well. Formal planning is critical to the successes of teaching. As the classroom teacher, you must be clear about your presentation each and every day. The students are your audience and how you interact with them through your daily planning is essential to a healthy learning environment. As a first-year teacher, you need to develop formal, detailed lessons. This ensures your confidence when presenting the information to students and shows your students that you are prepared and that you care about their learning. When teaching, being unprepared leads to classroom management problems and lack of interest among students. Students model the behaviors as they see them, so always remember, if you are unprepared, your students will be unprepared!

Preparation and organization compensates for your lack of experience as a beginning teacher. Although experienced teachers may not necessarily need to write extensive plans for each class, novice teachers (that is you) need to do it to be effective. Please note that what we are about to present is not a prescriptive format. Rather, it is a list of what should be included in lesson plans. We realize that some internship programs and some administrators mandate a particular lesson format. You should find each of the components we list here in any format you encounter. If a format is not mandated, develop one that suits you. A lesson plan is a perfect place for you to frame the purposefulness of your instruction, take account of student perspective, frame particular examples and nonexamples, and set students up to be able to both consolidate the lesson and do well on homework or other assignments. A completed daily lesson plan should contain the following:

1. Topic
2. Goals/objectives statement(s): the purpose, concepts, knowledge that the students will learn, and alignment with standards.
3. Setting:
   a. Motivation (How will you get your students excited about what you are teaching them?)

b. Tie to previous learning (How will you tie what you are about to teach with what they already know, readiness, and so on?)

4. Teaching sequence:
   a. How will you introduce the lesson?
   b. What is your instructional outline?
   c. What upper-level questions will you ask?
   d. What is your closure?
   e. What are your special needs adaptations and ESOL students?
   f. How will you connect this lesson to other material?
5. Materials
6. Assessment

The topic to be covered should be included not only for your benefit, but also as a contingency plan in case someone else needs to read your lesson. You know what you are teaching, but someone else may not. The goal helps focus on what are you trying to accomplish by teaching this topic. Why is this topic important for the students' development? Objectives are a must for any lesson plan. Why is this topic being covered? As you rationalize why a topic is being taught, remember to look at it from the students' perspective. You as an adult might see future applications of the topic, but the students want to know where they can use it today. You eventually will have to establish your own style for writing objectives. The important point is that objectives are necessary for a lesson plan.

There must be a reason for having your class learn material. What is it? It is also assumed that the focus is on the students being able to perform tasks they could not do prior to the lesson. For example, suppose you are going to teach someone to bake banana nut muffins. This will be the first time the person will have done such a thing. You say:

"Get the mix."
"Get a big bowl."

"Get a spoon."
"Get one egg."
"Get the milk."
"Get the measuring cup."
"Get the muffin pan."
"Put a paper baking cup in each hole in the pan.

At this point, YOU proceed to do the following:

Turn the oven on to preheat to 400°.
Empty the mix into the bowl.
Measure a third of a cup of milk.
Pour the milk into the bowl with the mix.
Break the egg and put it into the bowl.
Blend the ingredients.
Fill each muffin cup until it is half full.
Bake 13 to 15 minutes or until golden brown.
Remove the muffin pan from the oven.
Let the muffins cool.

Now, you say to the person:

"We baked muffins."

You did not let the person measure the milk because of potential spills, or perhaps an inability to deal with a third of a cup. You did not let the learner break the egg because of the possibility of shells getting into the mix. Similar excuses can be made for other events that would occur during the making of the muffins.

The muffin example shows that "we" did not make muffins; you did. You used the individual as a "gofer" by saying "go for this" or "go for that." The objective in this case was to make muffins. If the objective had been behaviorally stated and learner oriented, the instructions would have had the learner doing each of the steps, or at least most of them. As lessons are considered in the framework of this text and the mathematics classrooms described, it is assumed that they will be behaviorally oriented. If that assumption is not correct, the teacher could become a dispenser of information, paying no attention to whether or not it is received. More significantly, you run the risk of having an environment where the students are not active participants in learning the mathematics they will need to become functional citizens.

A well-formulated plan includes all materials that will be needed in the lesson. Because the lesson is planned in advance, there is a good chance you may forget an important manipulative or demonstration prop needed for teaching the concept. If you list your materials ahead of time you can gather them before you begin to teach the lesson that day. Nothing is worse than having to stop an effective lesson because you have forgotten needed materials. This can be a distraction to students and to you because it stops the flow of the lesson and requires refocusing.

Questions, lesson notes, and examples are major ingredients for any plan. Each of these is equally significant to the overall development and delivery of the plan. They help you model and stimulate mathematical thinking. Remember you are trying to stimulate thought in your students because they are active learners. Consider the level of questions you are asking. If all of your questions are on the knowledge level, there is little or no thought involved because the student is merely repeating previously encountered information. Your lesson plans should include higher-order questions, which are generally defined as anything more complex than knowledge level, using Bloom's taxonomy. Higher-order questions usually cannot be generated quickly, although it does become easier and more reflexive as you mature within your career. Higher-order questions require careful thought in advance of the

class. Do not worry about including exact wording. You will be able to phrase the question within the context of the class as long as you have the idea in the plans. As you teach your lessons, distractions will occur which may cause you to get slightly sidetracked. Without having your higher-order questions listed it is likely you will simply forget to ask them.

Questioning is not easy. A knowledge-level question, while still important, should be fairly reflexive. Similarly, it is not necessary to state the name of the student who will be called upon to respond. It is assumed you will distribute participation throughout the class. Higher-order questions are designed to make students think and reflect about what they are learning. They strengthen students' reasoning ability and communication skills. Usually questions requiring thought are not easy for students to answer. "How?" and "Why?" can be higher-order questions when connected to a response given by a student. Many questions asked in a classroom are lower order. Probably the most likely reason for the preponderance of lower-order questions is that higher-order questions are difficult to create extemporaneously.

Your lesson outline notes should reflect the things you will say, as the students progress from a point of not knowing something to a point of knowing it. You should initially assume that your students do not know the material you are helping them learn. If they know the topic of the day, why are you teaching it? The notes should contain the major points that comprise your discussion or development of the topic. There is no need to write out a word-by-word description of what will be said, just the major points. Some form of an outline (not necessarily formal) is most beneficial. You should be able to quickly skim the outline and determine if all the salient points have been covered. Your outline should help answer, "What essential points do you expect the students to see? What reactions do you expect them to have? Where do you intend the discussion to lead?" These ideas should be a part of the notes. Otherwise there is a risk that the discussion will become a random talk session with no apparent point or central theme.

Most students are curious about things and have questions. Students need to learn to be willing to ask. The following situation was used to stimulate questions. The students entered the classroom to find the teacher sitting on a chair, which had been placed on the teacher's desk. The students asked each other what was going on. Some inquired of others whether or not they should call the principal or another teacher. The level of uncertainty and inquisitiveness was quite high. After a few minutes of this, the teacher hopped off the chair and removed it from the desktop, saying to the class, "Isn't it interesting that you had several questions but no one asked me. Since I was the one sitting in the chair, wouldn't it be reasonable to ask me why?" The moral of the story—know what to ask and know whom to ask.

Examples are equally as important as questions. Examples are the ideal forum for modeling mathematical thinking. You should be willing to make public your thoughts, questions, confusions, and insights as you help peel layers of cloudiness off the onion of understanding for your students. Students need to know what each example is an example of. They also need to see nonexamples—samples that illustrate incomplete thinking, misapplication, common errors, exceptions, or overgeneralization. It has been said, "If you want to know what a duck is, you have to know what a goose is." Specific examples must be carefully thought out as each lesson is planned. Many students learn by observ-

ing examples. Although it is ideal to have students develop and discover mathematics, there will be times when you will be explaining things to them. When you are explaining a situation that requires an example, each new problem type should have one written example in your plans, solved in complete detail, just as you expect your students to do it. This should not be an example worked in the text. You will probably use more than one example in your lesson for each type of problem, but one worked out in complete detail should be sufficient for your planning. If students are not to skip steps, your example should include all steps they are expected to present in their discussion. Warning: be very careful here! It is not to be assumed that the students must do the problem the way you do it. Often the problem could be done in a variety of ways, any of which should be acceptable, as long as it is mathematically legal. Furthermore, do not limit the example discussion to working problems. Manipulatives, literature, technology, activities, games, experiments, demonstrations, journaling, reporting, and so on all fit into this idea as well.

Assessing Your Lessons

Assessment can be incorporated into your lesson plans to determine student (and your—remember the mirror test?) progress. You can give a homework assignment and then check it to see if the subject has been mastered. Quizzes, tests, portfolios, group work, reports, individual projects, and software programs as well as a plethora of other means can all be used to provide insight into the progress of students. You need to determine how successfully you created an environment in which the students could learn the material, and whether or not the class understood what was covered. Deciding how well you did is not always easy. Some of us tend to be too critical of ourselves. Others are quite lenient when it comes to self-examination and decide that it had to be good because "I" did it. Somewhere between those two extremes is probably where most of us will land. A few moments for reflection can be very revealing:

- Were the examples clear and pertinent?
- Did the students ask similar questions repeatedly?
- How were the questions I asked answered?
- Did the students show reflection and thought?
- Were the students able to relate the topic to prior work?
- Were the applications clear to the students?
- Could the students see the relevance of the topic?
- Did I act excited and interested throughout the lesson?
- Can the presentation be improved? Where? How?
- Would this lesson be effective with another class?

This is not an exhaustive list of questions to ask as you go over your self-evaluation, but it is a start. Video- or audiotaping a class can prove quite revealing. You may also want to create a lesson checklist for yourself. At the end of the day (when you have time), go through the checklist and make notes regarding the effectiveness of the lesson. Be sure to use checklist items that are important to you. Remember this list is a self-assessment of your lesson. You will probably be the only one to see it, but that does not excuse you from doing the self-evaluation.

Another form of lesson assessment can be from student feedback. Have students keep a small notebook that can be used as a math journal or anonymous comments handed in on index cards. Periodically, ask your students to answer questions such as the following:

- What was the most fun in mathematics during the past week?
- What gave you the most trouble?
- What would you like to learn more about?

Collect the students' journals every week or two. This can be extremely valuable for assessing both lesson effectiveness and student progress throughout the year.

Sample Lesson Plan

The following lesson plan involves the whole class in problem solving, decision making, and communicating mathematics.

1. Topic: fractions
2. Goals/objectives statement(s): students will be able to investigate, apply problem-solving processes, and model fractions as part of a whole.
3. Procedures:
a. Motivation—The following is similar to problems typically posed to students: "You just came home from shooting hoops with friends. You helped yourself to a piece of chocolate cake and a can of soda. Someone had already eaten part of the cake because only two thirds of it was left. After taking your piece, only half of the cake remained. What part of the cake did you eat?"
b. Tie to previous learning—Students have had prior experiences working with problem-solving strategies and working with fraction models.
4. Teaching sequence:
a. How will you introduce the lesson? After posing the initial setting, ask students

to begin brainstorming about possible problem-solving strategies. These can include modeling, acting, drawing, diagrams, simplifying, looking for patterns, and so on.

b. What is your instructional outline? Direct students to analyze the problem for knowns and unknowns. Introduce strategies to help students arrive at possible solutions. Draw diagrams, patterns, and model fractions to show one half and two thirds. If needed, include other strategies for student understanding. If students are having difficulty interpreting knowns, and unknowns, then pose other problems for understanding and generating data.

c. What higher-order questions will you ask? Ask students if they can predict what part of the cake was eaten, based on the question posed. Why or why not? What part of the cake was eaten? How did you arrive at your conclusion? What portion of the cake was left? How did you determine this to be true? What strategies were used to determine your solution? Can you construct a diagram showing your results? Why did you choose this particular procedure? Can you model the fractional parts using a manipulative? Can you simplify your solution or state it in different terms? How did you organize your strategies to solve the problem?

d. What is your closure for the lesson? Have students share their solutions and discuss them. Have students summarize their understanding of these solutions in their mathematics journal.

e. What are your special needs adaptations and those for ESOL students? These can include peer modeling, diagrams, models, pictures, acting, drawing, simplifying the problem, and so on.

f. How will you connect this lesson to other material? Many books and resources (see end of this chapter) abound that relate to problem solving and fractions. Incorporating books into the classroom environment will help build reading and language arts skills.

5. Materials:
   Manipulatives
   Markers
   Poster board, chart paper, or chalkboards.

6. Assessment: The following rubric may be used. Don't forget to look for error patterns. Examples can be found in TAG 8.22.

Problem interpretation (5 points)

5 = Interpreted the problem correctly

3 = Interpreted only parts of the problem

0 = No interpretation is evident

Appropriateness of chosen solution strategy (5 points)

5 = A correct strategy was chosen for a correct solution

3 = Strategy chosen was questionable

0 = No strategy or attempt was made for solution

Solution strategy implementation (5 points)

5 = Correct solution was implemented successfully

3 = Partial solution was implemented or had errors

0 = No solution was implemented

Verification of solution (5 points)

5 = Solution was verified using an alternate strategy

3 = Used alternate solution but was incorrect

0 = No attempt was made using alternate strategy

The lesson just presented emphasizes the teacher facilitating and controlling students' thought processes. Now look at the same lesson plan with activities and incorporated cooperative learning strategies. The upcoming version of this lesson allows for more student interaction, communication among peers and teacher, and group goal accountability.

1. Topic: fractions
2. Goals/objectives statement(s): in groups, students will be able to investigate, apply problem-solving processes, and model fractions as part of a whole.
3. Procedures:
a. Motivation—Pose the following to students: "You just came home from shooting hoops with friends. You helped yourself to a piece of chocolate cake and a can of soda. Someone had already eaten part of the cake because only two thirds of it was left. After taking your piece, only half of the cake remained. What part of the cake did you eat? How can this be determined?"
b. Tie to previous learning—Students have had prior experiences working with problem-solving strategies and working with fraction models.
4. Teaching sequence:
a. How will you introduce the lesson? After posing the initial setting, students will be encouraged by the teacher and peers to draw upon prior knowledge of problem solving strategies.
b. What is your instructional outline? Students will be placed in groups. Each group will have an assigned coordinator/manager, secretary/recorder, evaluator, and reporter. (Other roles will be assigned if needed: reader, checker, praiser, gofer, or timekeeper.)

The coordinator/manager will have all students brainstorm the details of the problem. Recorders will write the information on the poster board or chart paper.

Reporters will elicit one or two known facts to the whole class. Other facts may be added to charts after each group has reported. This will continue until all known facts have been listed.

Each group will be responsible for analyzing their data of knowns and unknowns for the question posed, determining what is and is not important. Each of these is listed by the recorder. The teacher will probe groups for further information that may be missing during their discussions.

Coordinators/managers will lead the discussion for solutions presented in the group. Possible strategies could include pictures, diagrams, numbers, manipulatives, dissecting information, organizing data, translating, predicting, simplifying, composing, creating, estimating, and so on.

The best strategy as determined by the group will be implemented to solve the problem. The recorder will illustrate how the group arrived at its conclusion. The reporter will describe how the group worked together to find the solution to the problem. The evaluator will discuss how each group member participated in the activity.

c. What higher-order questions will you ask? Can your group predict what part of the cake was eaten? Why or why not? What part of the cake was actually eaten? How did your group arrive at your conclusion? What portion of the cake was left? How did you determine this to be true? What strategies did your group use to determine your solution? Can you construct a diagram showing your results? Why did you choose this particular procedure? Can you model the fractional parts using your manipulatives? Can you simplify your solution or state it in different terms? How did you organize your strategies to solve the problem? What did each of you contribute to the brainstorming discussion?

d. What is your closure for the lesson? Students will be asked to find an alternative solution to the problem and present it to the whole class. Each of the groups' responses will be displayed and discussed.

e. What are your special needs adaptations and those for ESOL students? This includes group work, peer modeling, diagrams, models, pictures, acting, drawing, simplifying the problem, and so on.

f. How will you connect this lesson to other material? Many books and resources abound (see end of this chapter) that relate to problem solving, fractions, and cooperative learning. Incorporating such books into the classroom environment will help build reading and language art skills.

5. Materials:

Manipulatives

Markers

Poster board, chart paper, or chalkboards

6. Assessment: The following rubric may be used. Don't forget to look for error patterns. Examples can be found in TAG 8.22.

Problem interpretation (5 points)

5 = Interpreted the problem correctly

3 = Interpreted only parts of the problem

0 = No interpretation was evident

Appropriateness of chosen solution strategy (5 points)

5 = A correct strategy was chosen for a correct solution

3 = Strategy chosen was questionable

0 = No strategy or attempt was made for solution

Solution strategy implementation (5 points)

5 = Correct solution was implemented successfully

3 = Partial solution was implemented or had errors

0 = No solution was implemented

Verification of solution (5 points)

5 = Solution was verified using an alternate strategy

3 = Used alternate solution but was incorrect

0 = No attempt was made using alternate strategy

Comments

We are showing this lesson again using cooperative learning because it is an instructional approach that increases students' participation, communication, and learning in all subject areas. Johnson and Johnson (1987) emphasized that implementing cooperative learning experiences promotes greater competencies in critical thinking, more positive attitudes toward subject matter, greater competencies working collaboratively, greater psychological health, and stronger perceptions of the grading system's failures. It should be noted that, even though grouped, each student should accept responsibility for his or her own personal learning structure.

So what are you asked to do? You are charged with making this process successful and workable. How do you do that? The implications for you as the classroom teacher are as follows:

- Cooperative learning procedures may be used successfully with any academic task, although they are most successful when conceptual learning is required.
- Whenever possible, cooperative groups should be structured so that controversy and academic disagreements among group members are possible.
- Students should be encouraged to keep each other on task and to discuss the assigned material in ways that ensure elaborate rehearsal and the use of higher learning strategies.
- Students should be encouraged to support each other's efforts to achieve, to regulate each other's task-related efforts, to provide each other with feedback, and to ensure that all group

members are verbally involved in the learning process.

- Cooperative groups should contain low-, medium-, and high-ability-level students if possible to help promote discussion, peer teaching, and justification of answers.
- Positive relationships among group members should be encouraged. (Johnson & Johnson, 1987, p. 40)

Kagan (1994) presents several structures for implementing cooperative learning in the classroom. Think–Pair–Share is one form of cooperative learning. The problems presented earlier could be used in this manner by asking students to work individually for a few minutes; pair to share, compare, and check findings, and as a group write a short report for another few minutes; and share final solutions with the whole class. This will give students the chance to use written and verbal communication. Also, this will provide a good opportunity to share and compare approaches: Which one of the approaches is more appropriate? Which one of these approaches is more elegant? Are there similarities between the approaches? You should always be looking for ways to help them communicate mathematics effectively. They should notice that there are many acceptable, effective, and stylish ways to solve a problem, and should learn to respect each other's efforts in a supportive environment. Students need exposure to hearing about, reading about, and listening to the thoughts of others. To share ideas and thoughts with others through writing or talking forces us to think more deeply. When we think more, we deepen our understanding and can communicate more clearly.

What are we saying here? Not all students learn the same way. That is why learning modalities are discussed in education classes. You are responsible for knowing your students well enough to determine the best method of introducing a topic. Given all the pedagogical options that are available today, a majority of instruction still uses the lecture method, even though it is known to be a very ineffective method for student learning. The teacher tells the students how to do a problem and the class mimics the model (cookie cutter mathematics). Little student thought is required in this format. Thinking and flexibility are not highly valued. It basically becomes the teacher saying, "Here is how you do this. Trust me, I would not lie to you. Don't think about it, just do it." That is a sad commentary, but it is a lot closer to the truth than many of us would like to admit.

You can be a catalyst for change in the middle school classroom. Use technology and manipulatives. Find real-world applications that relate to the students. Create and use models. Insert activities. Establish expectations. You can take a student from an entrance or beginning level to higher ground. You need to try to reach each student. That is why the variety of approaches is so important. The preceding statements are easy to make. The reality is that they might be difficult for you to implement and the reason is tragically simple. Almost all of your mathematical education has been via the "teacher telling" model. The preceding statements are asking you to break that pattern; the trouble is that you have very few examples to refer to. You lack experience in two facets: teaching and creating lessons. Teaching experience comes with time. Your lesson-creating skills can be practiced and developed starting right now!

The basics have been discussed as far as establishing a lesson plan. However, there is another consideration. You should know more than what you will be teaching. But, your mathematical content is compartmentalized into classes and topics. You need to take the time to reflect on the breadth of mathematical knowledge you have and begin to devise ways to cross between the different compartments. That will create new and stimulating ideas for you and your students. As you do this, you should consider taking additional mathematics courses to strengthen your knowledge base. You do not want to be caught in the situation where you are teaching at the precipice of your own knowledge.

We have given you ideas to think about when constructing lesson plans. Many schools and states have prescribed forms and procedures for lesson plans. If you examine those predefined forms, you will notice many of the same ideas. Incorporating these ideas into your lessons will only help you as you begin to teach mathematics. Now it is up to you to begin. How do you establish these communication skills? You need to know a multitude of things. We have covered the basic ideas here. You need to investigate the NCTM communication standard in greater detail. You need to go beyond that though, and expand your horizons through continual professional growth (reading journals, attending in-service activities, going to conferences and workshops, taking classes, and joining professional organizations). As you do that, and as you gain teaching experience, your flexibility will increase, as will your ability to present your knowledge in a variety of ways.

CONCLUSION

Communication is not easy. You know that, just from life. As you begin your classroom experiences via internship, you will become aware of the need for a whole new level of communication skills. Up to now, you have been working mostly with one individual at a time as you present your thoughts. In the classroom, you will be responsible for getting your thoughts across to as many as 35 or 40 students at one time. Add to that number the idea that they will not all be paying attention, they will not all see things from the vantage point you do, they may not all have the background skills necessary to deal with the topic, and who knows what else, and you see the tremendous communication difficulties. Getting through to students is not always easy, but it is most gratifying when a student says, "I get it." That is what teaching is all about!

STICKY QUESTIONS

5.1. How do you create an atmosphere that prompts each student to want to learn and communicate knowledge of mathematics?

5.2. In business it can be said that a product is only as good as the workers, manufacturing process, and raw materials used. In school, the workers are the teachers, the manufacturing process is the curriculum, and the raw materials are the students. How can you get students who do not want to learn to communicate with you about mathematics?

5.3. Would you have thought of those five different ways of showing $\angle BEF + \angle EFG + \angle FGD = 360°$ presented in the text? Why or why not? Can you come up with at least one more solution?

5.4. Imagine that you are a middle school teacher of mathematics and the parents of one of your students feel that their child is spending too much time talking and writing about mathematics. How will you respond?

5.5. Interview a middle school teacher of mathematics who uses cooperative learning strategies. Ask how the class is organized and what activities are implemented using this instructional approach? If you cannot find a teacher who uses cooperative learning, inquire about why these teachers do not use this instructional approach.

TAG

5.1. A mouse will gain 2 grams of weight every day eating as much cheese as possible. Not eating results in losing 3 grams of weight per day. If the mouse gained 5 grams over 20 days, how many days were spent not eating for the mouse?

5.2. If n is a real number, find the smallest possible real value for the expression: $n^2 - 3n + \sqrt{n-3} - \sqrt{n+3}$.

5.3. When you divide your favorite number by 7, you get a remainder of 5. What is the remainder if you multiply your favorite number by 5 and then divide by 7?

5.4. The pattern ABBCCCDDDD-EEEEE...ZZZ...Z repeats continuously such that after the final Z the letters ABBCCCDDDDEEEEE...begin again. What will be the 3000th letter in the pattern?

5.5. You drive to and from school over the same route each day. On Friday, you drive at an average rate of 52 kph and are 1 minute late. On Monday, you drive at an average rate of 60 kph and are 1 minute early. If you left home at the same time each day, how far do you travel from home (one way) to school?

5.6. The counting numbers 1–500 inclusive are placed in a hat. What is the probability that the first randomly chosen number from the hat is a multiple of 6 or 19?

5.7. Determine the exact sum of all 10-digit numbers.

5.8. The average of two 4-digit positive integers is found by placing a decimal point between the two numbers. Find the sum of the two 4-digit numbers.

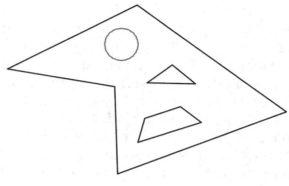

FIG 5.6.

5.9. The game of passing a saying around a group and determining how it changes because of communication can be used in the classroom. Start with the statement, "A square is a polygon that is a regular quadrilateral, parallelogram, rectangle, and rhombus." Was that the expression the last participant gave?

5.10. Pair the students. Have one person create a simple collection of geometric figures like the one shown in Fig. 5.6. That person describes the work to the partner (who does not see the finished product that was created), who is to create a duplicate from the description. Compare results.

RESOURCES (BOOKS AND SITES)

Book List

The following is a listing of useful books and Web sites appropriate for elementary, middle, and high school students. We opted to include all levels because all middle school students are not at the same ability level. Read on!

Number Concepts

Adler, D. (1996). *Fraction fun* (N. Tobin, Illus.). New York: Holiday House.

Connections to our world are central in this introduction to fractions. Equal-sized parts and the meaning of numerator and denominator are discussed with examples.

Burns, M. (1992). *Math for smarty pants* (M. Weston, Illus.). Boston: Little, Brown & Co.

This book explores a variety of topics and intriguing stories. It includes benchmarks for developing number sense.

Carle, E. (1994). *Very hungry caterpillar.* New York: Putnam Publishing Group.

A hungry caterpillar eats a variety of foods throughout the week. On the last day the caterpillar feels sick, rests, and wraps himself in a cocoon soon becoming a butterfly. This book can help students with addition and subtraction word problems.

Christaldi, K. (1996). *Even Steven and Odd Todd* (H. B. Morehouse, Illus.). Mechanicsburg, PA: Scholastic.

Even Steven likes even numbers. Everything in his life is even. One day his cousin Odd Todd shows up. Todd likes odd numbers, and everything in his life is odd. Odd Todd drives Even Steven crazy with all of his odd numbers. The book describes classroom activities.

Clement, R. (1991). *Counting on Frank.* Milwaukee, WI: Gareth Stevens Children's Books.

This book looks at estimation of numbers and measurements. It offers hilarious illustrations of the two characters investigating new and outlandish situations.

Giganti, P. (1998). *Each orange had 8 slices* (D. Crews, Illus.). Mechanicsburg PA: Scholastic, Greenwillow Books.

This book can be used to introduce multiplication without mentioning the word. "On my way to school I saw 3 little kids. Each kid rode a tricycle. Each tricycle had 3 wheels." The book then goes on to ask questions concerning the kids and the tricycles. This is how the entire book is formatted.

Hutchins, P. (1986). *The doorbell rang.* Mechanicsburg, PA: Scholastic.

The Doorbell Rang focuses on how to share so each person receives the same amount. It starts off with only two children, and then four, and so on. It introduces division, too.

Juster, N. (1961). *The phantom tollbooth.* New York: Random House.

This work offers ideas and activities on infinity, finding averages, and understanding number versus numeral.

Moore, I. (1991). *Six dinner, Sid.* New York: Simon & Schuster Books for Young Readers.

An intelligent cat lives at Pythagoras Place.

Schwartz, D. (1985). *How much is a million?* (S. Kellogg, Illus.). New York: Lothrop, Lee & Shepard Books.

Mathematical Magician Marvellosissimo introduces his friends to the magnitude of large numbers through thought-provoking situations.

Scieszka, J. (1995). *Math curse* (L. Smith, Illus.). New York: Viking.

Almost everything is a math problem. A young student finds mathematics problems in everything she sees and does. After waking from her dream, she realizes that all problems have solutions.

Sitomer, M. (1976). *How did numbers begin?* New York: Thomas Y. Cromwell.

This nonfiction book describes how numbers arose from need and how they were named and used.

Slobokina, Er. (1998). *Caps for sale.* London, England: HarperCollins.

A peddler sells caps, which he has sorted and stacked on his head. The caps are stolen by monkeys. He gets his caps back, recounts, resorts, and continues his selling.

Number Systems

Adler, D. (1977). *Roman numerals* (B. Barton, Illus.). New York: Thomas Y. Crowell.

A variety of activities are presented as a think-through process using Roman numerals.

Fisher, L. (1982). *Number art: Thirteen 123's from around the world.* New York: Four Winds Press.

The history and development of Arabic, Armenian, Brahman, Chinese, Egyptian, Gothic, Greek, Mayan, Roman, runic, Sanskrit, Thai, and Tibetan number systems are introduced.

Friedman, A. (1995). *The king's commission* (S. Guevara, Illus.). Mechanicsburg, PA: Scholastic.

This is a hilarious view of the king's demand to get a count of his appointments.

Leedy, L. (1992). *Money book.* New York: Holiday House.

Several concepts are introduced: value of money, how to run a business, profits and losses, budgets, and banking.

Massin (1993). *Fun with numbers* (L. Chats Peles, Illus.). San Diego, CA: Creative Editions.

Numeration systems other than base 10 are introduced along with the historical origins of metric and inch-foot-pound measurement.

Numbers and Operations

Michelson, R. (2000). *Ten times better*. Tarrytown, NY: Marshall Cavendish.

This is a poem about multiplying by 10.

Pinczes, E. (1995). *A remainder of one* (B. Mac-Kain, Illus.). Boston: Houghton Mifflin.

The book introduces division concepts.

Rockwell, T. (1990). *How to get fabulously rich*. New York: Dell.

This book is about winning the lottery. It includes a discussion on concepts of large numbers.

Rockwell, T. (1997). *How to eat fried worms* (E. McCully, Illus.). New York: Bantam Doubleday Dell.

The book offers connections with division, combinations, and Roman numerals.

Statistics and Probability

Ash, R. (1996). *Incredible comparisons*. New York: Dorling Kindersley.

The text is brief but offers many illustrations that use scale drawings and other models to convey relative sizes effectively. It explores number, size, and how data can be represented.

Cushman, J. (1991). *Do you want to bet? Your chance to find out probability* (M. Westo, Illus.). New York: Clarion.

The characters become involved in everyday situations that deal with probability. Drawings are used to illustrate the story and concepts.

Morgan, R. (1997*). In the next three seconds* (R. and K. Josey, Illus.). New York: Lodestar Books.

A numerical wizard uses seconds, hours, days, months, years, and decades in a collection of statistics and predictions. There is also a suggestion for readers to calculate their own unique predictions.

Patterns and Relationships

Adler, I. (1990). *Mathematics* (R. Miller, Illus.). New York: Doubleday.

The text offers connections between number and geometry with extensions to simple computer programs. Number and space are briefly described using historical approaches. Topics include integers, rectangular numbers, primes, perfect, amicable, and sociable numbers, Fibonacci numbers, and the number of degrees in a polygon.

Anno, M. (n.d.). *Anno's magic seeds*. New York: Philomel Books.

This book focuses on number patterns and relationships as the characters journey through the planting of a magic seed.

Anno, M. (1987). *Anno's math games*. New York: Philomel Books.

This book introduces attributes that we can measure, and those that cannot be measured. A comparison to height leads to indirect measures using bar graphs, spring scales, and other instruments. A wealth of ideas appear that can be extended to other areas of mathematics.

Anno, M. (1989). *Anno's math games II*. New York: Philomel Books.

The characters discover relationships of age, number, doubling, shape, one more than, and similarities and differences.

Barry, D. (1994). *The rajah's rice: A mathematical folktale from India* (D. Perrone, Illus.). New York: Scientific American Books for Young Readers.

The power of doubling and measuring are explored and embedded throughout the story.

Burns, M. (1975). *The I hate mathematics! book* (M. Hairston, Illus.). Boston: Little, Brown.

This book shows the reader how much fun mathematics can be by including interesting facts, questions, experiments, ratios, volume, estimation, prediction, measurement, spatial relationships, clock arithmetic, strategy games, and probability.

Hayes, C., & Dympna, H. (1988). *Number mysteries* (P. MeEwen, S. Doyle, R. Rowden, and J. Schuster, Illus.). Niagara Falls, NY: Durkin Hayes.

The text explores number puzzles, involving number and operation sense; beginning probability, ratio, and spatial relationships are embedded throughout with number lines, diagrams, models, graphs, tables, and patterns.

Kallen, S. (1992). *A mathmagical fun*. Edina, MN: Abdo & Daughters.

Thirteen "magical math tricks" involving numbers are explored through patterns and observations.

Markle, S. (1993). *Math mini-mysteries*. New York: Atheneum.

Many of the problems in this text are embellished with interesting facts and explanations about history, science, and other connections to the real-world ratios, measurement, geometry, patterns, data collection, interpretation and problem solving activities.

McKibbon, H. (1996). *The token gift* (S. Cameron, Illus.). New York: Annick Press.

Doubling and accumulating sums are depicted in a story about an invented game.

Sharp, R., & Seymour, M. (1990). *The sneaky square and 113 other math activities for kids*. Blue Ridge Summit, PA: TAB Books.

Problems appear to be tricks. However, investigation shows explanations for solutions embedded in algebra, spatial reasoning, logical reasoning, number theory, and number relationships. The focus is on problem solving, mental computation, and mathematical reasoning.

Reasoning

Pappas, T. (1991). *Math talk: Mathematical ideas in poems for two voices*. San Carlos, CA: World Wide Publishing/Tetra.

Twenty-five mathematical concepts are introduced through poetry.

Talbot, J. (1995). *An amazing picture-puzzle book*. New York: Dutton Children's Books.

The reader is asked to solve puzzles using riddles and rhyming form.

Measurement

Baumann, H. (1979). *What time is it around the world?* (A. Boratynski, Illus.). New York: Scroll Press.

The book offers progressive time forms to show how different places in the world are one hour apart in time as you move east.

Bendick, J. (1989). *How much and how many*. New York: Franklin Watts.

The historical development of weights and measures are introduced with activities.

Branley, F. (1993). *Keeping time: From the beginning and into the 21st century* (J. Weber, Illus.). Boston: Houghton Mifflin.

This book illustrates how time was kept in the earliest of days via the sun, moon, and stars. It defines the need now for seconds, minutes, and hours in today's lifestyle. Micro, nano, pico, and femtoseconds, standard and daylight time, time zones, reasons for 24 hours in a day, 60 minutes in an hour, 60 seconds in a minute, 7 days in a week, 12 months in a year, and whether days are getting longer are all introduced.

Estes, E. (n.d.). *The hundred dresses* (L. Slobodkin, Illus.). New York: Scholastic.

The kids at her school remind a girl from a poor neighborhood of her position by asking her how many dresses she has in her closet. This discusses time, place value, and measurement.

Fisher, L. (1987). *Calendar art: Thirteen days, weeks, months, years, from around the world*. New York: Four Winds Press.

The author presents various ways other cultures have recorded time. Aztec, Babylonian, Chinese, Egyptian, French, Georgian, Hebrew, Islamic, Julian, Mayan, Roman, and Stonehedge are introduced.

McKissack, P. (1992). *A million fish . . . more or less* (D. Schutzer, Illus.). New York: Alfred A. Knopf.

Covered topics include weights, measurement, place value, and time.

Singer, M. (1991). *Nine o'clock lullaby* (F. Lessac, Illus.). London, England: HarperCollins.

The author explores different time zones, offering activities for the hour and the culture visited at each time zone location. A brief discussion is included about how time changes as the earth rotates on its axis.

Optical illusions, unique measuring tools, collecting data, quantities, weights, temperatures, volume, area, and perimeter are developed. Multiple solutions, hands-on activities, problem solving and explorations, experiments, puzzles, and games round out this text.

Wells, R. (1993). *Is a blue whale the biggest thing there is*? Morton Grove, IL: Albert Whitman.

The development of number sense and comparative size are the focus of this book. The flipper part of a whale's tale is related to other creatures and Mount Everest to begin the process of contemplating the size of our universe.

Investigations

Smoothley, M. (1992). *Area and volume* (T. Evans, Illus.). New York: Marshall Cavendish.

Rhombi, hexagons, and formulas for areas of parallelograms and triangles are developed through paper-cutting activities. Connections of area are made to real-world experiences.

Smoothley, M. (1993). *Angles* (T. Evans, Illus.). New York: Marshall Cavendish.

Estimating angle sizes and exercises for measuring angles are offered in this text. Special angles, such as right, straight, acute, obtuse, and reflex are defined and included in classification activities.

Smoothley, M. (1993). *Circles* (T. Evans, Illus.). New York: Marshall Cavendish.

Activities include folding a circle to find its center to replicate attractive designs and patterns, determining which regular polygons or star polygons can be formed from 8- to 12-point circles. Connections are made to early uses of this relationship and to the different values of pi over time. Circles in our culture and in nature are discussed.

Smoothley, M. (1993). *Solids* (T. Evans, Illus.). New York: Marshall Cavendish.

Investigations include folding a box from a square piece of paper, drawing different pentominoes, and deciding which can be folded into a cube. It is an introduction for cubes, cuboids, and nets.

Smoothley, M. (1993). *Statistics* (T. Evans, Illus.). New York: Marshall Cavendish.

Tally charts, pie graphs, calculating averages, displaying data, and constructing pictographs are explained. Directions are given for making pie charts, how to measure angles, and how to calculate degrees and percentages.

Smoothley, M. (1993). *Time, distance, and speed* (T. Evans, Illus.). New York: Marshall Cavendish.

Connections are made to history, time measures, and instruments like sundials, obelisks, and calibrated candles. The text is in puzzle format using problem solving and a mystery.

Smoothley, M. (1993). *Triangles* (T. Evans, Illus.). New York: Marshall Cavendish.

Skill exercises and problem-solving activities are concepts found in the middle grades. Many definitions and questions are presented.

Smoothley, M. (1995). *Calculators* (A. Baum, Illus.). New York: Marshall Cavendish.

The reader is challenged to express different values using a digit several times with various operations.

Smoothley, M. (1995). *Codes and sequences* (T. Evans, Illus.). New York: Marshall Cavendish.

Directions for creating a cipher wheel are given so readers can decipher beginning codes or create their own. Activities are designed to explore averages, and frequencies. Connections include Morse code, bar codes, and patterns in music.

Sobol, D. (1979). *Encyclopedia Brown's record book of weird and wonderful facts*. New York: Delacorte Press.

Problem-solving activities are included to help students create mathematical story problems.

Vorderman, C. (1996). *How math works*. Pleasantville, NY: Reader's Digest Association.

This text helps develop an appreciation and understanding of the world of scientific discoveries. It is organized into chapters on numbers, proportions, algebra, statistics, measurement, shape, and thinking. Subtopics include a history of writing numbers, series and sequences, calculating tools, positive and negative numbers, fractions and decimals, estimation, powers, and number bases. Puzzles and tricks are also included.

Vorderman, C. (1997). *Triangles*. New York: Benchmark Books.

Toothpick puzzles and origami instructions for folding are covered. Connections to the real world include examining how the triangular form is used in the construction of bridges.

Shapes

ABC Quilts. (1992). *Kids making quilts for kids*. San Francisco, CA: The Quilt Digest Press.

Photographs and step-by-step instructions for constructing quilts are provided.

Stienecker, D. (1997). *Patterns* (R. Maccabe, Illus.). New York: Benchmark Books.

Linear patterns are explored through activities that involve stenciling, folding, and cutting paper chains: two-dimensional patterns, paper strips, and the exploration of tailings that use letters or geometric shapes. Other patterns use lines, mazes, and shimmering designs. Connections are made to Native American pottery and weaving.

Stienecker, D. (1997). *Rectangles* (R. Maccabe, Illus.). New York: Benchmark Books.

Magic squares, strategy games using dot paper, mazes, and toothpick puzzles are some of the activities described in this text.

Stienecker, D. (1997). *Shapes* (R. Maccabe, Illus.). New York: Benchmark Books.

Pyramids, cubes, prisms, spheres, optical illusions, cones, and cylinders are introduced. The reader is encouraged to find the many shapes in the world around them.

Geometry

Burns, M. (1994). *The greedy triangle* (G. Silveria, Illus.). New York: Scholastic.

A triangle is transformed into a quadrilateral, pentagon, hexagon, and so on. He finally realizes that he was happiest as a triangle. The book teaches shapes and connects them to real life. It is also a story with a moral, "the grass is always greener on the other side."

Emberly, E. (1984). *Ed Emberly's picture pie: A circle drawing book.* Boston: Little, Brown.

Circles are cut in halves, fourths, or eighths to create elaborations and patterns. There are numerous explorations of geometric designs and fractions.

Hansen-Smith, B. (1995). *The hands-on marvelous ball book* (K. S. Palmer, Illus.). New York: W. H. Freeman.

When spinning, a sphere becomes four smaller spheres, all touching one another and all contained within the outline of the original sphere. The story is told in a rhyme and includes appropriate mathematical material and terminology.

Lasky, K. (1994). *The librarian who measured the earth* (K. Hawkes, Illus.). Boston: Little, Brown.

Eratosthenes' questioning mind and how he measured the circumference of the earth is dis-cussed. His calculations were within 200 miles of today's calculations. The text is an excellent opportunity for the reader to learn and develop a sense of history and mathematics.

MacCarone, G. (1997). *Three pigs, one wolf, and seven magic shapes* (D. Neuhaus, Illus.). Mechanicsburg, PA: Scholastic.

This book introduces some of the cornerstones of geometry and provides a set of cardboard tangrams.

Ross, C. (1992). *Circles: Fun ideas for getting a round in math* (B. Slavin, Illus.). Reading, MA: Addison Wesley.

The circle and other round shapes are connected to our world and the historical significance is clearly defined. It includes lines, radial symmetry in nature, circle signs, cave dwellers, meteorologists, botanists, and building with circles.

Sarasas, C. (1964). *ABC's of origami.* Rutland, VT: Charles E. Tuttle.

Origami patterns for 26 objects are illustrated with sequenced diagrams.

Sharman, L. (1994). *The amazing book of shapes.* New York: Dorling Kindersley.

Connections to the real world are evident as the author discusses geometric patterns and shapes.

Simon, S. (1991). *Mirror magic* (A. Matsick, Illus.). Honesdale, PA: Bell Books.

How a mirror works and how to make a kaleidoscope, periscope, and a corner cube mirror are included.

Tompert, A. (1990). *Grandfather Tang's story* (R. A. Parker, Illus.). New York: Crown Publishers.

This story is an old Chinese tale told with tangrams and is very helpful for learning spatial sense.

White, L., & Broekel, R. (1986). *Optical illusions* (A. Canevari Green, Illus.). New York: Franklin Watts.

Illusions with examples are introduced in a text that seeing is not what you really see. Connections are made between mathematics and science.

Fractions

Leedy, L. (1994). *Fraction action.* New York: Holiday House.

This book uses cartoon characters to introduce number concepts using fractions. Models of circles, rectangles, and parallelograms divided into the appropriate number parts introduce fraction concepts. Halves, thirds, and fourths, and making whole sets into fractions and subtracting fractions are covered.

McMillan, B. (1991). *Eating fractions*. New York: Scholastic.

The book uses fruit to illustrate the halves, thirds, and fourths, provides extension activities, and emphasizes a multicultural approach.

Murphy, S. (1996). *Give me half!* (G. B. Karas, Illus.). London, England: HarperCollins Children's Books.

This story is about a brother and sister who are told to split pizza, juice, cupcakes, and cookies equally when they do not want to share their food. This book introduces the concept of halves using a simple rhyming story.

Pallotta, J. (1999). *The Hershey's milk chocolate fractions book* (R. Bolster, Illus.). Mechanicsburg, PA: Scholastic.

This book uses a candy bar to develop one as a whole, 3/3, 1/2, denominator, numerator, improper fractions, and so on.

Algebra

Burns, M. (1997). *Spaghetti and meatballs for all! A mathematical story* (D. Tilley, Illus.). Mechanicsburg, PA: Scholastic Press.

This story is about a dinner arrangement using 32 chairs and 8 tables. Guests have their own ideas for the seating arrangements, rearranging the chairs and tables. Every time they think they've got it, more family members arrive. Connections can be made to addition multiplication, subtraction, division, perimeter, area, and angles.

Sachar, L. (1978). *Sideways arithmetic from wayside school*. Mechanicsburg, PA: Scholastic.

Kids attend wayside school to help the reader solve problems. There are optional clues and hints listed, along with answers.

Silverstein, S. *Where the sidewalk ends*. London, England: HarperCollins.

This book is a collection of poems. Connections are made through measurement, size, comparison, money, number sense, multiplication, and addition.

Site List
Geometry

Anyangle   http://www.riteitem.com/Anywin.htm

Anyangle is a geometry solver, which includes an interactive scientific calculator and will solve any triangle, given appropriate information.

Big Chalk, Geometry Section
http://www.bigchalk.com

Big Chalk is students, teachers, and parents. Geometry is broken into many subtopics. Each topic links to another page that breaks the subject down more. The site includes instruction, tutorials, practice, sample tests, and quizzes.

Cabri Geometry II
http://www.Education.ti.com/product/software/cabri

Cabri Geometry is interactive and allows the user to manipulate drawings. Teacher instructions with reproducible activity worksheets are available.

Cinderella   http://www.cinderella.de

Cinderella is in Java and is highly interactive. Users can compare a construction in Euclidean, hyperbolic, or elliptic geometry. The online help for Cinderella is extensive.

Color Mathematics
http://www.geocities.com/Athens/6172/index.html

Color Mathematics can be downloaded at no cost. You will find programs for geometry, algebra, trigonometry, and calculators.

Conjectures in Geometry   http://www.geom.umn.edu/~dwiggins/mainpage.html

This Web site was created in 1996 by three high school students for high school students to assist in learning the basic concepts, conjectures, and theorems in geometry. The Web site provides definitions, sketches and explanations, and interactive demos of the conjectures.

Connecting Geometry
http://www.k12.hi.us/%7Ecsanders/Welcome.html

Connecting Geometry uses computer technology and the Internet to explore and discover the principles and concepts of geometry. Connecting Geometry is designed to meet the high school one-year geometry requirement and students can enroll through the Web site. There are 12 chapters which include lessons, exercises, and projects.

Cynthia Lanius Site   http://math.rice.edu/~lanius/Geom/

You will find a plethora of links that provide access to lessons or activities students can do online, including questions. Answers can be submitted, graded, and checked online. A link to a glossary of geometric terms is provided throughout the Web site.

Dave's Math Tables
http://math2.org/math/geometry/areasvols.htm

The site contains formulas dealing with area (including Heron's formula), volume, and surface area.

Euclid's Elements
http://aleph0.clarku.edu/~djoyce/java/elements/elements.html

This Web site is essentially a translation and study of the 13 books of Euclid's elements. The author has included a summary of the main points of each book.

Exploring the Shape of Space
http://geometrygames.org/ESoS/index.html

Exploring the Shape of Space has many different games that can be used for geometry, both two- and three-dimensional. The students learn by example, using paper-and-scissors activities, pencil-and-paper games, and computer games.

E-Z Geometry   http://www.e-zgeometry.com

This site is into lesson notes, practice quizzes, interactive support, geometry glossary, math Web links, Web-based projects, in-class projects, Geometer's Sketch Pad assignment, video footage, java applets, GSP demonstrations, e-z Weekly update, problems, quotes, journal topics, e-z student section, feedback form, math games, e-z parent section, school calendar, and email teachers.

FX Draw 2   http://www.mathsnet.net/software.html

FX Draw 2 is a Windows-based package that allows the user to draw angles, graphs, normal distribution curves, Venn diagrams, right-angled triangles, and much more.

Game Aquarium   http://www.gamequarium.com/geometry.html

This has a lot of different geometry games and activities for geometry arranged by difficulty.

Geocomputer   http://www.download.com

This software gives you the ability to draw and color all types of geometric figures by using a grid.

Geometer's Sketchpad
http://www.keypress.com/sketchpad/

Sketchpad is interactive software that covers geometry, algebra, calculus, and conic sections. It is a building and discovery tool for students and teachers.

Geometria: Interactive Geometry Software
http://www.geocentral.net/geometria/

This downloadable provides definitions for the terms with a three-dimensional picture. The site links to other geometry sites.

Geometry   http://library.thinkquest.org/2647/geometry/geometry.htm

This site provides a simplified geometry textbook on the Web with a glossary of definitions and symbols, as well as a list of theorems and practice problems.

Geometry   http://pittsford.monroe.edu/jefferson/calfieri/geometry/geoframe.html

This site is about space figures, polygons, symmetry, volume, area, perimeter, lines, angles, rays, and coordinate geometry. It does have several quizzes in certain topics.

Geometry Blaster by Davidson
http://www.e-dealsusa.com/2372.htm

Geometry Blaster covers a full year of geometry curriculum as it develops triangles, angles, circles, polygons, the Pythagorean theorem, perimeter, and area.

Geometry in Action
http://www.ics.uci.edu/~eppstein/geom.html

The page links to other helpful pages involving real-world applications of geometrical concepts. There is a reference page with formulas and basic information.

Geometry in Motion
http://www15.addr.com/~dscher/

This Web site brings geometric figures to life with animation. Each problem is interactive. There are many open-ended questions that make the student think about WHY this is happening to the figure.

Geometry Junkyard
http://www1.ics.uci.edu/~eppstein?junkyard/teach.html

There are links to sites, lessons, and activities. There is a link to 12 downloadable activities, including 2 for MACs.

Geometry Puzzles http://www.einstein.et.tudelft. nl/~arlet/puzzles/geometry.html

Geometry Puzzles contains word problems that are not just simple word problems, along with answers and explanations.

Geometry Step-by-Step from the Land of the Incas http://agutie.homestead.com

The site contains several geometry problems and theorems, and their solutions/proofs are given in step-by-step fashion. There are quizzes, geometry problems, puzzles, games, and quotes from mathematicians and philosophers.

Geometry Super http://www.newtechdirect.com/ geomsuptut.html

The site includes lessons on circles, triangles and quadrilaterals, parallel and perpendicular lines, coordinate and space geometry, angle measurement and vectors, points, area, circumference, planes reasoning, equality and similarity, plus non-Euclidean geometry along with quizzes and tests.

Geometry World Middle Grades Interactive Explorer http://www.mathrealm.com/CD_ ROMS/GeometryWorld.htm

This software allows students to interactively explore geometric principles and includes lessons to teach concepts and tools that allow students to create and analyze geometric figures.

Geomview http://www.geomview.org/windows/

Geomview is free and runs on most Unix platforms including GNU/Linux. It is an interactive three-dimensional program and allows manipulation of three-dimensional objects.

GRACE—Graphical Ruler and Compass Editor http://www.cs.rice.edu/~jwarren/grace/

GRACE is an interactive and compass construction editor for use in teaching basic geometry concepts to high school students. Proofs are verified by an automatic method based on linear algebra.

Interactive Mathematics Dictionary http://www. intermath-uga.gatech.edu/dictnary/homepg.asp

This site is part of a larger geometry complex of sites. It will give the student or teacher quick reference to a dictionary on mathematical topics in the middle school curriculum. This dictionary doesn't just give you a word dictionary meaning but in most cases gives an example.

Interactive Mathematics Miscellany and Puzzles: Geometry Page http://www.cut-the-knot.org/ geometry.shtml

Problems about symmetries of a triangle, squaring a circle, squares inscribed in a circle, and Pythagorean theorem are solved.

Kaleidomania http://www.keymath.com

Kaleidomania is an interactive symmetry software that includes all kinds of symmetry. Students can rotate, reflect, and transform images using patterns.

KaleidoTile http://geometrygames.org/Kaleido Tile/index.html

This downloadable software allows you to experiment with tessellations of the sphere, Euclidean plane, and hyperbolic plane.

Kids Newsroom http://www.kidsnewsroom.com/elmer/infocentral/ geometry/

This site provides practice problems, games, and activities. It helps students understand their material beyond the classroom.

Math for Morons Like Us http://library.thinkquest. org/20991/geo/index.html

Math for Morons ranges from parallel lines, shapes, areas, and volumes, giving a brief overview of the selected topic.

Math League http://www.mathleague.com/help/ geometry/geometry.htm

This site covers basic geometry terms, angles, figures, polygons, areas and perimeter, coordinates, and solids. Each section covers the definition of the various terms and their attributes and then provides descriptions with samples and comparisons.

MSTE Java http://www.mste.uiuc.edu/java/default. xml?category=Geometry

Most introductions are technology based with applets or games to illustrate the concepts. It makes abstract ideas so concrete.

NonEuclid Software http://math.rice.edu/~joel/NonEuclid

Points, lines, segments, circles, perpendiculars, and parallels all can be constructed, reflected, translated, and measured.

Poly http://www.peda.com/poly/

Poly is a program for exploring, constructing, and manipulating polyhedra.

Mighty Math Cosmic Geometry http://www.riverdeep.net/products/math/index. jhtml

With this program, students explore attributes of shapes and solids, constructions and transformations, two- and three-dimensional coordinates, and the relationships among length, perimeter, area, and volume. Students get involved in different learning activities.

PBS   http://www.pbs.org/teachersource

This site offers 17 lesson plans and activities that are integrated across the curriculum.

Sacred Geometry   http://www.intent.com/sg/index.html

This Web site offers geometric topics and their history as well as links to several other sites. There are lots of ideas here.

Scienceu   http://www.scienceu.com/geometry/

Shapes, patterns, and symmetry are the central themes at this interactive site that offers step-by-step directions.

Tessellations   http://www.shodor.org/interactive/activies/tessellate

Tessellations allows the student to make their own.

The Geometric Supposer   http://www.mathforum.org/dynamic/classroom.html

Construct your own objects from scratch. You can construct points, circles, lines, angles, triangles, quads, and other polygons. It measures perimeter, area, distance, length, and angles.

The Geometry Center   http://www.scienceu.com/geometry/

The site contains interactive geometry online, puzzles, activities, articles, facts and figures, and step-by-step instructions.

Thinkquest Geometry
http://library.thinkquest.org/2647/geometry/geometry.htm?tqskip1+1&tqtime=0531

The site describes itself: "This [site] is where you'll find almost everything you'll ever need to know about Geometry."

Algebra

Absurd Math   http://www.learningwave.com/abmath/

Several of the challenges are brain teasers and multistep word problems. There are mathematical references to various topics including anxiety, and in-jokes that kids will like.

Algebra I Home Page/Mrs. Carlton   http://www.bonita.k12.ca.us/schools/ramona/teachers/carlton/index.html

This site has tutorials that could be helpful to students. A brief history of algebra, a few links, an over-the-top problem of the week, a cartoon problem of the week, and an area called shenanigans is included.

Algebra II Class   http://www.wkbradford.com/mta2.htm

Some of the tasks this software performs are algebraic expressions, equations, word problems, area and volume applications, linear programming, and exploration environment. It also provides a test generator.

Algebra Cheat 2
http://www.bacsoftware.co.uk/algebra/

Algebra Cheat 2 is able to simplify any algebra expression, simplify any algebra equation, add, subtract, and multiply any algebra expression, solve any simple linear equation, solve simultaneous linear equations of up to five variables, solve any quadratic equation of one variable, factor quadratic equations of one variable, and includes detailed explanation of the work.

Algebra.Help   http://www.algebrahelp.com/index.jsp

Algebra.Help provides online lesson plans for just about every algebra topic. The site also offers calculators, worksheets, and resources. The calculators will show step-by-step solutions and are programmed for each algebra content area.

Algebra Homework Help at Algebra.Com
http://www.algebra.com/

From homework help, word problems, and algebra worksheets to a math forum, there are tons of ways to find help with and learn algebra. There are explanations on graphs, imaginary numbers, polynomials, and so on.

Algebra One on One   http://www.sheppardsoftware.com/algebra1.htm

This program covers 21 functions and has a practice area and a game area.

Algebra Online   http://www.algebra-online.com/

This site assists students, parents, and teachers and is not limited to the discussion of algebra. One of the features of the site is free tutoring.

Algebra Proficency Tests   http://www.orange.k12.oh.us/depts/ohs/math/profweb/pages/algebra.html

This site offers math proficiency tests for algebra. It has links that connect to pages for review, tutorial, or practice tests.

Algebra Solutions   http://www.gomath.com/algebra. html

This site has many pre-algebra and algebra links with lots of good topics, each of which has a mini-lesson, and a worksheet with answer key.

Algebra Solver   http://www.cyberedinc.com

The student can enter any problem into the solver and get a step-by-step solution. It solves algebra problems involving equations, expressions, graphs, inequalities, and radicals, up to college algebra. There is an explanation with each solution and it is printable. The printout can also include a graph with an explanation.

Algebra Stars—Sunburst/Hyperstudio http://www. sunburst.com/resources/productcomm/ ALSTARS/

This software allows the students to build their understanding of algebra by constructing, categorizing, and solving equations, and classifying polynomial expressions using algebra tiles. This software provides games, activities, and a glossary.

Algebra World   http://www.cogech.com

Algebra World software is designed for middle school students and focuses on concepts, problem solving, reasoning, applications, and appreciations. The software outlines expressions, negative numbers, equations, ratios, proportions and percent, and geometry. The software includes real-world applications.

Algebrator   http://www.softmath

Algebrator is a computer algebra system meant to be used by students as well as teachers. Users can enter almost any problem and it is solved step by step. Algebrator will generate problems and make up tests or homework sheets.

Astro Algebra   http://www.edmark.com/prod/math/

Astro Algebra is designed for Algebra students in grades 7–9. The student becomes a captain of a spaceship in this intergalactic adventure. It also contains an online algebra help manual.

Astro Algebra   http://www.riverdeep.net/products/ math/mm_astro_al.jhtml#features

Astro Algebra guides students in their understanding of the concepts and enhances problem-solving skills necessary to learn basic algebra. It contains hundreds of problems that deal with expressions, equations and inequalities, functions, graphing on number line and coordinate grid, ratios and proportions, slope and intercept, fractions, decimals and percents, exponents, problem solving and reasoning, and algebra terminology and notation.

Basic Algebra Shape-Up http://www.algebra-software.com/index.html

Basic Algebra Shape-Up offers numerous questions and contextual help and feedback to guide the students. The software includes step-by-step tutorials.

Beginning Algebra   http://www.aw.com/altsupps/ 0,3483,0201434555,00.html

Beginning Algebra corresponds directly with Addison Wesley text chapters. The software offers exercises, sample problems, and guided solutions, which explain in a step-by-step manner, prompting students for responses.

BoxerMath   http://www.boxermath.com

Boxer can be used as supplemental materials or as a full curriculum. The program offers extra practice questions, experiments that relate to each topic, and sections on math in science and math in art and literature.

Discovery School   http://school.discovery.com/.

This Web site has lesson plans, a place where they will help you to create your own lesson plans, "Brain Teaser" questions, and worksheets.

Ed Helper.com   http://www.edhelper.com/algebra. htm#S1

Any topic you can imagine in algebra is covered. Click on a topic, and you get a worksheet with practice problems you can print. Parents can click on the answer key link to check work.

Education World http://www.education-world.com/a_tsl/archives/ math.shtml

There are 21 lesson plans on how to construct and use these games. Each lesson plan has a link to its individual page of instructions.

Felicia's Algebra Tutor   http://algebra.freeservers. com/springridge1.html

This site offers step-by-step tutorials on how to solve algebraic problems. It allows students to begin at various levels of competence. There are also links to other algebra sites.

Gnarly Math   http://www.gnarlymath.com/

Gnarly Math teaches algebra, geometry, trig, probability, topology, and numbers, using computer tricks and capabilities to make these subjects fascinating and understandable.

Grade Builder Algebra 1
http://www.superkids.com/aweb/pages/reviews/
   math/algebra/1/builder1/merge.shtml

This software includes 60 interactive lesson topics, tutoring, and games to test understanding. Instead of being a simple drill program, this software makes the effort to help teach the subject.

History of Algebra
http://aleph0.clarku.edu/~djoyce/mathhis/algebra.
   html

This site gives a history of math and algebra as well as links telling about famous mathematicians. The site can help students realize algebra is more than solving for x and y. The site has a topic index for algebra and gives a list of mathematicians who were born and died on the day the site is accessed.

Holt Algebra   http://www.hrw.com

This site is an interactive encyclopedia, which includes definitions, explanations, practice problems, statistical plots, a graphing calculator, and manipulatives for algebra and other math subjects.

Homework Help: High School Subject—Mathematics / Algebra   http://www.thebeehive.org/school/
   high/subjects.asp?subject=35

This site is essentially a homework help site for algebra. It has compiled, easy-to-access links to numerous sites that offer online homework help, lessons, practice exercises, problem solvers, calculators for algebraic functions, formulas, proofs, games, and quizzes; all are helpful and all offer immediate feedback. An added bonus for teachers is the free worksheet generator.

Information Please   http://www.infoplease.com/ipa/
   A0113430.html

Information Please gives brief and informative sports information in an easy to use format. The information is listed by type of sport. Listed are the size of balls, length of field, and so on. It offers lots of good, practical, and accurate information.

Interactive Learning Algebra   http://www.iln.net

Interactive learning offers both group and personal tutoring. There is a reference page with formulas, definitions, diagrams, and study tips.

Math Blaster
http://kidsdomain.com/review/kdr/mbalg.html

Math Blaster deals with pre-algebra developmental skills using fractions, decimals, integers, word problems dealing with everyday situations, ratios, proportions, percents, order of operations, and logical thinking.

Personal Algebra Tutor   http://www.cyberedinc.
   com/

The Personal Algebra Tutor solves algebra problems involving equations, expressions, graphs, inequalities, radicals, and so on. Enter your equation, expression, inequality, or graph data; click OK to solve it; and it displays your step-by-step solutions, explanations, or graphs. They also have an Algebra Word Problem Solver where all you do is enter your word problem in English, click on Solve to display your step-by-step solution with the traditional Find, Let, Given setup and receive a step-by-step solution with explanations.

Purple Math   http://www.purplemath.com/

Purple Math Web site is called "your algebra resource" and there are extensive links. "How do you really do this stuff?" is a page of topics with explanations that include examples, hints, common errors, and are cross-referenced with each other.

SOS Mathematics—Algebra   http://www.sosmath.
   com/algebra/algebra.html

Explanations and examples on topics such as fractions, conversions, quadratic equations, factorizations, solving linear equations, and so on are on this site, including step-by-step examples with notes and rules for all the topics.

Standard Deviants   http://standarddeviants.school.
   aol.com/pls/brain/cerebellum.show_
   subject?p_subject_id=25

There are new algebra trivia facts posted weekly. The site provides sample tests, interactive quizzes, puzzles, games, printable cards, and algebra links to the real world.

Your Other Teacher
http://yourotherteacher.com/algebra.htm

This Web site will deliver over 19 hours of streaming video algebra lessons. This is a pay-as-you-go Web site.

Calculators

Activities for the fx-7400G Mini Graph Calculator
  http://www.casio.com

This resource unit offers a practical application of fractions, data graph, scatter plot, mixed numbers and improper fractional equivalents, data table, equations, lists, combinations, numbers raised to a power, averages, squaring of numbers, graphing of equations, repeated use of expressions, scientific notation, zooming, exponential notation, and the meaning of mathematical errors.

Activity Calorie Calculator   http://www.primusweb.
  com/fitnesspartner/jumpsite/calculat.htm

Calorie Calculator provides the user a way to calculate how many calories you burn for 158 different activities in a user-specified amount of time.

Calculator Tutor
http//:oscar.ctc.edu/precalc/ReferenceCenter/
  Tech.html

This site offers instructional guides of over nine different calculators. It allows the student to choose from several topics and gives a detailed tutorial on how to accomplish the task using that particular calculator.

Casio CFX-9850G Calculator Programs
http://home.online.no/~kstordah/casio.htm

There are several programs available from puzzles to creating fractals on the Casio screen. Other programs include graphing programs and different algebra function programs.

Casio FX-270W Plus Scientific Calculator   http://
  www.casio.com/calculators

Casio's two-line display shows formulas and results simultaneously. Change the numbers and recalculate without having to input the entire calculation. This calculator has a single variable statistics feature. It has the ability to instantly convert fractions to their decimal equivalents.

Casio Solutions   http://www.cworks.starwon.com.
  au/casio.html

This is a resource for Casio graphic calculators users and the CFX, FX 1.0/2.0, and FX7400 ranges in particular. However, much of the contents can be adapted to other makes and models as well. The site offers over 100 games that can be downloaded free. The site also offers links to other technological Web sites.

Davidson Web Conversion Utility
http://www.davidson.com.au/tools/convert

This is an online conversion calculator that will convert from whatever unit you are working with to whatever unit you need.

Graphics Calculator   http://archives.math.utk.edu/
  calculator/

There are lab activities and worksheets that you can use for different lesson plans. It includes links to different calculator Web sites such as Casio, Texas Instruments, and others.

Graphing Calculating Resources for Students
  http://fym.la.asu.edu/~fym/GraphCal/Graphing.
  html

This site contains links for Casio and TI calculators. The site is very easy to navigate and find information for your specific calculator. It has links for the entire manual for all TI graphing calculators.

Graphing Calculator   http://www.pacifict.com

This graphing calculator solves for zero, finds the intersections, identifies min and max, and solves numerical expressions. It recognizes polar coordinates, and rectangular, cylindrical, and spherical coordinate systems. The calculator also includes animation. Type in the equation and the graph appears!

Graphing Calculators Resource Materials   http://
  www.vent-pub.com/Graphingbks.html

Resource Materials contains a listing of books that focus on how to use graphing calculators effectively in the classroom. Each book is geared toward a specific subject and a specific calculator. The calculators used in the books are all Texas Instruments and range from models TI-73 to TI-89. The subjects covered range from middle school math to AP calculus.

Hewlett Packard 40G   http://www.hp.com/
  calculators/graphing/40g_info.html

The HP 40G calculator is an easy-to-use algebra graphing calculator with a built in computer algebra system, which enables you to perform algebraic functions such as factoring and systems of linear equations.

HP 49G Graphing Calculator
http://www.technoplaza.net/calculator...

The HP 49G graphing calculator allows equations to be solved or manipulated even when they include variables. It is useful for general solutions and equations.

HP Calculators   http://www.hpcalc.org

HP's Calculators site provides applications, games, graphics, programming, applets, utilities, and PC emulation for their HP48 and HP49 calculators with links to older models.

Lesson Plans for the Graphing Calculator   http://euphrates.wpunj.edu/clubs/itm/Lessonpl/calc/calc.html

This site contains lesson plans for the graphing calculator on parallel lines and properties of slope. The plans give step-by-step procedures of how to introduce the material, objectives of the activity, and questions to ask the student to ensure understanding.

Math Teacher Link: TI-82 Tutorial   http://mtl.math.uiuc.edu/non-credit/basic82/ti-tutorial/ti-tutorial.title.html

Math Teacher Link is an interactive site to learn how to use a TI-82. There is a table of contents that will take you right where you need to go.

Online Calculator http://www-sci.lib.uci.edu/HSG/RefCalculators.html

This site links to thousands of different online calculators listed in categories and subcategories.

Pacific Tech Graphing Calculator http://www.nucalc.com

This will turn your computer into a big graphing calculator. The software allows you to enter an equation with that equation graphed for you in two, three, or four dimensions. It will solve for zeros of any curve.

Resource Central   http://www.resourcehelp.com/qsercalculations.htm

There are calculators that can be used straight from the site, so nothing has to be downloaded. There are other more complicated calculators that can be downloaded, however. It will convert the ancient measurements of the Greeks and Romans. A credit card calculator can give estimates for interest and the land area calculator can give acreage estimates for various shapes.

Texas Instruments   http://education.ti.com/educator/support/support.html

Texas Instruments has dedicated sections on their Web site for educator support. Among some of the selections are training, programs, and resources.

Various Mathematics Topics

A Plus Math   http://www.aplusmath.com

A Plus Math is designed to help improve math skills from addition to fractions. It has flashcards, games, homework helper, and worksheets.

AAAMath   http://www.aaamath.com

This site has information for almost every topic in math that a student through middle school could use. It has an interactive section that allows students to practice their work.

About School http://www.aboutschool.com/3math.htm

Teachers can use the many skills found at this Web site to provide the best education possible for students. There are plenty of problem-solving situations that students can practice.

Allmath.com   http://www.allmath.com

You can find games, problem-solving solutions and steps, teacher references, teacher resources, as well as articles containing information on mathematics.

Awesome Library   http://awesomelibrary.org/classroom/mathematics/Middle-High_School

This site has connections to math standards by state and by subject (algebra, geometry, etc.). The NCTM standards are also included. There are connections to games, lesson plans, projects, and discussions.

Basket Math Interactive   http://www.scienceacademy.com/BI/index.html

The site has problems that deal with addition, subtraction, multiplication, division, rounding, and orders of operations. Students choose the section they need help on and go through as many questions as needed for practice.

Color Math Pink   http://www.colormathpink.com

Color Math Pink is designed to help middle school and high school girls excel at math. Students must register and become a member in order to use some of the help offered at the Web site and the membership fee is $25 per year. Students then have unlimited access to plans to improve their math weaknesses, peer tutors, diagnostic tests, problem solver bulletin board, FAQ center, game center, career corner, and pink links to the best math Web sites around.

Cool Math   http://www.coolmath.com

Cool Math offers lessons, games, and puzzles for all general math, algebra, and geometry. The site gives access to calculators that go from basic to graphing. It gives game ideas and a link center to a wide range of specific math topics. For parents, it offers advice on how to help with homework and access to games.

Discovery   http://school.discovery.com/ homeworkhelp/webmath/

Discovery is geared toward helping students with specific math homework questions. It also has links for teachers to use to help them create lesson plans and activities such as brainteasers and puzzles.

Dositey.com Educational Site http://www.dositey. com/

Many lessons, exercises, worksheets, educational games, and open-ended problems are given. The site includes many games and interactive exercises that help kids better understand math and reinforce ideas. It also includes many printable worksheets. Topics range from addition and subtraction to telling time and rounding decimals.

Education World   http://www.education-word.com

This Web site includes a list of wonderful sources for educators such as search engine for educational Web site, lesson plans, practical information for educators, information on how to integrate technology in the classroom, articles written by education experts, and so on.

Figure This   http://www.figurethis.org/

Figure This offers students, parents, and teachers tips on helping students. There are links to other Web sites that offer assistance on homework questions.

Free Math Help   http://www.freemathhelp.com/

Students interact by reading and offering math question which are posted on message boards. There are links to other math sites that answer math questions, math games and puzzles, glossary of math terms, math lessons, study tips, and practice worksheets. This site also includes a calculator for solving variable equations.

Fun Brain   http://www.funbrain.com/

The activities range from simple addition and subtraction to long division and it is all made fun with games. There are also quizzes for students to test their skills along with a link to homework help with links for teachers and parents.

Get Smarter   http://www.getsmarter.org

This site has user-friendly quizzes with good diagrams for geometry and interactive animation relating to celebrities and catchall funny phrases. The explanations that appear when the wrong answer is selected provide good hints and clues to make the user try again before giving the correct choice. The student page gives excellent links to other math sites for glossary, math help, math forums, and math careers.

Glencoe   http://www.glencoe.com/sec/math/index. html

Teacher resources cover key concepts, puzzle makers, state and national resources, and teacher sites.

Go Math   http://www.gomath.com

Go Math is a free online mathematics tutor designed to assist students and parents. This Web site offers message boards, Q-banks, a search engine if you are looking for a specific topic within the domain, games, an autograph, and formulas/rules from pre-algebra to calculus.

Homework Spot
http://homeworkspot.com/elementary/math/

General sites are listed that link to other math Web sites which vary from helping with math problems to games and puzzles.

Hot Math   http://www.hotmath.org

Holt Math provides math homework help for algebra, geometry, precalculus, and calculus. The site contains solutions for the most commonly used textbooks.

I Know That
http://www.iknowthat.com/com/L3?Area=L2_Math

I Know That includes short animated movies that are followed by math problems related to the previous cartoon. The site also features areas dedicated to increasing student's computation speed, counters, geometry, and shapes.

InfoMath   http://www.infomath.com/

The infomath's online tutor program offers basic math, flash cards, tables, pre-algebra, algebra, and precalculus.

Interactive Math Activities Online
http://www.globalclassroom.org/authors/florida/ math/interactive.html

There are many math activities for students as well as lesson plans and examples. There are background grids to show the hundreds, tens, and ones groupings or the ones, tenths, and hundredths if a flat is used as the unit, base 10 blocks, interactive pattern blocks, and integer bars (same as Cuisenaire Rods).

Internet Resources for Elementary Mathematics Teachers   http://www.math.ttu.edu/~dmettler/title.html

Designed for teachers, potential teachers, and students of mathematics, each main link has links to other sites, so there are hundreds of resources available. It has sections for lesson plans, teacher resources, professional organizations, software, commercial materials, and Internet search engines.

King's List of Online Math Activity http://www.k111.k12.il.us/king/math.htm

This Web site has a variety of math topics, from beginning math to probability and integers. Help is given to students at an elementary level to a well-advanced level in all aspects of mathematics.

Math www.math.com

Ranging from basic math to calculus, the site provides practice problems, homework help, calculators, and games. Students can use the site for homework help or to select a topic for a complete lesson on a specific concept.

Math for Morons Like Us http://library.thinkquest.org/20991/home.html

Math for Morons Like Us was designed by three high school students. Tutorials, sample problems, and quizzes are provided. The assumption is made that you know basic concepts but need some reinforcement. Many math links are provided to other math Web sites.

Math Forum   http://www.mathforum.org

The site is multifaceted and can give an enormous amount of assistance. Due to the variety of options, a visitor to the site is not restricted to just one area of mathematics or to a particular knowledge level.

Math Games   http://www.kidsdomain.com/games/math2.html

Many interactive math games for all age types are generated on this site. Skills such as strategy, patterns, angles, and logic are used and practice.

Math Goodies   http://www.mathgoodies.com

There are a variety of lessons for different grade levels and resources for parents, students, and teachers.

Math Real   www.mathreal.com

This software contains tools for teachers and students. It includes subjects like pre-algebra, algebra, data analysis, and trigonometry. It provides lessons, learning tools, and exploration activities with interactive tutoring.

Math Today
http://www.usatoday.com/educate/mathtoday/index.htm

Math Today is part of *USA Today*. It shows students how the use of graphs, data analysis, mean, median, mode, percentages, patterns, and so on can and are being used to relay information about current events and real-world concerns of today. The teacher site has concepts, objectives, and prerequisite skills.

Math Word Problems for Children
www.mathstories.com

There are over 10,000 interactive/noninteractive math word problems to improve critical thinking skills. The problems are available in English or Spanish.

Mathbiz   http://www.mathbiz.com/

This Web site lets students practice math problems including addition, subtraction, multiplication, division, rounding numbers, multiples, and factors, among others. You can click on a subject and attempt to do a variety of examples. The site will give you an example of how to do a similar problem if you are stuck.

Mathematical Journey Through Time   http://nunic.nu.edu/~frosamon/history/math.html

This is a very visually stimulating site that takes students through the early journey of mathematics all the way through present-day discoveries. It has links for games and word problems relating to particular time periods. The site has information and pictures of the great mathematicians.

Mathsoft Studywork
http://www.studywork-sonline.com/

Studyworks is an interactive software available for math and science and includes a graphing calculator with animation capability. There is a resource center that is helpful for problem solving. There is a library of identities and formulas. There are Web links for additional help for students and teachers.

Math2.org (formerly Dave's Math Tables) http://www.math2.org/

Reference tables for all topics of mathematics are here. The Web site also lists several resource sites. It provides all the information in French, Spanish, and English.

Mathworld   http://mathworld.wolfram.com

This site is a comprehensive and interactive mathematics encyclopedia covering many areas of mathematics. It clarifies and defines subjects and concepts in fields such as algebra, geometry, and number theory by including links to articles on current mathematical news from possible new discoveries to important mathematicians.

MegaConverter2   http://www.megaconverter.com/mega2/

The MegaConverter provides conversion interfaces for speed, volume, area, mass, weight, power, pressure, financial interest and payments, length, fractions to decimals, Roman numerals, and much, much more. It provides links to other conversion sites for measurements that are not featured.

Mega-Mathematics   http://www.c3.lanl.gov/megamath

This site takes simple everyday activities and shows how they are related to mathematics.

Merit Software   http://meritsoftware.com

Algebra Shape-Up helps students master specific algebra skills and provides teachers with measurable results. Some of the topics covered are ratios, proportions, integers, simple and multistep equations, and variables. Students start with an assessment and are given immediate feedback. The program is self-paced and self-monitored.

Mrs. Glosser's Math Goodies   http://www.mathgoodies.com

This is a great math site for teachers, parents, and students and offers interactive lessons, homework help, and solutions to problems. The site covers many concepts such as percents, statistics, and geometry.

Ms. Lindquist   http://www-2.cs.cmu.edu/~neil/

This is a tutoring program that teaches students to form workable problems from word problems. It

can carry on a running conversation, ask probing questions, and break down problems.

Mudds Math Fun Facts http://www.math.hmc.edu/funfacts/

This Web site is hosted by the Math Department of the Harvey Mudd College in Claremont, CA. It has fun math facts that you can use in your classroom to generate student interest.

Professor Friedman's Math Help www.mathpower.com

Professor Friedman's math help site offers a variety of resources about basic math and algebra skills. The site has an entertaining way to learn math and algebra by providing animations and music throughout the various links.

Project Interactive Activities   http://www.shodor.org/interactivate/activities/

These interactive applets can be used to instruct the class or for individual student discovery. This Web site provides interactive mathematics activities based on the NCTM *Principals and Standards for School Mathematics*.

Project SkyMath
http://unidata.ucar.edu/staff/blynds/Skymath.html

It is designed for middle school mathematics teachers and is tied to NCTM standards. The curriculum uses real-time weather data, involves classrooms in hands-on mathematics, elicits higher-level thinking, engages students in purposeful projects, and calls for reflection and communication.

Sportsfigures   www.sportsfigures.espn.com

Lesson plans are clearly categorized by target subject like physics, algebra, some science, and geometry. It offers links to written lesson plans in a variety of content areas such as batting average, kinetic energy, slope, velocity, and acceleration.

SuperKids.com Worksheet Creator
http://www.superkids.com/aweb/tools/math/

The worksheet creator can be used for drills and worksheets for addition, subtraction, mixed addition and subtraction, multiplication, division, fractions, rounding, and greater than/less than. This site allows you to customize worksheets. This site also includes links to other educational tools like vocabulary builders and games!

SureMath   www.suremath.com

This product concentrates on solving word problems in a "fun and easy" way. The problems and equations are as easy to enter as if typing in a word processor that understands math. It will also graph several equations at once.

Surfnetkids   www.surfnetkids.com

Tutoring, games, links to other sites for specific help on a topic, and other interesting facts are provided. It allows the user to type in a function and the program will graph it.

Teach R Kids   http://www.teachrkids.com

You can choose your own grade level for online worksheets. It introduces math topics in a variety of creative and challenging ways. It covers topics through decimals, fractions, and division, and beyond.

The World of Math Online   http://www.math.com

Each section is divided into mini lessons to assist students in pre-algebra, algebra, and geometry.

White House Kids   www.whitehousekids.gov

Weekly problems are generated for all grade levels. Students receive feedback on whether or not their answer is correct and can get a certificate for correct responses.

REFERENCES

Huetinck, L., & Munshin, S. (2004). *Teaching mathematics for the 21st century. Methods and activities for 6-12.* NJ: Merrill Prentice Hall. Upper Saddle River.

Johnson, D., & Johnson, R. (1987). *Learning together and alone: Cooperative, competitive, and individualistic learning.* Englewood Cliffs, NJ: Prentice Hall.

Kagan, S. (1994). *Cooperative learning.* San Antonio, CA: Kagan Cooperative Leaning.

National Council of Teachers of Mathematics. (2000). *Principles and standards for school mathematics.* Reston, VA: Author.

6
Reasoning and Proof

FOCAL POINTS

- Why prove things?
- Informal proofs
- Teacher responsibility in developing reasoning and proof
- Conclusion
- Sticky questions
- TAG
- References

Students in middle school can appear to be quite sure about what they know and what all those around them do not know. Those confidences are about their world, and often spill over into their academic life, too. Yet these same students hold a raft of insecurities and that mentality can also be seen in their school life. It is amazing how they can "just know" so many things and still be uncertain about other things. We, as teachers of mathematics, need to capitalize on the uncertainties and steer the students toward a need for convincing arguments to counteract what they think they do not know. That is, we need to show them the need for reasoning and proof and, at the same time, convince them that these are invaluable skills to possess in both the academic and world environments.

They will have seen proof positive many times in their world. It will have come through advertisements that tell how a shoe will make them run faster, jump higher, and so on, just like the person endorsing it. They will have heard how a prod-

uct cleared up the zits for a friend and that is all the proof they need that it will work for them, too. While those may be acceptable evidences for them, the academic demands differ and are all too often rejected. Your responsibility will be to convince them of the need for a more formalized process that adheres to a defined logic.

Mathematical proofs require an understanding of definitions and logic, but they also depend on insight into how and why things are connected. This can be a level of sophistication that is developmentally beyond some middle school students. Prerequisite skills to formal proof include independent thinking, conjecturing, acquiring the ability to wonder why things are as they are, seeing appropriate examples of informal proofs, and stimulating a need for precision of language, definition, and expression.

WHY PROVE THINGS?

That question is not as illogical as it first appears. You have heard that "seeing is believing" and you are probably aware of optical illusions. For example, are the line segments in Fig. 6.1 horizontal and straight, or not (BWH Ventures, 2004a)? How do you know?

Figure 6.2 shows two different vertical line segments, each in a rectangular box (BWH Ventures, 2004b). Which of the two vertical line segments is longer? Explain your reasoning to someone in your class.

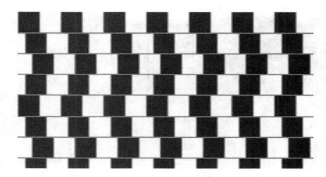

FIG 6.1.

FIG 6.2.

FIG 6.3.

Figure 6.3 shows an image similar to some you may have seen. What do you see? So, is seeing believing?

You may have heard something like, "If 10,000 people agree, it must be correct." Is that a reasonable statement to make? Is it possible that all 10,000 are not in agreement? Could it be that all 10,000 people were given some false, but convincing information? Have you heard, "The figures do not lie"? For example, suppose some superstar graduated as a mathematics education major from a program that saw a total of 10 people complete the program in the given year. The superstar gets a $20,000,000 signing bonus and earns $10,000,000 the first year after gradua-

tion. The other 9 graduates start teaching in a middle school, earning $32,000 each. The average salary for the first year of the 10 mathematics education graduates is reported to be $3,028,800. Oh, the report neglected to include any comments about the superstar. All it said was that the average first-year income of the mathematics education graduates of that year was $3,028,800. The report is questioned and the number is confirmed as true. Still there is no comment about the inclusion of the superstar. It seems like something is not right, and yet the report is confirmed. Thus, it must be true as reported, all agree. The figures may not lie, but having all the facts could make a difference. How would you like to be a graduate of that program? A quick examination of the computation would show one first-year income to be $30,000,000, which would clarify the situation. Reasoning and proof can do wonders for eliminating misunderstandings.

We know that mathematics is the creation of the human mind as we attempt to describe, order, and expand our understanding. How do we convince students that proof is necessary, especially when many of them are convinced that all of mathematics was chipped in stone and handed down on a mountain long ago? We can give them the optical illusions in Figs. 6.1, 6.2, and 6.3, hoping to stimulate questions and discussions. We can give them situations that defy their sense of truth and then convince them of our position. Consider the following example that deals with repeating decimals.

You know that $0.\overline{9} = 1$. To convince students that is true, typically they see the following algebraic presentation:

Let $x = 0.\overline{9}$ (1)

Then $10x = 9.\overline{9}$ (2)

$$\begin{array}{r} 10x = 9.\overline{9} \\ -\;x = 0.\overline{9} \\ \hline 9x = 9 \end{array}$$ Subtracting (1) from (2)

$x = 1$ Dividing both sides of the equation by 9.

Although this is mathematically correct, most students will deny that $0.\overline{9} = 1$. They struggle to accept that $0.\overline{9}$ is equivalent to $0.999\ldots9$, where the 9s continue forever. Everything they have encountered prior to repeating decimals appeared finite and the idea that the 9s repeat eternally is beyond them, masked by the associated psychological dilemma. In truth, $0.\overline{9}$ is fundamentally different from other numbers. Many people, middle schoolers included, struggle to think that something that seems to be more dynamic can be compared with, let alone equal, a static quantity. The reality is that $0.\overline{9}$ means that the string of 9s continues forever, never ending, but approaching the limit of 1. Thus, we see that there is a psychological component of the reasoning and proof.

So, we, as well-versed teachers of mathematics, provide them with a different defense that $0.\overline{9} = 1$, which usually entails the following:

$$\begin{array}{r} 0.\overline{3} = \frac{1}{3} \\ +\;0.\overline{6} = \frac{2}{3} \\ \hline 0.\overline{9} = 1 \end{array}$$

While they can be convinced that $0.\overline{3} = \frac{1}{3}$ and that $0.\overline{6} = \frac{2}{3}$, and they

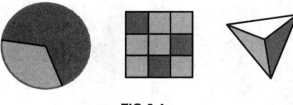

FIG 6.4.

know that $\frac{1}{3} + \frac{2}{3} = 1$, they will still resist the idea that $0.\overline{9} = 1$.

They know that pictures like those in Fig. 6.4 show that $\frac{1}{3} + \frac{2}{3} = 1$. The pictures are convincing as far as fractional parts are concerned, but when the repeating decimal is inserted into the discussion, many students are no longer convinced, even though the definitions are known. So the need to prove is established, but how is that step accomplished?

INFORMAL PROOFS

Readiness comes into play immediately, and it takes two forms. First, have these students seen any proofs in their earlier grades? The assumption here is that the proofs would not be formal in the sense that we think of mathematical proofs, and yet the students will have seen convincing arguments of some sort, even if it is only the use of things like Fig. 6.4 to show that $\frac{1}{3} + \frac{2}{3} = 1$. Any exposure like the pictures is a foundation because the beginnings of answering why something is so are established. Second, are middle school students developmentally ready to handle the complexities of a formal proof?

Diane van Hiele-Geldof and her husband Pierre van Hiele both dealt with students learning geometry. They developed an assessment tool that consists of five levels: visualization, analysis, informal deduction, formal deduction, and rigor. The van Hieles contended that students could move from one category to another via appropriate experiences. Each of the five levels could be defined as follows, going from lowest to highest (Crowley, 1987; van Hiele, 1986):

Visualization (Level 0)—Students are aware of space. Geometric shapes are recognized holistically by their appearance without paying attention to component parts. Students functioning at this level can recognize geometric shapes and can reproduce them upon request. These students recognize squares and rectangles but do not realize the presence of right angles, opposite sides of the same length, and so forth.

Analysis (Level 1)—Students begin analysis of geometric concepts. Parts of geometric figures are recognized. Generally, definitions are repeated but not understood. Relations between properties are not explained. Students would be able to conclude that opposite angles of a parallelogram are congruent. They may not believe a figure can belong to more than one general class. For example, they might accept that a square is a quadrilateral, but they might resist the idea that that same square is also a parallelogram or rectangle or both.

Informal deduction (Level 2)—Definitions now make sense. Informal arguments about why things are as they appear begin to be formulated. Students know there are relations between properties of a figure. For instance, if opposite sides of a quadrilateral are congruent and parallel, the figure must be a parallelogram. They also become aware of connections between groups of figures, like all squares are rectangles but not all rectangles are squares. These students know there is a collection of rules and axioms, but they cannot put them together via deductive techniques yet. They can follow formal proofs, but the logic of connections is not fully understood. Changing the order of steps in a proof confuses

them. These students are essentially unable to construct an original proof when starting with different material.

Formal deduction (Level 3)—Students understand the role of axioms, rules, terms, theorems, definitions, and how they are interwoven. The ability to construct, not just memorize, proofs emerges. Doing a proof more than one way is within the sphere of these students. This means they are ready to study geometry as a formal mathematical system. As a part of that study, they will be able to write formal proofs using "if-then" type logic.

Rigor (Level 4)—Abstractions are comprehended. Students can investigate and compare different geometries (van Hiele, 1986).

Research indicates that appropriate van Hiele questions can lead teachers to know where students are developmentally on the geometry readiness continuum (Burger & Shaughnessy, 1986; Geddes, Fuys, & Tischler, 1985; Grouws, 1992; Hoffer, 1983; Lindquist, 1987; Usiskin, 1982). That would be useful information as far as determining how ready middle schoolers would be for informal proof. One thing that does seem clear is that the typical student entering a high school geometry course is functioning at a van Hiele Level 2, whereas the course is essentially defined for students at a van Hiele Level 3. Thus, either the course must be watered down or the typical student is doomed to failure. If nothing else, this should be a warning as far as expecting too much along the lines of proof and reasoning out of middle school students.

Piaget's research seems to indicate a different outline of how geometric reasoning proof develops. Piaget contended that logical operations develop in individuals independent of the content in which they are working. These operations, according to Piaget, can be applied in a variety of mathematical knowledge. A student who knows that both squares and rectangles contain only right angles, and that their respective opposite sides are congruent and parallel, along with the idea that a square also has adjacent sides congruent, could deduce that all squares are rectangles. This would be an application of the Piaget idea in which known information is used to create new information.

The van Hiele and Piaget thinking represent two major positions on the learning of geometry. Research can be gathered to support either posture, as is the case in so many things. In reality, the situation is not one where either belief is totally correct. More than likely, there is some combination that adequately reflects how most students learn geometry. Either way, there is an implication for the study of reasoning and proof in the middle school (Brumbaugh & Rock, 2001).

TEACHER RESPONSIBILITY IN DEVELOPING REASONING AND PROOF

Now you are in a bind. The Piaget/van Hiele discussion indicates that there is uncertainty about how much reasoning and proof middle school students are ready to absorb. We know that high school students are most likely at van Hiele Level 2, placing middle school students no higher than that, and probably lower. Is it safe to assume that entering middle school students have much experience with reasoning and proof? Perhaps not. They may have seen some reasoning in their elementary exposures, but mathematical proof of any sort is unlikely. From the van Hiele discussion, that is not surprising. Yet, your charge is to provide at least formative experiences. Think about that last statement for a moment. In a study conducted by McCrone and Martin (2004), teachers who taught honors classes included more dis-

covery investigations in their lessons than non–honor class teachers. These teachers involved students and used proofs as a basis for building and justifying relationships. Furthermore, students in the honors classes were encouraged to look back on complete proofs to determine if there were other valid methods for establishing the same relationship or if steps could be eliminated to create more concise proofs. These different processes were also modeled during class. So what are we saying here? Although you may not all be teaching honors-level classes you are still teaching. Are you responsible for productive student learning? Yes! Are you responsible for providing many opportunities for discovery and proof? Of course! Are you responsible for setting high expectations for all students regardless of ability level? Absolutely!

Before reading the next paragraph, please draw a rectangle on a sheet of paper. You should do this! Youngsters have a feel for mathematics and school begins a formalization process for them. The formalization begins to create areas of confusion too, often in subtle, unrealized ways. For example, "standard position" of a geometric figure usually means that one side of the figure is drawn parallel to the bottom of the board or page. Consider a rectangle. Most of the rectangles students see are in standard position. Teachers draw them that way. Books show them that way in pictures and special ideas presented in rectangular-shaped boxes that are in standard position. Consider the multiple-choice question shown in Fig. 6.5, where the student is to select one option.

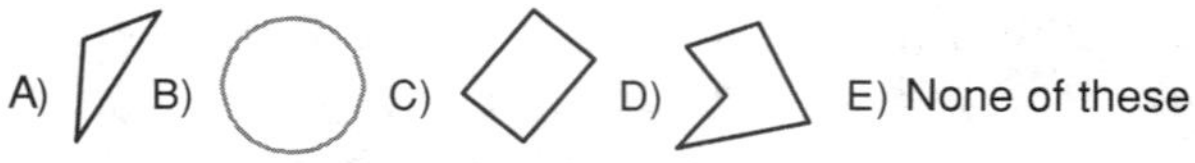

A) ▱   B) ◯   C) ◇   D) ⬠   E) None of these

FIG 6.5.

The number of students who select option E in this example is amazing. Do you have any idea why they might select E?

Before reading on, look at the rectangle you drew earlier. Was it in standard position? Now, please color your rectangle. There is no need for you to get out your crayons; just mark the rectangle in some manner that indicates it is colored. Did you fill the inside? That is not the rectangle! That is the rectangular region. The rectangle is the set of line segments that comprise the border of the figure.

The reason you were asked to draw and color a rectangle is to emphasize a problem faced in the teaching of mathematics. You have the advantage of having had several college mathematics courses. Yet you probably drew your rectangle in standard position and colored the interior. If so, you indicate a tendency to not be mathematically precise. If we, as teachers of mathematics, are not accurate, how can we expect our students to be?

Your Turn

6.1. Describe how you would get your students to not draw polygons in standard position.

6.2. Describe how you would convince your students that coloring the polygon means coloring the segments that make up that polygon, not the interior.

What is the ratio of the long side length and the short for the rectangle you drew? It is probably close to 1.61803399, which is the golden ratio, or golden section. Why did we have you draw the rectangle and then measure its sides to end up with what we predicted? This should give you a feel for what we mean about your students having a feel for mathematics. You do some things reflexively, probably not even realizing it, or formalizing it, just like your students.

Your students come to you with a background. They know (we hope) number facts, basic geometric shapes, are able to operate with fractions and decimals, have covered place value (including exponents), and the list goes on. How do you, the teacher of middle school mathematics, convince students they need to begin formalizing the proof process? Suppose the students have had a concrete exposure to adding fractions, either through egg cartons (see http://pegasus.cc.ucf.edu/~mathed/egg.html), Cuisenaire rods (see http://pegasus.cc.ucf.edu/~mathed/crods.html), or a fraction kit (see http://pegasus.cc.ucf.edu/~mathed/fk.html). Also suppose they are able to get the following results:

$$\frac{1}{2} + \frac{1}{3} = \frac{5}{6}$$

$$\frac{1}{3} + \frac{1}{4} = \frac{7}{12}$$

$$\frac{1}{3} + \frac{1}{5} = \frac{8}{15}$$

Now, you need to steer the discussion. The students need to notice two things: adding the denominators of the addends gives the numerator of the sum, and multiplying the denominators of the addends gives the denominator of the sum. Did you know that? The natural follow-up question is, "Does that always work?" That question establishes that a conjecture has been made and there is an implied need for a proof or counterexample.

Actually there are two conjectures that could come out of that set of three examples. The fact that all three problems contain $\frac{1}{3}$ as an addend is misleading. It is possible that someone would conjecture that as long as one of the addends is $\frac{1}{3}$, the process of adding the denominators of the addends to get the numerator of the sum, and multiplying the denominators of the addends to get the denominator of the sum, will work. Notice how a poor set of examples could cause a false conjecture. The message is to pay attention to the examples given so this does not happen.

Your Turn

6.3. Did you notice that the addend denominators in each problem from the set just discussed in the text are relatively prime? Will the process work for unit fractions with denominators that are not relatively prime?

The second conjecture that this newly discovered process might work all the time requires a little reasoning (a skill you need to help your middle schoolers develop). The logic you would apply with the students is that, if the routine worked all the time, wouldn't someone have used it rather than giving the rule about finding the least common denominator (LCD), dividing the denominator of the fraction addend into the LCD and multiplying the numerator of that fraction by the answer, repeating the process for the next fraction addend, and finally adding the products you got and putting that answer over the LCD? Thus, the conclusion is that the rule does not work all the time. But, don't be too quick to leave the idea that came out of the problem set.

Look at the addends for each problem. Each addend is a unit fraction. It is the case that, as long as the fractions are unit fractions, the process will work. Now consider a different set of problems where each addend denominator is still relatively prime but one of the two addends is not a unit fraction. Examine the example $\frac{1}{4} + \frac{2}{3} = \frac{11}{12}$. The idea of multiplying the addend denominators to get the denominator of the sum still works. However, the idea of adding the addend denominators to give the numerator of the sum does

not work. But, do not abandon the adding idea. Looking at the denominators of the addends: is there a way to get 11 out of them? We can check that $4 + 3 + 3$ *does not* give 11. However, $4 + 4 + 3$ *does* give 11. That could be expressed as two 4s + one 3 or $(2)(4) + (1)(3) = 11$. Wow! Check that out! $\frac{1}{4} \times \frac{2}{3}$ Multiplying one numerator by the other denominator and adding the two products gives the numerator of the sum. That should sound vaguely familiar. Why? Because some people use the concept of cross-multiplication when adding fractions. Now you have just seen how that idea can be reasoned into being for middle school students. In the process, some level of understanding should be developed. That level of understanding and reasoning is the foundation of proof that you need to instill in your middle school students.

You have seen a couple examples of how to start your students along the course of proving things. The stimulus can be much less involved though. One easy way is to ask seemingly ridiculous questions that can be answered. For example, When does $4 - 4 = 8$? Figure 6.6 shows the solution. More than likely you will get some groans on that one, and comments like, "I didn't think of that." Seize the moment and talk about the need to think outside the box.

Number novelties can stimulate the desire for proof too. Do the following with a

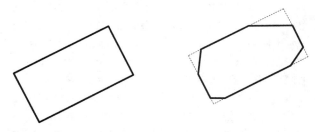

Cut 4 corners off a rectangle (4-4) and get 8 corners.

FIG 6.6.

friend who is not in the class that uses this textbook.

Direction	Example
Pick a number	7
Double it	14
Add 4	18
Divide by 2	9
Subtract 2	7
What did you get?	7

Generally the person will say, "The number I started with." More than likely, that statement will be followed by, "How does that work?" Another typical response is, "Does that work every time?" Either response implies that there is a request for some verification, or proof. Most middle school students can understand the proof of this trick.

Direction	Example	Proof	Algebraic proof
Pick a number	7	□	n
Double it	14	2□	2n
Add 4	18	2□ + 4	2n + 4
Divide by 2	9	$\frac{2\square + 4}{2} = \square + 2$	$\frac{2n + 4}{2} = n + 2$
Subtract 2	7	□	n
What did you get?	7	□	n

Notice we gave two different proofs, one using □, and the other using algebra. Most students will have seen □ used in an equation to represent a variable and, thus, it might be easier for them to comprehend an explanation (proof) using familiar symbols. Ideally, they would easily migrate to the same explanation using a letter for the initial number.

CONCLUSION

You should now have some ideas of how to stimulate a desire for proof in your students. They are naturally curious. You just have to figure out ways to capitalize on that curiosity. Once you get them to ask you

how or why something works, you have them where you want them. It will be easy to keep providing them with more situations that have them asking for proof. In that venue, you are giving them invaluable mathematical background.

STICKY QUESTIONS

6.1. Rationalize why it would be advisable for a future teacher of middle school mathematics to take a mathematics methods course designed to meet the needs of future elementary teachers of mathematics.

6.2. Describe where you could find resources that would provide material that could be used to encourage students to ask for verification (proof) of what they see.

6.3. Explain why there is or is not value in teaching truth tables (conjunction, disjunction, if-then) to middle school students?

6.4. Explain why you believe or do not believe that middle school students are capable of the depth of reasoning required to do mathematical proofs.

6.5. Prove that a segment joining a vertex of a triangle to the midpoint of the opposite side divides the area of that initial triangle in half.

6.6. A vehicle travels 30 miles an hour. How fast will the vehicle have to cover a second 30 miles so it will average 60 miles an hour for the total distance?

6.7. A number trick asks students to write a three-digit number without repeating any digits. The selected number is then reversed and the smaller three-digit number is subtracted from the larger. Reverse the answer and add the reversal to the initial subtraction answer. If the answer is 99, it must be written as 099. The sum will be 1089. Explain how this works.

TAG

6.1. Determine the values of a, b, and c given that $a^3 + b^3 + c^3 = 6396$, $(a)(b)(c) = 935$, and $a + b + c = 33$.

6.2. A 5-digit number is represented by ABCDE. If we affix the digit 1 at the left end of ABCDE, giving 1ABCDE, then the product of 1ABCDE and 3 will be the 6-digit number ABCDE1. What is the original five-digit number ABCDE?

$$\begin{array}{r} 1ABCDE \\ \times 3 \\ \hline ABCDE1 \end{array}$$

6.3. Sometimes problems that appear complex can be approached from a surprising direction. Looking at the following problem, calculators and most interactive algebra software will struggle to work the problem because of the magnitude of the numbers involved. What is $\dfrac{1000! - 996!}{997!}$?

6.4. A right triangle with integral side lengths has an area of 756 square units. What is the hypotenuse of this right triangle?

6.5. A 44-foot rope is attached to the top of a vertical 20-foot flagpole. When the other end of the rope is stretched tight and touched to the ground, a right triangle is formed. What is the area of the largest circle that can be drawn using this rope attached to the top of the pole, assuming the rope does not wrap around the pole at all as the circle is drawn?

6.6. It is known that 40% of boys and 28% of girls in a school are soccer players. If the school contained an equal number of boys and girls, what is the probability that a randomly selected person in that school is a soccer player?

6.7. To square any 2-digit number starting with 5, add 25 to the ones digit and you will have the thousands and hundreds dig-

its of the product. Then square the ones digit and that result becomes the tens and ones digits of the product. Note, you might need 0 for the tens digit of the final product if the ones digit of the number being squared is 0, 1, 2, or 3.

6.8. Using 3 different digits, form all possible 2-digit numbers (including repeating the digits). Add all 9 of the 2-digit numbers you form. Divide this sum by the sum of the original 3 digits. The answer will be 33.

6.9. How can these products be done quickly in your head?

$$(36)(34) = 1224$$
$$(53)(57) = 3021$$
$$(62)(68) = 4216$$
$$(41)(49) = 2009$$

6.10. What is wrong with the following calculations that seem to prove that 2 equals 1?

$a = b$	Let $a = b$
$aa = ab$	Multiply both sides by a
$aa - bb = ab - bb$	Subtract bb from both sides
$(a + b)(a - b) = b(a - b)$	Factor
$a + b = b$	Divide both sides by $(a - b)$
$2a = a$	Substitute a for b
$2 = 1$	Divide both sides by a

6.11. $23 \times 96 = 2208 = 32 \times 69$. Notice that the product of the left side of the equation is equal to the product of the digits reversed on the right side. Find another pair of 2-digit numbers that share the same product when their digits are reversed. Repeated-digit factors are not permitted (like 33 x 33). Prove why this is possible.

REFERENCES

Brumbaugh, D. K., & Rock, D. (2001). *Teaching secondary mathematics*. Mahwah, NJ: Lawrence Erlbaum Associates.

Burger, W. F., & Shaughnessy, J. M. (1986). Characterizing the van Hiele levels of development in geometry. *Journal for Research in Mathematics Education*, 17, 31–48.

BWH Ventures. (2004a). Optical illusions: Image gallery #1. Retrieved November 21, 2004, from http://www.eyetricks.com/0102.htm

BWH Ventures. (2004b). Optical illusions: Image gallery #3. Retrieved November 21, 2004, from http://www.eyetricks.com/0302.htm

Crowley, M. (1987). The van Hiele model of the development of geometric thought. In M. M. Lindquist and A. P. Shulte (Eds.), *Learning and teaching geometry*. Reston, VA: National council of Teachers of Mathematics.

Geddes, D., Fuys, D., & Tischler, R. (1985). An investigation of the van Hiele model of thinking in geometry among adolescents (Final Report). *Research in Science Education (RISE) Program of the National Science Foundation*. Grant No. SED 7920640. Washington, DC: National Science Foundation.

Grouws, D. A. (Ed.). (1992). *Handbook of research on mathematics teaching and learning*. A project of the National Council of Teachers of Mathematics. New York: Macmillan.

Hoffer, A. (1983). Van Hiele-based research. In R. Lesh & M. Landau (Eds.), *Acquisition of mathematical concepts and processes* (pp. 205–277). New York: Academic Press.

Lindquist, M. M. (Ed.) (1987). Learning and teaching geometry, K-12. In *1987 NCTM Yearbook*. Washington, DC: National Council of Teachers of Mathematics.

McCrone, S. S., & Martin, T. S. (2004). Assessing high school students' understanding of geometric proof. *Canadian Journal of Science, Mathematics, and Technology Education*, 4(2), 223–242.

Usiskin, Z. (1982). Van Hiele levels and achievement in secondary school geometry. *Final report, Cognitive Development and Achievement in Secondary School Geometry Project*. Chicago: University of Chicago.

van Hiele, P. M. (1986). *Structure and insight: A theory of mathematics education*. Orlando, FL: Academic Press.

7
Problem Solving

Ever have any problems? How did you solve them? As you ponder that for a moment, think about the steps you took to resolve whatever situation you were in. Problem solving in mathematics uses techniques similar to those you apply to real-life situations. Problem solving is one of the core ideas in mathematics and the main thing that mathematicians do. Because we all experience problems of one nature or another, learning how to be a good problem solver is important for everyone.

Problem solving is central to all disciplines, and one reason for including mathematics in all levels of the PreK – 20+ curriculum. According to NCTM (2000), "in everyday life and in the workplace, being a good problem solver can lead to great advantages" (p. 52). Problem solving should be an integral part of mathematical learning, not isolated. You need to have a problem solving plan. Care needs to be taken

to ensure that the degree of difficulty of the problem being presented is not too great for the students or beyond their skill and readiness levels. If it is, they will become discouraged about solving problems, and about mathematics as well. The students need to accept the challenge and believe they can solve the problem. On the other hand, if the problem is too easy, the students can get the impression that there are few challenges in mathematics. There is a delicate balance between hard and easy, and ready or not when considering problem solving. You and your students need to define that balance and all will benefit.

HISTORY OF PROBLEM SOLVING

The history of mathematics is rich with problem solving situations that can be used to attract student attention, connect mathematics with other disciplines, show applications, and provide challenges for individuals. The "Seven Bridges of Konigsberg" is a classic problem that Euler proved impossible (Newman, 1956). This problem can be the basis for an enthralling lesson.

As the story is told, the German town of Konigsberg (now Kallningrad, Russia) faced a difficult dilemma each year. The people planned an annual parade through their village and wanted the parade to follow a path that would march the procession across each of the town's bridges only once. The citizens of Konigsberg did not want the parade to pass any of its landmarks more than once. The Pregel River

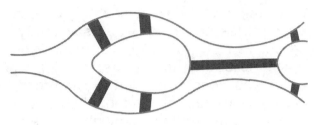

FIG 7.1.

flowed through the town and split in two on the other side, with one island existing within the town limits as shown in Fig. 7.1. This seemed like such a simple task, yet no one was able to plot a course for the parade to cross each bridge in the town once and only once.

Try placing this drawing or one similar on a board or poster in front of the class. Also, make copies of the diagram for students to work with at their desks. Tell the perplexing story of the Bridges of Konigsberg. Ask your students to try to trace a course that would cross each bridge once and only once.

After your students have attempted the problem for a while, tell them that the famous mathematician, Leonard Euler, showed in 1735 that it was impossible to complete the task as defined. Your students might surprise you by continuing to try the problem, even after being told that Euler proved it impossible. Attempting to find the path for the bridges of Konisberg led to the development of a branch of mathematics called topology.

Gauss intuitively "discovered" how to sum consecutive counting numbers while in his early school years (Beck, Bleicher, & Crowe, 1969). The teacher assigned the task of finding the sum of the first 100 consecutive counting numbers to Gauss, who quickly determined the sum to be 5050. This idea can be an interesting challenge for some students. A lesson could be built around it in the following manner. (T represents a teacher comment and S stands for something a student might say.)

T: What is the sum of the first 3 consecutive counting numbers?
S: 6
T: What is the sum of the first 4 consecutive counting numbers?
S: 10
T: What is the sum of the first 5 consecutive counting numbers?
S: 15
T: What is the sum of the first 6 consecutive counting numbers?
S: 21
T: What is the sum of the first 100 consecutive counting numbers? (You might do a few more numbers before asking for such a large value.)
S: That is too big to try (although some might work at it).
T: Is there a pattern we can look for?

Students could say a variety of things here. They could say yes or no to the pattern question and perhaps make suggestions about what to look for. Eventually you will need to lead the class in the following type of discussion.

T: Look at $1 + 2 + 3 = 6 = \dfrac{3 \times 4}{2}$.

T: $1 + 2 + 3 + 4 = 10 = \dfrac{4 \times 5}{2}$.

T: $1 + 2 + 3 + 4 + 5 = 15 = \dfrac{5 \times 6}{2}$.

T: $1 + 2 + 3 + 4 + 5 + 6 = 21 = \dfrac{6 \times 7}{2}$.

T: Do you see a pattern?
S: Each time the sum is half of the largest addend times itself plus one.
T: Explain that, please.
S: In $1 + 2 + 3 + 4$, the sum is 10, which is half of 4 times 5.
T: What is the sum of the first 100 consecutive counting numbers?
S: It has to be $\dfrac{100 \times 101}{2} = 5050$.

The Konisberg and summing the first 100 counting number lessons should provide insight into how much problem solving potential the history of mathematics holds. There are many other examples. The Egyptians measured land after the floods so ownership could be determined. Consider a herder who could not count but could keep track of the flock number by moving stacks of pebbles as the sheep came or went from their pen. We have calculators but so did the ancients: the abacus. Piles of stones, papyrus, an abacus, and calculators are all tools that have been used to help solve problems. The important thing to note is that a problem presented itself and it got solved somehow. That is a spirit you need to instill in your students.

Your Turn

7.1. The Seven Bridges of Konigsberg, a discussion of Gauss, and the Egyptians using geometry to measure flooded ground were given as examples of historical topics that could be inserted into the middle grades classroom. Find a different historical topic appropriate for middle schoolers. Give all pertinent bibliographic information and create a lesson plan that would incorporate your topic.

7.2. Read the parts in NCTM's *Curriculum and Evaluation Standards for School Mathematics* pertaining to problem solving in the middle school. Reflect on what the publication says and write your feelings about their position on problem solving in the elementary curriculum.

WHAT MAKES A PROBLEM A PROBLEM?

Problem solving is a daily activity for most people. Do all situations in mathematics require problem solving? No. Not every situation we encounter in daily life requires

problem solving. If we asked, "How much is nine times three?" you would say twenty-seven. In fact, you might roll your eyes if we implied that this was something for which you needed problem-solving techniques. However, one person's memorized fact might be another person's problem. Even the most difficult problem becomes just another exercise once you unlock the solution. Exercise and problem are often interchanged, but we distinguish between them by saying that an exercise is practicing an algorithm or technique, whereas a problem has no immediate or obvious solution. Also, a situation which starts as a problem or challenge might become an exercise after the student solves it. So what makes an exercise into a problem? How do you know when something will require problem solving? What makes a good problem solver?

For a situation to be a problem, it has to be something that cannot be answered by blindly applying a regular algorithm to get a viable answer. Nine times three could require problem solving for a child learning multiplication, but for you it is not problem solving. The criterion is important and means that, if you already have done a particular type of problem, even if you had to do problem solving to get the answer, it is no longer a problem-solving situation for you. It might still be a problem for others who have not seen it or resolved it.

The second requirement is that a problem needs to engage you or get your attention. If you are not engaged, or do not accept the challenge the problem presents, you will not attempt it. Anyone can be turned off if the problem presented is too difficult or if the individual does not have the necessary background to attempt a solution. Problems must be challenging, appropriate, and engaging for the learner. Engaging should not be overlooked. For example, suppose you want to know the distance between towns A and B. The question could be answered by a bike ride between the two. For some this would be a compelling question. For others, for a multitude of reasons, the temptation would be to ignore the situation as uninteresting. It is not realistic to think that all students will be compelled to solve each problem solving problem you present them. That statement, however, does not give license to the student to ignore all problem-solving situations you present because it is not engaging enough for them.

The third requirement for problem solving is tenacity—you must work on the problem and persevere long enough to come up with a solution. Making one or two attempts at a new problem is rarely sufficient for finding a viable solution. It is important to make conjectures about a problem as you work through it. Conjectures, even when they are wrong, often lead to a solution because they may eliminate false paths or provide insights to other possibilities. Sometimes we call this attribute stick-to-itiveness.

POLYA'S STEPS

Polya's Four Steps for Problem Solving

George Polya (1973) stated that there are four basic phases required to solve a problem, as shown in Fig. 7.2. The first step is to understand the problem. That is, the learner must read and correctly interpret the situation. You are probably saying to yourself, "Well, of course you have to understand the question before you can begin to solve the problem. How could you even start if you didn't understand?" Some possible questions you can ask are:

- What is the unknown, challenge, or question?
- Are there any words to define?

Polya's 4 Steps for Problem Solving

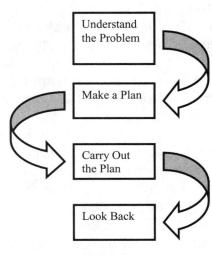

FIG 7.2.

- Have you taken into account all the information?
- Can the problem be simplified or paraphrased?
- What is the information or data given in the problem?
- Is there any extraneous, redundant, unnecessary, contradictory, or insufficient information?
- Where can I get more information?

Polya's second step is to make a plan, which will help you solve the problem. Some possible questions you can ask at this point are:

- Is this problem familiar?
- Has all the information been considered as a plan is devised?
- Is there a strategy or theorem that could be used?

Any plan you develop will be based on your prior knowledge and experiences and may combine ideas in new or different ways. Nonetheless, you may be saying, "Of course the next step is to make a plan."

Polya's third step is to carry out the plan. Your plan may require revision or perhaps you will scrap it and develop a new one after attempting to carry out the original. You may even go back to make sure you understood the problem correctly, make an entirely new plan (for example, select a different strategy), and try it. You are probably saying to yourself, "Duh? How else would you ever get a solution?"

We distinguish between the words *answer* and *solution*. The answer to 9 times 3 is 27. When you solve a problem, you come up with a solution. The solution is the process used to solve a problem. There may be more than one solution or answer for a problem, depending on the situation. A solution also implies that there is some sort of rationale or reasoning behind your method.

Polya's fourth step is to look back and make sure your understanding, plan, and execution of the plan resulted in a solution that makes sense and resolves the original situation. This is the time to look for errors, other possible approaches and answers, and connections to different contexts. Some possible questions you might ask are:

- Can the solution or argument be checked?
- Can the solution be proven?
- Is there more than one way to solve the problem?
- Is there more than one solution?
- Are the steps correct?
- Does the solution make sense?
- Can the solution be used to solve other problems?

You should also examine your solution for faults in your plan or difficulties in the execution of your plan. Are you saying, "I know I should always check my answers, but sometimes I forget or get in a rush?"

Polya's four steps for problem solving or some of the other instructional varia-

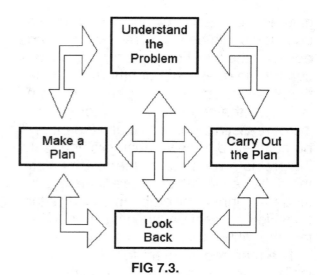

FIG 7.3.

tions of this model make sense. Understand the problem, make a plan to solve the problem, carry out the plan, and look back and check your work. It seems like just plain common sense. Then why do we struggle with problem solving? Take a look at Fig. 7.3, which indicates the interconnectedness of the four problem solving steps. You will see that, although the steps themselves seem simplistic, their interconnectedness and interdependence veil a complexity the steps themselves do not necessarily evoke. Sometimes we are not as sequential in our approach to problem solving, as indicated in Polya's steps. Some might feel that a solution to the problem evolves (maybe intuitively) before going through each one of the problem-solving steps. This flexibility of thought is important as students tackle a problem. It does not develop easily, or at any given time; it is a developmental/readiness thing. The problem-solving steps become more important as students try to present feasible approaches to solving problems.

The problem-solving steps are also useful teaching and evaluation tools. The teacher could consider students' attempts to solve a problem by assessing where they are along the process. For example, one student might be trying to understand the problem and need help with this aspect, while another might be already applying a strategy to solve the problem and need help in a different form.

STRATEGIES

Now that we have discussed what makes a problem a problem and the steps you take to find a solution, you are ready to explore different strategies for solving problems. Will we give every possible strategy? No. The strategies we are about to discuss, just like Polya's problem-solving steps, will seem natural and for the most part straightforward, and could be used or combined as you solve problems. These, coupled with your continued growth in problem solving, should provide the tools you will need to become an effective problem solver.

Probably one of the most popular strategies used by students is guess, test, and revise (also known as guess and check). After reading, your plan for solving the problem is to guess, test the solution, and then revise your guess according to the results of testing. Try and solve the following: "I am a number between one and twenty. I can be written as a base raised to a power to obtain myself. Exchange the base and the power and you still get me. The base is not equal to the power. What number am I?"

You can start by guessing any number, say four, our first conjecture. We test four and find that four is two to the second power. The power and the base are equal, so looking back, four is not the solution. You could guess nine as your next conjecture. Nine is three to the second power, but two to the third power is eight, not nine, so looking back, nine doesn't work either. Guessing six leads to all sorts of difficulties, so that one gets eliminated in the test-

ing phase. Continue to guess, test, and revise until you solve the riddle.

How'd you do? You probably started thinking about using another strategy to help keep track, like making a list. Did you make a list of the numbers between 1 and 20? Another handy strategy for this problem is eliminating impossible answers. Did you cross out 1 and the prime numbers? That would leave 4, 6, 8, 9, 10, 12, 14, 15, 16, 18, and 20. What could you do next? You could cross out all the numbers that can't easily be written as a power of another (4, ~~6~~, 8, 9, ~~10~~, ~~12~~, ~~14~~, ~~15~~, 16, ~~18~~, ~~20~~), then show the remaining numbers using exponents $4 = 2^2, 8 = 2^3, 9 = 3^2$, $16 = 4^2$. Now what are you thinking? How about eliminating 4 because the power (2) is equal to the base (2)? Can you eliminate any more numbers? Notice that $2^3 \neq 3^2$, thus taking out both 8 and 9. Now you're getting somewhere. What's left? We know that $4^2 = 16$, so we test $2^4 = 2 \times 2 \times 2 \times 2 = 16$, and so the solution is 16: $16 = 4^2 = 2^4$.

We are trying to help you think about your thinking, a process called metacognition. Thinking about your thinking and being able to communicate about your thinking is one of the NCTM process standards. Many standardized tests now require explanations. It would be wise for you to articulate your thinking process to your partners in class. (The problem solving steps would be especially useful for this task.) Verbalizing your thinking helps clarify it. When working in a group, it helps in two ways: first, by letting you know others were thinking similar things, and second, knowing what others are thinking reduces overlap in the group effort.

Making a chart or a table can be helpful in solving some problem types. Consider this: "Suppose you are in charge of a 128-team single-elimination softball tournament for which all tie games will go into

128-Team Elimination Tournament

Number of Teams	Number of Games	Number of Winners
128	64	64
64	32	32
32	16	16
16	8	8
8	4	4
4	2	2
2	1	1
Total	127	

FIG 7.4.

extra innings until a winner is determined. If no team forfeits a game, how many games will have to be played before the tournament winner is declared?" What categories will you need for your chart or table? Would software be helpful?

You may have played in tournaments and recall the diagrams used to pair teams. If that is part of your previous knowledge base, you might try solving the 128-team tournament problem by drawing a picture or diagram like that in Fig. 7.4. Your past experiences and comfort level with a particular type of strategy often determines whether or not you use it. We encourage you to draw pictures as a strategy, because they often provide insight that makes a difficult-appearing problem easier.

Before leaving this tournament problem, is there another way to solve it? You might ask why we would bother to do that since the problem has already been done. There are a couple of reasons. First, a student could solve a problem different from how you do it and it is imperative that you be flexible enough in your thinking to consider it. Second, there just might be a simpler way to solve it. Third, if you practice thinking about problems from different perspectives, you will be amazed at how much more versatile your thought patterns become. So, take another look at the tournament problem. There are 128 teams in a

single-elimination tournament and the task is to determine the number of games to declare the tournament winner. If it is a single elimination tournament, then every team but one has to lose. That means one out of 128 teams wins all its games. All other 127 teams lose a game, meaning there must be 127 games.

One of the key strategies used for any problem is looking for a pattern. Much mathematics is based on one type of pattern or another. Before you see the pattern, solving the problem seems improbable, if not impossible. Once you see the pattern, the problem may become trivial. Looking for a pattern is a subgoal of almost every problem-solving strategy. You might think of the tournaments in which you have played and use them as examples for the 128-team problem, even if they involved far fewer than 128 teams. Using a simpler version of a problem can provide the needed insight for solving a complicated or complex problem.

Some problems lend themselves to solutions involving algebraic models. Restating the problem to use an algebraic strategy more effectively sometimes helps. Take a look at this one: "If the Loch Ness monster is 20 meters long plus half of its own length, how long is Nessie?" Your understanding of the English language is important in solving problems such as this. Certainly this problem begs for an algebraic model, but would restating the problem help you avoid an error during the process of translating the English into the algebraic model? Although phrases add descriptive information and clarity to English sentences, they are sometimes movable or removable in mathematical situations. Would you understand the question of how long Nessie is if we rewrote and translated? Let's see. How long is Nessie if the length is 20 meters plus half of its own length? How about forming an algebraic model like this one? How long is Nessie (L = Nessie's length) if the length is 20 meters plus half of its own length?

$$L = 20 \text{ meters} + \frac{L}{2}$$

Combine like terms by subtracting $\frac{L}{2}$ from both sides of the equation. Then $\frac{L}{2} = 20$ m. Multiply both sides of the equation by 2, and L = 40 m, the length of Nessie, the Loch Ness monster.

Some people shy away from doing story problems because they struggle with forming algebraic models. Problems in the real world are not stated in mathematical terms. Understanding the English structure of problems goes a long way toward helping you become more proficient at solving problems, because it helps you translate situations into algebraic terms.

Have you ever wondered what purpose the answers in the back of your book might have—other than to see if you are right? One reason we provide a solution manual (not just answers, but how we got them) is to give you the opportunity to work backward. Sometimes, if you know the answer you can work your way back to the question.

Your Turn

7.3. "You have been contracted to use gold to guild the page numbers in a reproduction of an ancient manuscript, starting with page 1. Because of the expense and time required for this process, you will be paid by the number of digits you guild. If you guild a total of 642 digits, how many pages did you number in the manuscript?" Try your hand at using the working-backward strategy to come up with a solution.

Did you get the gilded page problem? Perhaps the very first strategy for solving any problem is to use reasoning to deter-

mine how to proceed. Few problem solving strategies work well in isolation. One of the important aspects of the reasoning strategy is the estimation of an answer and checking the reasonableness of a solution. An estimate of 500 pages for this problem should seem unreasonable to you. Why? Did you use Polya's step number four, looking back, before you looked up the answer? If so, you put the reasoning strategy to good use. Every time you check back you are using this strategy!

Your Turn

7.4. Consider the following problem: "In the early days of movie making, a villain might do things that cannot be done in real life. In today's movie making, directors often use consultants to avoid this type of blunder. A director has asked you to determine if it is reasonable for the villain to grab a $1,000,000 ransom, in one-dollar bills, and run. You know a dollar bill weighs about one gram. Is the scene reasonable?"

7.5. Find a list different from the four steps Polya presents for problem solving. Describe the similarities and differences between the list you found and Polya's.

7.6. List the four components for problem solving. Explain how these components will help you in preparing for instruction.

7.7. Provide examples of different types of problems. How can you use them in the classroom to teach problem solving to middle schoolers?

TEACHING PROBLEM SOLVING

Why teach problem solving? For many, mathematics is problem solving. One thing problem solving can do is connect the classroom to real life. It also provides an opportunity to join different mathematical topics. Suppose a student is asked to use 100 feet of fence to provide a maximum

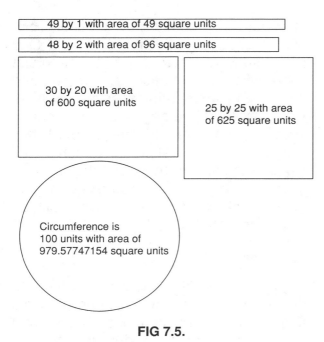

49 by 1 with area of 49 square units

48 by 2 with area of 96 square units

30 by 20 with area of 600 square units

25 by 25 with area of 625 square units

Circumference is 100 units with area of 979.57747154 square units

FIG 7.5.

play area for a dog. Figure 7.5 shows some of the possible shapes and areas. The student learns that, when a perimeter is fixed, the maximum area comes from a circle. In the process of investigating, a useful generalization is developed.

If you are going to be teaching problem solving, you have to be a problem solver. You do not need to do every problem, but you do have to practice what you preach. As you talk the talk and walk the walk of problem solving, your excitement will spill over into other teaching areas. Your class cannot be constantly problem solving. You and your students need time for explaining, discussing, elaborating, generalizing, algorithm building, and practice of known mathematical content.

There are several things to keep in mind as you integrate problem solving into your curriculum. First and foremost, do it consistently. As you do it, pose problems appropriate for all levels of your students. Keep textbook problems in perspective. (Your textbook is not the only source of problem-solving problems.) Put a premium on think-

ing and creative solutions. Consider posting the work of a student who has done an exceptionally clear or innovative solution. It is not just how much you know that counts. It is how you use what you know, when you need it. Sometimes in problem solving, that can be difficult. Problem solving should lead to more mathematics and stimulate a need for mathematics. Your plan for problem solving should start with reasonably easy problems and build toward more difficult ones to avoid discouraging students.

Each of us must do problem solving. In the process of doing, appropriate problem-solving behavior is modeled. How did we learn to solve problems? In most cases, the ability has taken years to evolve, and there was little, if any, conscious awareness of its development. Now the expectation is that you teach this ability to students. How can students be taught to become problem solvers without our modeling the desired result? Do not be afraid to let yourself think out loud for the students. The examples done in class are prepared in advance to teach the concepts and skills we want students to acquire. As the lesson develops, student questions and responses the teacher did not anticipate can provide opportunities that might become part of their problem-solving skills. Do not be afraid to solve problems with the class. As this is done, describe each thought process, thus giving students insights into how the total picture is developed. Such an approach involves risk. A problem may be encountered for which no solution is immediately visible. Students are conditioned to believe that the teacher can immediately see the solution to a given problem. When they become aware that you are not functioning at that level, their confidence in you might be shaken. Do not panic. You are not the answer machine. They will learn to understand the thought process you are demonstrating to them. The value of your thinking in front of the class is too crucial to disregard. They need to become aware of how they should be examining problems to arrive at a satisfactory solution. This discussion about thinking in front of a class does not preclude the demand that lessons must be planned in advance. Thinking on your feet is not the same as not being prepared for a class. When a student works a problem out loud in class, others have the opportunity to observe their classmate's problem-solving process. At times students can comprehend a peer's thought process better than the teacher's. We can learn from each other!

As problem-solving skills are developed, several issues warrant consideration. Most middle school students spend time doing specialized problem types: number problems, rate problems, age and coin problems, percent problems, mixture problems, and so on. The trouble is that, if the first week is spent doing age problems and then percent problems are done the second week, at the end of the second week the students typically have forgotten how to do the age problems. This is a result of working with specialized problem types. It is easy to avoid this scenario by providing a wide variety of problems. The problems presented must be appropriate for all ability levels and, yet, fit into the curricular topics being covered. Presenting problems appropriate for students who have different ability levels is not overly difficult, thanks to the multitude of resources now available. However, using problems appropriate for the curriculum being presented is not always that easy; planning is crucial. One factor that should be considered is how frequently problem solving should be integrated into each lesson. The easy answer is, "as often as possible." The thing is, that response does not provide much information. Problem solving can be invigo-

rating and stimulating as well as frustrating, tedious, and tiring. The frequency of presentation requires a delicate balance. Part of the question can be resolved by establishing a program whereby a problem solving exercise is presented at least once a week. This problem may or may not be related to the curriculum being covered. As problems are offered, time must be allowed for discussion of solutions. A possible reaction of some students is not to accept the challenge of the problem and, therefore, they will not be interested in the solution. The discussion could be held during a time you have allotted for seatwork, for example. This allows those who are not interested to engage in other constructive objectives. Alternatively, discussing the solution during seatwork time can be viewed as punishment by those who accept the challenge. The allocated time could not be used to do the seatwork because of the problem-solving discussion, but the assignment is still due. These considerations are part of a delicate balance that must be maintained. A very important component of this whole problem-solving picture is that problem solving should not be restricted to the "problem of the week," extra credit, or to a given day. Problem solving is mathematical thinking!

DIFFERENT TYPES OF PROBLEMS

The idea of different problem types goes beyond nonspecialization. You need to incorporate problems appropriate for varying student ability levels, gathered from different subject areas, exemplifying a variety of real-world applications, and designed to reach a multitude of objectives. Many of these problems do not need to be invented. They do exist in resources like your textbook for the class, the Internet, other books, colleagues, classes you could take, workshops, professional development opportunities, and so on. The major difficulty becomes one of being able to compile a set of problems appropriate for your classes. Because there is such a wealth of information available, time will be required to get familiar with the resources and then make appropriate selections. It is necessary to go beyond the resources provided by your textbook if you are to have a stimulating problem-solving program in your classes.

One interesting source of problems is the students themselves. Have them create problems that appeal to them and offer those creations to their peers as a challenge. Surely they are likely to use topics that interest them. You will also learn things about the world of the students and what they value.

As students conceptualize problems, evidence of creative thinking will surface. This will be especially apparent in strong problem solvers. It also becomes an avenue that can be pursued as problem solving skills are developed. Students need to be made aware of the value and rewards available for creative thinking. As students begin to become problem solvers, their inventiveness can progress to extremely intricate levels. Encouragement of such developments, in turn, stimulates flexible thinking processes. As this is done, a spiral is started in which the problem-solving skills and excitement begin to fuel each other.

Planning a problem-solving program is another essential ingredient in building problem-solving skills. This statement cannot be given enough emphasis. Good problem-solving programs do not just happen. They require a lot of reflective thinking on the part of the teacher. This thinking involves deciding which problems to use

and where to insert them into the curriculum. Allowances must be made for alterations because of the discovery of a new problem or of differing student needs. The problem-solving program is a constantly evolving process. The textbook may have the framework of a plan you can work with, but you will undoubtedly need to expand it. Include problems not directly related to the curriculum that are designed to attract the attention of your students to problem solving.

As problem-solving skills are developed, care must be taken to ensure that problem solving and new content are not taught at the same time. Problem-solving problems can be used to generate a need for new content. New content might provide the background for an exciting problem. Teaching the two new things at once may lead to confusion and should be avoided. There will be times when, through coincidence, it will happen that the two will appear at the same time, but it should not be planned that way. The difficulty with introducing two new things at the same time is that some students will do creative mathematics by combining parts of each of the two things into some new whole. This new whole is not useful to the student because of the flaws inherent in combining parts from two different entities.

The difficulty level of any particular problem is dependent on the background knowledge of the problem solver. Difficult for one person may be easy for another, not because one is smarter but because they have had experiences with a type of problem or they have the background and tools to solve the problem. Another influencing factor, and a big key to solving almost any problem, is how much tenacity a problem solver possesses. One or two attempts at a problem are often insufficient. Take a look at all of the problems here. Anyone can do "easy" problems. These may not be so easy. Take this opportunity to challenge yourself (and in the future, your students) to do the TAG problems, even the ones you perceive as "difficult." Please note they may not be arranged in ascending degree of difficulty for you.

REAL-WORLD PROBLEMS

Discussion within the NCTM standards deals with the idea that mathematics students need problem-solving problems from their world. It is common to find examples in a middle school setting that involve students "purchasing" stocks and tracking market movement. Is investigation into the workings of the stock market as interesting or relevant to a middle school student as creating a study of current fashion trends, comparing prices of skateboards, or shopping for the best deal on CDs? Certainly the stock investigation permits them an opportunity to act grown up, but would other topics hold more interest for them?

The standards say that, as students mature mathematically, problem situations spring from within the study of mathematics. Problem-solving questions can resolve dilemmas from the students' real world and from their world of mathematical growth, as was often the case for ancient mathematicians. It should be noted here that the *Standards 2000* and the addenda series (NCTM, 1989) contain a variety of settings that could be used to develop problem-solving skills with students.

Your Turn

7.8. Identify two topics that would be of interest to middle school students and the mathematics related to those topics. Determine the grade level or subject in which each topic could be used to introduce the defined mathematical concept(s).

BECOMING A PROBLEM SOLVER

If you have been working the problems in this chapter as we have gone along, you are polishing your problem-solving skills. If you are going to expect your students to be problem solvers, you must model appropriate behavior. Trying the problems presented in this text is a great beginning. If you do not accept the challenges of these problems, how can you, in good conscience, expect your students to attempt the problems you pose for them? It becomes a matter of practicing what you preach. One beauty of becoming a problem solver is that your excitement about learning will spill over into other areas of teaching. Then both you and your students will benefit.

So, how do you spot a good problem solver? Certainly we are not all equally adept at doing everything and that includes problem solving. It is a struggle for some and easy for others. Problem solving is a valuable skill so it is important to encourage those who are good at it. One indicator is that the individual is willing to try problems. Another involves persistence. Many times a good problem solver is able to skip steps as a situation develops, generally reflecting a clear understanding of what is happening. Finally, good problem solvers frequently talk to themselves. In the process they learn what questions are helpful to ask and what to do with the answers they derive.

CONCLUSION

Polya (1973) provided the general four-step process for solving problems. We added a group of common strategies and insights into what makes a situation a problem versus an exercise. We also gave you opportunities to practice Polya's four-step process and use a variety of strategies to solve problems as they were presented to you. As you solve a greater variety of problems and use different strategies, your problem-solving abilities will grow. It is up to you to become a good problem solver, but, like any other worthwhile endeavor, becoming a good problem solver requires interest and practice on your part. This is only the beginning of a discussion on problem solving. *You* need to be a problem solver. The literature abounds with many successful problem-solving examples from various classrooms. It is your responsibility as a professional to learn problem solving and to lead by example. Solve on!

STICKY QUESTIONS

7.1. Is it reasonable to expect problem solving to be interwoven throughout the entire curriculum? Why or why not?

7.2. Is it possible to assimilate a reasonable collection of problem-solving problems appropriate for a given heterogeneously grouped middle school class? Defend your answer.

7.3. Can you effectively teach problem-solving problems you have not solved yourself? Defend your response.

7.4. What do you say to the teacher your students had last year who does not believe in teaching problem solving?

7.5. What do you say to a former student who reports that the teacher they now have for mathematics does not believe in incorporating problem solving into the curriculum?

7.6. Is using technology (excluding the Internet) "cheating" to a problem-solving problem? Why or why not?

7.7. Is using the Internet "cheating" to a problem-solving problem? Why or why not?

TAG

7.1. A farmer had 26 cows. All but 9 died. How many lived?

7.2. A uniform log can be cut into 3 pieces in 12 seconds. Assuming the same rate of cutting, how long will it take for a similar log to be cut into 4 pieces?

7.3. How many different ways can you add four odd counting numbers to get a sum of 10?

7.4. What is the sum of the first 100 consecutive counting numbers?

7.5. How many cubic inches of dirt are there in a hole that is 1 foot deep, 2 feet wide, and 6 feet long?

7.6. How many squares are there in a 5 by 5 square grid?

7.7. A little green frog is sitting at the bottom of the stairs. She wants to get to the tenth step, so she leaps up 2 steps and then slides back 1. How many leaps will she have to take if she follows this pattern until she reaches the tenth step?

7.8. If there are 7 months that have 31 days in them and 11 months that have 30 days in them, how many months have 28 days in them?

7.9. TTTTTTT9: What number does this represent?

7.10. You are given 5 beans and 4 bowls. Place an odd number of beans in each bowl. Use all beans.

7.11. You are to take a pill every half hour. You have 18 pills to take. How long will you be taking pills?

7.12. If you got a 40% discount on a $150.00 pair of sport shoes and 20% off a $200 set of roller blades, what was the percent discount on the total purchase (assuming no taxes are involved)?

7.13. Where should the Z be placed and why?

```
A      EF   HI  KLMN        T    VWXY
  BCD      G    J      OPQRS    U
```

7.14. Estimate how old will you be in years if you live 1,000,000 hours?

7.15. A child has $3.15 in U.S. coins, but only has dimes and quarters. There are more quarters than dimes. How many of each coin does the child have?

7.16. There are 3 children in a family. The oldest is 15. The average of their ages is 11. The median age is 10. How old is the youngest child?

7.17. A famous mathematician was born on March 14, which could be written as 3.14. This date is the start of a representation for pi. It is interesting that this mathematician was born on "pi day." Give his name.

REFERENCES

Beck, A., Bleicher, M. N., & Crowe, D. W. (1969). *Excursions into mathematics*. New York: Worth.

National Council of Teachers of Mathematics. (1989). *Addenda series*. Reston, VA: Author.

National Council of Teacher of Mathematics. (2000). *Principles and standards for school mathematics*. Reston, VA: Author.

Newman, J. R. (1956). *The world of mathematics* (Vol. 1). New York: Simon & Schuster.

Polya, G. (1973). *How to solve it* (2nd ed.). Princeton, NJ: Princeton University Press. (Original work published in 1945)

8
Number and Operations

Number and operations encompasses a plethora of concepts from a variety of mathematical venues, all of which are intertwined to form the basic platform from which most future mathematical studies grow. Each element is a critical piece of the total mathematical landscape and demands attention and mastery. Most view arithmetic as the first step in this overall picture. It has been said that:

> The depressing thing about arithmetic badly taught is that it destroys a child's intellect and, to some extent, his/her integrity.
>
> Before they are taught arithmetic, children will not give their assent to utter nonsense; afterwards they will.
>
> Instead of looking at things and thinking about them, they will make wild guesses in the hopes of pleasing the teacher. (W.W. Sawyer, personal communication, September 2, 2004)

There is no question that arithmetic background is essential to understanding the world of mathematics. Alas, to many, arithmetic is mathematics when, in reality, it is only a small part of the field. Because of their microscopic view of mathematics as being only arithmetic, these folks fail to see the beauty and power of the subject. It is your responsibility to overcome that view and broaden the perspective of each student in your class. Your task is a daunting one because that is the view often held by the parents of students, some other teachers these students have, school administration, and a large segment of society. Still, you must fight on!

READINESS

Although we would like to assume that all students entering middle school have mastered the basic facts and are functional with operating (add, subtract, multiply, divide) with whole numbers, fractions, and to some extent decimals, we know that is not the case. For the sake of discussion, a basic fact involves three numbers, at least two of which must be digits. Thus, $3 + 4 = 7$ and $9 + 5 = 14$ are addition number facts because each of those examples contains at least two digits. On the other hand, $7 + 11 = 18$ is not an addition fact because only one of the three numbers involved is a digit. You will face the entire gamut of the arithmetic knowledge base, and it will be your challenge to prepare each and every student you see for future mathematical study.

Your Turn

8.1. Give three examples of subtraction facts and one counterexample.

8.2. Give three examples of multiplication facts and one counterexample.

8.3. Give three examples of division facts and one counterexample.

8.4. Write a definition that will describe a number fact, no matter what operation is used.

The background established in middle school provides the basis for more mathematical studies. Can you imagine solving linear equations without the ability to perform basic addition, subtraction, multiplication, or division on real numbers? Would you attempt to work with rational expressions without knowledge of simplifying fractions? Do you fathom working with data analysis, probability, and statistics without knowledge of equivalence between fractions and decimals? How would you approach formalized geometry without knowledge of shapes, angles, points, lines, and planes?

The cold, hard fact is that students leaving middle school must be adequately prepared to meet the challenges and rigor of high school mathematics. The reality is that many of those students are woefully underprepared to deal with the middle school mathematics they will face. You must get them ready for what is coming. But how do you do that when the spectrum of students facing you is so broad?

We will provide you with some alternate algorithms to operating with numbers, which could be used for enrichment with students who have already mastered these necessary skills. At the same time, the substitute algorithms could be used as alternates when the method you use does not

make sense to some students. It is your responsibility to come up with an approach that does register with them. We have called this section readiness and, although the implication is that we focus on student readiness, we also want to highlight the need for you to have adequate preparation. You have undoubtedly had several college mathematics courses as a part of your program. Those courses are far beyond what you will be teaching and yet, it is imperative that you know more than what you will be teaching so that you know where the students are headed. Even more significant, those advanced courses are designed to provide you with a broad background and understanding of the wonderful world of mathematics, making you better prepared to ignite interest in each of your students. That last sentence is a lot easier said than done, but it is the charge given to you as a teacher of mathematics. Readiness!

We are aware that you are preparing to teach middle school mathematics. Understanding that some of your students will not have an adequate background, we encourage you to incorporate an elementary mathematics methods course into your program if at all possible. There, you will learn invaluable lessons on what needs to be done to provide your students with a sufficient background so they can learn the foundational material they need to be able to deal with middle school mathematics. For example, in an elementary mathematics methods course you will see specific sequences that begin at the concrete level via manipulatives; move to the semiconcrete (also called representational or pictorial) level through pictures of those manipulatives; then pass to the semi-abstract level of development with shorthand representations of those pictures; and finally to the abstract stage where the student becomes functional with numbers and operations. Typically, it takes years to go through these stages. We have found though that middle schoolers can move through them quickly and yet each step is essential. Why is it that a student is unable to comprehend abstract subtraction? Perhaps the student never saw manipulatives in the formative development of subtraction. Maybe the student was taken directly from the concrete to the abstract stage of subtraction, skipping the all-important two middle steps. Who knows? What we do know is that if you start the student at the beginning of the sequence and move them along, many of them will progress quickly to full functionality at the abstract level. Then they are ready to deal with the middle school mathematical curriculum.

Please note that if the student does need manipulatives (meaning there is a need to start at the beginning of the learning sequence), there is a need for some free play with the manipulatives. Let them build towers of the blocks, for example, until they fall. That removes the novelty and temptation to do it again. It is highly likely that middle schoolers will resist using manipulatives, saying that such materials are too childish for them. Your understanding of the need for them to obtain a solid basis must override their argument on this point. However, you cannot do it in an "I told you to do it" manner. Rather, you need to convince them of the value. Be prepared for a lot of resistance, but overcoming it is worth it for you and, more important, for your students.

There are two huge implications in the discussion about moving a student along a subtraction-type continuum from concrete to abstract. First, you have to know each of the steps and be prepared to convince the student of the need to cover them. Second, and even more significant, is the student's desire to learn. If that aspiration is not present, learning will not take place. It becomes your responsibility to sell each student on the need to learn. That too is an awesome task!

Please do 312 − 147 now, showing your scratch work.

Please do the problem before reading on! That you do the problem now is important to your understanding of what we are about to say and do.

Did you do it?
More than likely your work looks something like

$$\begin{array}{r} 2\ 10\ 12 \\ \cancel{3}\ \cancel{1}\ \cancel{2} \\ -1\ \ 4\ \ 7 \\ \hline 1\ \ 6\ \ 5 \end{array}$$

This is the way most people do the subtraction by hand (sometimes called the subtraction computation decomposition method). One of the authors learned the borrow-payback (also called equal-addition) method for subtraction and would do that same problem this way:

$$\begin{array}{r} 11\ 12 \\ 3\ \ \cancel{1}\ \ \cancel{2} \\ 2\ \ 5 \\ -\cancel{1}\ \ \cancel{4}\ \ 7 \\ \hline 1\ \ 6\ \ 5 \end{array}$$

That probably looks strange to you, and yet the way you probably did the subtraction looks strange to those of us who use borrow-payback (which is considered a low-stress algorithm by some because less emphasis is placed on knowledge of place value). The point is, the same problem can be done more than one way. If a student does not understand one process, the other one can be presented. Caution to avoid confusion must be exercised, of course, and great care and consideration must precede any different approach, maybe even going so far as starting with the concrete stage of the new process and moving through the stages to abstract functionality. The bottom line is that a student who, for whatever reason, did not grasp the subtraction algorithm used by most people now has a means of doing the problem and understands the process being used. As we progress through this chapter, we will provide you with other examples of alternate algorithms that you should learn and use with your students, either as enrichment or as a different way of doing a problem. Notice the implied readiness for both you and the students in these alternate approaches.

TECHNOLOGY AND NUMBER AND OPERATIONS

"Technology is essential in teaching and learning mathematics; it influences the mathematics that is taught and enhances students' learning" (NCTM, 2000, p. 24).

It is time for you to experiment and learn about the tools that have become commonplace as the 21st century continues. Technology will not eliminate the need for arithmetic basic skill proficiency, but technology can save time and effort that can then be focused on decision making, reflection, reasoning, and problem solving. Using technology can deepen and extend your understanding of when and why to make connections within middle school mathematics. This understanding can enhance your comprehension of why you do some arithmetic operations as you do. It is important for students to memorize number facts and the functions involved in operational (computation) algorithms. Those certainly are a part of the curriculum. However, they are not the only part. Technology should not be used to just to get answers. Skillfully used, technology can stimulate student learning and inquisitiveness into the world of mathematics. Technology can provide opportunities to open a variety of windows for your students.

An important aspect of learning mathematics is conjecture posing, which occurs when multiple examples, representative forms, and possibilities can be investigated quickly and efficiently. Once basic skills have been mastered, technology enables examination of real-life problems and connections much more efficiently and effectively by eliminating paper-and-pencil computations.

We hope you will examine different technology. Begin your investigation with the four-function calculators, followed by scientific calculators, and, finally, graphing calculators. You should not confine your investigation to any one brand, but rather experiment with different models, including the types of logic used by each. Begin your inquiry by visiting Web sites provided by the manufactures of different calculators:

Casio   http://www.casio.com/
Hewlett Packard
    http://www.hewlettpackard.com/
    (handheld/calculators)
Sharp   http://www.hewlettpackard.com/
    (business/calculators)
Texas Instruments http://education.ti.
    com

These sites are commercial but they provide information about product features. Many of the manufacturers are willing to lend classroom sets for examination and experimentation.

Internet investigation will provide a great deal of information about mathematics-based software. Many programs can be described as plug-and-chug, simply transferring worksheets to the computer screen. Such programs are useful as practice or review but we question the value of using a tool like a computer as a drill machine. However, there are powerful programs available that allow and, indeed, encourage experimentation and learning of important concepts in all areas of mathematics. Here are a few sites to get you started:

http://matti.usu.edu/nlvm/nav/index.html
http://www.mste.uiuc.edu/java/default.php
http://www.arcytech.org/java/integers
http://mathforum.org/
http://mathcentral.uregina.ca/

For additional Web sites check out the Resources list in chapter 5.

Technology can add confusion to the mathematical concepts students encounter in the curriculum. Throughout this text, we have represented fractions with horizontal vinculums $\frac{3}{4}$, and you should adopt that practice. If two and three fourths is written as $2\frac{3}{4}$, there is no question about the value. However, if it is written as 2 3/4, some could interpret it to mean $\frac{23}{4}$. Horizontal vinculums resolve the issue. A few calculators show the horizontal vinculum or pretty print form of $\frac{3}{4}$. Many calculators express three fourths as 3/4, whereas some will show it as 3 ⌋ 4. Many will shift the representation to 0.75 with the touch of a button. You become comfortable with one way, but easily gravitate to another because you understand that all those forms are different ways of saying the same thing. Your students need to become conversant with the different ways of saying the same thing too.

If we asked you for the answer to a long division problem, would you do it by hand, or would you grab a calculator? Why would you reach for the calculator? Might you have rationalized that long division is too painful to do, the calculator is faster, and the calculator is a lot more accurate? All of that makes sense to us. Still, a very critical issue has been raised.

When do you use a calculator? Students need to know the number facts and the basics of the operations. OK, when do you say that a sufficient level of competency has been reached and it is time to use technology? We cannot answer that for you, but we are willing to bet it is after the division facts and long before a problem like $358\overline{)2495618}$. Our point is that technology has a place. We cannot tell you when to permit student calculator use; that is your decision. However, when you decide to use or not to use technology, you must be able to defend your position. Saying technology is out of place because you had to do a certain kind of problem by hand is inappropriate. At the same time, deciding to use technology for generating a number fact because it has not been memorized is equally unacceptable. Of course, that last statement is too broad because it does not consider students with learning disabilities, who may be able to do some good mathematics if only they can get beyond the basic fact level. We are attempting to help you make an informed decision, rather than a blanket statement.

SETS AND NUMBER PROPERTIES

Sets establish a critical background for the study of mathematics. We start by looking at collections of things. From that, the cardinal number (total number of elements in the set) is established. Then the focus shifts to operating on sets (union, intersection, cross products, set subtraction), which leads to operations with the cardinality of sets. The basics of arithmetic are established through our work with sets. Once one has arithmetic under control, the sky is the limit.

Union of disjoint (no common elements) sets leads to addition. The beginning would form a union between your 3 toys and my 2 toys, giving a total of 5 toys.

The process might be slow for a beginner, but it gets shortened to $3 + 2 = 5$ at the abstract stage and shows a developed number fact. The entire learning sequence would be (spread over time as follows):

Concrete (*objects*)	$\{Y, \text{\&}, \text{\&}\} \cup \{\text{\&}, \text{\&}\} =$ $\{Y, \text{\&}, \text{\&}, \text{\&}, \text{\&}\}$
Semiconcrete (*pictures of objects*)	$\{Y, \text{\&}, \text{\&}\} \cup \{\text{\&}, \text{\&}\} =$ $\{Y, \text{\&}, \text{\&}, \text{\&}, \text{\&}\}$
Semi-abstract (*tally represents object*)	/// // → /////
Abstract	$3 + 2 = 5$

This sequence of development from concrete to abstract is repeated not only for building number facts, but also as algorithms begin to emerge. If you go to http:// matti.usu.edu/nlvm/nav/vlibrary.html, click on Number and Operations and then select Base Blocks Addition, you could see how base 10 blocks can be used to create addition problems beyond facts. This approach, too, grows out of the concept of sets.

Set multiplication or cross products establish the foundation for multiplication. Suppose set A = {e,o} and set B = {r,g,d,b} Cross products form all possible pairings of elements from each set, with order mattering. That is, if you are talking A × B (read A cross B), every element of A would be paired with every element of B. In this case, A × B = {(e,r), (e,g), (e,d), (e,b), (o,r), (o,g), (o,d), (o,b)}. The ordered pairs within the cross product could be in a different sequence, but care needs to be taken that all are present. Now, the cardinality of A is 2, B is 4, and A × B is 8. Thus, the basis for multiplication is established. Figure 8.1 depicts the situation more concretely. Figure 8.2 shows

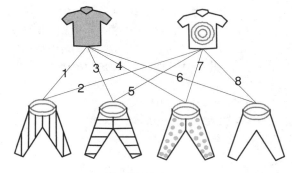

FIG 8.2.

the same setting using shirts and pants to determine the number of possible outfits, which might prove helpful for students who are not functioning abstractly.

Some sets commonly used in the world of mathematics will occur often throughout this text. Please take the time to refresh your memory about these sets:

Digits or D = {0, 1, 2, 3, 4, 5, 6, 7, 8, 9}
Natural numbers, counting numbers, or N = {1, 2, 3, 4, ...}
Whole numbers or W = {0, 1, 2, 3, ...}
Integers or Z = {... $^-3$, $^-2$, $^-1$, 0, $^+1$, $^+2$, $^+3$, ...}
Rational numbers or Ra = {$\frac{a}{b}$ where b ≠ 0} (a and b ∈ Z, b ≠ 0).

Although some people use Q to represent the rational numbers, we will use Ra.

Irrational numbers or IRa = {numbers that cannot be written $\frac{a}{b}$ (π or $\sqrt{2}$)}
Real numbers or R = {Ra ∪ IRa}
Complex numbers or C = {a + bi where a and b are real numbers, $i = \sqrt{-1}$}
Universal set or U = all the elements needed to describe a situation.

This is not the end. For example, can you define a quaternion?

There are properties, rules, axioms, and ideas that are consistently true as we study numbers. The Field Axioms is a basic collection of 11 properties that are used throughout the mathematics curriculum.

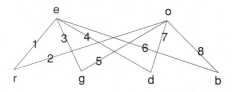

FIG 8.1.

These properties are fundamental to the development of mathematical knowledge. As one progresses to the study of more advanced mathematical topics, some of the properties are removed to create groups, loops, rings, and other topics in the study of abstract algebra. So, what are these properties?

Commutative property of addition on a set

Commutative property of multiplication on a set

Associative property of addition on a set

Associative property of multiplication on a set

Identity element for addition on a set

Identity element for multiplication on a set

Inverse element for addition on a set

Inverse element for multiplication on a set

Closure property of addition on a set

Closure property of multiplication on a set

Distributive property of multiplication over addition on a set

As we discuss these important properties in detail, we will use proper terminology as opposed to slang (yet commonly accepted) terms. Any discussion of a property must begin with a set of elements and an operation.

The commutative property of addition is true for all the sets we will discuss (digits ($3 + 5 = 5 + 3$), counting numbers, wholes, integers, rationals, reals, and complex). The significant thing is that an operation (addition) and a set of elements have been identified. In our discussion of $3 + 5 = 5 + 3$, we did not merely mention the commutative property. It was called the commutative property of addition on the set of counting numbers. Although

you might know what is meant when someone mentions the commutative property or commutativity, there is a need for precision of language in the world of mathematics. We all must be careful to differentiate between the commutative property of addition on the set of counting numbers and the commutative property of multiplication on the set of integers.

Stating the properties with letters rather than specific numbers generalizes the idea. In the instance of the commutative property of addition on the whole numbers, we could say $a + b = b + a$, and then list the set from which a and b are taken. This is a convenient way of summarizing the statements for all sets because any number could be substituted for either a or b. Your students need to develop this generalized concept (which is related to one of the conceptions of algebra).

There is a difference between the commutative property of addition on the set of whole numbers and the commutative property of multiplication on the set of whole numbers. This is generally not difficult to see with $2 + 3 = 3 + 2$ and $2 \times 3 = 3 \times 2$. The addition gives a sum of 5 and the multiplication gives a product of 6, so saying whether or not you are commuting 2 and 3 over addition or multiplication is important. However, you could have $2 + 2 = 2 + 2$ and $2 \times 2 = 2 \times 2$, each of which gives an answer of 4, implying that saying commutative alone is sufficient. These examples with the 2s raise important issues. First, sometimes it does not matter whether or not you state the operation because the answer is the same either way. Second, using different numbers in your examples is important as a means of helping students track them. With all those 2s, if you say to the class to consider the 2, which one do you mean?

As the development of the concept of commutativity on a set continues, your students need to realize there is no commutative property for subtraction on the set of integers. For that statement to be true, it must be the case that $6 - 2 = 2 - 6$, which is not a true statement because $6 - 2 = 4$ while $2 - 6 = {}^-4$. As you continue the discussion, at some point you would need to develop the idea that there is not a commutative property for division on sets. This development of the generalized notion of the commutative property does not happen all at once. It slowly develops as the concept is revisited with different sets of numbers and operations. With addition, students are willing to generalize quickly that the property exists for all sets, which is true, even when dealing with advanced situations like matrices. Subtraction, however, is a different story. In general, there is no commutativity for subtraction. Still, to enhance understanding of the generalized concept, discussion should take place, and that discourse should include exceptions. For example, subtraction on the integers does commute when $a = b$ because $a - b = b - a = 0$. Somewhere along the line, the students need to learn to never say never.

The concept of closure within a set for any operation is difficult for some to grasp. Fraternities and sororities are examples of closed groups. Whereas guests are welcome to many functions, only members are permitted to attend business meetings. In such an exclusive situation, who is and who is not a member is clearly known. The concept of closure on a set of numbers is similar. For example, think of any two counting numbers. Add them. Is the sum a counting number? Of course, you say (and so will your students). That is the beginning of the development of the generalized concept of closure of an operation on a set. As with commutativity, examples from different sets and operations need to be considered before a generalization is established.

It is your responsibility to create that background for each student.

The identity elements for addition and multiplication take on special characteristics that your students need to realize. Zero is the identity element for addition and one is the identity element for multiplication within any set that contains these respective elements. Consider $3 + 0 = 3 = 0 + 3$. The commutative property for addition on the set of wholes is implicit in the example. We cannot generalize from a single example but we assume that you are already familiar with the idea that zero is the additive identity (identity element for addition). You may have seen $a + 0 = a$, where a is an element of any set that contains 0. Although that is a correct statement, it is not correct for discussing the idea that zero is the identity element for addition on a set. That discussion should include the idea of commutativity of addition too. That is, it should be stated as $a + 0 = 0 + a = a$. Similarly, one is the identity element for multiplication starting with the counting numbers, typically shown as $a \times 1 = a$, where a is an element of any set that contains 1. Again, proper expression would be $a \times 1 = 1 \times a = a$. Why the big fuss, you say? You do not want to give your students false impressions. If they see no need to consider commutativity of multiplication, what happens when they encounter left and right identities in matrices? They have to unlearn something that is deeply rooted by that time, unless it is properly developed at the beginning.

The inverse element for an operation on some set is easily conceptualized, yet difficult to express. You need to work through the development from simple examples with integers and on to more difficult representations with real numbers. As with the other number properties we have discussed, this growth will not take place in a few days. It is a long process that must be carefully presented. At some point along the continuum, the idea will become intuitively obvious to each student. That is when you ask about some weird exception to help them cement the total picture. Then, they are ready for the generalization.

One property is unique in that it is the only one combining two operations. You have seen something like $3 \times (4 + 5) = (3 \times 4) + (3 \times 5)$. Notice that the order of the elements is maintained, which is significant. You probably call this the distributive property even though it is properly called the left distributive property of multiplication over addition because the 3 is being distributed via multiplication from the left over the sum of 4 and 5. This property is crucial as background for algebra and thus merits careful development as a readiness skill. Because the times sign looks so much like a variable, you might have seen an expression or equation involving juxtaposition, or implicit multiplication, such as $4yz + 12z = 4z(2y + 3)$ where multiplication is indicated, but the multiplication symbol is absent and implied or understood to be there. Still, you can recognize this as the left distributive property of multiplication over addition on a set of numbers. All of this type of thinking needs to be incorporated into the development of the generalization of the distributive property of multiplication over addition.

Your Turn

8.5. You might see texts where the commutative property of addition on the set of counting numbers is initially listed as a + b = b + a. Explain why that is, or is not, the best way to do things?

8.6. If there are examples beyond $2 + 2 = 2 + 2$ and $2 \times 2 = 2 \times 2$, list one. If there are not, explain why this is a unique example.

8.7. Provide an example where the commutative property of subtraction on the set of integers is true.

8.8. Provide an example where the commutative property of division on the set of reals is true.

8.9. Is there any example of adding two counting numbers where the sum is not a counting number?

8.10. True or false—the digits are closed for multiplication?

8.11. Develop a continuum for helping students arrive at a generalized conceptualization of each of the 11 field axioms.

8.12. Is there a right distributive property of division over addition?

8.13. Is there a left distributive property of division over addition?

WHOLE NUMBERS

We present alternate algorithms for adding, subtracting, multiplying, and dividing whole numbers to expand your knowledge base and provide you with substitute means of helping students understand the operations. Which routine you choose will be determined by personal preference and the text you are using. It makes sense that you use the format described in the text because that avoids confusion for the students. However, the text should not determine the curriculum! You should make choices based on your students' readiness, background, and mathematical prowess.

We will provide a detailed development of addition of whole numbers to give you an idea of how a concept can be built from the concrete through the semiconcrete, semi-abstract, and abstract stages. After that we will present different procedures for doing operations and leave you to develop the sequencing for other number sets and operations, as your students need it. Here again, more than likely, the textbook will be your primary source but do not neglect the caveat about your students' readiness. We suggest again that you consider an elementary mathematics methods course, or at least an elementary mathematics methods text (see, for example, Brumbaugh, Rock, Brumbaugh, & Rock, 2003, *Teaching K-6 Mathematics*) if you find your students are not ready for middle school whole number computational demands.

Addition of Whole Numbers

The following list of steps is a beginning of the sequence that leads students to the ability to do all whole number addition problems. Although each of these steps is given abstractly, the assumption is that the progression from concrete to abstract will have been followed for the developmental sake of each student. You might have to supply that sequence for some students. At some stage in the sequence each student should realize the same process is being repeated in each place value. At that point, the generalization of the addition algorithm is established and such fine detailing as shown here is no longer necessary.

you are going to see students who have not mastered the ability to add whole numbers. Most textbooks do not break the sequence into such fine detail, something that is necessary for a student to build the conceptual framework that accompanies the ability to add whole numbers. The likelihood is that the small steps will help all students understand the addition concept better, and in most cases you cannot assume that if a student knows how to, for example, add a three-digit addend and a one-digit addend with regrouping the ones, the student will also be able to add three digits to two digits with regrouping out of both the tens and ones places. It is important to note that a similar sequence could be developed for each of the other operations.

You should notice that the examples given avoid duplicating digits, which could add unnecessary confusion for some students. This is not to be construed as saying that digits should not be duplicated. Rather, in the initial examples

Addition Facts	
Sums <10 (Need place value of 2 digits before going on) $10 \leq sum \leq 18$	
Multiples of 10 + multiples of 10 (sums < 100)	Example: 20 + 30
2 digits + 1 digit with no regrouping	Example: 23 + 4
2 digits + 2 digits with no regrouping	Example: 23 + 45
2 digits + 1 digit with regrouping of the ones	Example: 27 + 8
2 digits + 2 digits with regrouping of ones only	Example: 27 + 38
(Need place value of three digits before going on)	
2 digits + 2 digits with regrouping of tens only	Example: 85 + 91
2 digits + 2 digits with regrouping of both places	Example: 87 + 45
Note: Some three-digit problems could be done before all two-digit types are completed.	
3 digits + 1 digit with no regrouping	Example: 246 + 0
3 digits + 2 digits with no regrouping	Example: 246 + 30
3 digits + 3 digits with no regrouping	Example: 246 + 301
3 digits + 1 digit with regrouping of the ones	Example: 246 + 7
3 digits + 2 digits with regrouping of ones only	Example: 426 + 57
3 digits + 2 digits with regrouping of tens only	Example: 482 + 91
3 digits + 2 digits with regrouping of tens and ones	Example: 417 + 96
3 digits + 3 digits with regrouping of ones only	Example: 317 + 608

And so on.

Some might argue that this addition sequence is overkill, particularly at the middle school level. The harsh reality is that

avoid duplication of digits for the benefit of your students. Eventually duplication of digits must occur.

Although all the sequence examples are listed horizontally, students need to be comfortable dealing with both horizontal and vertical formats. Also, you should sometimes place the smaller addend first, especially in $4 + 23$ and $\begin{array}{r} 4 \\ +23 \\ \hline \end{array}$. This mixed listing will enhance the students' understanding and stimulate the awareness of the commutative property of addition on the set of whole numbers.

The order listed in the sequence is not absolute. The facts (which should have been mastered by all middle schoolers, but you might encounter some who have not) should come first. The advantage of splitting them into sums less than 10 followed by sums of 10 through 18 is related to place value. For example, students could work with sums of three addends, where the sum is less than 10 if they have not mastered the place value idea to tens. They can work with number families (all the pairs that give a sum of seven, for example). They can begin to learn the basics of the commutative property of addition on the set of whole numbers, the associative property of addition on the wholes, and the additive identity on the wholes. These property exposures should continue throughout the development of addition with whole numbers and beyond.

We now move well into the addition of whole number sequence with the assumption that the students are ready to do $289 + 427$. That means they have dealt with hundreds place value and re-groupings out of the ones and tens places. We further assume they are familiar with the base 10 blocks. We start with the base 10 blocks to amplify the need to have students progress through the various learning stages from concrete to abstract with each new problem type until the generalized algorithm is intuitively obvious for them. Here, rather than picturing the

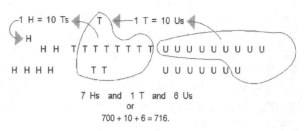

7 Hs and 1 T and 6 Us
or
700 + 10 + 6 = 716.

FIG 8.3.

base 10 blocks, we have used H for the flat or hundred, T for the long or ten, and U for the unit or ones place. You could do this problem with base 10 blocks by going to http://matti.usu.edu/nlvm/nav/vlibrary.html, clicking on Number and Operations, selecting Base Blocks Addition, creating the problem, and solving it with pictures of the blocks. Of course, you could go concrete and use the blocks themselves, too. In Fig. 8.3, we show you the semi-abstract solution to the problem.

Notice that nine of the Us from one addend are combined with one U from the other addend to make one T. Any combination of Us could have been used, even five from each addend. The point is that 10 ones are used to make 1 ten. There are not 10 more Us that could be combined to make another T. Then, the regrouped T and nine others are combined to make 1 H. Again, there are not enough Ts left to make another H. At this point, all of the regrouping has been completed and the only thing left to do is to count the number of each block representative that is left. In this case there are 7 Hs, 1 T, and 6 Us, which are equivalent to 716.

The importance of the concrete to abstract sequencing is brought out with $289 + 427$. Our assumption here is that the students have done this problem first with base 10 blocks (concrete) and then with pictures of the base 10 blocks or software (semiconcrete). We used Fig. 8.3 to present the semi-abstract approach.

Abstractly, the problem could be done as

$$
\begin{array}{r}
11 \\
289 \\
+\ 427 \\
\hline
716
\end{array}
$$

where the 1 above the 8 depicts the regrouping of 10 ones (U's in Fig. 8.3) to become one ten (T in Fig. 8.3). Similarly, the 1 above the 2 shows a regrouping of 10 tens (Ts in Fig 8.3) to make 1 hundred (H in Fig. 8.3). Notice how the 1s connect with the semi-abstract stage. Once the student sees that connection and generalizes it to the point of saying something like, "it does not matter what place value is being considered, the process of regrouping is always the same idea," it is likely that the student is functioning abstractly with that operation and the lead-up developmental stages can be eliminated. One should not assume that, because a student functions abstractly for addition on the set of whole numbers, student is capable of functioning abstractly with addition on other number sets or that student is able to deal abstractly with other whole number operations. As was the case with whole numbers, the developmental sequence from concrete to abstract should be used until the student generalizes the setting.

Figure 8.4 shows the development of $289 + 427$ in a different format, making a step-by-step connection between the semiconcrete and abstract solutions.

Well, there you have it; a careful development of how you probably do addition of whole numbers. That discussion and sequence should make sense to you. It is imperative that you digest the beginning stages, which may or may not be a part of your background. Current research clearly shows that the concrete, semiconcrete, and semi-abstract stages are necessary for understanding. Heddens and Spears (2001) indicated that students are not prepared to learn a concept at the abstract level until they have sufficient experiences with the concept (or skill) at the concrete level. In most cases, students are conditioned by their own experiences in mathematics. That is, students may not choose the best or most efficient method to solve a problem if prior experiences have not included relevant knowledge. Even though you may not have had those stages in your background, you should provide them for your students.

You may have been asking what you are expected to do with the students who are functioning abstractly with addition of whole numbers while you help struggling students develop that ability. We shift the emphasis now to alternate computation algorithms. These could be used as challenges for those who have mastered adding with whole numbers.

The partial sum approach to addition assumes the students realize that $500 + 700$ is very much like $5 + 7$ only the five and seven are not in the ones column. They would also need to be aware of the basics of zero being the identity element for addition on the set of whole numbers. With that background, a problem like $896 + 784$ would be done as follows:

$$
\begin{array}{r}
896 \\
+\ 784 \\
\hline
10 \\
170 \\
+\ 1500 \\
\hline
1680
\end{array}
$$

    10   (the sum of 6 and 4)
170   (90 + 80, not 9 + 8 as is commonly said)
1500   (800 + 700, not 8 + 7 as is commonly said)

You should notice that the 1 in the sum of 4 and 6 is the regrouped value, as is the case with the 1 in the hundreds column, coming from 8 tens plus 9 tens. As you would do the problem normally, those 1s would be above the tens and hundreds columns, respectively, as your carry. This

Represent 289 with 2 flats, 8 longs and 9 units, and 427 with 4 flats, 2 longs and 7 units under 289.	289 + 427	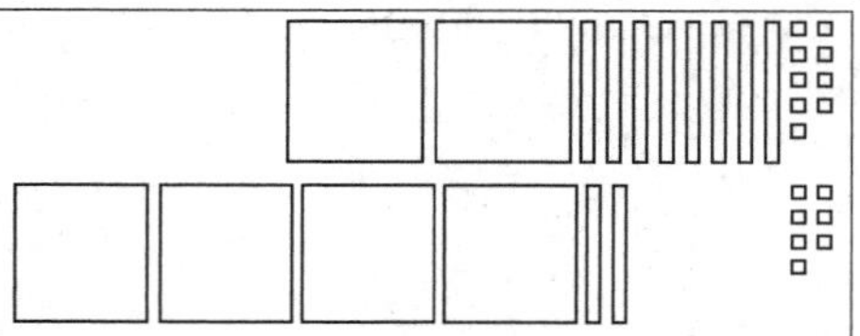
Add the units: 9 + 7 = 16 units.	289 + 427	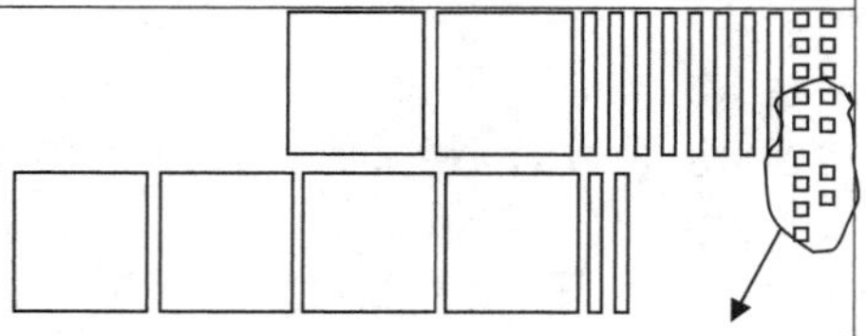
Trade 10 units for 1 long. Add the longs: 8 + 2 + 1 = 11 longs	1 289 + 427 6	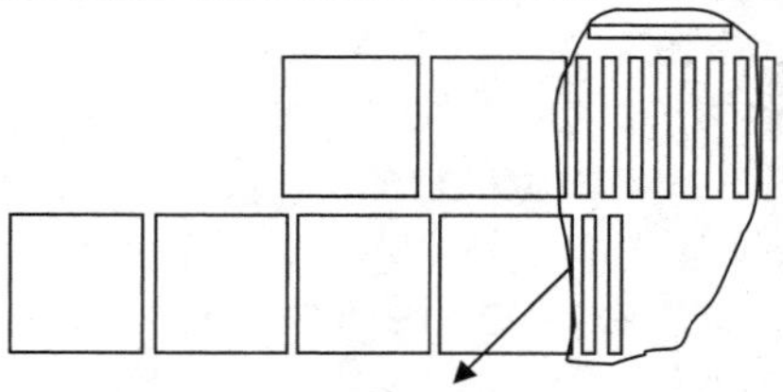
Trade 10 longs for 1 flat. Add the flats: 2 + 4 + 1 = 7 flats	1 1 289 + 427 716	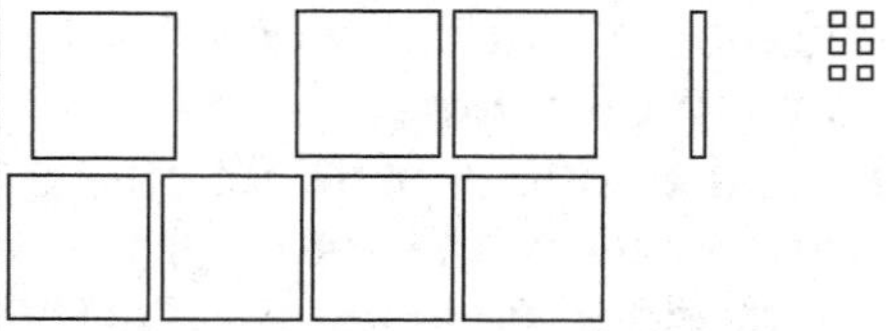

FIG 8.4.

is a powerful way to connect the base 10 block approach to our standard addition algorithm. This would be an added step to the sequence between the semi-abstract Us, Ts, and Hs and the standard algorithm, but it could prove helpful to struggling students.

Reading involves motions going from the left to the right. The standard addition algorithm starts at the right and moves left. Look again at Figs. 8.3 and 8.4 and you should see how the trades can be made in any sequence. That is, the first one could involve trading ten 10s for one 100 followed by swapping 10 ones for one 10. The end result would still be the same. That says

that the partial sum approach could start with any place value.

A modification of the idea of starting anywhere is the basis for the *scratch method* for adding whole numbers:

$$
\begin{array}{r}
8\,9\,6 \\
+\,7\,8\,4 \\
\hline
1\,\overline{5}70 \\
6\,8
\end{array}
$$

Notice that the 5 is *scratched* out and a 6 is placed below it. Starting from the left, the first sum is 800 + 700, which is 1500. The 15 is written as a part of the sum in the appropriate place values and the zeros are not shown. Then, the addition in the tens column is completed, giving a sum of 17 (really 170). The zero presents no problem since it is the additive identity. The 7 is written in the tens place of the sum. However, that 1 that is regrouped (really 100) has to be accounted for. The 100 is shown by scratching out the 5 (which is really 500) and inserting a 6, for 600. If developmental steps were shown, the problem would be

$$
\begin{array}{r}
896 \\
+\ 784 \\
\hline
1500 \quad (800+700) \\
170 \quad (90+80) \\
+\quad 10 \\
\hline
1680
\end{array}
$$

where the regrouping "1s" are at the bottom of the hundreds and tens columns, which could prompt the scratch method.

There is another method, developed by Barton Hutchings, that can be intriguing and useful for students. Suppose the task is to find the sum of 9, 8, 9, 7, 9 in column addition. Before showing Dr. Huchings' Low-Stress Addition, consider what is going on in your head as you find this sum. The first part, $9+8$, is easy because it is a fact, yielding a sum of 17. The next step is to find the sum of 17 and 9, which is not a fact. Students will have worked this problem but in the formative stages of their development it probably would be formatted as follows:

$$
\begin{array}{r}
1 \quad \text{(regroup 10 ones as one 10)} \\
17 \\
+\ 9 \\
\hline
26
\end{array}
$$

The difficulty is that many students are unable to do a problem such as this in a mental format. As 17 is added to 9, what really happens in your head is that the 17 is expressed as $10+7$. The

"10" is *remembered* and the sum of 7 and 9, which is a fact, is determined to be 16. That 16 is actually $10+6$ so now the aggregate is $10+(10+6)=(10+10)+6=20+6=26$. Granted, you do the problem much more reflexively than that but if you think about it, that is what is going on in your head.

The Low-Stress algorithm eliminates the need to remember all those multiples of 10 and keeps the problem as a collection of addition facts. The following demonstration shows the addition of $9+8+9+7+9$:

$$
\begin{array}{rll}
9 & & \\
8 & & \\
1 & 7 & \\
9 & & \\
1 & 6 & (7+9=16) \\
7 & & \\
1 & 3 & (6+7=13) \\
+\ 9 & & \\
\hline
1 & & (10 \text{ from } 3+9) \\
\hline
& 2 & (\text{from } 3+9) \\
+\ 40 & & (\text{sum the 10s at the left}) \\
\hline
& 42 & (\text{partial sum not normally used here})
\end{array}
$$

This method can be used with more than digit addends. You only need a little more space between columns, and any regroup from a value is placed at the top of the respective next column. Students sometimes are confused by a sum like $3+4+9$ when using Low-Stress Addition but it reacts like the others:

$$
\begin{array}{rl}
3 & \\
4 & \\
7 & (3+4=7) \\
+\ 9 & \\
1 & (10 \text{ from } 7+9) \\
\hline
6 & (6 \text{ from } 7+9) \\
+10 & \\
\hline
16 & (\text{partial sum not normally used here}).
\end{array}
$$

These are not the only alternate methods for adding whole numbers. The basis for you to provide students with different ways of finding sums is here, though. The rest is up to you.

Your Turn

8.14. Do $967 + 579 + 418$ using the partial sum method.

8.15. Do $967 + 579 + 418$ using the scratch method.

8.16. Do $967 + 579 + 418$ using the Low-Stress method.

8.17. Explain the scratch method to someone who does not know how to add that way.

8.18. Explain the Low-Stress method to someone who does not know how to add that way.

Subtraction of Whole Numbers

Traditionally subtraction has followed addition in the school curriculum sequence. That makes sense on one hand because they are opposite operations. Developmentally, in the formative stages, students are more ready to deal with multiplication before subtraction. Why? Because multiplication uses groups resembling the approach used for addition as in the model for successive addition (Heddens & Spears, 2001). That also makes sense because multiplication is a short way of adding. Multiplication can be defined as repeated addition and some students learning facts will describe $3 + 3 + 3 + 3 + 3 = 15$ by saying that five 3s are 15, which is also one way the multiplication setting of $5 \times 3 = 15$ can be stated.

We are not going to provide a detailed sequencing to lead into the different ways of doing subtraction. Furthermore, we are going to assume basics like subtraction facts and place value. Students who do not possess this background are doomed

to failure in your arithmetic sessions with subtraction. It is your responsibility to develop that background with them and your approach with them should follow the careful development given in the whole number addition section of this chapter.

With that said, we move to subtraction algorithms. More than likely, the one found in your textbook will be the one you learned and the one you will prefer to teach. You would probably do $426 - 189$ as follows (assuming you do not use a calculator):

$$
\begin{array}{r}
11 \\
3 \; 1 \; 16 \\
\cancel{4} \; \cancel{2} \; 6 \\
-1 \; 8 \; 9 \\
\hline
2 \; 3 \; 7
\end{array}
$$

In that format, you recognize the 16 as coming from a 10 regrouped out of two of the 10s in 426 (there actually are 42 tens in 426 if you think about it), leaving one 10 in the 10s column. With that regrouping done, the subtraction fact $16 - 7$ is used. With one 10 left in the 10s column, another regrouping is necessary, as shown by the 11 in the top row of the solution. This time the regrouping takes one hundred and expresses it as ten 10s, giving a total of 11 tens. That 11 represents 11 tens or 110, even though most of us say 11. Developmentally, students should be aware of that subtle difference in wording and its impact. Now the subtraction problem $110 - 80$ is done, resulting in 30. The idea that zero is the additive identity surfaces here, allowing the 3 to be placed in the tens place of the answer with no impact on the ones. Finally the $300 - 100$ is done and the 2 is placed in the hundreds place of the answer. Once again, the zeros have no impact on the tens and ones places.

We would be willing to say that you have probably not analyzed problems like $426 - 189$ with the detail we just went through. More than likely you reflexively do the different regroupings and give no thought to the place value implications, proper statement of the different settings, and so on. Still, if you are going to effectively help your students understand all the implications of the subtraction algorithm they use, you need to cover these issues with them. This could be a hard sell though, because they are all going to tell you they know how to subtract, even if they do not do it correctly. Why would they say such a thing? Well, they have seen subtraction problems like 426 − 189 before. What else is there? More than likely they do not want to bother with the whole subtraction issue and the easy way to deal with it is to say that they know how to do it. Thus, convincing them of the need to go through the algorithm and understanding all the associated subtleties can be a foreboding task. But, you are a professional in the making and, as such, it is your responsibility to prepare to do that careful development with each of your students.

Another subtraction algorithm is called borrow-payback (also referred to as the equal-addition method) and it relates to take-away subtraction. You start with the sum and take away an amount, leaving the missing addend. The problem 426 − 189 would be done as follows:

```
    1     10 ones added to sum (minuend)
  426
 -189
 ─────
```

```
    1
  42 6
     9    Additional 10 subtracted. Ten
 -1 8 9   has been added to the sum
 ──────   (minuend) (10 ones) and to the
          missing addend (subtrahend)
          (1 ten) so the problem is not
          changed.
```

```
    1
  4 2 6
      9
 -1 8 9
 ──────
      7    16 − 9 = 7
```

```
  1 1
  4 2 6        10 tens added to sum
      9
 -1 8 9
 ──────
      7
```

```
    1     1
  4   2   6
  2       9       Additional 100 subtracted.
 -+   8   9       100 has been added to
 ─────────        the sum (minuend) (10
          7       tens) and to the missing
                  addend (subtrahend)
                  (1 hundred) so the
                  problem is not changed.
```

```
    1     1
    4 2 6
9
  -+  8 9
 ────────
      3 7    120 − 90 = 30 (Note zeros
             not written on problem)
```

```
    1     1
  4   2   6
  2       9
 -+   8   9
 ─────────
  2   3   7    400 − 200 = 200.
```

Borrow-payback subtraction may seem confusing but it could be because it is new to you. Do a few subtraction problems that way and it will not seem so difficult. It is a method some students who struggle with the standard algorithm can learn to be comfortable with. It is your obligation to teach your students how to subtract. Notice that the last sentence did not say it is your obligation to teach your students to subtract the way you do!

Before leaving the borrow-payback subtraction, notice the use of zero expressed in different way in the process, like 1 hundred showing up as 10 tens. The concept of expressing zero in different formats is handy in a multitude of places in higher mathematics. For example, when completing the square in something like $x^2 - 6x + 7$, you add $(-3)^2$ to both sides of the equation. But that is zero, expressed in the form of $9 - 9$ if it is written on one side of the equation.

The integer subtraction method uses the idea of taking the little number from the big one in each column, which is a common error (for a complete discussion of error patterns, see the TAG section of this chapter, starting with TAG 8.22). The problem $5123 - 1684$ would be

$$
\begin{array}{rrrr}
5 & 1 & 2 & 3 \\
-1 & 6 & 8 & 4 \\
\hline
 & & & -1 \quad (3 - 4 = -1) \\
 & & -6 & 0 \quad (20 - 80 = -60) \\
 & -5 & 0 & 0 \quad (100 - 600 = -500) \\
+4 & 0 & 0 & 0 \quad (5000 - 1000 = 4000) \\
\hline
3 & 4 & 3 & 9 \quad (4000 - 500 - 60 - 1 = 3439) \\
\end{array}
$$

Notice that, in each place value, the smaller number is subtracted from the larger number. To motivate the idea of regrouping in subtraction, students are often told that a large number cannot be subtracted from a smaller one. That is not true in the set of integers. Thus, an important issue is raised. Extreme caution should be exercised when making absolute-sounding statements. The intent of motivating regrouping by saying a big number cannot be subtracted from a smaller one is well founded, but it is not a true statement. Later, when that student

encounters integers and a big number can be subtracted from a little one, that student is in a quandary as to what to believe as true.

As the subtraction is done in $5123 - 1684$, three of the partial steps are listed as negative. That is because, when taking 80 from 20 for example, the answer is -60. There is $5000 - 1000$, which gives a $+4000$. The only remaining task is to compile the results: $+4000 + (-500) + (-60) + (-1)$, which is 3439. As with borrow-payback subtraction, this probably seems very strange. Yet, if you try a few, it will make sense.

Integer subtraction is an unusual method and would not be appropriate for most students learning to subtract whole numbers, particularly because of the use of integers. However, students who are accustomed to playing card games where the score can go in the hole have been known to do quite well with this method. We assume you noticed the reliance on the ability to subtract multiples of tens (or hundreds and thousands) from multiples of tens (or hundreds and thousands). That would be a prerequisite skill, along with integer exposure if this method is given to students.

The problem $3001 - 487$ can generate the incorrect answer 624 when students are unclear about regrouping. Students enjoy a variation, which makes this problem very easy to do. Rewrite 3001 as $2999 + 2$. The problem is then done $(2999 - 487) + 2$ and the real beauty is that all regrouping in the subtraction has been eliminated. By the way, we assume you noticed the use of the associative property of addition as we went from $(2999 + 2) - 487$ to $(2999 - 487) + 2$. This procedure can be extended to something like $5023 - 1469$, which would become $(4999 - 1469) + 24$. Try it; you'll like it.

Most students think subtraction cannot be done moving from left to right. That is not the case. Consider $523 - 176$ and the scratch method, which would be shown as:

$$
\begin{array}{ccc}
 & 12 & 13 \\
5 & \not{2} & 3 \\
-1 & 7 & 6 \\
\hline
\not{4} & \not{5} & 7 \\
3 & 4 &
\end{array}
$$

Starting from the left, $500 - 100 = 400$. There is a need to have more than 2 tens in the center column since the task is to subtract 7 tens from 2 tens. Regrouping involves scratching out the 4 in the subtraction answer and making it a 3, writing the 3 below the 4. Now the answer is $300 + 50$ (remember the zeros are typically not written but they help clarify this discussion). Moving to the ones shows a need to regroup again to get $13 - 6$. That is accomplished by scratching out the 5 in the tens column of the answer and writing a 4 below it. Now the 7 ones are placed in the answer and the problem is done, giving 347. We have presented another unusual method for subtracting.

There are other ways to subtract whole numbers but this should get you started. The start is twofold: to give you different ways to subtract and to enhance your own understanding of how subtraction works. It is imperative that you have the ability to explain even the minutest part of subtraction so that you are able to help each student understand the operation. Today's students need to comprehend what they are doing and not just be good arithmeticers.

Your Turn

8.19. Provide an analytical discussion of $7436 - 2518$, where you discuss regroupings, place value, and so on.

8.20. Do $67953 - 18476$ using the borrow-payback method. Describe your thought process as you do it.

8.21. Do $67953 - 18476$ using integer subtraction. Describe your thought process as you do it.

8.22. Do $5007 - 2345$ by renaming 5007 as $4999 + 8$. Do you think this is a good method to show students? Explain why or why not.

8.23. Do $5007 - 2345$ using the scratch method for subtraction. Do you think this is a good method to show students? Explain why or why not.

Multiplication of Whole Numbers

We are again going to assume that you could develop a sequence leading to a multiplication algorithm. Students should be exposed to unusual formatting for problems before getting too far in the process. Typically 27×9 is shown as $\begin{array}{r} 27 \\ \times 9 \\ \hline \end{array}$, but there is no reason it could not be shown as $\begin{array}{r} 9 \\ \times 27 \\ \hline \end{array}$, even with the expectation that it be done in this format. Of course, if the student is beginning to suspect the existence of the commutative property of multiplication on the set of whole numbers, this formatting change could stimulate that development. Perhaps you would want to format problems this way to kindle the expansion of the concept of commutativity for multiplication on the wholes.

As with addition and subtraction of whole numbers, the multiplication facts must be mastered before moving on. Multiplication offers a few new hurdles. Suppose for the sake of this discussion that we consider only problems written vertically. The students will have seen multiplication facts written as

$$
\begin{array}{r}
6 \\
\times 7 \\
\hline
42
\end{array}
$$

However, when they start dealing with a multiplication algorithm, they will encounter situations where one factor is not directly over the other. For example, in

$$\begin{array}{r} 5\ 7 \\ \times\ \ 8 \\ \hline \end{array}$$

the 8 × 7 appears natural but the 8 × 50 is different because of the alignment. This very slight alignment variation might not be a big deal for you, but for a student who is struggling with the basics of multiplication it can be catastrophic. Notice also the readiness of 8 × 50, assuming the skill of multiplying digits by multiples of ten. This not only assists in the conceptual development of multiplication but also reinforces the idea of place value as shown with 2 × 6 = 12, 20 × 6 = 120, and 200 × 6 = 1200.

Traditionally, students have been told to do 4 × 23 by putting the 2 of the 12 below the 4, and the 1 of the 12 above the 2 of 23. Then they were told to multiply the 4 by 2 (really 20) and, upon getting that product, add the 1, which was carried, placing the sum to the left of the 2 from the 12. The entire process would look like this:

$$\begin{array}{r} 1 \\ 2\ 3 \\ \times\ \ 4 \\ \hline 9\ 2 \end{array}$$

This should make sense to you because that is how you probably do the problem. However, it sure could seem confusing to a beginner.

Partial product multiplication can alleviate part of the dilemma. Assuming the appropriate background, the problem 23 × 4 can be treated as (20 + 3) × 4,

which becomes (20 × 4) + (3 × 4), thanks to the distributive property of multiplication over addition on the set of whole numbers. Both 20 × 4 and 3 × 4 are old problems and you are actually employing a good teaching technique—taking a new problem and breaking it into parts that the students have already mastered. This problem shown in a vertical format would be

$$\begin{array}{r} 2\ 3 \\ \times\ \ 4 \\ \hline 1\ 2 \quad \text{(from } 4 \times 3) \\ 8\ 0 \quad \text{(from } 4 \times 20) \\ \hline 9\ 2 \end{array}$$

From here, it is relatively easy to convert to a standard algorithm.

Partial products can be used to dissect problems into simpler, known information, but it also connects the problem with previous work. If the partial product process is developed from the beginning of instruction in multiplication after concrete exposures, it is a simple matter for the partial product to be abandoned in favor of a standard algorithm.

One of the beauties of the partial product approach to multiplication is the established background for future work in multiplication. The process can be applied to multiplication of decimals and fractions and extended to the algebraic environment with (2n + 3) × 4, where the problem could be written

$$\begin{array}{r} 2n + 3 \\ \times\ \ \ \ 4 \\ \hline +12 \quad (4 \times 3) \\ 8n \qquad (4 \times 2n) \\ \hline 8n + 12 \end{array}$$

The partial product method is a viable option for those who are not ready for a standard algorithm. Even with larger factors, the partial product works well:

```
          3   4   6   9
      ×   5   8   7
                  6   3   (7 × 9)
              4   2   0   (7 × 60)
          2   8   0   0   (7 × 400)
      2   1   0   0   0   (7 × 3000)
              7   2   0   (80 × 9)
          4   8   0   0   (80 × 60)
      3   2   0   0   0   (80 × 400)
  2   4   0   0   0   0   (80 × 3000)
          4   5   0   0   (500 × 9)
      3   0   0   0   0   (500 × 60)
  2   0   0   0   0   0   (500 × 400)
1 5   0   0   0   0   0   (500 × 3000)
2 0   3   6   3   0   3
```

That problem looks long compared with a standard algorithm, but it is a process that works and condenses when the student is ready. (Teacher, can't I just use a calculator?)

The statement, "If you know your multiplication facts and can add, you can do any whole number multiplication problem in the world" is going to get almost any student's attention. It just sounds too good to be true. The statement can be used as a lead-in for lattice multiplication, which would show 248 × 39 as

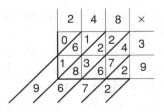

The row and column containing digits in the factors intersect in a square cell that has a diagonal segment through it. The two digits in the cell comprise a multiplication fact. The tens digit of the product is placed above and to the left of the diagonal in the appropriate cell and the ones digit is below and to the right of that same diagonal. Once all the products are entered, the values in the respective diagonals are added, giving the product for the entire problem. For some students, lattice multiplication is too tempting and they learn in spite of themselves. Eventually, they will ask if there is an easier way and then they are ready to look at a standard algorithm.

Before leaving lattice multiplication, look at the connection between that and partial products. Doing 248 × 39 in partial product format gives

```
          2   4   8
      ×       3   9
              7   2
          3   6   0
      1   8   0   0
          2   4   0
      1   2   0   0
      6   0   0   0
      9   6   7   2
```

Look at that same problem in lattice format, with the lattice rotated 45° in a counterclockwise direction:

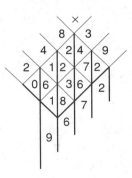

Do you see the same columns in what were the lattice diagonals (now verticals) as in the partial product format, with the zeros missing? This is a connection that

should be presented to your students. So much of our mathematical world is compartmentalized when, in reality, there are connections that are missed.

Another appealing challenge could be: "If you know how to multiply by 2, divide by 2, and add, you can do any whole number multiplication problem in the world." That statement leads to one more method we will visit, called the "simple halving doubling" (Russian peasant) method for multiplication. We will use this opportunity to show how you can connect different areas of our mathematical world. In 248×39, one factor will be "halved" repeatedly until the result is 1; each time one factor is halved, the other is doubled, thus the halving doubling name. The first question is which factor to halve. In this example, the temptation is to halve 248 because it is even. That works fine at first because the halving sequence would be $248 \rightarrow 124 \rightarrow 62 \rightarrow 31$, and so eventually an odd value is encountered. The goal is to get the halving column to one, and so it is advisable to start with the smaller factor. Starting with the larger factor will yield the same result, but it will involve more steps. The process looks like this:

Double column	Halve column
248	39
496	19
992	9
~~1984~~	~~4~~
~~3968~~	~~2~~
7936	1

Once the halving factor is selected, a process is repeated. In this example, the first step would be to find half of 39, which is $19\frac{1}{2}$, 19.5, or 19 with a remainder of 1. Typically students will say it is $19\frac{1}{2}$, which is fine. After they say that, tell them to forget the half. It does not take many

repetitions before they will say that half of 19 is 9, something you cannot permit them to say. Half of 19 is $9\frac{1}{2}$, forget the half. After arriving at 1 in the halving column (doubling in the other column for each halving step made), any row having an even value in the halving column is eliminated, as shown by the double strikethroughs. The remaining doubling values are added, including the initial factor if it is not crossed out. In this example the product is $248 + 496 + 992 + 7936$, which gives the sum 9672. WOW! That is what we got in lattice multiplication, and so it checks out.

Now look at that same problem only with an additional column that involves base 2:

Double column	Halve column	Base 2
248	39 half of 39 is 19, remainder 1	1×2^0
496	19 half of 19 is 9, remainder 1	1×2^1
992	9 half of 9 is 4, remainder 1	1×2^2
~~1984~~	~~4 half of 4 is 2, remainder 0~~	~~0×2^3~~
~~3968~~	~~2 half of 2 is 1, remainder 0~~	~~0×2^4~~
7936	1 half of 1 is 0, remainder 1	1×2^5

The halving factor can be expressed in base 2 numeration, and the problem is restated as $248 \times 111001_2$. That is, $248 \times (32 + 4 + 2 + 1)$. Sixteen and 8 are not considered because there is a zero in the 2^4 and 2^3 places. Therefore, the rows containing 2 with 3968 and 4 with 1984 are eliminated. The product is $7936 + 992 + 496 + 248$, or 9672. You have worked with bases. You have been exposed to proofs. Yet, each of those seems to stay in its own compartment, with one idea not being used in the other area. If you decompartmentalize and apply your knowledge about bases to the process in Russian peasant multiplication, the proof is fairly simple. It is impossible to show you all of these intricacies. You must capitalize on your background and develop the connections between the various mathematical exposures you have had.

There are other ways to multiply but the ones given here provide you with alternatives. You should not present these methods unless you need to have something to challenge some students or you need another way to multiply for students who labor with a standard algorithm. Eventually struggling students conclude that even though these ways work, there has to be a simpler way. When they ask, you can show them the world's slickest, quickest way to multiply (short of technology), which is a standard algorithm. Yes, you tried to show them earlier and they resisted. Now they are asking for it. Big difference!

Your Turn

8.24. In the "simple halving doubling" routine for multiplying two numbers, one situation exists where the halving factor will always be even except for one. Describe the situation and how it occurs.

8.25. Compare the Russian peasant method with the lattice multiplication approach. Which do you prefer and why?

8.26. Compare lattice multiplication with the partial product method. Which do you prefer and why?

Division of Whole Numbers

Division is complex to say the least. The question in $4\overline{)24}$ is "how many 4s are in 24?" or "can you estimate how many 4s are contained in 24?"—something that is not stressed enough. Notice that mastery of multiplication facts would be helpful with the estimation. Although there are other ways to say that we want to know how many 4s are in 24, clarification of that idea in the beginning of division discussions will

bear fruit. Not only will students have a better understanding of the process, but also later, when dealing with the division of fractions, the background will simplify the process significantly.

Do $47\overline{)27401}$ by hand—no calculators allowed here. As you do the division, record the possible places where errors could be made. We respectfully request that you build the division potential error list before reading on. After you have done the exercise, your list should include rounding, estimation, place value, mental arithmetic, multiplication, subtraction, as well as unusual formats for doing whole number algorithms. Identification of these potential problem spots requires close examination of student work. It is important to define and correct division difficulty spots as quickly as possible.

Background for division should be established concretely. One component of that development involves the physical partitioning of a group of items with a one for you, one for me, approach. As this is done, emphasis should be given to associating the problem and answers with the resultant numbers. That is, if there is a pile of 28 items to be divided equally between you and me, we can do the one for you, one for me, routine to determine that there are 14 objects for each of us. The related discussion would focus on how a group of 28 items being shared equally by two people results in 14 things for each participant. Ultimately the situation is expressed by

$$28 \div 2 = 14 \text{ or } 2\overline{)28}^{\,14}.$$

Another approach that is often overlooked is called repeated subtraction division. If this is done before dealing with the standard algorithm, students encounter fewer difficulties. With the standard division algorithm, estimations must be precise. In the repeated subtraction approach to division, it is acceptable for estimations to be low or precise. Considering how weak the estimation and rounding skills of most students are, this is a significant asset. Students need to be familiar with multiplying digits by multiples of 10 when doing repeated subtraction division, but this should have been developed earlier and, therefore, is not a hurdle.

The easiest way to visualize how repeated subtraction division works is to think of a large pile of sticks. Consider 27401 ÷ 47 and you have a pile of 27,401 sticks. The question is, "How many 47s are in 27,401?" Certainly we could remove one group of 47 from the 27,401 sticks, leaving 27,354 sticks. Another batch of 47 could be removed, leaving 27,307 sticks. This process could continue 581 more times and we would learn that a total of 583 sets of 47 are contained in 27,401 sticks. Even the most patient of individuals would tire of that process before too long.

Using multiples of 10, shortcuts begin to appear. Suppose after the second group of 47 is removed, leaving 27,307 sticks, it dawns on the person to remove 10 bunches of 47 or 470 sticks. After that, 2 more sets of 10 bunches of 47 sticks could be removed. At this stage, 32 bunches of 47 sticks have been removed, leaving 25,897. We still have a long way to go.

The idea of multiplying 47 by 10 extends to multiplying by 100 or 1000. Alas, 1000 is too big and is eliminated. Someone usually realizes that multiple bunches of 47 could be removed 200, or 300 at a time as well. Now old skills come into play because quick mental multiplication of 300 by 47 with 14,100 removed, leaves 11,797 sticks. We can't take out 300 more bunches of 47 because 14,100 is greater than 11,797, but we could take out 200 bunches of 47,

leaving 2397 sticks. We have already done 47 × 300, and so 47 × 30 should come quickly and then we could take out 20 more bunches of 47, leaving 47 sticks. Someone might want to try 50 × 47, which is fine. Either way, there is one bunch of 47 sticks left. The only question remaining is how many bunches of 47 have been removed all together? The answer is 1 + 1 + 10 + 10 + 10 + 300 + 200 + 50 + 1 or 583, which is the missing factor. The significant part of this discussion is that estimates on or below the actual value are acceptable. As estimation skills increase, the repeated subtraction division method collapses to the standard algorithm.

The 27401 ÷ 47 discussion would be shown as

```
47) 27401
    - 47        1
    27354
    - 47        1
    27307
    - 470      10
    26837
    - 470      10
    26367
    - 470      10
    25897
  - 14100     300
    11797
   - 9400     200
    2397
   - 2350      50
      47
    - 47        1
       0      583
```

The number of bundles of 47 removed is recorded to the right of each removal. The recording could also be above the ⌐, which has the advantage of collapsing into the standard algorithm:

$$
\begin{array}{r}
1 \\
1 \\
10 \\
10 \\
10 \\
300 \\
200 \\
50 \\
1 \\
\hline
47)\overline{27401} \\
-47 \\
\hline
27354 \\
-47 \\
\hline
27307 \\
-470 \\
\hline
26837 \\
-470 \\
\hline
26367 \\
-470 \\
\hline
25897 \\
-14100 \\
\hline
11797 \\
-9400 \\
\hline
2397 \\
-2350 \\
\hline
47 \\
-47 \\
\hline
0
\end{array}
$$

As the student's estimation skills increase, the repeated subtraction approach gets closer and closer to the standard algorithm.

One could justifiably ask why we used the example $27401 \div 47$ as opposed to one with smaller values. It is a good question. This problem should give you a good feel for how repeated subtraction works. You might say that a calculator should be used with a problem like this. We agree. Having said that though, we are also aware of the fact that many text series and tests require students to be able to do problems such as $28567 \div 49$ by hand. Be-

tween repeated subtraction and technology is the division algorithm you have grown to love. ☺ It is imperative that you carefully develop how that algorithm works so that each of your students achieves a reasonable level of understanding.

Another way to model the division algorithm is by using partition or sharing division instead of repeated subtractions. This model requires a different type of questioning. The underlying assumption here is that we are discussing whole numbers only. Thus, remainders and fractions are inappropriate, but they are coming. The question in $4)\overline{24}$ is "how many 4s are in 24?" or "can you estimate how many 4s are contained in 24?" In this case, the end result will be six groups of four. The step-by-step division algorithm using this model and base 10 blocks is illustrated for $135 \div 3$ in Fig. 8.5.

Your Turn

8.27. Multiply a 2-digit number by a 2-digit number. Use the product and the 2-digit factor to create a division problem, making the other 2-digit factor into the missing factor. Now, do the division problem using the repeated subtraction approach. *You may not estimate accurately!* Give a low estimate for both the ones value and the tens value as shown in the example in the text.

8.28. Write a summary of your impressions on the advantages and disadvantages of repeated subtraction division.

FRACTIONS

Fractions are not as transparent to students as they think they are. Ask a youngster to tear a piece of paper in half and you could see something like Fig. 8.6. Because of unspecific daily language use, they may not have an accurate interpretation of what

Represent 135 using 1 flat, 3 longs and 5 units, and 3 sets. Start by trying to divide the highest place value (in this case the hundreds, or the flat).	3)135	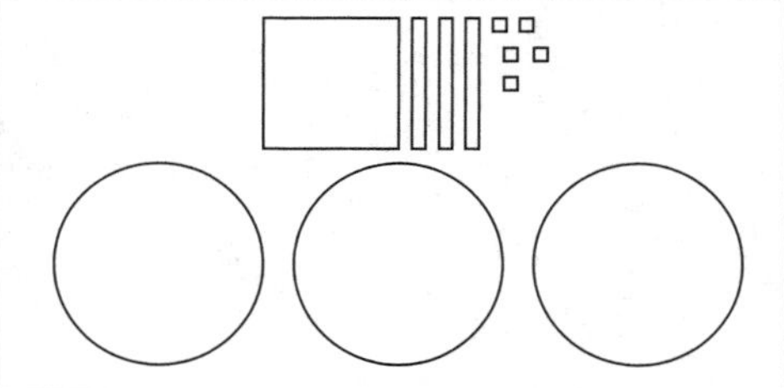
Since this will not work, trade the flat for 10 longs, giving a total of 13 longs and 5 units.	3)135	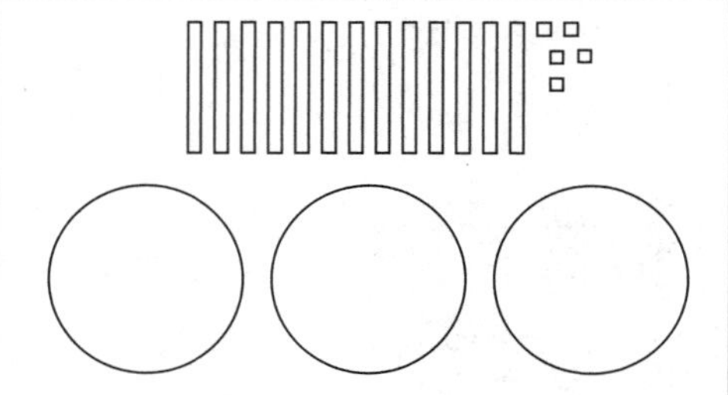
Estimate how many longs can be used in each of the 3 groups, assuming each group gets the same number. Then distribute them: place 4 longs in each group. Now you have 1 long and 5 units left.	4 3)135 12 1	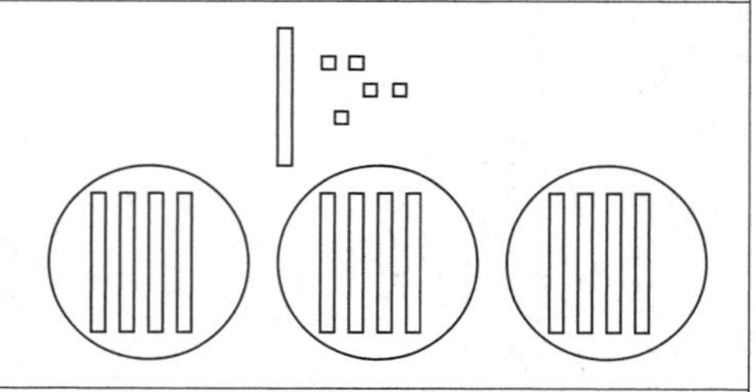
Trade the remaining long for 10 units, giving a total of 15 units.	4 3)135 12 15	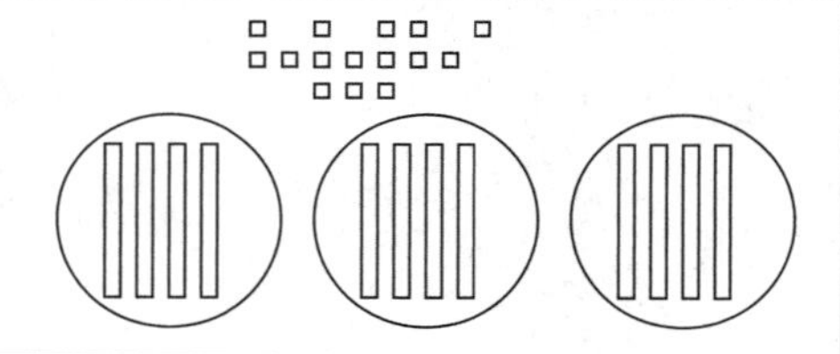
Estimate how many units can be used in each of the 3 groups. Then distribute them: 5 units in each group.	45 3)135 12 15 15 0	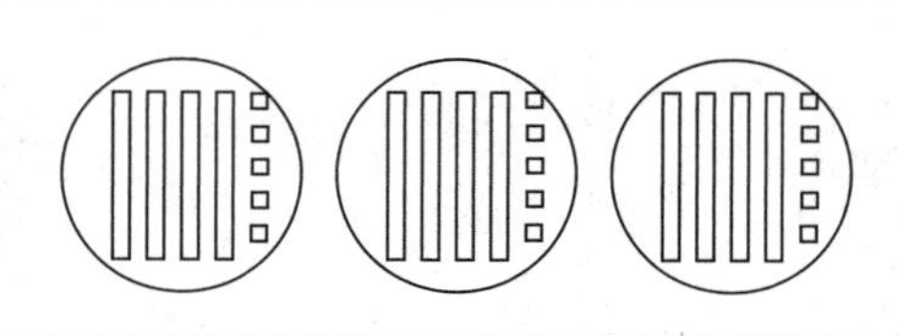

FIG 8.5.

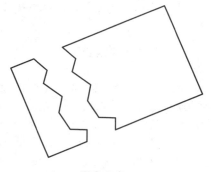

FIG 8.6.

is being conveyed. For example, what is "half of a cookie"? As adults we know the intent and accept that "pretty close" is usually good enough.

When teaching fractions, is "pretty close" good enough? NO. It is important that students are aware that a half means one of two equal-sized pieces. Later, the approximations and inaccuracies accepted in our common language will suffice, but not in

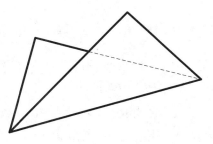

FIG 8.7.

the learning stages of fractions. So, what do we educators do?

The idea of a half can be conveyed at an informal level by using a candy bar as a manipulative. The assignment would be to share the candy with a friend. One "breaks" the candy in "half" and the friend picks first. It is amazing how well the concept of half is now understood.

Have your students fold a piece of paper in "half" and then ask them how they know it is a half. Ultimately, they will say the edges match for the two sides, or something like that. With students who have a better grasp on the idea, you might want to fold a piece as shown in Fig. 8.7 and ask if that piece of paper is folded in half. This should prompt some discussion and alteration of their definition, which should lead to halves being equal-sized pieces. Another potential discussion point that comes out of tearing a piece of paper in half is that of ratio with one of the two pieces being 1 to 2 or 1:2.

The development of the concept of fractions is just as critical as that of whole numbers. There are useful manipulatives that provide considerable insight for a struggling student and you should be conversant with them. If you go to http://pegasus.cc.ucf.edu/~mathed and click on Courses, followed by MAE 2801 Resource Page, and then scroll down to Egg Carton Fractions, Cuisenaire Rods, and Fraction Kit, you will find resources for teaching fractions. There is a developmental sequence with each resource that could

prove beneficial, particularly for struggling students.

Equivalent Fractions

It is relatively common to see equivalent fractions discussed prior to exposure to the idea of multiplication of fractions. That does not make a lot of sense because, to show $\frac{1}{3} = \frac{2}{6}$ we show $\frac{1 \times 2}{3 \times 2} = \frac{2}{6}$, which is a modification of $\frac{1}{3} \times \frac{2}{2} = \frac{2}{6}$. You will encounter students who have memorized the routine but have no idea what is really happening. Manipulatives remove the mystery. It is imperative that students realize that equivalent fractions stem from multiplying or dividing the numerator and denominator of a fraction by the same value before moving into operations on fractions.

Figure 8.8 shows how paper folding can help build the concept of equivalent fractions. For this discussion, we will assume a rectangular sheet of paper is folded in half with an initial fold that is parallel to one of the edges. After the first fold, shade one of the two halves. Then, refold the paper along the fold segment. Now, fold the paper in half again. Your discussion should focus on the idea that the paper has now been folded into four equal-sized pieces and that one of those pieces represents $\frac{1}{4}$. Once that is established, open the paper so that the entire shaded section is visible. You should ask, "how many pieces are shaded now?" You should get both 1

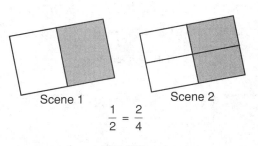

Scene 1 $\frac{1}{2} = \frac{2}{4}$ Scene 2

FIG 8.8.

out of 2, and 2 out of 4 as responses. Then ask if any more shading has been done. The students should conclude that $\frac{1}{2}$ and $\frac{2}{4}$ are different names for the same thing. Additional folds could be made to show $\frac{1}{2} = \frac{2}{4} = \frac{4}{8} = \frac{8}{16}$, but most middle schoolers will catch on to what is happening rather quickly.

After the folding activity, the students need to discuss the relations between the different fraction representations and how, because they are equivalent, there is an abstract way to go between them. Undoubtedly, your students will have seen the abstraction before coming to you, but it is important that you work with them to create a mental image and understanding of how equivalent fractions work.

Multiplication of Fractions

You might be asking why we start with multiplication of fractions. Think about it. When you add fractions with different denominators, you are going to need equivalent fractions. But equivalent fractions use multiplication, at least at an implied level. Besides, multiplication of fractions only has one simple procedure to follow.

When sequencing fraction multiplication, the first problem type would involve a whole number times a fraction. Figure 8.9 shows five unit squares side by side (a 1×5 rectangle in standard position). Each of the units is also divided horizontally into fourths and so each row of Fig. 8.9 represents $\frac{1}{4}$ of 5. At the same time, within any one of the unit squares, each row represents $\frac{1}{4}$ and there are five $\frac{1}{4}$s on

each row, representing $\frac{5}{4}$. Counting the total number of little shaded $\frac{1}{4}$s gives $\frac{15}{4}$. This shows the product for the problem as $5 \times \frac{3}{4}$. If addition has been developed then this product could also be shown in the repeated addition format. Did you notice that the shading in Fig. 8.9 is not typical? We opted to do it as shown to call attention to doing things differently from what is expected. You will be amazed at the discussion and learning that can be stimulated by such a simple move.

The array method for showing multiplication of fractions is probably the easiest to produce. The discussion here will focus on the product of two fractions. If there is a need to physically show the product of more than two fractions, one way is to find the product of the first two and then use that product with the third fraction, repeating the process until all fraction factors are considered. Any product will result in a rectangle. Fig. 8.10 shows the array method for $\frac{2}{3} \times \frac{5}{7}$. Notice there are no common factors in the two fractions. Certainly, problems like $\frac{2}{3} \times \frac{3}{4}$ must be discussed. At first, it is best to avoid making matters any more complicated than necessary.

Looking at the figure, you see 21 unit rectangles (who said they had to be squares?). Of the 21 unit rectangles, 14 (or $\frac{2}{3}$) of the total as marked with diagonal slashes, and 15 or $\frac{5}{7}$ are shaded. The

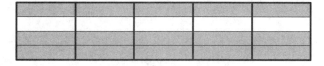

FIG 8.9.

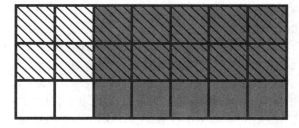

FIG 8.10.

overlap region represents $\frac{2}{3}$ of $\frac{5}{7}$ or $\frac{5}{7}$ of $\frac{2}{3}$ of the total number of unit rectangles. So, $\frac{2}{3}$ of $\frac{5}{7}$ or $\frac{5}{7}$ of $\frac{2}{3}$ is $\frac{10}{21}$ and the product is shown as the overlapped region.

Traditionally students are asked to express answers for $\frac{2}{3} \times \frac{6}{8}$ in lowest terms (often referred to as reduce, simplify, or divide out common factors). You could get $\frac{12}{24} = \frac{12}{24}$, something smaller which is what reduced means. We know that is not the intention of the statement, but in the strictest sense, the fraction has been reduced. A similar discussion could be made about "simplify" from the standpoint of asking why one fraction is simpler than one of its equivalent forms. Again, we know what we mean by simplify, but the word is not overly descriptive. Divide out common factors is a good prerequisite skill for an algebraic setting like $\frac{m+2}{m}$, where some students will say $\frac{\cancel{m}+2}{\cancel{m}} = \frac{1+2}{1} = 3$. With divide out common factors, clarification of the algebraic process is a lot easier. The point is that so much of what is done in middle school mathematics is critical groundwork for future study. Your care as you explain the basics makes the mathematical lives of your students much easier as they progress through the curriculum. Your colleagues will appreciate the effort too!

The exercise $\frac{2}{3} \times \frac{6}{8}$ raises one more issue. If we, as teachers, insist that students divide out common factors in their work, how do we justify using $\frac{6}{8}$? Should we not set a good example?

Your Turn

8.29. Show someone who is not in your class how to "reduce" a fraction and describe their reaction.

8.30. Should students be expected to express fractions where the greatest common factor (GCF) between the numerator and denominator is one? Explain your reasoning.

Having already dealt with equivalent fractions, students should be ready to handle the intricacies of $\frac{2}{3} \times \frac{6}{7}$ by expressing it as $\frac{2 \times 6}{3 \times 7}$, which gives $\frac{12}{21}$. The traditional task now is to find an equivalent form of $\frac{12}{21}$, where the numerator and denominator are relatively prime (GCF of the numerator and denominator is 1). Prior work with equivalent fractions should make this a manageable task. Is there a better way to get the numerator and denominator to be relatively prime? Here, $\frac{2}{3} \times \frac{6}{7} = \frac{4}{7}$. Students should be encouraged to look for patterns. From equivalent fractions, they should know that going from $\frac{12}{21}$ to $\frac{4}{7}$ involves both the numerator and denominator being divided by three. They should conclude that the division could be done before multiplying, thus the phrase "dividing out common factors." That would generate the form you are familiar with: $\frac{2}{\cancel{3}_1} \times \frac{\cancel{6}^2}{7} = \frac{4}{7}$. It is not incorrect to multiply the numerators and denominators first and then divide out common factors, but it is not as efficient. Errors can occur because larger numbers are involved. Eventually students encounter something like $\frac{2}{3} \times \frac{3}{4} \times \frac{4}{5} \times \frac{6}{7} \times \frac{7}{8}$, which is much easier to do if the common factors are divided out initially as opposed to dividing out the common factors of $\frac{1008}{3360}$.

Your Turn

8.31. Describe how you would help a student see the advantage of dividing

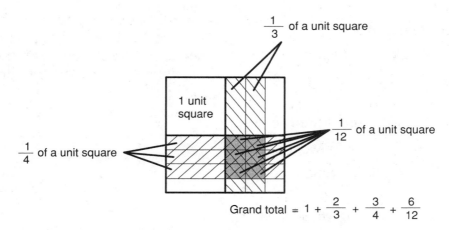

FIG 8.11.

out common factors first in problems like $\frac{2}{3} \times \frac{3}{4} \times \frac{4}{5} \times \frac{6}{7} \times \frac{7}{8}$.

Students should generalize how to multiply fractions as quickly as possible, but not without understanding the process. When the students are functioning at the abstract level for multiplication, mixed numbers are easy to deal with because they can be converted to improper fractions.

The product of mixed numbers can be shown concretely with an array in a manner similar to that used for finding the product of whole numbers. Figure 8.11 shows $1\frac{2}{3} \times 1\frac{3}{4}$. Each of the entire length of a cross-slashed (lower left to upper right) strip represents $\frac{1}{4}$ of the bottom 2 unit squares. A similar discussion would hold for the $\frac{1}{3}$ vertical strips that are cross-slashed from upper left to lower right. Notice the region where the $\frac{1}{4}$ strips and $\frac{1}{3}$ columns intersect. Each of those small rectangular regions represents $\frac{1}{3}$ of $\frac{1}{4}$ or $\frac{1}{12}$ and there are 6 of them or $\frac{6}{12}$. If the

students are familiar with showing partial products, they should be able to understand this presentation.

You should have noticed that our explanation for $1\frac{2}{3} \times 1\frac{3}{4}$ uses addition of fractions. Addition of fractions has not been discussed in the sequencing used in this text and so readiness would become a consideration. If the traditional sequencing is followed, this would not be a problem. An alternative would be to do equivalence and some fraction multiplication first. Next, deal with addition of fractions, and simply delay discussion of multiplying mixed numbers. After addition involving different denominators has been developed, return to multiplication of mixed numbers.

Grouping equivalent fractions with multiplication of fractions makes sense because the skills of multiplication are used in equivalent fractions. Even if your text sequences the treatment of operations of fractions in the traditional manner, we have still shown you an alternate route. Along the way, we have also demonstrated how concrete exposures can enhance explanations and increase the opportunity for understanding. These lessons should prove invaluable to you regardless of the sequence used.

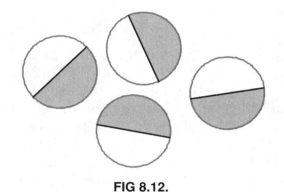

FIG 8.12.

Your Turn

8.32. Create a model for explaining $2\frac{1}{4} \times 3\frac{1}{3}$.

Division of Fractions

As the division sequence for fractions is constructed, consideration should be given to the problems that result in answers that are whole numbers first. A whole number divided by a fraction should be done prior to a fraction divided by a fraction. Figure 8.12 shows how many halves are in four. The circles from Fig. 8.12 easily shift to how many halves are in three circles. These humble beginnings stimulate conjectures in students' minds.

Shift now to $\frac{1}{2} \div \frac{1}{8}$, where the question is how many eighths are in a half. Pictorially, Fig. 8.13 shows how the question can be answered. The unit rectangle is divided into eight congruent rectangles, each of which represents an eighth. The segment parallel to the long sides of the unit rectan-

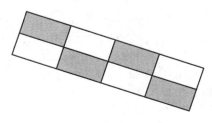

FIG 8.13.

gle divides it in half. Counting the eighths on either half shows there are 4 of them. The conclusion is that there are 4 eighths in a half, or $\frac{1}{2} \div \frac{1}{8} = 4$. Several more problems like this need to be done. For example, when the students solve several problems like $\frac{1}{3} \div \frac{1}{6} = 2$, $\frac{1}{4} \div \frac{1}{20} = 5$, and $\frac{1}{5} \div \frac{1}{15} = 3$, they will begin to arrive at some conclusions about what is happening. For those who do not see, you can stimulate their thinking. For $\frac{1}{2} \div \frac{1}{8} = 4$, you could ask for a connection between the denominators and the answer. If that does not work, you could ask how a 2 and 8 could be used to give a 4. The response eventually should be $8 \div 2 = 4$.

Now you begin asking how $\frac{1}{2} \div \frac{1}{8} = 4$ could be changed to give the answer in terms of dividing the 8 by the 2. Because the students have experience with multiplication of fractions, they should recognize that $\frac{1}{2} \times 8 = 4$ and more specifically that $\frac{1}{2} \times \frac{8}{1} = 4$. Your next question focuses on how this last problem of $\frac{1}{2} \times \frac{8}{1} = 4$ is related to $\frac{1}{2} \div \frac{1}{8} = 4$. It should not take long for the idea of inverting the second fraction and changing from division to multiplication to develop.

The groundwork is now established. Only after several divisions such as $\frac{1}{2} \div \frac{1}{8} = 4$ are done should the students encounter $\frac{2}{3} \div \frac{3}{4}$, where the question is how many $\frac{3}{4}$s are in $\frac{2}{3}$. What if the problem is $\frac{3}{4} \div \frac{2}{3}$? Now the question is, how many

$\frac{2}{3}$s are in $\frac{3}{4}$? Either way, knowing the question is not sufficient to solving the problem. Perhaps, between doing problems like $\frac{1}{2} \div \frac{1}{8} = 4$ or their prior exposure to dividing fractions, students will come up with the idea of inverting the second fraction and following the rules for multiplication of fractions. However, if they do not understand the ramifications of what they are doing, it is necessary to work through it with them.

Fraction division is clouded by remnants of whole number division difficulties, unclear impressions of fractions, and the fact that this format is different from any division they have experienced. The familiar $6\overline{)42}$ is gone. But, there is hope because fractions can also be placed in that familiar format for division. This approach can be introduced as easy to do because it uses familiar skills: finding the least common denominator (LCD), equivalent fractions, and the familiar division format. Suppose the problem is $\frac{1}{2} \div \frac{1}{8}$. The LCD is 8; $\frac{1}{2} = \frac{4}{8}$; and the format would be $\frac{1}{8}\overline{)\frac{4}{8}}$. The question still is how many $\frac{1}{8}$s are in $\frac{4}{8}$. But, because the denominators are the same, the question translates to how many 1s are in 4. The completed fraction division would be

$$\frac{1}{8}\overline{)\begin{array}{c} \frac{4}{} \\ \frac{4}{8} \\ \frac{4}{8} \\ \hline \frac{4}{8} \\ \hline 0 \end{array}}$$

Assuming students are familiar with division with remainders expressed as a fraction, the equivalent fraction process can be used. The exercise $\frac{3}{4} \div \frac{2}{3}$ becomes

$\frac{9}{12} \div \frac{8}{12}$ or $\frac{8}{12}\overline{)\frac{9}{12}}$. It does not take many problems in this format before students realize they could just do $8\overline{)9}$ and the new, seemingly difficult problem is just like something that has been done many times before. Think about the idea of finding the LCD first and then dividing the numerators. Doesn't this seem easier than how you learned when you were in school? Doesn't it make you wonder why division of fractions is not taught this way? If you thought that, there is a loud and clear message to you—you should use the method to help your students understand fraction division.

You know $\frac{3}{4} \div \frac{2}{3}$ becomes $\frac{9}{12} \div \frac{8}{12}$, but rather than expressing it as $\frac{8}{12}\overline{)\frac{9}{12}}$, express it as $\frac{9 \div 8}{12 \div 12} = \frac{9 \div 8}{1}$, which becomes $\frac{9}{8}$ or $1\frac{1}{8}$. Notice (as should your students) that this acts a lot like multiplication of fractions. That should make sense if the equivalent fraction generalization included either multiplying or dividing both the numerator and denominator by the same value. Another approach could focus on the idea that dividing by 5 is the same as multiplying by $\frac{1}{5}$. Either approach should suffice, depending on the past experiences of your students.

Your Turn

8.33. Do $\frac{4}{5} \div \frac{7}{8}$ using the equivalent fraction process. Make up at least two more fraction division problems where the denominators are unrelated and do them using the equivalent fraction process. After you have done at least those three problems, describe your feelings of the equivalent fraction division process.

8.34. Find a student (or adult not in your class) with the appropriate background to be dividing fractions and demonstrate equivalent fraction division. Describe their reaction to what you show them.

Students routinely make one of two basic errors when doing fraction division: inverting the first fraction rather than the second; or arithmetic. Even though the arithmetic errors vary, they should be relatively easy to control and correct, assuming the requisite readiness skills are met. Inverting the first fraction rather than the second and then multiplying is also rather easy to control. First, it is important to do the problems concretely. That should lead the students to the conclusion of inverting the second fraction and multiplying. The second thing, and this is critical, is that, when the rule for division of fractions is stated, the students should say, invert the second fraction and multiply. They should not say invert and multiply.

One objective of modern mathematics education is to provide students with real-life examples. When asked to provide a real-life example of a fraction divided by a fraction (for now, exclude factors where the denominator is 1), a common response involves halving a recipe, which actually means to divide by two. In the desired context, a fraction divided by a fraction would be something like $\frac{4}{5} \div \frac{7}{8}$ or even $3 \div \frac{1}{2}$, where the factor is a fraction. Examples such as this are not easy to find, and yet the world is full of them. Your task is to find such an example.

Your Turn

8.35. Find an example of a fraction divided by a fraction, something like $3 \div \frac{1}{2}$.

For this assignment, dividing something in half would be like dividing by $\frac{2}{1}$ and is not acceptable.

We mention one last situation for your consideration. Converting mixed numbers to improper fractions is the easiest way to deal with that problem type. In that format, $8\frac{3}{5} \div 2\frac{1}{7}$ would look like

$$
\begin{aligned}
8\frac{3}{5} \div 2\frac{1}{7} &= \frac{43}{5} \div \frac{15}{7} \\
&= \frac{43}{5} \times \frac{7}{15} \\
&= \frac{43 \times 7}{5 \times 15} \\
&= \frac{301}{75} \\
&= 4\frac{1}{75}
\end{aligned}
$$

This process should be relatively easy for most students because it comprises prior skills.

Division of fractions causes problems for many students. Ironically, it is a relatively easy process for them to understand with a background that considers sequence, concrete exposure, and the equivalent fraction method for division of fractions. A relatively difficult task can be made comparatively easy to understand if you go beyond telling them the rule for dividing fractions.

One vocabulary point comes out of that last paragraph. The proper name for fraction is fractional number and the proper name for decimal is decimal fraction. Still, their common names are fraction and decimal, respectively. We have opted to use the common names. At some point in their careers, your students should become aware of the two different names.

TABLE 8.1

	Unit	Nonunit	Mixed
Same denominators	$\frac{1}{7}+\frac{1}{7}$	$\frac{2}{7}+\frac{3}{7}$	$1\frac{2}{7}+8\frac{3}{7}$
Related denominators	$\frac{1}{7}+\frac{1}{14}$	$\frac{3}{7}+\frac{5}{14}$	$1\frac{3}{7}+8\frac{5}{14}$
Unrelated denominators	$\frac{1}{5}+\frac{1}{7}$	$\frac{2}{5}+\frac{3}{7}$	$4\frac{2}{5}+6\frac{3}{7}$
Quasi-related denominators	$\frac{1}{4}+\frac{1}{6}$	$\frac{3}{4}+\frac{5}{6}$	$2\frac{3}{4}+11\frac{5}{6}$

Addition of Fractions

Addition of fractions ranges from adding two unit fractions with the same denominator through adding mixed numbers with denominators that share a common factor. Between those two are several situations involving addition of fractions. Table 8.1 represents all the basic fraction addition problems. Only two addends are used but you should deal with more than two addends along the way. Not all possible two-addend fraction addition problems are presented in Table 8.1. An intermediate example like $\frac{1}{7}+\frac{2}{7}$ could be inserted between the left two entries of the top row. This might be essential to enhance the understanding of some students because it contains one unit fraction. Similar insertions could be made in other locations.

The examples in Table 8.1 avoid duplication of digits. Many students learn processes by tracking numbers in the examples. If the examples do not contain redundancy of digits (except for the same denominators), they are easier for the students to follow. Eventually digits will be used more than once within a problem type.

By the time students investigate addition of fractions with unlike denominators they will have had experience with equivalent fractions. Typically, the requirement is to express a fraction sum with all common factors divided out. It is not advisable to present them with that requirement during their early encounters with addition of fractions. As with repeating digits in a problem, eventually sums that do not have all common factors divided out are dealt with, but avoiding them at first can help avoid confusion for some students. TAG 8.21 provides a game approach for students to experiment and practice with addition of fractions. Ortiz (2000) and Burns (2003) provide further adaptations and discussions of this game.

The sums of many of the examples in Table 8.1 are all less than one. As with dividing out common factors, ultimately conversion of a sum from an improper fraction to a mixed number will be encountered. However, in the spirit of helping students master the task at hand, avoid expecting them to perform this extra maneuver when beginning fraction addition. Later, when the students are more experienced and conversion between improper fractions and mixed numbers is reflexive, this ceases to be an issue.

There are many ways to progress through the examples presented in Table 8.1. Certainly one could do all of the types where the denominator is the same with possible additions like $\frac{1}{7}+\frac{2}{7}$ between the first two entries of the top row. Doing this would mandate the introduction of mixed numbers, but that could be done.

After all the problem types involving the same denominator are completed, the skills necessary for students to do the second row of problem types could be addressed, followed by the third and fourth rows. The examples in Table 8.1 could be addressed in a multitude of different sequences, however. For example, rather than doing all problem types with the same denominator first, $\frac{1}{7} + \frac{1}{7}$ could be followed by $\frac{1}{7} + \frac{1}{14}$ with the possible inclusion of $\frac{1}{7} + \frac{2}{7}$ between $\frac{1}{7} + \frac{1}{7}$ and $\frac{1}{7} + \frac{1}{14}$ to make smaller steps between concepts.

The path followed through the examples in Table 8.1 is influenced by student readiness. In addition, consider whether or not the past few concepts presented were easy for them. If they were, it might be appropriate to offer them a more challenging topic. That would indicate which problem type would be next. By the same token, if the students have found the last few concepts difficult, it might be time to implement something they would find relatively easy.

Typically, textbooks do not provide such precise considerations of topic sequencing. They can't! The text authors do not know your students, their background, or their readiness level. You are the local authority for your students. As such, you make the decisions. Following a prescribed sequence may not be the best route for your students. That is why careful consideration of the topics presented in Table 8.1 is so critical.

Rather than developing each example type, we will focus on $\frac{1}{3} + \frac{1}{4}$, assuming you could do a comparable development with any fraction addition problem type. Logically, manipulatives would be used with each fraction addition problem type. We refer you again to http://pegasus.cc.ucf.edu/~mathed/ (Courses, MAE 2801 Class Resource Page, scrolling down to Egg Carton Fractions, Cuisenaire Rods, and Fraction Kit) and http://matti.usu.edu/nlvm/nav/

index.html (Virtual Library, Number & Operations) for manipulative approaches you could use with your students. Manipulatives help students understand why operation rules work as they do. Frequently, they are given a procedure and told to follow it when presented with $\frac{1}{3} + \frac{1}{4}$. Here is an algorithm typically given for adding fractions:

- Find the least common denominator (LCD).
- Divide the denominator of the first fraction into the LCD.
- Multiply the numerator of the first fraction by the answer you got when you divided the first denominator into the LCD.
- Divide the denominator of the second fraction into the LCD.
- Multiply the numerator of the second fraction by the answer you got when you divided the second denominator into the LCD.
- Add the two new products.
- Put the sum over the LCD.

More than likely you were given that procedure in your elementary or middle school experiences. Undoubtedly, it has become engrained in your head.

Read that preceding list of statements pertaining to adding two fractions onto a cassette tape. Read it as fast as you can. Play the tape back and you will get some feel for how that string of directions sounds to a student who does not comprehend the procedure. Granted, you would speak much more slowly with a class, but the intent is to note how it could sound to someone who does not understand the process.

Now look carefully at adding two unit fractions with unrelated denominators. Ideally, assuming the students do not know how to add something like $\frac{1}{4}$ and $\frac{1}{3}$, the development would be concrete based. Certainly they should not be given an algorithm and told to use it. The development we build could be duplicated for several different fraction addition problems. With that, assume you have developed the following and the results are known by the students: $\frac{1}{3} + \frac{1}{4} = \frac{7}{12}, \frac{1}{2} + \frac{1}{3} = \frac{5}{6}$, and $\frac{1}{2} + \frac{1}{7} = \frac{9}{14}$. It is hard to tell how many examples like this need to be done, but eventually some enterprising student is going to develop a generalization saying that all you need to do is multiply the denominators of the addends to get the denominator of the sum and add the denominators to get the numerator of the sum. AHA! That student is well along the way of discovering the rule used to add fractions. Granted these are unit fractions and additional work would be necessary to complete the concept, but a powerful foundation has been established.

Something like $\frac{2}{3} + \frac{1}{4}$ can be used as a next step in developing the algorithm for adding fractions. Again, we assume a concrete development of the sums and not following the given algorithm. If the students are given the algorithm, there is no need for the development. Yes, giving them the algorithm makes the entire situation easier for you and for the students, but the cost of that is a lack of understanding. That price is far too great! After several problems like this are done, a discussion similar to the one used when finding the sum of two unit fractions can lead the students to a more inclusive generalization. Suppose the examples are $\frac{2}{3} + \frac{1}{4} = \frac{11}{12}$, $\frac{2}{5} + \frac{1}{3} = \frac{11}{15}$, and $\frac{3}{7} + \frac{1}{5} = \frac{22}{35}$. The product of the denominators of the two fraction addends still gives the denominator of the sum. Adding the denominators of the addends to yield the numerator of the

sum will not work now. In $\frac{2}{5} + \frac{1}{3} = \frac{11}{15}$ you need to ask how to get 11 from 5 and 3. The sum of 5 and 3 is not enough. Using different combinations leads to the conclusion that the only way to get 11 using 5s and 3s is to have two 3s and one 5 or $3 + 3 + 5 = 11$. But $3 + 3$ can be written as $(2)(3)$ and a major piece of the complete algorithm for adding fractions is supplied. Some extension of this discussion will finalize the desired algorithm. Ultimately, you end up with one of the ways used to teach addition of fractions with unrelated denominators: multiply the denominator of each addend by the numerator of the other, and add the products to get the numerator of the sum of the two fractions. The process for determining the denominator of the sum of the two fractions has already been established. Notice, however, this slow and careful development has focused on the students generalizing from solved examples and ultimately building the algorithm typically used in the classroom.

Did you notice that in the last set of three examples all of the numerators in the sums are multiples of 11? If you did, give yourself a pat on the back. You are beginning to be sensitive to issues that can give students wrong impressions and perhaps even generate an error pattern. In this case, a student could conclude sums of a unit and nonunit fraction with unrelated denominators will always have a numerator that is a multiple of 11. Stranger things have happened.

There are many more aspects of fraction addition that need to be developed before the algorithm is completely established. That can be seen from the examples given in Table 8.1, but the basics have been covered. It is your responsibility as a professional to continue the process so that each of your students understands the background of the algorithm for adding fractions. If the students know how to find the LCD, there is no need to do this careful and tedious sequencing and discussion because the abstract approach to solving these problems is already present (or at least trying to be). If the students are not comprehending the abstractions they should use a manipulative, but it will take a significant effort on your part to sell them on the idea. Once abstractions are started, a concrete approach is often visualized as being too childish. Remember, the ultimate goal is to have the students use and understand the algorithm commonly applied when adding fractions. (Listen to that tape you made earlier.)

One common error when adding fractions has the numerators of the addends being added and placed over the sum of the denominators of the addends. This could be an outgrowth of multiplication of fractions because the process works there. Manipulatives can help prevent that error before it happens. Consider $\frac{2}{7} + \frac{3}{7}$, which frequently generates the incorrect response of $\frac{5}{14}$. Often this error is corrected by telling a student that the denominators are not added. This is a fact the student must simply believe. Depending on the individual, you might need to proceed from the concrete to the abstract application of the algorithm. Your knowledge of the student, content, and pedagogy will help you place the student properly in the sequence.

Your Turn

8.36. Has all of this discussion caused you to rethink technology? There are calculators that work directly with fractions in pretty print, divide out common factors, present equivalent fractions, and so on. Should we just use them and forget all of this development stuff? Explain your thoughts.

8.37. A student says $\frac{2}{3} + \frac{1}{8} = \frac{3}{11}$. Describe how you would help the student understand that the sum is $\frac{19}{24}$.

8.38. Define an error pattern for adding fractions that is different from placing the sum of the numerators over the sum of the denominators of the addends. Describe how you would help a student making such an error to correct it. (For ideas see TAG 8.23.)

Addition of fractions is not easy. The examples discussed are only a part of the picture. It is critical that you do the different problem types concretely. A clear sequence that pays attention to small details as influenced by the readiness and ability levels of your students needs to be established. You should work concretely with problem types different from those we described to ensure that you could create the necessary learning environment that is most productive for your students. Practice these skills now. You will be extremely busy when you start full-time teaching.

Subtraction of Fractions

There are some unique situations that occur with subtraction that do not happen with addition. For example, what is the answer when one unit fraction is subtracted from another unit fraction when the denominators are the same? Similarly, if a unit fraction is subtracted from another unit fraction where one denominator is a multiple of the other, is there a pattern? Questions such as these can be investigated as a part of developing a sequence for subtracting fractions.

Typically, not all addition topics are completed before subtraction is introduced, regardless of what set of numbers is being used. When students operate on fractions, they will have seen subtraction of whole numbers. Thus, it is likely that the beginning topics for subtraction of fractions could occur along with, or soon after, the beginning topics for addition of fractions. This is not too illogical; particularly if manipulatives are used in the formative stages. Your students will have seen subtraction of fractions with some having mastered at least the basics while others are not functional. Your task will be to place each student at the appropriate point on the fractions subtraction continuum. Some of them might be at the concrete level, which, as you know, will require a sales effort from you to get them to use manipulatives.

Your Turn

8.39. Create a sequence for student development for subtracting fractions starting with two unit fractions with the same denominator and ending with mixed numbers with quasi-related denominators.

8.40. As the addition sequence for fractions was developed, some discussion focused on providing steps that were not listed in the table. For example, $\frac{1}{7} + \frac{2}{7}$ was listed as a potential entry between $\frac{1}{7} + \frac{1}{7}$ and $\frac{2}{7} + \frac{3}{7}$. Does the sequence you created in exercise 8.39 allow for such detail or would this detail need to be added?

Manipulatives are as essential when dealing with the subtraction of fractions as they are when introducing any operation. It is not prudent to assume all of your students will be capable of dealing with the abstractions related to subtraction of fractions. It is possible that the students would be able to move through those concrete parts quickly because of the exposure in the formative stages of adding fractions. The weaker the background with other operations, the more difficult it will be for students to call on those experiences as they encounter new concepts to be learned. We refer you again to http://pegasus.cc.ucf.edu/~mathed/ (Courses, MAE 2801 Class Resource Page, scrolling down to Egg Carton Fractions, Cuisenaire Rods, and Fraction Kit) and http://matti.usu.edu/nlvm/nav/index.html (Virtual Library, Number & Operations) for manipulative approaches you could use with your students. Manipulatives help students understand why operation rules work as they do.

A few problems like $\frac{5}{7} - \frac{2}{7} = \frac{3}{7}$, $\frac{7}{9} - \frac{5}{9} = \frac{2}{9}$, and $\frac{11}{13} - \frac{6}{13} = \frac{5}{13}$ should be done early on. We assume here that these missing addends were generated concretely. If the standard fraction algorithm is used, there is no need for all this development. Did you notice that none of these exercises involve dividing out common factors? There is no sense muddying the water at first. Assuming exercises like this were done with addition of fractions, the desired generalization about the answer having the common denominator and the smaller numerator being subtracted from the larger for the numerator of the answer should follow quickly. Notice the last sentence says the smaller numerator is subtracted from the larger. At this stage of development, that is adequate. However, eventually the students will need to realize that the larger numerator could be subtracted from the smaller, resulting in a negative missing addend. Do not let the students generalize that you can't subtract the larger numerator from the smaller. Although they may not see negative fractions in middle school, you know it is coming. It is important not to confuse the students for their mathematical future.

Something like $\frac{1}{7} - \frac{1}{14}$ would be next in the sequence. This might not be the best choice because the addend and missing addend are the same. Still, doing several problems like $\frac{1}{7} - \frac{1}{14}$, $\frac{1}{3} - \frac{1}{6}$, $\frac{1}{11} - \frac{1}{22}$, and $\frac{1}{5} - \frac{1}{10}$ could stimulate a generalization. If the idea of the addend and missing addend being the same bothers you, you could use a set of problems like $\frac{1}{5} - \frac{1}{15}$. Sticking with the initial set of examples, there are some things students should be able to conclude. First, the second denominator is twice the first in each problem. Second, the addend and the missing addend are the same in each case. These may not be monumental conclusions, but they are a means of helping students learn to look for unusual happenings. This ability to notice different things can be an asset as they progress through their mathematical future.

Your Turn

8.41. Suppose you asked your students to do a series of problems like $\frac{1}{4} - \frac{1}{12}$, $\frac{1}{5} - \frac{1}{15}$, $\frac{1}{6} - \frac{1}{18}$, and so on. What generalization could they be expected to develop?

8.42. If the problems from exercise 8.41 were followed by sets of problems like $\frac{1}{4} - \frac{1}{16}$, which would be followed by problems like $\frac{1}{4} - \frac{1}{20}$, which would be followed by problems like $\frac{1}{4} - \frac{1}{24}$, and so on for as long as necessary, what generalization could students be expected to develop?

All of the typical subtraction error patterns, and some that are unique, could appear here in subtraction with fractions.

For example, when doing $\frac{1}{5} - \frac{1}{7}$, the students could conclude that the denominator should be the product of 5 and 7 as they did in addition of unit fractions with unrelated denominators. They would subtract 5 from 7 and get 2 for the denominator. We know the order of the denominators in the problem will influence the sign of the missing addend, and they may or may not realize that. The point is that they use absolute value and get the correct signed answer. Unless you are paying very close attention, an error pattern could be generated.

Subtraction of fractions is not easy. The examples we presented are only a part of the picture. It is critical that you do the different problem types concretely, *NOW*! Doing problem types different from those described will help you develop the skills to build the necessary learning environment that is most productive for your students.

DECIMALS

Prior to adding decimals, students should have a solid understanding of place value and regrouping. The students have probably already dealt with fractions and they need to be aware that decimals are another way of writing fractions in which the denominator is some power of 10. They should realize that $\frac{7}{10}$ means $7 \div 10$ or $10\overline{)7}$, which can also be expressed as 0.7. Calculators with an F<->D key can be an asset. Enter $\frac{3}{10}$ and then touch the F<->D key. The result will be 0.3 (some calculators might not put the zero in front of the decimal point). It should be noted that the more exposure the students have had to working with money, the easier the work with decimal could be. Also, do not forget the manipulatives, particularly the base 10 blocks.

In introducing decimals there is a temptation to provide oral drill where you would read something like, "Five thousand seven hundred ninety-eight and one hundred twenty-three thousandths." Avoid that practice. Sure the students need to recognize that five thousand seven hundred ninety-eight and one hundred twenty-three thousandths is a word expression of 5,798.123. However, oral drill involving such statements sets students up for failure in some instances. First, consider your enunciation skills. Do you say things clearly enough that students are able to distinguish between thousands and thousandths. Certainly if you concentrate the difference is obvious. However, if you are in normal speech pattern, is it still so obvious? The students' listening skills are even more critical. Alas, students do not listen as well as we would like them to. Thus, when you start with thousands and thousandths, the opportunity for difficulty arises.

Addition of Decimals

Traditionally, students have done ragged addition problems ($3698 + 2 + 10 + 547$) by being told to line up the "last number." If they have lined up the ones, rather than the last number, decimal addition is much easier. With that background, $3698 + 2 + 10 + 547$ would appear as

$$\begin{array}{r} 3698 \\ 2 \\ 10 \\ +547 \end{array}$$

and the student should understand there are unwritten zeros holding places in the problem. That is, inserting zeros so that the problem becomes

$$\begin{array}{r} 3698 \\ 0002 \\ 0010 \\ +0547 \end{array}$$

can help some students. Thus, alignment difficulties may be resolved. Perhaps reference to a digital clock where 5 o'clock is 05:00 will help some students. Characteristically, all left-side zeros are not written. Student understanding can be helped by asking how they wrote their age when they were 9 years old. Did they write 09? They could have, but we typically don't. Why not?

Before being ready to deal with addition of decimals, the students also must realize that $0.4 = 0.40$. They should have encountered the idea that $\frac{4}{10}, \frac{40}{100}, \frac{400}{1000}, \ldots$ are equivalent fractions. If they have done that, and if the concept that $\frac{4}{10} = 0.4$ has been developed, the notion that $\frac{4}{10} = \frac{40}{100} = \frac{400}{1000}$ leads to $0.4 = 0.40 = 0.400 = \ldots$ should be present.

In their whole number experiences, students learned that putting zeros at the end of a number changes it. Now they are hearing that it is permissible to put zeros at the end of a decimal value. We understand that the decimal point makes a huge difference in the discussion, but students may not. Thus, this takes careful development and the result will be much less confusing, particularly when adding ragged decimals.

Your Turn

8.43. Create a lesson plan using the calculator to help students discover that $\frac{3}{10} = 0.3$.

8.44. What happens when you enter 0.700 in your calculator and touch =, enter, or EXE? Do this activity with a friend and explain the result.

8.45. Create a lesson plan to help students realize that $0.32 = 0.320 = 0.3200\ldots$

By the time students encounter a formalized approach to addition of decimals, they should have command of addition facts, regrouping, place value, addition of multidigit addends, addition involving addends with a varying number of places, and the idea that $0.8 = 0.80 = 0.800$. If the students are in control of these factors as well as the requisite decimals basics, decimal addition should be relatively easy. Without an adequate background in addition, place value, and regrouping, the student could be destined to suffer some difficult times.

When adding decimals students are usually told to line up the decimal points and then proceed as if adding whole numbers. If they write decimals properly, where seven tenths is shown as 0.7, there is no need for that rule, assuming they learned to line up the ones in whole number addition. For 0.7, the ones digit is zero. Lining up the ones automatically lines up the decimal points. This might not seem like a big deal to you, but if you use that with your students, you just eliminated one thing that has to be memorized. That helps your students.

Given the discussion about lining up the ones digits, the sequence for adding decimals is pretty much under control, assuming that the students have mastered whole number addition. If they have not, why are you are asking them to add decimals?

There is one new hurdle in addition of decimals. Ragged decimal values like $0.35 + 6.941 + 295.7$ can be a source of difficulty because of the missing zeros at the end of the addends. The students are accustomed to seeing the last digits aligned in vertical form. Look at what can happen with the ending zeros missing:

$$\begin{array}{r} 0.35 \\ 6.941 \\ +295.7 \\ \hline \end{array}$$

Because they have dealt with the idea that $0.35 = 0.350$ and they elect to have an alignment for the rightmost digits, the difficulty can be corrected by inserting the appropriate zeros. The earlier example of $0.35 + 6.941 + 295.7$ would become

$$\begin{array}{r} 0.350 \\ 6.941 \\ +295.700 \\ \hline \end{array}$$

This should look familiar, except for the decimal point, but that too should be an old issue.

The calculator has already been discussed as a means of introducing decimals. In fact, if students have the opportunity to use calculators, the likelihood is quite high that they will be asking about decimals before they work with them in the school curriculum. The reason for that is simple. They see decimal answers on their calculator when they experiment. Calculators: don't leave home without them.

Error patterns that appeared while adding whole numbers should be corrected by now. If that is not the case, then, any of those behaviors could reappear. The risk of errors in addition of decimals is minimized by the assurance that the students have the appropriate readiness skills. See TAG 8.24 for error patterns involving adding decimals.

Your Turn

8.46. Suppose a student consistently shows $3.2 + 0.98 + 4.657 = 47.87$, $2.178 + 4.6 + 0.35 = 22.59$, and $0.46 + 1.3 + 5.278 = 53.37$. Describe how the decimal is being placed in the answer. Outline how you would correct the error.

Subtraction of Decimals

Subtraction of decimals will have undoubtedly been encountered prior to formalized study. Good bets for exposure would still be in the realms of money and calculators. It is assumed that the concept $0.7 = 0.70 = 0.700 = \ldots$ has been developed.

Typical subtraction error patterns will appear unless they have been resolved earlier. Ragged decimal problems hold the potential to create difficulties. Base 10 blocks or some other manipulative can help avoid most misconceptions if used appropriately.

You should expect that the students have command of subtraction facts, subtraction involving regrouping, place value, and decimal basics. Given this background, things should move rather smoothly. Without this background, how do you justify asking them to subtract decimals?

The sequence for subtraction of decimals should parallel that of whole numbers. It is assumed that the manipulative of choice will be available, even though the students should move from the concrete to the abstract stage rather quickly. Initially, problems like $0.8 - 0.5$ should be done and generalized that the subtraction is essentially an application of known facts except for the presence of the decimal points. A concrete introduction similar to those used for whole number subtraction will facilitate the learning.

Ragged decimals are still a potential source of difficulty, especially with something like $1.8 - 0.93$. The idea of showing $1.8 = 1.80$ and renaming to $1.7 + 0.10$ is critical. With that, $1.8 - 0.93$ becomes

$$\begin{array}{r} 1.7 + 0.10 \\ -0.9 + 0.03 \\ \hline 0.8 + 0.07 = 0.87 \end{array}$$

If they have been used previously, the base 10 blocks become an invaluable asset for showing how and why this renaming can be done. Without that concrete exposure, you are asking for trouble.

Besides the base 10 blocks, a calculator can prove invaluable for experimenting with the subtraction of decimals. It provides the opportunity to see what the answer is supposed to be. In many cases, students will correctly conclude that decimal subtraction is a lot like whole number subtraction. If the emphasis has been placed on lining up the ones, there is no need to discuss lining up decimal points. Furthermore, many students will surmise that $1.8 - 0.93$ is a lot like $180 - 93$ with the alignment taken care of automatically. Ironically this approach can amplify the $1.8 = 1.80$ idea.

With the ability to add zeros to the right of the decimal point after the last digit of a number ($3.45 = 3.45000$), any of the alternate methods for subtracting whole numbers (borrow-payback, integer, scratch) can be employed. The assumption is that the students know to line up the ones as well, but that should have been established in operations with the whole numbers.

Any of the error patterns that occur with whole number subtraction can reappear. That is another reason why it is so important to spot and correct the errors early on. Problems like $4.7 - 1.635$ present a whole new opportunity for errors because of the unexpressed zeros in the hundredths and thousandths places of the sum (4.7). Even after those zeros are inserted the difficulties associated with subtraction problems having sums ending in zeros can occur. In $4.700 - 1.635$, you could still use the idea of converting 4.700 to $4.699 + 0.001$ and reexpressing the problem as $4.699 - 1.635 + 0.001$. As we said with whole number subtraction, this renaming helps avoid difficulties. However, the complications associated with decimals might increase the degree of difficulty for some students. See TAG 8.24 for error patterns involving subtracting decimals.

Multiplication of Decimals

Your students will have probably been exposed to decimal multiplication, experimented with it on calculators, and perhaps begun to formulate conclusions about what is happening. By middle school, they should be aware that the world of mathematics is ever expanding, building on prior experiences. It is important that you help them see that each new topic adds power to their abilities to manage their mathematical world.

Multiplication facts, a multiplication algorithm, place value, decimal placement, insertion of zeros in decimals, and dealings with money are all part of the readiness skills for multiplication of decimals. Any weakness in those and related topics will only lead to difficulties as students multiply decimals. The need for concrete exposure before proceeding toward the abstract algorithm may be present for some students.

If students are not aware of the fact that there is a decimal point to the right of any integer, it should be established. The idea is necessary for when decimal places will be counted in products involving decimal factors. This becomes an extension of the likes of $0.8 = 0.80$, which they should be comfortable with by now.

Sequence-wise, start with something like 4×0.3, showing it with the number line, an array, base 10 blocks, or the calculator. The problem and answer should be recorded upon completion. Soon, students should conclude they are multiplying the 4 and 3 like they always do and the product is changed only by the placement of the decimal point. At this juncture, it will not be clear that the decimal point is located by counting from the right. It is a beginning because they are seeing the need to have the decimal point in the answer.

Problems like 4×0.03 should be done next, again recording the factors and product. They should generalize there are two decimal places in the problem and two in the answer. With 0.12, they should conclude that the counting comes from the right. At this point, you could proceed to other problems like 6×0.27 or even

6×0.027. Notice however, that the product is such that there is no need to insert a zero into it to accommodate the appropriate number of decimal places. That zero insertion problem type should be delayed until the students are more comfortable working with decimals in products. The careful sequencing is essential if you want to provide the easiest curriculum path for learning decimal multiplication.

So far we have dealt only with two factors; a whole number and a decimal. Problems like 4.2×3 could be next. This would amplify and strengthen the idea of placement of the decimal point in the product. Eventually, you are going to need to consider problems where both factors contain a decimal part.

Problems like 0.3×0.4 are a reasonable place to start because they can easily be shown with an array like Fig. 8.14, which can help rationalize why the decimal point is placed as it is in the product. This should not prove to be too much of a hurdle if the appropriate prior exposure to decimal products has been developed in a manner similar to what we have described. As in all the other problem types, 0.4×0.3 should be recorded along with the product. Once some similar problems have been done, the students should conclude the

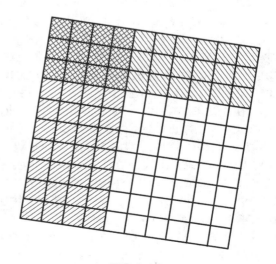

FIG 8.14.

location of the decimal point in the product. Something like 0.7 × 0.43 could be another consideration for exploration. If you establish the appropriate background early, the generalization should develop quickly. Still avoid any situation where there is a need to insert a zero.

Eventually you are going to need to deal with 0.2 × 0.3 problem types. Calculators or arrays can be used to generate suspicions in your students, who will quickly become aware of the need to have more digits to make the decimal placement correct; that of counting decimal places from the rightmost digit in the product; and that the total number of decimal places in the two factors gives the number of decimal places in the product. The missing element is the idea of inserting a zero between the decimal point and the 6 at this juncture. In all of their mathematical lives, students have been discouraged from adding digits to a number because of the impact on the answer. Now, you need to rationalize for them why it is OK to insert zeros in this situation. With this last piece of information, students should be able to derive the general rule that will work for multiplying any decimals.

We have outlined the basic sequencing continuum for decimal multiplication, starting with manipulatives and technology. Your students will have probably been exposed to some decimal multiplication, and as usual, they will be at different stages of development. Once again, it is your responsibility to plug students into that continuum at the appropriate readiness level for each one of them. The students could use calculators to do problems like the ones discussed here. The more work you and your colleagues have done with these students on patterns and generalizations, the easier it will be for them to draw the appropriate conclusions.

Given the concept of decimal location in products, any of the alternate methods for multiplication can be used with decimal factors. As discussed with whole number multiplication, one of these alternate ways might be the preferred method of multiplication for some students. Partial product can provide some interesting review of place value and zero insertion. Lattice multiplication is done exactly like it was with whole numbers—the only difference is decimal placement. Don't forget about Russian peasant multiplication. With this one, you would need to treat the factors as whole numbers for the sake of simplicity and then place the decimal at the end of the work. Notice that this assumes the student already knows how to locate the decimal point in the product.

Your Turn

8.47. Create a three-digit (hundredths) times a two-digit problem (tenths) and do it using partial product, lattice, and Russian peasant multiplication.

Most of the errors typically found in multiplication should have been corrected by this time. However, there might be remnants of any of them and so there is a need to watch carefully. Multiplication of decimals introduces one new error pattern: proper placement of the decimal point in the product. Thus, the need for the careful sequencing is amplified. See TAG 8.24 for error patterns involving multiplying decimals.

Division of Decimals

If the students have gotten beyond division with no remainder in their work with fractions, decimal division is easier to master. Some might question the reasonableness of putting division and easy in the same sentence. Without exposure to division with remainders, decimal division is still manageable given appropriate introductions. Remainders in division must be considered because sometimes a problem with a remainder makes sense and sometimes it does not. A dozen cookies shared by eight people, where each gets a cookie and a half, makes sense. On the other hand, dividing a dozen ball bats between eight people does not make sense.

Certainly students need to be able to do division problems by hand. However, there is debate over how much is enough. Just as with whole number division, the facts are a foregone conclusion. Certainly it would seem reasonable that a student should be able to do something like $3.8 \div 2$ mentally, or at least by hand. Similarly, it would seem unreasonable to expect a student to do $43.81025 \div 796.38624$ by hand. Somewhere between those two problems is a cut-off point where technology becomes acceptable.

Your Turn

8.48. Provide a written defense for when it is appropriate to permit students to use technology when doing decimal division problems.

8.49. Assume your position for permitting the use of technology in decimal division differs from that of your department, school, district, or state standards. What do you do and why?

Prior to starting division with decimals, the students need to be well founded in the basics of division, place value, equivalent fractions, rounding, approximation, estimation, multiplication, and subtraction. If the students have encountered equivalent fractions, division of decimals can be broken into four categories: $\frac{whole}{whole}$, $\frac{decimal}{whole}$, $\frac{whole}{decimal}$, and $\frac{decimal}{decimal}$. Each of these types can be expressed as $\frac{whole}{whole}$ through equivalent fractions

achieved by multiplying both the numerator and denominator of the given fraction by an appropriate power of 10. Students should soon realize that only the denominator of the fraction needs to be a whole number. That is equivalent to moving the decimal point the appropriate number of places in both the factor (divisor) and product (dividend).

The ultimate objective is to have students generalize how to move the decimal points in the factor and product to yield our standard algorithm, which is essentially dividing something by a whole number. As long as there is a remainder of zero in division, the situation is not overly difficult. That should be developed already. Now there is a need to go beyond. Initially division excess is expressed as a remainder, then as a fraction, and finally as a decimal. If the students have encountered fractions, they more than likely will have seen excess expressed in terms of something like a half. Then, conversion of that half to 0.5 is relatively simple and the stage is set for decimal division involving situations that have remainders.

Most whole number division problems these students have done so far could be converted and done with decimals rather easily. Even something like $78)\overline{735.54}$ should not present much of a challenge, IF the student knows how to divide and has an inkling of where to place the decimal point in the missing factor (quotient). A problem like $7.8)\overline{73554}$ may present a challenge because of the need to reset the decimal point in the factor and in the product. However, with equivalent fractions, this is a relatively simple task. The problem can be restated as follows:

$$\frac{73554}{7.8} = \frac{73554}{7.8} \times \frac{10}{10}$$
$$= \frac{735540}{78}$$

More than likely, you were taught the rule that said to move the decimal point to the right end in the factor and then move it the same number of places in the product. Multiplying the numerator and denominator by the same power of 10 explains why that motion is appropriate. The only other clarification involves amplification of the decimal point at the right end of any whole number. That ending decimal point might need to be inserted in the product to provide proper placement of a decimal point in the missing factor of a division problem involving decimals.

Your Turn

8.50. Make up a problem involving a whole number divided by a decimal. Explain how to convert your problem to one where it is a whole number divided by a whole number.

8.51. Make up a problem involving a decimal divided by a decimal. Explain how to convert your problem to one where it is a whole number divided by a whole number.

Manipulatives can be used with division but they become cumbersome quickly. Technology is a wonderful ally at any stage of learning, but that is particularly true with division of decimals. An organized set of decimal division problems done with technology, where the problem and results are recorded and analyzed, can lead the students to the generalization about moving the decimal point in division problems.

The easy way to do repeated subtraction division with decimals is to convert the problem to a whole number divided by a whole number. But, if the student can do that converting, and if the student has the appropriate readiness skills, one could question why the student would be asked to do long division using any method other than the standard algorithm.

All whole number division error patterns may still show up with decimals. The hope is that these errors would have been corrected. Location and movement of decimal points in division provides fertile ground for errors, particularly involving left to right or right to left and where to start the counting. Aside from those rather standard errors, you need to carefully examine a student's work to determine exactly what is happening.

PERCENTS, EQUIVALENTS, AND CONNECTIONS

Percents may be a new topic for your students. The coverage should be based on concrete exposures and relate to work with fractions and decimals. You have seen charts similar to the one in Table 8.2, showing the relation between fractions, decimals, and percents. It also gives a strong message on how important fractions and decimals are as readiness skills. If students are unable to convert between fractions and decimals, and understand the relationship, they will struggle with percents. They need to become familiar with the idea that $\frac{1}{2}$, 0.5, and 50% are different names for the same thing. Without this understanding, the students will be memorizing more information. Although these are things they need to memorize, students need to have understanding and feeling too. Otherwise, their minds are filled with what appears to be disconnected facts. It is imperative that we instill connections and

TABLE 8.2

Fraction	Decimal	Percent
$\frac{1}{2}$	0.5	50%
$\frac{1}{4}$	0.25	25%
$\frac{1}{8}$	0.125	12.5%

understandings between the different materials students learn.

Ability to switch between fractions and decimals (going either way) can be used to develop the concept of percents. Begin with the idea of a unit being divided into a number of equally sized parts. For fractions, this was the denominator. For decimals, it was implied that the denominator related to a power of 10. Assuming that the fractions and decimals background exists, focus on the idea of dividing a unit into 100 equally sized pieces. As with the decimal point being used to express integral powers of 10 denominators, the percent symbol can be used to express denominators of 100.

The most common percent values are between 1% and 100% and students generally learn those rather quickly, if only because they are so closely related to decimals. Assuming the students are well versed in changing fractions with denominators of 10 or 100 to decimals, the transition from decimals to percents goes rather smoothly. The percent symbol can be made by having the 1 from the denominator of 100 represent the diagonal slash with one of the zeros from the 100 being placed above and to the left of the slash and the other below and to the right. This explanation helps students make connections between the two expressions.

Things greater than 100% might be difficult for students to conceptualize because they get the idea that 100% is all of something and nothing more can happen. You know percents greater than 100 can happen because your stock portfolio has increased 150% weekly for the past year (don't you wish). Things less than 1% are difficult for students to deal with because of the need to add zeros to express them as a decimal. This should not be new because they wrote 3 one-hundredths as 0.03, for example. Still, this is foreign to many students and will take time. Once the ability

to go above 100% and below 1% is established, the rest of the development should proceed rather smoothly.

Base 10 blocks could be used to show percents, starting with the flat as the unit. A long is one of 10 equal pieces of a unit, or 0.1 and discussion about how to write that 0.1 in terms of a percent is assumed so the transition should be easy. This approach creates a strong connection between expressing a value as either a decimal or a percent, making it much easier for students to fill blanks in Table 8.2 extended to more values. The unwritten zero to the right of the 1 in 0.1 becomes significant as 0.1 is written as 10%. Similarly, the small square is 0.01 of the unit and is expressed as 1%.

For values larger than 100%, you would have more than one flat. Two flats would represent 200% of something. One flat and three longs would represent 0.3 more than one flat or 130%. Students should be familiar with this idea from their work with decimals. They should also be familiar with the idea that three-tenths more of something would result in that amount being affixed to the right of the unit, showing it as 1.3. Because they should already be familiar with the idea that 1 can be expressed as 100% by moving the decimal point two places to the right, the transition to expressing 1.3 as 130% should be rapid and natural for most students. After this, they should be able to express values greater than 100% and understand what is being said.

A base 10 big cube (10 by 10 by 10) can be designated as the unit, or 100%. Then the flat becomes 10%, the long is 1%, and the little cube is 0.1%. Students should realize that the little cube is one tenth of 1% because the little cube represents one tenth of a long. Their prior work should help them understand that expressing a tenth of some percent value would result in moving the decimal point one place to the left. Thus, a tenth of 1% would be expressed

0.1%. This approach is dependent on the realization that a decimal point exists at the right end of any whole number but is typically not written. Values to 0.9% can be shown by taking more little cubes to comprise part of a long.

All of these transitions are predicated by the thought that concepts have been developed concretely throughout the curriculum. This concrete evolution will provide the ability to visualize changes and mentally manipulate pieces. Eventually the associated abstractions replace the manipulatives. At that stage of development, the student is functioning at the abstract level for that concept. However, because of the concrete development of the concept, the student possesses the ability to re-create the ideas if necessary.

Percent error patterns focus on decimal point location and conceptualizing percents greater than 100 and less than 1. Decimal placement ranges from just not putting one in to moving it the wrong way. By the time students are learning percents, they should have begun developing some feel for numbers. After assuming that, one way to correct decimal placement problems is to encourage the students to visualize the amount in question and relate it to a unit. That vision should give a feel for how much larger or smaller than the unit the amount is, which in turn should provide some strong clues about decimal placement.

Your Turn

8.52. A student consistently moves the decimal point the correct number of places when converting a decimal to a percent or vice versa, but always in the wrong direction. Describe what you would do to help stimulate understanding of the error.

8.53. When values are greater than 100%, a student consistently omits the hundreds (237% is shown as 37%). Describe what you would do to help stimulate understanding of the error.

8.54. When values are less than 1%, a student consistently omits the necessary zeros (like 0.05% would be expressed as 5%). Describe what you would do to help stimulate understanding of the error.

INTEGERS

The existence of negative numbers needs to be established. Traditionally, this is done with discussions about temperature (Florida students have trouble thinking in terms of below zero), below sea level (Colorado students have trouble identifying with this), debt (most middle school students will know the word but might not have an understanding of the concept), or above or below ground level. You need to identify a means with which your students can identify.

By the time students consider operations on integers, they should be well versed in operating with whole numbers, fractions, and maybe decimals. With integers we make a big deal about rewriting $4 + 3 = 7$ as $^+4 + ^+3 = ^+7$, talking about a positive four plus positive three equals positive seven. We are preparing them to deal with negative numbers. We know that, but the students do not. Eventually, the students are told there is no need to worry about saying positive four plus positive three equals positive seven, and saying four plus three is seven is acceptable because everyone knows the numbers are positive if no sign is present. Some students have got to be thinking, "Why don't they make up their minds? First I do it without signs; then they insist I say positive; then they say to not worry about the signs." They have a point, don't they?

Your Turn

8.55. Describe your opinion of having students add positive numbers without signs, then insisting that they insert the signs, and later telling them not to worry about the signs.

Addition of Integers

Integer addition is difficult for students who are not proficient with addition of whole numbers. Ironically, they have to be proficient at subtraction of whole numbers as well because addition of integers with opposite signs involves subtraction. Addition of integers is a binary operation. More than two addends can be considered, but, no matter how capable the students are, they can only deal with two addends at a time. Once the sum of two addends is determined, that sum becomes one addend and the next addend would be considered. Thus, we will deal with two addends. Integer addition covers four problem types:

$$^+4 + {}^+6 = {}^+10$$
$$^-4 + {}^-6 = {}^-10$$
$$^+4 + {}^-6 = {}^-2$$
$$^-4 + {}^+6 = {}^+2.$$

Addends with the same sign should be considered first and then generalized to adding the absolute values and giving to the answer the common sign. Addition of positive values should be easy. Using technology, they should notice that, when adding two negative values, the answer is the sum of the two addends, but the sign of the sum is negative. With those conclusions, the generalization relating to normal adding and giving to the sum the common sign of the addends should develop quickly.

After completing the work where the signs of the addends are the same, introduce problems where the addends have opposite signs. Initially, have students do problems with the first addend positive and the second negative where the absolute value of the first is greater than the absolute value of the second. For example, with $^+5 + {}^-3 = {}^+2$, focus on the numbers involved and ask how a 2 can be derived out of a 5 and a 3, looking for a response of $5 - 3 = 2$. Relate that $5 - 3 = 2$ and $^+5 + {}^-3 = {}^+2$ are two different ways of expressing the same thing. Focus on how one can be changed to the other. Next should come the idea that the sign of the second number is changed, and the operation is changed from addition to subtraction. The students should generalize that, when adding numbers with unlike signs, they should subtract the smaller absolute value from the larger absolute value and give to the answer the sign of the larger absolute value. Some students will want to say they are subtracting the little number from the big one. That statement should be discouraged because that will not always be true. Using the absolute value keeps the ideas much clearer.

Approach problems like $^-5 + {}^+3 = {}^-2$. As before, $5 - 3 = 2$ is essentially what they will be doing. The answer gets the sign of the larger absolute value, which is what happened before. Focus the discussion on the two problems and how the two different ways of doing the problem can be interchanged. The students should conclude that, when adding numbers of opposite signs, they should subtract the smaller absolute value from the larger absolute value and give to the answer the sign of the larger absolute value.

Colored chips could be used to show integer addition, too. Suppose blue (B) is positive and green (G) is negative. The problem $^+2 + {}^+3$ is translated to be 2 Bs put together with 3 more Bs, giving a total of 5 Bs or $^+5$. The students should not need to do many problems like this to become comfortable with the idea that adding two positive integers yields a positive integer for the sum. Using Gs for problems like $^-2 + {}^-3$ should lead to a similar conclusion for negative addends. At this point, the students should combine these two ideas into one generalization stating that, when the signs of the addends are the same, the sum is determined by "regular addition" and holds the common sign of the addends.

The essential ingredient for adding values with opposite signs is that the students realize that a B and a G together counterbalance each other or yield zero. Given that, $^-2 + {}^+3$ would be expressed by 2 Gs and 3 Bs. However, 2 Gs could be paired with 2 Bs and they would be the same as zero, leaving only one B as the sum. That would be interpreted as $^+1$, showing that $^-2 + {}^+3 = {}^+1$. Similarly, $^+2 + {}^-3 = {}^-1$ because, after the pairing, one G would be left. At this point, you would develop the generalization described earlier.

Technology can be an ally when teaching integers. Give them problems grouped as discussed, having the students write the problem and the answer. As they look for patterns, they should generalize the rule for adding integers. If they are accustomed to looking for patterns and generalizing, this should go rather quickly.

Your Turn

8.56. How could absolute value be explained to your students?

8.57. Describe how technology could be used to help develop generalizations about adding signed numbers.

Integer addition errors generally involve incorrect signs, omission of signs, or subtraction errors when integers of unlike signs are added. Concrete beginnings, precise work as the concepts are developed, and an emphasis on paying attention to what is being done help avoid such difficulties.

Subtraction of Integers

The integer subtraction generalization that will be built says that you change the sign of the second number and follow the rules for addition. However, the generalization for addition of integers with unlike signs states that you subtract. So, to subtract, you think add, which really involves subtracting some of the time. You probably said those last three sentences are pretty confusing and yet that is what you were taught. IF students develop the ideas for subtraction of integers with technology or colored chips, the idea of changing the sign of the second number and adding is relatively easy to generate and comprehend. There is a message in that last statement. Did you get it? Concrete introduction is critical.

At this level, sequencing is not much of a factor. The goal is to have students establish the idea that, when subtracting integers, they should change the sign of the second number and follow the rules for addition of integers. The four problem types the students will encounter are as follows:

$$^+8 - {}^-3 = {}^+11$$
$$^-8 - {}^+3 = {}^-11$$
$$^+8 - {}^+3 = {}^+5$$
$$^-8 - {}^-3 = {}^-5.$$

We will focus on colored chips and on technology to develop the concept of subtracting integers. You should not assume that these are the only ways available. Any of the colored chips or technology activities involve the student doing several problems similar to $^+8 - {}^+3 = {}^+5$, $^-8 - {}^-3 = {}^-5$, $^+8 - {}^-3 = {}^+11$, or $^-8 - {}^+3 = {}^-11$, recording the problem and answer, and then drawing conclusions.

Again, the colored chips involve the idea that zero can be expressed in a multitude of convenient ways. Here, a positive (B) and a negative (G) counterbalance each other when paired to give a net result of zero. When additional chips of a given color are needed to solve a problem, adequate pairs of chips representing zero can be inserted.

With the chips, subtraction is viewed as a take-away model. Suppose you had to do $^+2 - {}^-5$ with the colored chips. You would start out with 2 Bs to represent the $^+2$. The problem indicates that you need to remove 5 Bs. Inserting zero in the form of 3 Bs and 3 Gs gives a set consisting of 5 Bs and 3 Gs, allowing the removal of 5 Bs. That leaves 3 Gs, which are interpreted as a negative three. Thus, $^+2 - {}^+5 = {}^-3$ has been shown with the chips. Your students should do several similar problems and then draw conclusions.

With $^+2 - {}^-6$, the need is to remove 6 Gs. To accomplish that, 6 Bs and 6 Gs should be placed with the existing 2 Bs. Now you have 8 Bs and 6 Gs and the $^-6$ can be removed, leaving $^+8$, the answer. All problem types would be developed in a similar manner.

Your Turn

8.58. Describe how you would lead a class to the generalization for changing the sign of the second number and following the rules for addition when dealing with the subtraction of integers.

8.59. Create a lesson plan covering each of the four problem types for subtracting integers represented by colored chips. Be sure to include detailed examples and questions that would lead to the desired generalizations.

With technology, you would give the students several of one problem type, recording each problem and the result. Each time, discussion would focus on how the given numbers would yield the indicated result. As a generalization from a problem type is made, discussion could focus on compiling the partial conclusions into one bigger generalization. The students should specify that the rule (about changing the sign of the second number and adding) works for all integer subtraction problems.

Multiplication of Integers

There are two conclusions students need to generate for multiplication of integers: assuming none of the factors is zero, an even number of negative factors gives a positive product, and an odd number of negative factors gives a negative product. These both should develop relatively quickly, given students with the appropriate background. Some argue that we should just tell the rules, but that makes students dependent on an outside source to tell them what to do. Our goal is to teach them to think through things on their own.

By the time the students get to multiplication of integers, they *should* have mastered their multiplication facts. They *should* be adept at using a multiplication algorithm. They *should* be familiar with working with signed numbers. They *should* have some background with colored chips or technology through addition and subtraction of integers. If all of that holds true, multiplication of integers will not be too difficult. It may be prudent to provide a quick review of addition and subtraction of integers before introducing multiplication, particularly if it has been a while since the students have worked with integers.

With appropriate readiness skills, the magnitude of the factors involved with the multiplication of integers is not significant. Still, digit factors can make the learning a little easier for the students because the focus can be on the signs of the factors as opposed to multiplication skills.

If more than two factors are involved, the product of two factors must be found first and then that product becomes one of two factors that generate a new product, until all factors are considered. If the students know how to deal with two factors, they should be able to work with more than two rather quickly. With that, multiplication of integers considers four problem types:

positive times positive,
positive times negative,
negative times positive, and
negative times negative, taken in that order.

Technology, colored chips, or another medium can be used to develop the ideas that follow. If the students know multiplication as repeated addition, multiplication of two positive factors has essentially already been done. They should have completed a problem like $4 \times 3 = ?$. The only difference now is that the problem is $^+4 \times ^+3 = ?$. This does reiterate the issue of excluding signs, and then insisting they are present, followed by the conclusion that everyone knows the signs are there when positive, so they can be omitted. No wonder they get confused.

Following the positive times a positive problem types with a positive times a negative is significant. Students should quickly be able to generalize that a positive times a negative yields a negative product because of experiences with repeated addition with negative addends.

Assuming the students have dealt with the commutative property of multiplication on whole numbers, fractions, and maybe decimals, they should suspect that there is a commutative property for multiplication on integers. With that in mind, a negative factor times a positive factor can be commuted into a positive factor times a negative factor. Technology can quickly confirm this suspicion. Therefore, three of the four problem types are done.

The fourth problem type, which involves two negative factors, presents a little more of a challenge to explain to students.

Technology can certainly be used to get students to conclude that a negative factor times a negative factor yields a positive product. Patterning is another way to develop the idea, assuming the students know how to do the other three integer multiplication problem types. In the following sequence, each time from the second problem on, there is a comparison between the respective problem and the preceding one, and the written words (or something similar) must be uttered by the group:

$$^-6 \times ^+6 = ^-36$$
$$^-6 \times ^+5 = ^-30$$

Comparing the second line with the first line, the students would say, "first factor stays the same, second factor decreases by 1, product increases by 6."

$$^-6 \times ^+4 = ^-24$$

"first factor stays the same, second factor decreases by 1, product increases by 6."

$$^-6 \times ^+3 = ^-18$$

"first factor stays the same, second factor decreases by 1, product increases by 6."

$$^-6 \times ^+2 = ^-12$$

"first factor stays the same, second factor decreases by 1, product increases by 6."

$$^-6 \times ^+1 = ^-6$$

"first factor stays the same, second factor decreases by 1, product increases by 6."

$$^-6 \times 0 = 0$$

"first factor stays the same, second factor decreases by 1, product increases by 6."

$$^-6 \times ^-1 = ^+6$$

"first factor stays the same, second factor decreases by 1, product increases by 6."

The set of problems needs to be long enough so students reflexively say the "stays the same, decreases by one, increases by six" phrases. By the time they get to $^-6 \times {}^-1 = {}^+6$, they will say the words without thinking. BANG! They just got a positive product out of two negative factors.

Two final generalizations should be developed after all four integer multiplication problem types are done: if the two factors have the same sign, the product is positive; if the two factors have different signs, the product will be negative. These can then be extended to the conclusion that, assuming no factors of zero, if the number of negative factors is even, the product is positive, and if the number of negative factors is odd, the product is negative.

Your Turn

8.60. Do the sequence of problems that started with $^-6 \times {}^+6 = {}^-36$ and ended with $^-6 \times {}^-1 = {}^+6$ with someone not in the class using this text. As you do it, focus on their reaction to the comments as a problem is compared with the preceding one. Write your reflections to their responses and actions.

8.61. Describe how you would convince students that the product of two factors with the same sign is positive.

8.62. Describe how you would convince students that the product of two factors with opposite signs is negative.

Colored chips could be used to show several problems like $^+4 \times {}^+3 = {}^+12$. Using the set definition for multiplication, this problem represents putting together four sets of positive three. If blue (B) represents positive, then the student would have four sets of 3 Bs. Compiling all of the chips

yields 12 Bs or $^+12$ and the problem is completed.

The product of a positive and a negative would be done in a very similar manner to that of a positive times a positive. If the problem is $^+3 \times {}^-6$, the student would need three sets of $^-6$, or three sets of 6 Gs. Combining all of the chips would yield 18 Gs or a product of $^-18$. Several problems of this type would need to be done to lead the students to the appropriate conclusion.

Earlier, you should have been thinking that the "commutative property of multiplication on the set of integers" approach was rather abstract. Technology is the easiest way to develop a set of problems that would be recorded along with the respective products. After several are done, the appropriate conclusion that settings like $^+3 \times {}^-6$ and $^-6 \times {}^+3$ yield the same product no matter the order should lead to the idea that there is a commutative property for multiplication on the set of integers.

Division of Integers

When signed numbers are involved, the ultimate goal is to generalize that, in division, if the signs are the same, the answer (missing factor) will be positive, and if the two signs are opposite, the missing factor will be negative. These are the same generalizations that were developed in multiplication of integers.

Integer division develops like multiplication did. Start with problems like $^+4\overline{)^+20}$ or $\dfrac{^+20}{^+4}$ and $^-4\overline{)^-20}$ or $\dfrac{^-20}{^-4}$, concluding that, when the signs are the same, the sign of the missing factor will be positive. Then cover problems like $^-4\overline{)^+20}$ or $\dfrac{^+20}{^-4}$ and $^+4\overline{)^-20}$ or $\dfrac{^-20}{^+4}$, concluding that, if the numbers involved in the division are of opposite signs, the missing factor will be negative.

Manipulatives for Division of Integers

Technology is the most efficient means for developing the generalizations for integer division. Start with a set of problems like $+4\overline{)+20}$ or $\dfrac{+20}{+4}$ only, and have students list the problem and the answer. When enough have been done, they should state their conclusion in writing. Next, deal with problems like $-4\overline{)-20}$ or $\dfrac{-20}{-4}$ only, having them list the problem and the answer. Again, when enough problems have been completed, they should state their conclusion in writing. After they have finished both of these problem sets, they should combine the two conclusions into one that deals with division problems where the signs of the two numbers involved are the same.

The third set of problems should be like $-4\overline{)+20}$ or $\dfrac{+20}{-4}$. (They could do problems like $+4\overline{)-20}$ or $\dfrac{-20}{+4}$ first.) They should list the problem and the answer, stating their conclusion in writing. Finally, they should work on problems like $+4\overline{)-20}$ or $\dfrac{-20}{+4}$ (or $-4\overline{)+20}$ or $\dfrac{+20}{-4}$), presenting their written conclusion. After they have completed the third and fourth problem sets, they should combine the two conclusions into one that deals with division problems in which the signs of the two numbers involved are opposites.

You just got the quick story on integers. It was probably more elaborate than what was done with you when you were in middle school. Yet, we went very fast. As a professional, it is your responsibility to create an atmosphere that helps students understand the story behind the rule or generalizations. To do that, you have to expand your horizons and go beyond simply telling them to do what you model abstractly for them. This method is a lot harder on you, but it is better for your students. True professionals rise to the challenge!

NUMBER THEORY/PATTERNING

For some, number theory is viewed as a tool that bridges the various branches of mathematics because of its broad-based connections. Number theory also includes divisibility rules, greatest common factor (GCF), least common multiple (LCM), factors, multiples, proof, factorials, abundant numbers, deficient numbers, perfect numbers, and all sorts of number oddities. At higher levels of instruction, number theory is studied as a distinct topic.

Factor and multiple, essential ingredients of number theory, are confused by many students, even those who typically do well in mathematics. Much of the dilemma arises over definitions. The product of two numbers is obtained by multiplying two factors. Therefore, 3 and 4 are factors of 12. Multiples of a number come from multiplying the given number by a counting number. For example, the multiples of 3(3, 6, 9, 12, 15, ...) are found by multiplying 3 by 1, 2, 3, 4, 5, ... Some authorities say 0 is a multiple of 3 and others say it is not. When factor and multiple are taught separately, little trouble occurs. Finding the factors or multiples of a given number after both terms are taught is when the difficulty arises.

Prime Factorization

All composite numbers can be expressed as a product of prime numbers. This may seem apparent to you as a teacher of mathematics, but it is not intuitively clear to neophytes. After factors, the idea of prime factorization can be introduced. One method of displaying the prime factors of a composite number is through the use of a factor tree. Figure 8.15 shows two factor trees,

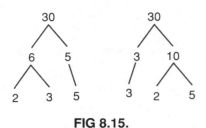

FIG 8.15.

representing the prime factorization of 30. Notice that the bottom row in each setup shows 2, 3, and 5, primes that yield 30 as their product. Observe that 5 and 6 were selected in the left example as the first choices. Next, the student decides if either of these factors is prime. Because five is a prime, it can be left where it appears, or extended down as shown. Many people prefer extending the primes down so they are not overlooked once all prime factors are identified. Six is not a prime and requires factorization. Because 2 and 3 are both prime, the process is terminated. The process could be extended, if needed. Notice that the right-most example shows 30 factored differently at first, and yet the end result is the same. The fundamental theorem of arithmetic ensures that will always be the case, stating that any number is uniquely factorable into a product of primes, excluding order. Factor trees provide excellent time for exploration and discovery.

Fundamental Theorem of Arithmetic

The fundamental theorem of arithmetic helps clarify one trouble spot for some students. Is 1 prime or composite? It is neither. Composites have factors other than 1 and themselves. The number 1 does not fit that definition. Primes are factorable only by 1 and themselves. Even with those definitions, questions arise. We need the assurance that, when dealing with whole numbers, there are no numbers other than 3 and 5 that will provide a product of 15, for example. Without that assurance, we

would not be able to multiply. Similarly, if 1 were a prime, the fundamental theorem of arithmetic would lose the uniqueness part of the definition, and that is a critical element. If 1 were considered prime, then the prime factorization of 6 would be 2×3, $1 \times 2 \times 3, 1 \times 1 \times 2 \times 3, \ldots$. Although we have listed the factors in ascending order, it is not necessary to do that; however, it is convenient for keeping track of things.

Greatest Common Factors (GCFs)

When introducing the idea of GCF, starting with just two numbers, it is important to examine two components:

the factors of the numbers involved, and

the factors that the involved numbers share.

Using 18 and 24, the factors of 18 are 1, 2, 3, 6, 9, and 18 and the factors of 24 are 1, 2, 3, 4, 6, 8, 12, and 24. The common ones are 1, 2, 3, and 6. The greatest factor they share, or GCF, is 6. Figure 8.16 shows the process in a different manner, with the common factors looped. After that, the largest looped value is identified as the GCF.

The GCF can also be found using the prime factorization of each number. To determine the GCF of 24 and 36, find the prime factorization of 24 ($2 \times 2 \times 2 \times 3$) and 36 ($2 \times 2 \times 3 \times 3$). The prime factors they share are 2, 2, and 3. Therefore, the GCF is $2 \times 2 \times 3$ or 12. The prime factorization could be accomplished with factor trees or more abstractly, as was done here.

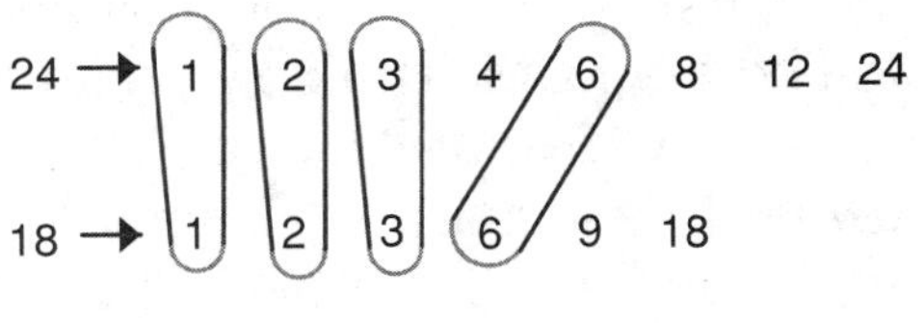

$24 \rightarrow$ 1 2 3 4 6 8 12 24

$18 \rightarrow$ 1 2 3 6 9 18

FIG 8.16.

The prime factorization approach opens the door to another means of determining the GCF of two or more numbers. Using 24 and 36 again, the factors could be expressed with exponents: $24 = 2^3 \times 3^1$ and $36 = 2^2 \times 3^2$. We are looking for 12 as the GCF, which could be expressed as $2^2 \times 3^1$. Observation should lead to the conclusion that the factors of 12 are expressed as the smallest listed power of each of the common factors. These three methods provide the opportunity to deal with different levels of student maturity as the GCF is covered.

Least Common Multiples (LCMs)

When finding the LCM of two numbers, two components are considered:

the multiples of the numbers involved, and

the multiples the two numbers share.

Using 6 and 10, the multiples of 6 are 6, 12, 18, 24, 30, 36, 42, 48, 54, 60, 66, ..., whereas the multiples of 10 are 10, 20, 30, 40, 50, 60, 70, ... Two common multiples, 30 and 60, are shown but there are infinitely more. The LCM is the least-valued they have in common, or 30. As with GCF, it is important to provide several examples. Be sure to include types of exercises such as finding the LCM of 15 and 45. Notice that the multiples of 15 are 15, 30, 45, 60, ... Do the multiples of 45, which are 45, 90, 135, ..., need to be listed? Students should quickly become aware that 45 is a multiple of 15 and therefore is the least multiple that they have in common.

A factor tree of both numbers can be used to find the LCM. The only prime factor that 12 and 15 share is 3, which could be shown with a factor tree. Therefore the GCF of 12 and 15 is 3. The LCM is the product of the GCF and the prime fac-

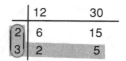

FIG 8.17.

tors that are not shared, which for 12 and 15, are 2, 2, and 5. Therefore the LCM of 12 and 15 is $3 \times 2 \times 2 \times 5 = 60$. This method tends to be a bit confusing for some students but it does provide a visual representation.

Exponents could be used to determine the LCM, too. Staying with 12 ($2^2 \times 3^1$) and 15 ($3^1 \times 5^1$), we know we need 60 as the LCM. Examination of a few examples shows that the largest power of each factor shown (common or not) will give the desired result. Again, you have three different routines to arrive at the desired conclusion, allowing the option to meet the developmental needs of all students.

Figure 8.17 shows the L method for finding the GCF and LCM of 12 and 30. Starting with 12 and 30 as shown, ask what number other than 1 divides them both. Although there are a couple options, start with 2 to show how the process works, writing it to the left, outside the vertical segment. After taking 2 out of both 12 and 30, 6 and 15 are left. The procedure is repeated, taking out a 3 from both 6 and 15, and 2 and 5 are left. The process is complete because the remaining two missing factors are 2 and 5 and they are relatively prime. The GCF is found by multiplying the looped numbers on the left side. The LCM comes from multiplying all the numbers in the shaded region. Notice the L, which stands for LCM.

Your Turn

8.63. Can the GCF of two numbers be greater than both numbers? How would you explain this to a student?

8.64. Will the GCF of two numbers always be less than both numbers? How would you explain this to a student?

8.65. Can the LCM of two numbers be less than both numbers? How would you explain this to a student?

As a teacher, it is important to realize that sometimes it takes several methods, carefully and patiently developed, before some students see the light. Other students may pick up a particular concept in a matter of seconds. After students are comfortable with finding the GCF and LCM of two numbers, ask them to find the GCF or LCM for three numbers. This process can be difficult for some students because you cannot simply find the factors that all three have in common and multiply them by the remaining noncommon factors to obtain the LCM. Furthermore, with three numbers, the LCM could be much larger than the numbers the students have worked with so far. With larger numbers comes the increased chance for arithmetic errors.

Divisibility Rules

Divisibility rules could be presented as a diversion, novelty, motivator, or stimulus for proof. To accomplish the idea of proof, students need to be aware that, if a number is divisible by some value, any multiple of that number will also be divisible by that value. For example, because 12 is divisible by 4, any multiple of 12 is also divisible by 4. In addition, students need to be able to deal with expanded notation, expressing a number in different ways, and all of the whole number operations.

How do you know if a number is divisible by 2? The typical answer is something like, "The last digit will be even," or "The last digit will be a 2, 4, 6, 8, or 0." Either one is acceptable. The bottom line is that many students know a number is divisible by two because the number is even. But why does the rule work, or where is its emanation point? Discussion for proving divisibility by 2 often becomes cyclic, and students struggle for a way to begin. Consider any number Xy where X is any integer and y is any digit. In 7,354 X is 735 and y is 4. Xy can be written in expanded notation as $(X)(10) + y$. No matter what integer is used for X, $(X)(10)$ must be divisible by 2, because 10 is always divisible by 2. One term of the expanded form is guaranteed to be divisible by 2. If the other term is also divisible by 2, a 2 can be factored out of the expanded form and the original number written as 2 times something. This verifies that the original number is divisible by 2. But, when can a 2 be factored out of both terms? Only when y is even, or 0, 2, 4, 6, or 8, which gives the rule statement and the proof is completed.

The proof for divisibility by 5 and even 10 is similar to that for 2, except that the y must be either 5 or 0 for divisibility by 5 and only 0 for divisibility by 10. It should not be too difficult for students to produce these proofs once they have seen the one for 2.

Divisibility by 4 does not use the expanded expression of the number being considered as $(X)(10) + y$ because 10 is not divisible by 4. The first counting number power of 10 that is divisible by 4 is 100. So, the number being considered needs to be written as Xyz where X is any integer and y and z are any digits. The number is then written as $(X)(100) + yz$ (note y and z represent the tens and ones digits of the number and are not multiplied). Because 100 is divisible by 4, and any multiple would also be divisible by 4, attention is turned to the last two digits, yz. If they are divisible by 4, the whole number is. If yz is not divisible by 4, then the initial number is not, because 4 cannot be factored out of both terms. For example,

$$5{,}732 = 57(100) + 32$$
$$= 57(4)(25) + 4(8)$$
$$= 4[57(25) + 8]$$

If the initial number is 5,731, four cannot be factored out of 31. Thus, 5,731 is not a multiple of 4.

The divisibility rule for 8 can be considered in a manner similar to that of 2 and 4 with one variation. The expanded version of the number being checked for divisibility by 8 is expressed as $W(1000) + xyz$, where x, y, and z are digits and are not multiplied. The 1000 is used because it is the first counting number power of 10 that is divisible by 8, and the only remaining question is whether or not xyz is one of 8's multiples. Looking at the proofs of divisibility for 2, 4, and 8, notice the parallel between the exponents of 2 and 10.

The proofs of divisibility by 3 uses expanded notation along with that of having each term in the expansion expressed as a multiple of 3, allowing a 3 to be factored out. Suppose you want to know if the three-digit number XYZ, where X, Y, and Z are all digits, is divisible by 3. The rule says to find the sum of the digits. If that sum is divisible by 3, then the original number is also. The 3 rule could be repeated. Mathematicians often use the known answer as a clue for how to proceed with a proof. Rewrite XYZ as $(X)(100) + (Y)(10) + Z$, which highlights a useful proof technique. The answer is known; the desire is to have the sum of the digits as a part of expressing XYZ. Using that information, XYZ needs to be rewritten somehow so $X + Y + Z$ are some of the terms of the sum. Focus on $(X)(100)$ because once it is seen how to rewrite this, the rest are similar.

How can $(X)(100)$ be expressed so it is a sum of X and something? We know that one term of the final answer needs to be X, and so 100 needs to be expressed in a manner that will give an X when things are all done. Listing $(X)(100)$ as $(X)(99 + 1)$ yields $(X)(99) + (X)(1)$ or $99X + X$. The X is now isolated. Using the same technique for $(Y)(10)$,

$$XYZ = (X)(100) + (Y)(10) + Z$$
$$= (X)(99 + 1) + (Y)(9 + 1) + Z$$
$$= (X)(99) + (X)(1) + (Y)(9) + (Y)(1) + Z$$
$$= 99X + 9Y + X + Y + Z$$

It is known that 99X and 9Y will always be divisible by 3, assuring the ability to factor 3 out of those two terms. The only thing left to consider is $X + Y + Z$, which is the sum of the digits. If the sum $X + Y + Z$ is divisible by 3, then the original number can be expressed as a multiple of 3. If the sum of the digits is not divisible by 3, the original number cannot be expressed as a multiple of 3.

Divisibility by 9 works exactly like that of 3 except that the sum of the digits must be divisible by 9. Divisibility by 6 uses a combination of the 2 and 3 rules. If the number in question is even, then apply the 3 rule to determine if it is divisible by 6. The discussion about why divisibility for 6 uses the 2 and 3 rules should include items dealing with the prime factorization of 6.

Divisibility by 7 provides exploration opportunities for more inquisitive students. The rule states, double the last digit in the number and subtract that product from the original number with the last original digit deleted before subtracting. If the subtraction answer is divisible by 7, the original is. If the subtraction answer is not divisible by 7, the original is not. The process may be repeated. To check if 2065 is divisible by 7, the process is:

2	0	6	5	Double last digit (5)
−1	0			Subtract 2 ×5 from rest after deleting 5
1	9	6		Repeat the process—double 6
−1	2			Subtract from rest after deleting 6
	7			Because 7 is divisible by 7, 2065 is also.

The essence of the proof lies in the idea of eliminating the last digit before subtracting twice its value from what is left. If X is the last digit, eliminating it is like subtracting it from the initial value. Doubling it and moving that product one place to the left is akin to multiplying X by 20. So, essentially the setting involves removing 21X from consideration. Since 21 is a multiple of 7, 21X must be divisible by 7 too. The process becomes 210Y, and so on as it is repeated.

Proof of divisibility by 11 is relatively simple, revolving around renaming 10 as $11 - 1$ and using the concept of expanded notation. Consider $(11 - 1)^2$, which when expanded yields $11^2 - 2(11)(1) + 1^2$. Because 11 is a factor of two of the terms in the expansion, that sum must be divisible by 11. Expanding $(11 - 1)^3$ gives all terms except 1^3 as a multiple of 11. The situation is similar for all cases of $(11 - 1)^n$, where n is any counting number—all terms except for 1^n will be multiples of 11. The sign of 1^n will be negative for odd values of n, and positive for even ones. Using this information to check for divisibility by 11, on the number UVWXYZ where U, V, W, X, Y, and Z are any digits, UVWXYZ would be rewritten as $U(10)^5 + V(10)^4 + W(10)^3 + X(10)^2 + Y(10)^1 + Z(10)^0$ or as $U(11 - 1)^5 + V(11 - 1)^4 + W(11 - 1)^3 + X(11 - 1)^2 + Y(11 - 1)^1 + Z(11 - 1)^0$. From the earlier discussion, expansion of this polynomial will yield a set of terms that are multiples of 11 plus some residue, which is −U, +V, −W, +X, −Y, and +Z. Inspection shows the rule to be the rightmost digit minus its left neighbor, plus the next left neighbor, and so on, until all digits are considered. Another way of saying this is that the sum of every other digit is subtracted from the sum of the rest of the digits (for divisibility, the sign is not important). Only if that missing addend is a multiple of 11 will the original number be divisible by 11.

Your Turn

8.66. Should students be required to prove a divisibility rule? Why or why not?

Factors, multiples, expanded notation, place value, exponents, renaming, and whole number operations play key roles in the developmental picture of algebra and beyond. Once these terms are introduced.

CONCLUSION

There are a multitude of topics and examples we have not developed with you (perfect numbers, abundant numbers, deficient numbers, amicable numbers, and so on). Yet, we have given you examples, ideas, and alternatives in a broad variety of number dealings with whole numbers, fractions, decimals, integers, and number theory. There is a lot more to be considered. At some point, it is your responsibility to take the knowledge you have gained in your education and mathematics classes and combine it in manners that create new views of the mathematical world for your students. It is your responsibility to present topics in ways that entice them to dig deeper, just like we are asking you to do now.

STICKY QUESTIONS

8.1. Suppose you have a group of sixth-graders who have very weak mathematical backgrounds and the fact can be traced to a particular school. What do you do? Do you accept them where they are and build the needed background? Do you ask your administrators to speak with the administrators from the school? Do you approach the fifth-grade teacher directly?

8.2. Assuming you have a group of students who do not have the mathematical sophistication to deal with the mandated objectives of your class, is it reasonable to attempt the work anyhow? If you say no, the implication is that you must build the necessary background with your students. If you say yes, the implication is that you are dooming those students to fail. Now what?

8.3. Most states mandate passing a high stakes mathematics test in the middle school. Is that reasonable? Rationalize your response.

8.4. Assuming your state requires passing a high stakes mathematics test in the middle school, could that lead to a state-defined mathematics curriculum that must be followed? Assuming that mandated curriculum comes to fruition, is that a good thing? Rationalize your response.

8.5. Should all teachers of seventh-grade mathematics in a school be required to use the same book and teach the same lesson on the same day? Rationalize your response.

8.6. Suppose your school has a capable group of students going into the eighth grade. They have mastered algebra 1 and are ready to move on mathematically. Should they take algebra 2, geometry, or something else? Rationalize your response.

8.7. Suppose your school has a capable group of students going into the eighth grade. They have mastered algebra 1 and are ready to move on mathematically. Next year they will move to ninth grade at the high school. You have just been told that the high school will not accept middle school credit for geometry or algebra 2, and would require the students to retake either course as a part of the high school mathematics curriculum. Describe the action you would take.

8.8. Most districts offer the sequence algebra 1, geometry, and then algebra 2. Describe why the courses are offered in that order. Rationalize why the algebra 1–geometry–algebra 2 sequencing is the best way to offer the courses, or, if you disagree, present your desired arrangement and defend your position.

8.9. Rather than offering the algebra 1–geometry–algebra 2 sequence, some districts (and publishers) present an integrated sequence of courses that blends topics from algebra 1, geometry, and algebra 2 over a three-year period. Defend or argue against such an approach.

8.10. How do we justify having students attempt operating with decimals if they are not competent adding whole numbers?

TAG

8.1. Square a number ending in 3. Last digit is a 9.

+ 60 times the rest of the number (left of the 3)

+ 100 times the rest of the number (left of 3 squared followed by 00)

$73^2 = 9 + 60(7) + 100(7^2)$ $123^2 = 9 + 60(12) + 100(12^2)$

$\quad\quad = 9 + 420 + 4900$ $\quad\quad\quad = 9 + 720 + 14400$

$\quad\quad = 5329$ $\quad\quad\quad = 15129$

Why does this work?

8.2. Place the first 10 counting numbers, one each on a card. Arrange the cards so that when you start with the top card and spell the number word "one," moving a card to the bottom of the stack for each letter said, after the card for "e" is moved to the bottom of the stack, the numeral 1 is showing. Remove the 1. Spell "two," and after the third card is placed on the bottom of the stack, the numeral card 2 is showing. Remove it. Continue through all 10 counting numbers, spelling each and removing the card associated with the word spelled. What is the original sequence of cards that makes this work?

8.3. Tell someone you will race their calculator skills in multiplying a 2-digit number by 55.

Ask for a 2-digit number.

Divide the selected number by 2.

Move the decimal point one place to the right (call this number A).

$B = 10A$

Find $A + B$

Examples

Pick 28.	51
$28 \div 2 = 14$	$51 \div 2 = 25.5$
Decimal one to right 140 (=A)	$255 = A$
$B = 10(140) = 1400$	$B = 2550$
$A + B = 140 + 1400 = 1540$	$A + B = 255 + 2550$
So $28 \times 55 = 1540$.	So $51 \times 55 = 2805$

(Source: BEATCALC@aol.com)

Note: BEATCALC is great source of number oddities. A new one is produced each week and it is free!

8.4. A person likes 225 but not 224; 900 but not 800; 144 but not 145. Which would be preferred, 1600 or 1700? Why?

8.5. Place digits 1 through 6 in the circles so each triangle is a correct sum (see Fig. 8.18).

8.6. Use three 6s and addition, subtraction, multiplication, and division to get 20. HINT: You will need a decimal.

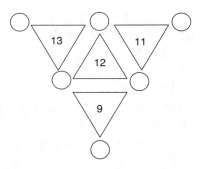

FIG 8.18.

8.7. Use three 9s and a minus sign to make 1.

8.8. Which number becomes larger when it is turned upside down? The number of correct answers is infinite.

8.9. A farmer threw 9 ears of corn in the barn. A rat came in and left with 3 ears each day. It took the rat 9 days to take all the corn. Why?

8.10. Ask for a 3-digit number comprised of the same digit. Ask that the number be doubled and then divided by 37. The answer will be 6 times the selected digit. How does it work?

8.11. How can you quickly square numbers made up of 9s up to 9 digits long?

8.12. In the pattern O T T F F S S, what comes next?

8.13. What is two times a half of 456,789?

8.14. Take a bus between two towns. The bus travels at an average speed of 30 miles per hour. How fast would the bus have to travel on the return trip for the average speed of the round trip to be 60 miles per hour?

8.15. The people on a certain island are divided into two groups—the truth-tellers and the liars. The truthtellers always tell the truth. The liars always lie. There are no half-truths or half-lies.

A stranger comes to the island one day and sees three of the natives standing together. The first native says, "I am not a liar." The second native says, "He's lying." The third native says, "They are both lying."

What is the third native—a truth-teller or a liar?

8.16. Did you know that the Hindu Arabic number system was illegal for years in Europe? The thinking was that because it came from Hindus and Arabs, it had to be unclean. By using the system, it was assumed that the individual was doing the work of the devil.

8.17. Ask an individual to give a 3-digit number. Have the individual duplicate the digits in the order given, yielding a 6-digit number. Divide that 6-digit number by 7; divide that answer by 11; divide that answer by 13. The result will be the original three-digit number. How does that work?

8.18. Ask an individual to give a 3-digit number. Have the individual duplicate the digits in the order given, yielding a 6-digit number. Divide that 6-digit number by 7; divide that answer by 13. You can give the answer much faster than the individual can do it, even with a calculator. How does that work?

8.19. Mnemonic to remember division by zero: $\frac{O}{K}$ and $\frac{N}{O}$. Describe other mnemonics for remembering fraction rules.

8.20. Try the Fraction Squares Game (adapted from Ortiz, 2000) with middle school students using the game board (Fig. 8.19) and game rules for addition version. Make some annotations of the students' work as they use the game.

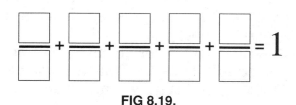

FIG 8.19.

1	1	2	2	4	4	8	8
1	1	2	2	4	4	8	8
1	1	2	2	4	4	8	8
1	1	2	2	4	4	8	8
1	1	2	2	4	4	8	8
1	1	2	2	4	4	8	8

FIG 8.20.

a. Number of Players: Two to four individual players, or teams of two to three players.

b. Materials: 40 game pieces (see Fig. 8.20) and fraction kit (optional). This provides game pieces for halves, fourths, and eighths, and enough game pieces for four players or teams. You need 10 game pieces per player or team. Copy and enlarge this page on cardboard and cut each.

c. Place the game pieces face down in front of the players for round 1 of the game.

d. Each player (or team of players) takes turns randomly selecting 10 game pieces each.

e. After selecting the game pieces, use as many of your game pieces to form fractions that add up to one (1) on the game board (see Fig. 8.19). You will earn one point for each game piece that you use correctly. The more game pieces you use the more points you earn. There may be many possible correct combinations that can be played during a given round, but you may only play one of the possible combinations of the game pieces to add up to one whole. For example, if you use 1, 1, 2, and 2 out of your selected game pieces to form $\frac{1}{2} + \frac{1}{2} = 1$, then you will earn 4 points for this round.

f. (Optional) You may use a fraction kit or Cuisenaire rods to represent one whole,

TABLE 8.3

Name/Team	Round 1	Round 2	Round 3	Round 4	Final Scores
1.					
2.					
3.					
4.					

halves, fourths, and eighths, to help you find the best possible answer.

g. After deciding your choice for the first round, count the number of game pieces that you were able to use, and record your points for round 1 of the game in the scoring table (see Table 8.3). Every player or team should have a turn.

h. After every player or team has had a chance to play, place the game pieces face down, scramble them, and randomly select 10 new game pieces.

i. Record the score for each player or team at the end of the round (see Table 8.3). Repeat the preceding steps for the other three rounds of the game.

j. The player or team with the most points at the end of four rounds wins the game! EXTENSION: Alternative game pieces for thirds, sixths, and twelfths (see Fig. 8.21) could be used instead of or in combination with the game pieces illustrated in Fig. 8.20, and game board for subtraction (see Fig. 8.22).

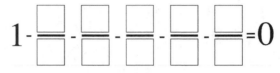

FIG 8.22.

8.21. Each of the following set of problems involving whole numbers is done incorrectly the same way. Determine the error pattern, solve the fourth and fifth problems using that pattern, describe it in your own words, indicate possible reasons for the error, and describe ways to help the student overcome the misconception. (For more information on error patterns, see Ashlock, 1998.)

a.

$$
\begin{array}{ccccc}
23 & 64 & 27 & 82 & 34 \\
+4 & +5 & +4 & +9 & +6 \\
\hline
9 & 15 & 13 & &
\end{array}
$$

b.

$$
\begin{array}{ccccc}
38 & 52 & 27 & 64 & 81 \\
+47 & +83 & +39 & +59 & +28 \\
\hline
715 & 135 & 516 & &
\end{array}
$$

c.

$$
\begin{array}{ccccc}
 & 1 & 4 & & \\
342 & 74 & 385 & 282 & 279 \\
+631 & +43 & +667 & +723 & +836 \\
\hline
973 & 18 & 9116 & &
\end{array}
$$

d.

$$
\begin{array}{ccccc}
32 & 245 & 524 & 458 & 241 \\
-16 & -137 & -298 & -372 & -96 \\
\hline
24 & 112 & 374 & &
\end{array}
$$

1	1	3	3	6	6	1	1
1	1	3	3	6	6	1	1
1	1	3	3	6	6	1	1
1	1	3	3	6	6	1	1
1	1	3	3	6	6	1	1
1	1	3	3	6	6	1	1

FIG 8.21.

e.

```
  578      479      554      195      355
+ 179    + 578    + 256    + 589    + 256
  647      947      700
```

f.

```
 8 17     6 16     7 14
19 7↗    17 6↗    38 4↗     273      385
-4 3     -2 3     -5 9      - 51     - 39
1414     1413     32 5
```

g.

```
 8         2          51216
19 1↗     3 25↗      7 2 6↗     638      638
- 43      -1 51      -3 4 9     - 349    - 129
 443       174        2 8 7
```

h.

```
  2
 23      53      28      45      48
+39     +26     +45     +35     +36
 71      79      91
```

i.

```
 313      210      524      135      345
 × 4      × 15     × 34     × 463    × 36
1252      210     1576
```

j.

```
32      42      31      23      42
× 3     × 4     × 8     × 3     × 3
 6       8       8
 9      16      24
15      24      32
```

k.

```
34      27      18      24      35
× 2     × 4     × 3     × 4     × 3
68      88      34
```

l.

```
27      43      62      38      28
× 5     × 6     × 7     × 6     × 5
255     308     494
```

m.

```
  233      221      231
2)176    4)824    3)713    3)639    4)518
```

n.

```
  33        25        78
3)99      7)364     8)696     4)192     6)528
  90        35        64
   9        14        56
   9        14        56
   0         0         0
```

8.22. Each of the following sets of problems involving fractions is done incorrectly the same way. Determine the error pattern, solve the fourth and fifth problems using that pattern, describe it in your own words, indicate possible reasons for the error, and describe ways to help the student overcome the misconception (for more information on error patterns, see Ashlock, 1998).

a.

$$\frac{4}{5} + \frac{1}{2} = \frac{5}{7} \qquad \frac{1}{4} + \frac{1}{4} = \frac{2}{8} \qquad \frac{1}{6} + \frac{3}{4} = \frac{4}{10} \qquad \frac{3}{4} + \frac{1}{3} = \qquad \frac{5}{8} + \frac{1}{9} =$$

b.

$$\frac{1}{2} = \frac{2}{4} \qquad \frac{1}{3} = \frac{3}{9} \qquad \frac{3}{5} = \frac{6}{10} \qquad \frac{1}{7} = \qquad \frac{1}{5} =$$
$$+\frac{1}{4} = \frac{2}{4} \qquad +\frac{2}{3} = \frac{6}{9} \qquad +\frac{1}{10} = \frac{2}{10} \qquad +\frac{3}{14} = \qquad +\frac{5}{6} =$$
$$\frac{4}{4} = 1 \qquad \frac{9}{9} = 1 \qquad \frac{8}{10} = \frac{2}{5}$$

c.

$$3\frac{1}{2} = \frac{3}{6} \qquad 2\frac{2}{5} = \frac{4}{10} \qquad 8\frac{1}{4} = \frac{5}{20} \qquad 5\frac{1}{6} \qquad 3\frac{1}{5}$$
$$+2\frac{1}{3} = \frac{2}{6} \qquad +8\frac{2}{10} = \frac{2}{10} \qquad +7\frac{3}{5} = \frac{12}{20} \qquad +3\frac{3}{12} \qquad +2\frac{3}{6}$$
$$\frac{5}{6} \qquad \frac{6}{10} \qquad \frac{17}{20}$$

d.

$$\frac{1}{8} \times 1 = \frac{1}{8} \qquad \frac{2}{3} \times 3 = \frac{6}{9} \qquad \frac{4}{5} \times 2 = \frac{8}{10} \qquad \frac{3}{9} \times 4 = \qquad \frac{1}{9} \times 5 =$$

e.

$$\frac{2}{3} \times \frac{3}{5} = 90 \qquad \frac{1}{5} \times \frac{3}{4} = 60 \qquad \frac{2}{3} \times \frac{2}{5} = 60 \qquad \frac{3}{6} \times \frac{1}{7} = \qquad \frac{5}{6} \times \frac{3}{7} =$$

8.23. Each of the following sets of problems involving decimals is done incorrectly the same way. Determine the error pattern, solve the fourth and fifth problems using that pattern, describe it in your own words, indicate possible reasons for the error, and describe ways to help the student overcome the misconception (for more information on error patterns, see Ashlock, 1998).

a.

```
  0.3      0.4      0.4      0.5      0.9
+ 0.9    + 0.7    + 0.8    + 0.6    + 0.9
 0.1 2    0.1 1    0.1 2
```

b.

```
 3.6 9    5.3 2    7.1 8    8.9 7    6.3 4
-  2.8   -  4.3   -  3.5   -  5.8   -  4.3
   1.1      1.9      4.3
```

c.

```
   4 12     6 12     4 14
  .5.3.2    7.22     5.34     7.67     9.85
- 0.08    - 0.06   - 0.09   - 0.08   - 0.08
  4.34      6.26     4.35
```

d.

```
  2.7      8.36     0.765     4.64     5.65
× 0.6    ×  6     × 2.6     × 0.5    ×  7
 16.2     50.16     4590
                    1530
                   19.890
```

e.

```
    0.543      9.062     27.871
6)3.27     4)36.26    3)83.62    4)78.65    5)78.68
  30          36          6
  27          26         23
  24          24         21
   3           2         26
                         24
                         22
                         21
                          1
```

REFERENCES

Ashlock, Robert. (1998). *Error patterns in computation.* Upper Saddle River, NJ: Prentice Hall.

Brumbaugh, D. K., Rock, D., Brumbaugh, L. S., & Rock, M. (2003). *Teaching K-6 mathematics.* Mahwah, NJ: Lawrence Erlbaum Associates.

Burns, M. (2003). *Teaching arithmetic: Lessons for extending fractions, Grade 5.* Sausalito, CA: Math Solutions Publications.

Heddens, J., & Spears, W. (2001). *Today's mathematics.* New York: John Wiley & Sons.

NCTM. (2000). *Principles and standards for school mathematics.* Reston, VA: Author.

Ortiz, E. (2000). A game involving fractions. *Teaching Children Mathematics*, 7(4): 218–222.

9
Measurement

Measurement grew out of necessity. Early on, as property ownership developed, there was a need to know how much ground was being dealt with. The standard units of measure we use today have evolved over many years. Early measurements were based on human anatomy, making standardization problematic. Tailors once measured cloth using the distance from the tip of one outstretched hand to the center of the chest as a unit. Who would you hire, a tailor with long or short arms? The cubit (length from elbow to longest fingertip) was common to several cultures. The Egyptian Royal Cubit, used to build the pyramids, was 20.63 inches, whereas the Greek Olympic Cubit was 18.93 inches. There was a need for standardization.

You can count discrete objects, but measuring involves a continuous property. You need a measurable attribute (a characteristic that can be quantified by comparing it to a unit, directly or indirectly) of an object or event: length (direct), area (direct), mass (indirect), or time (indirect). The process, however, is the same for each attribute: the measuring unit is chosen and the object or event is compared to this unit. The end result is a number and a unit: 23 km, 3.5 hours, 45 inches, 9 m^2, 64 cm^3, 90°, 5 cups, and so on. Measurement is always a reasonable approximation. Improving the selection of instruments and measuring process increases accuracy and precision, subject to the skills of the individual using them. In middle school, students should be familiar with the ruler (length), pan balance (mass), graduated beaker (capacity), protractor (angles), thermometer (temperature), and clock (both analog and digital for time).

Measurement is a fun topic to work with because there are so many things that can be done to involve students. How big? How far? How long? How heavy? How much? These are all questions your students will have heard and asked. Each of these questions and all the related ones come naturally out of their world. What an invitation for you to pique their interest in getting answers to their questions, and by engaging them with the wonderful world of mathematics.

Did you notice "their world" in the last paragraph? Some of the exercises and activities teachers ask students to do fit nicely into a discussion of the concept at hand, but can be a turn-off for students. For example, there is a problem about a kid who sees 36 animal legs in a barnyard. It is known that there are only pigs and chickens involved and there are at least 2 of each animal. The question asks how many of each animal could be present. Although this is a nice problem-solving situation that provides a set of answers, the context is not sensible for a lot of students. The quick logic of many students would be to count the number of each animal type and be done with it. If you can see the legs, you can see the animal; that would be the basic mentality. That makes sense. Thus, many students write the problem off as being dumb and another exposure to mathematics becomes a turn-off, or joke to them. It is imperative that the exercises and activities come from the student world as much as possible. Experiencing measurement can be fun!

READINESS

By the time they come to you in middle school, the students should be at the operational stage as described by Piaget. That is, they should be conserving length, for example. Visualize two wooden pencils, both of which have been sharpened. Are they the same length? Assuming they are not, Fig. 9.1 shows how they would be placed

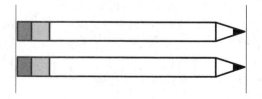

FIG 9.1.

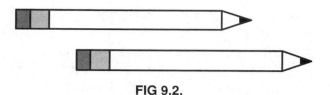

FIG 9.2.

as the student agrees they are the same length after the longer one is sharpened to be shorter. The vertical line segments are there to help confirm the agreement as to the pencils being the same length. The discussion involves the student agreeing the pencils are the same length.

While the student is looking at the configuration in Fig. 9.1, one of the pencils is moved to create Fig. 9.2, as shown. After the movement, the student is asked if these pencils are the same length. Words like "still" are omitted from this new question. The verbiage should be the same or parallel to that used with the initial discussion. Students who are conserving length will agree the pencils are still the same length, often commenting that movement does not impact their length.

Nonconservers would say that the lengths of the pencils are no longer the same. A transitional conserver will think there is something going on, not believing what is perceived, and need a closer look (maybe by taking the pencils and comparing them). To conservers, that last sentence seems preposterous. We are conservers of length and it is difficult to imagine how someone could conclude that the motion changed the length of the pencils. Most, if not all, middle schoolers are functional conservers. That simplifies the options for measurement activities.

Although we have discussed only conservation of length, similar activities exist for determining if students are conserving things like area, volume, and weight. You need to be sure your students are ready for the things you are asking them to do.

For example, suppose a student is not conserving length. Asking for a 4.5-foot board to be measured using a foot-long ruler is an impossible task because when the ruler is moved, to the nonconserving student, the length changes. Essentially you are asking that the measurement be made with a rubber ruler. Does that make sense?

Your students will have participated in measurement activities before they arrive at middle school. More than likely, they will have measured lengths with paper clips, pencils, hand spans, and so on, as preliminary events to show the need for standard units. By the time you see them in class, they will probably be convinced of the need for standardization. As you deal with inch-foot-pound and metric systems of measure, you might encounter the, "My mind is made up, don't confuse me with facts" attitude. You are going to need to be a salesperson for metric, so you better prepare for battle.

NEED FOR MEASUREMENT

Seeley (2004), in her National Council of Teachers of Mathematics President's message said, "[W]e can raise the bar on mathematical proficiency by choosing fewer topics to focus on at each grade level and by teaching those topics in greater depth" (p. 3). That statement leads one to ask what topics get selected. Measurement has to be one of them because there are too many unanswered questions in the student world if that part of the curriculum does not get adequate focus. It could be said that the students will get that later, but when?

Two people were measuring to cut a board. One read the ruler as "3 little marks past the 7 mark." What does that mean? The answer to that one depends on how many marks are between the 7 and 8 mark. Are we talking inch-foot-pound or metric systems? If we are using inch-foot-pound, did that mean sixty-fourths, thirty-seconds, sixteenths, eighths, or quarter inches? If we are talking metric, are we talking centimeters? Although rare, we could be talking inches divided into tenths (see engineer scales on some rulers). Would you want something made by the person who said "3 little marks past the 7 mark" if a consideration is accuracy?

Measurement questions start early in life and continue. "How many do you have?" starts initially and may refer to dolls, toy trucks, blocks, or a multitude of other objects. In middle school the focus could be on CDs, a brand of shirt, concert tickets, or who knows what. You soon will be asked how many classes you teach, how many students are in each class, the total number of students you have this year, the percentage of Fs in a marking period, and on and on. Other adult questions could be:

- How many years have you been teaching?
- How long before you retire?
- How many years have you been retired?
- How many siblings do you have?
- How many kids do you have?
- How many miles do you run a week?
- Etc., etc., etc.?

Think of the conversations you had yesterday. How many "how many" questions did you deal with, either as an initiator or as a respondent?

There are other basic questions that could have been used in that last paragraph:

- What time does ___ start?
- How far is it to ___?
- How fast does your ___?
- How long is your skateboard, ski, ___?

- What size (diameter) is your bike wheel, ___?
- How many ___ did you score?
- How big is your ___?
- How many days do we get off school because of ___?
- How much can ___ lift?
- How much will ___ hold?
- How much is in your ___ account?

There are more, but look at that list. Many of those questions arise from when your students were preschoolers. The object of the statement may change as a function of age, but the basic question continues through adulthood. For example, the collectibles could be stuffed animals or toy cars for a youngster, CDs for teenagers, and (baseball) cards, stamps, coins, motor cycles, old cars, and so on for adults. Measurement is everywhere.

When you hear "measurement," what topics do you think of? Length, width, height, area, volume, and weight are reflexive for most people. After some thought you will hear things like miles per hour, time, and money. Go back to length. That raises a natural question: are we talking inch-foot-pound or metric? Whereas a centimeter is about a half an inch, a meter is just a little longer than a yard, so not only do we need to know what system we are using, but the basic reference within that system. Confusion anywhere along that last sentence could mean dramatically different results. Talk about confusion; when we weigh something, are we really massing it?

Regardless of the system or question within it, measurement needs to be a focal topic within the curriculum, particularly at the middle school. Although your students will have encountered many of the basic topics, there will be a need for refinement. Right angles will have been defined by the time they come to middle school. They may have seen acute, obtuse, and maybe even straight angles by the time they meet you in middle school. With you, they will expand to measuring angles with a protractor to 180° and beyond.

The angle extension could be said for any other measurement topic. The point is, that measurement is needed to function in our daily world. We cannot focus on all topics so we will select some that are central to generate some thoughts for you. It is your responsibility to expand your horizons and those of your students by adding measurement topics to the list that are appropriate for your classes.

Your Turn

9.1. Describe how you would help students understand angle measure that exceeds 180°.

9.2. If you had the power to determine what measurement concepts would be focal points in the middle school curriculum, what would you list and why?

INCH-FOOT-POUND

Confusion was mentioned close to the end of the last section. The inch-foot-pound system has a bit of potential confusion built in. There are 16 ounces in a pound and 32 ounces in a quart. Pound is dry measure (avoirdupois) and the quart is liquid measure. You probably knew that. Did you know that both apothecary and troy pounds are 12 ounces? Wait a minute. Minute! Do you mean degree measure or do you mean time? Typically "wait a minute" refers to time, but it could refer to a shadow moving through angle measure as you are discussing the rate of spinning of the earth as we rotate about the sun. Did you know that a mil in the inch-foot-pound system refers to 0.001 inches? What is the difference between a long ton and a short ton? What is a grain (no, we are not talking sand here)? How many pennyweights in an ounce? Do you have scruples? No, we are not talking the conscience-type stuff here, but you should have those too! Wow, this is all getting pretty confusing.

Check out the inch-foot-pound system and you will find liquid and dry ounces, long and short tons, mils, drams, scruples, pennyweights, and a lot more. You probably knew some of the things we have mentioned and you probably did not know some of the things we have mentioned as units of measure in the inch-foot-pound system. What is the message here? We have used the inch-foot-pound system for years in the United States. What is the history of that system?

After we gained our independence from England, they, along with Canada, were our main trading partners. Thus, we used the same system they did, long called the English system. Since England now uses the metric system of measure, if we call our inch-foot-pound system English, what do we mean? Whoa more confusion! Typically, any measurement system that used body parts as reference points at the beginning, eventually became standardized. In the inch-foot-pound system, the distance from the tip of the thumb to the first thumb joint was an inch (some say it was the width of the thumb, while others say it was the length of 3 barleycorns, whatever they are). The foot was the length of the foot, some saying it was the king's foot. Either way, the foot evolved to be longer than most feet. Hhhmmm, that sounded confusing too, didn't it? The yard was the distance from the end of the nose to the tip of the middle finger on an outstretched hand, with the arm held straight out to the side. That eventually became defined as being 3 feet.

The whole system seems poorly defined and in disarray. Although there is not traceable documentation, it appears as if Henry I (1100–1135) of England standardized the inch (3 barleycorns), foot (36 barleycorns), and yard (108 barleycorns). Ironically, the yard was rumored to be the distance from King Henry's nose to the tip of his middle finger when he held his arm straight out. And so the story goes for all the other units of measure in the English (inch-foot-pound) system. Eventually the English Parliament, over the period of a couple hundred years, standardized all measurements into what we now know them to be. You can find detailed descriptions of the measurements and history of their development at several locations. Good ones to start with are:

http://regentsprep.org/Regents/math/
meteng/LesEng.htm
http://www.unc.edu/~rowlett/units/
custom.html
http://www.bartleby.com/65/en/
English-u.html.

Your Turn

9.3. Investigate the inch-foot-pound system of measure. List at least three units of measure you had not heard of, along with their definitions.

9.4. What is the connection between pace, rod, furlong, and stadium (stadia)?

9.5. Describe the historical development of 16-ounce and 12-ounce pounds.

9.6. Describe the history of the long and short ton and the connection with the metric ton, which is used as the standard for most shipping today.

9.7. Describe the history of the defining of a gallon.

Inch-foot-pound units are cumbersome because of all the strange connections and varied definitions. Still, these units are rich in cultural significance. They are a part of our mathematical and developmental history, deserving of consideration in our curriculum. Our 21st-century economy will probably go metric, but some vestiges of the inch-foot-pound system will surely linger. A centimeter will be about a half an inch, a meter will be a little more than a yard, a kilometer will be about two thirds of a mile, and so on. Both systems (metric and inch-foot-pound) still need to be presented to the students.

METRIC

The U.S. Metric Association, Inc. (USMA; www.metric.org) was founded in 1916. USMA advocates conversion to the International System of Units, called SI, which is also called the modern metric system. International trade uses SI along with product standards and preferred sizes accepted throughout the world.

The United States signed the 1875 Treaty of the Meter, which established, among other things, the International Bureau of Weights and Measures. Law in the United States authorized metric measure in 1866. Yet today, the United States is the only industrially developed nation, that has not established a national policy to facilitate conversion to the metric system.

World trade uses the metric system of measurement. U.S. industries that have international dealings are often compromised because of measurement deviations. They can be, and often are, excluded from business consideration when they cannot deliver goods measured in metric terms.

Some U.S. industries (automobile and beverage container, for example) discovered that changing to metric causes rethinking of production and takes advantage of size standardization. Redundant products are eliminated, interchangeability of parts is increased, and resource streamlining comes into play. The shift can stimulate examination and reevaluation of other business practices, often causing an economic wake-up call.

One immediate objection to shifting to metric is cost. It is expensive to retool an operation, but there is also a long-term cost in not switching resulting from lost business opportunities if metric units are required. Since 1975, some of our trading partners (England, Canada, Australia, and China, for example) have converted to metric and they want products shipped to them that are metric because of their switch. Exporting is only part of the picture. Products designed in one country may be produced in another and sold in a third. These products must be compatible with systems anywhere in the world.

Here in the United States, both metric and inch-foot-pound units are used. Thus, it is imperative that both systems be taught. Although there are many examples of it, we do not support converting between metric and inch-foot-pound units. Do it in the unit you want, and be done with it.

Measurement begs for activities and applications. Here are some things that have students use the metric system and have fun at the same time. You could also use similar activities with inch-foot-pound units. The neat thing is that, with the activities, they will be learning and not realize it. You could have a Metric Olympics event, which might be a collection of linear activities, or it may involve other arenas. If you decide to do all linear events, your imagination is the limit.

Standing long jump has a team of three or four students participating against other teams with the same number of participants. Put several meter sticks end to end on the floor in an open area. The first person stands with both toes on a line segment that is perpendicular to the beginning end of the meter sticks. The person does a standing long jump, landing on both feet (two-foot take-off and two-foot landing). That jump is measured by the official and announced. Suppose it is 2.1 m, for sake of discussion. The next person, who needs some recognition, starts at the point where the first person landed and jumps. This jump is announced to be 180 cm, which sounds a lot bigger than the first one. We know the real truth, but this might be a positive stroke for this student. Continue until all team members have jumped and than announce the total of all the jumps. Once all teams have competed, the winner is announced, determined by the largest total.

A second linear event can be total team foot length. If the number of members of each team is different, each team should select some people to go twice to equalize things. Participants stand heel to toe and the total foot length is determined. Decisions about shoes on and off are to be determined before the event starts. Prior to the event, you need to write shortest somewhere so that, after the event ends, you can announce that the shortest team total wins the event. This helps compensate for a team with all long legs (that usually are paired with bigger feet), thus giving all teams a better chance of winning the competition.

A punt, pass, and kick contest provides ample opportunities for measuring distances. A straight line segment, longer than participants can launch the ball, is established in an open area. The contestant punts, passes, or kicks the ball. The landing site of the ball is marked. If it is off the established line segment, a perpendicular from the point of impact to the segment is established. The point of intersection of the segment and the perpendicular becomes the radius center of an arc, which is marked toward the starting point. The intersection of the arc and the segment is the point used to establish the distance the ball traveled. The longest distance wins each event. The three measures could be totaled to establish a fourth winner.

Paper airplanes could be used along the same lines as the punt, pass, and kick contest. This capitalizes on the pastime of students as they make planes. Rules about weighted noses would need to be established.

Suppose there is an 8-lane 400-meter track around a football field. There are 8 contestants in a 400-meter race on the track. To make the race fair, there must be a staggered start, meaning that the person in the second lane from the inside appears to start in front of the person in the innermost lane. That stagger ensures that, if each of the 8 contestants stays in the assigned lane, they will all run 400 meters and a straight segment across the track can serve as the finish line. How far should each lane's starting point be ahead of that of the innermost lane to ensure that all runners travel the same distance?

Each end of the track is a semicircle. If the straight sections are each 110 meters long, there are 180 meters for the circumference of the circle formed by the two semicircles. Lane distances are measured at the inside edge. What is the radius of the curve to make the 180-meter circumference of the inside lane?

$$C = 2\pi r$$

$$180m = (2)\left(\frac{22}{7}\right) r$$

$$r = \left(\frac{(7)(180 \text{ m})}{(2)(22)}\right)$$

where $r \approx 28.64$ m, the radius of the inside edge of the inside lane. If a lane is 1 meter wide, the radius of the inside edge of the second lane would be approximately 29.64 meters long. That would make the circumference of the circle defined by the inner edge of the second lane from the inside to be $(2)\left(\frac{22}{7}\right)(29.64 \text{ m})$, or approximately 186.3 m. Thus, the stagger for the start sets the second lane starting point approximately 6.3 m ahead of that of the innermost lane. Each subsequent lane stagger

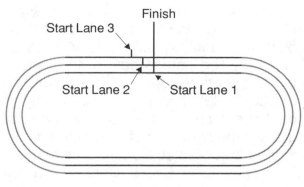

FIG 9.3.

will be about 6.3 m in front of the one on the lane immediately inside it. In the real world, the approximation would be removed from the discussion. Figure 9.3 shows the first three starting positions.

The activities done by the students do not have to be linear. For area, place a tennis-ball-sized chunk of soft clay close to the center of a sheet of centimeter grid paper. Have two members of a team each hit the ball one time, spreading it out. The second person would follow the first by spreading more than the first person had done. Trace the outer edge of the shape defined by the spread clay. Each team repeats the spreading and tracing process. There are three ways to get the area. Count all the full squares covered. Count each square touched. Count all the full squares and then combine the partial squares to generate the total number of full squares that are covered. Each method has advantages and disadvantages.

For volume, use a box and centimeter cubes. The box will probably be larger than the number of centimeter cubes you have, but that is OK. The length, width, and height of the interior of the box can be determined by the number of cubes that fit along each of the respective dimensions. The product of those measures gives the volume of the interior of the box.

There are other activities, but these should get you started. The important thing

is that you provide opportunities for students to use measurement. These activities show the different units in memorable settings and can be used for introduction, development, or review.

Your Turn

9.8. Investigate SI and present at least three rules that you did not know.

ESTIMATION

Check the driver's license manual for your state and you will find a statement that says you should start your turn signal 100 feet from where you plan to turn. Assuming you use your turn signal, how likely is it that you do it 100 feet from the point of turning? Most of us are lousy estimators.

Select the top-right corner and the diagonally opposite bottom-left corner in the room you are in (if you are not in a right rectangular parallelepiped [box] alter those instructions accordingly). ESTIMATE the distance between the two selected points before you measure. Estimate means just that. Do not count the number of ceiling tiles long and wide the room is and then calculate (this is approximating). Do not pace the length and width of the room. Just estimate that diagonal length. However, you can use referents (estimating another person's height by using your known height as a referent), chunking (estimating the area of a classroom by first mentally breaking the area into several workable parts), and unitizing (estimating the volume of a jar by mentally dividing it in smaller, equal glasses) as strategies for estimation. If you are in your classroom, compare your estimate with those of your peers. You might find a wide range of results. If you are interested, you could measure the diagonal using a piece of string, or compute it using the Pythagorean theorem. Either way, it is likely that your estimate was far from the actual length.

Estimation is a skill that comes in handy when measuring. It is a good idea to ask students to estimate before they measure in a given unit. This will help them internalize their understanding of the unit and develop visualization and perception skills. Furthermore, they could be challenged to predict the effects of using a larger or smaller unit. This will allow students to experiment with the inverse relationship between the size of the unit and the number of units used to measure the object. Ask them to verbalize the differences: How can two different answers be correct?

LENGTH

Almost anything can be used as a linear measuring unit (standard or nonstandard). You could express the length of this book in paper clips. A standardization problem would result if you used large paper clips and someone else used small ones. Activities like using paper clips for linear measure remind us how critical it is to provide two pieces of information when measuring—how many and what unit.

Whether using metric or inch-foot-pound for linear measure, precision becomes an issue. It is not necessary to put the zero part of a ruler at one end of the item to be measured, although it is convenient. The length to be measured can be located anywhere along the rules. Subtract the smaller from the larger reading to get the length. That makes using the zero mighty appealing. Be careful because some rulers have zero at the edge, whereas on others it is indented. Thus, the precision mandates that you know the tool. After that, the task at hand will dictate the precision level.

You know, and your students will know too, that linear measure means deter-

mining how long something is (usually a straight object, but not necessarily) or how far it is between two points (assumed to be straight). The natural outgrowth of those ideas is perimeter, the distance around an object. Would, "find the sum of the lengths of all the sides" be an appropriate way to discuss the perimeter of a triangle? Would that be an acceptable definition for finding the perimeter of a rectangle? How about any polygon? Is there a need for formulas? The fewer formulas we ask students to memorize, the more we can expect them to retain. Perimeter as the distance around an object is what we want understood. Isn't $P = 2L + 2W$ just a shortcut for finding the distance around a rectangle? Would it be bad to use $P = L + L + W + W$? Is it acceptable to use $P = 2(L + W)$? What about $P = W + L + W + L$ or $L + W + L + W$? How many formulas for the same thing do we need?

The distance around a circle is the circumference, or the product of the circle's diameter and the constant pi (π). Unfortunately, the formula $C = \pi d$ does not give any insight into how the circumference is determined. It also does not tell us where that strange number π came from.

A classic activity has students using a measuring device (ruler, meter or yard stick), string, calculator, and a variety of right circular cylinders. The task is to measure the circumference of each of the circular objects, not an easy thing to do with a ruler. One way to solve the dilemma is to wrap a string around the object and then measure that. A more uncommon approach is to mark a spot on the object and roll it along a smooth flat surface until that spot touches and, when it touches again, measure the distance between the touch points. Students should record each circumference in a table. The diameter still needs to be determined and there are a couple ways to do that. Using a string or ruler, determine the greatest distance across the circular end of the cylinder and record it. Placing the circular end of the cylinder between two cereal boxes on a smooth flat surface can enhance accuracy. Measuring the distance between the facing sides of the two boxes yields the diameter. Finally, divide the circumference of each object by its diameter, rounding the result to the nearest hundredth.

Students should look for similarities and differences in the calculations. Most results will be close to 3.14, a common approximation of π. It is important to notice that the ratios are all close to each other even though the diameters could vary significantly. Why do the ratios differ from each other if π is always the same? It is important to discuss the errors that can occur when measuring: human and lack of precision. Although there are potential errors associated with this activity, students can discover that π remains the same regardless of the circle's diameter.

How could one determine the diameter of a ball? The cereal box idea will work here too, with one variation. As shown in Fig. 9.4, the boxes must be oriented so that the two faces not touching the ball for each box are parallel to each other. With that, the distance between the two boxes is the diameter of the ball.

Hands-on experiences are important when finding the perimeter or circumference, or any linear measure. Those experi-

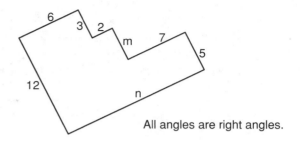

All angles are right angles.

FIG 9.5.

ences will prove beneficial when students encounter designs as shown in Fig. 9.5, where the missing dimensions are to be determined. Such configurations are common on standardized tests. Although often challenging for some, it is generally easier for students to derive a value for n than for m. The sum of 6, 2, and 7 yields n, whereas for m, the sum of 5 and 3 must be subtracted from 12, making it a more complex environment.

Linear measure is an integral part of the mathematics curriculum. Finding the perimeter or circumference of an object is a natural occurrence. We encourage you to seize the opportunity to put a little action into your students' learning environment by measuring and comparing a variety of objects.

Your Turn

9.9. Rationalize the need for several different formulas for finding the perimeter of a rectangle.

9.10. Does $\frac{22}{7} = \pi$? Explain your reasoning.

AREA

Whereas linear measure is one-dimensional, area is two-dimensional, being concerned with how many square units cover a surface. Square tiles carefully placed and counted can measure area. In real life, we consider area when dealing with hanging

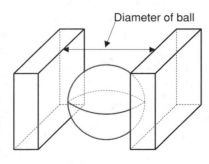

Diameter of ball

FIG 9.4.

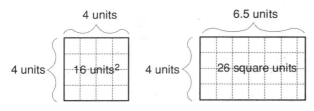

FIG 9.6.

wallpaper, tiling a floor, buying a countertop, carpeting a floor, and wrapping a present or box. It is important that students realize that any plane region that tessellates can be used as a unit but the standard measuring unit is a square with sides equal to one unit. A square inch is much larger than a square centimeter, so again measurement units are just as important as numbers. Some shapes are easily tiled, like the square and rectangle in Fig 9.6, where the action leads to formulas for their area. Although the rectangle is 6.5 units long, this is not overly taxing for most students.

Students' abilities with conservation of area should be taken into account when introducing the concept. A test of conservation of area can involve two same-size squares. After showing both squares to the student, as the student watches, cut one of the squares along a diagonal, rearranging these two pieces to form a triangle or parallelogram. Ask whether the two shapes (the remaining square and the rearranged square) have the same area and why or why not.

Right triangle area is relatively easy to determine out of rectangles. Visualize a rectangular sheet of paper with the appropriate length and width (or base and height) and fold it along the major diagonal. The resultant figure will be the desired triangle. That fold divides the rectangle in half, and so the triangle's area will be half that of the rectangle, giving the formula $A = \dfrac{bh}{2}$, or one of its variations. Notice that

length and width are not used in this common formula, establishing an argument for using base and height for the area of a rectangle. More on that matter later.

Sticking with tiles for now, consider the following triangle and a way to determine its area. Figure 9.7 shows triangle ABC with tiles on it. Determining the area of ABC is not easy, and yet it is not overly difficult. Students may know the triangle area formula, but it is important to be sure they understand its development. Thus, we elaborate on the idea of folding rectangular areas in half to get triangular areas. In this particular case, the first step to determining the area of ABC is to get the area of the surrounding rectangle ADEF, which is 32 square units. With that, areas will be subtracted until the resultant area of the triangle is determined. Rectangle BECG has an area of 8 square units and half of that is outside the triangle, and so 4 square units will ultimately need to be subtracted. Similarly, AHBF has an area of 16 square units, meaning 8 more square units will be subtracted. Finally, rectangle ADCJ has an area of 16 square units, resulting in another 8 square units to be subtracted. In all, 20 square units are subtracted from the area of the bounding rectangle, leaving the area of ABC to be 12 square units. Some students will be troubled by the overlap between rectangles BECG and ADCJ, so be prepared to discuss why that is not

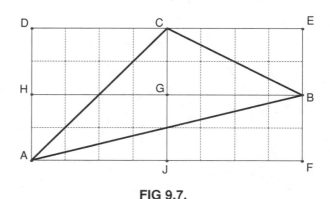

FIG 9.7.

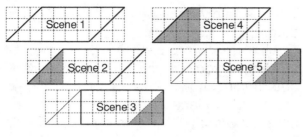

FIG 9.8.

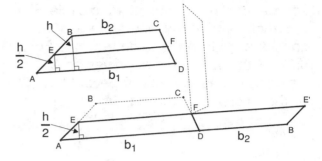

FIG 9.9.

a factor. It should be noted that we did not have a base and height for triangle ABC and yet we were still able to determine its area.

Others shapes are not easy to tile either, like the initial parallelogram in Fig. 9.8, for example. If the students are adept at considering half units in the form of right triangles, computation of the area is not overly demanding. There are other ways to determine the area of the figure. Notice though how the parallelogram in scene 1 can be transformed into a rectangle. Scene 2 marks a triangle at the left tip, which scene 3 shows as transformed to the right side of the parallelogram. Because the triangular area is not changed by the move, the parallelogram is transformed into a rectangle, something readily handled in terms of area. Scene 4 marks a shaded quadrilateral at the left tip, which scene 5 shows as transformed to the right side of the parallelogram. Again, the transformed area does not change with the move and the resultant rectangle has the same area as that of the original parallelogram. The initial parallelogram has three significant dimensions: base, which is typically the bottom segment length when the figure is in standard position; height, which could be shown by any of the perpendicular segments between the base and its parallel side in the initial figure; and the slant height, which is the length of the side of the parallelogram that is oblique to the base. Of those three dimensions, only the base and the height are needed to find the area,

as shown by the transformation of the parallelogram into a rectangle. You should notice how this leads to base times height, or bh, for the parallelogram area formula.

Now consider the Fig 9.9 nonisosceles trapezoid ABCD and focus on how to convert it to a rectangle. Points E and F are midpoints of their respective sides, making segment EF parallel to the bases AD and BC. Using F as a center, trapezoid BCFE can be rotated 180° to create ABE'E, a parallelogram. The parallelogram can be transformed to a rectangle and we are back to that basic shape again. We can determine that the area of the trapezoid must be $(b_1 + b_2)\left(\dfrac{h}{2}\right)$ or $\left(\dfrac{b_1 + b_2}{2}\right)(h)$. Although there are other ways of expressing the formula for the area of a trapezoid, focus on that last one. One of the ways it can be verbalized is "average of the bases times the height."

Using the "average of the bases times the height" idea, look at finding the areas for the Fig. 9.10 rectangle, parallelogram,

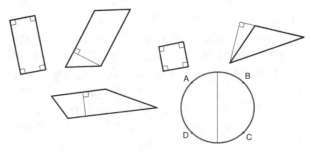

FIG 9.10.

square, trapezoid, triangle, and circle. The rectangle and parallelogram transformations are relatively straightforward. For a square, the area is usually given as $A = s^2$. Using that idea and the trapezoid formula of the average of the bases, the area of a square becomes $\left(\dfrac{side + side}{2}\right)$ (side) $= \left(\dfrac{2\,side}{2}\right)$ (side), which is s^2.

The triangle may seem confusing, but the lower base is the side to which the altitude is drawn and the upper base is the vertex at the other end of the altitude, and has a length of zero. Using the average of the bases times the height, $\left(\dfrac{base + zero}{2}\right)$ (height) $= \dfrac{(base)(height)}{2}$ or $\dfrac{bh}{2}$, the formula for the area of a triangle you have used all along.

The circle area with this one-formula-fits-all approach requires some editorial liberty. For this discussion, the base is a curved line segment, the length of which is one fourth of the circumference of the circle. That is, for this example, the length of arc AB = the length of arc CD = 0.5π. The diameter, or height in this case, will be 2r. Using the average of the bases times the height $\left(\dfrac{0.5\pi r + 0.5\pi r}{2}\right)$ (2r) $= \left(\dfrac{\pi r}{2}\right)$ (2r), which is πr^2, the formula you have grown to know and love.

Are you thinking, "Why didn't someone show me this before?" "Why don't we teach this method in the schools?" The easy answer involves preparation to get to the level where a student understands the average of the bases formula. Some are confused by the algebra involved. Before applying the formula, areas of rectangles and parallelograms have to be considered. Once those are done, is it reasonable to return to them and give a different formula? This average of the bases formula is rather obscure in the literature and not well known.

That certainly contributes to why it is not taught.

All of the discussion so far came out of tiling a region with unit squares and determining how many of them covered the area. A piece of grid paper or transparency with unit squares on it could also be used by placing it on top of the figure in question and applying processes similar to those discussed thus far for finding area. A geoboard could also be used to build the figures and then determine the area from there. With any of these mediums, the right angles in the tiles or grids remind us that the heights and bases used in algorithms must be perpendicular to one another. Your estimating skills may come in handy for finding some of these areas.

Why use square units to measure area? Typically people say, "because they fit so well into the figures being measured." That is true with rectangles, for sure. The previous discussion provides insight into how square units work for most polygons. But, could we not use rectangles as our basic unit of area measure? How about right triangles because they come out of rectangles? Certainly a plane could be tessellated with equilateral triangles so they too could be used as a unit of area measure. At this point you might be saying, yeah, but a square still works better. How well do squares cover circles? The circles in Fig. 9.11 are congruent. Even with the smaller unit squares, the fit is not always good.

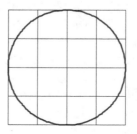
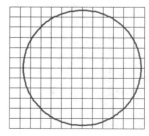

FIG 9.11.

Look at the bottom of a container for a 6-, 12-, or 24-pack of drinks. The boundaries form a rectangle and circles will cover it. That is a reversal of covering a circle with squares and yet it seems strange. In either instance there are leftover areas. Why do we use squares as our unit of area measure?

This is a foundational discussion of area. Many of your students will be somewhat comfortable with area, but enhancement and deepening of understanding can still occur in the middle grades. Repetition is good and additional foundation for formal geometry is essential. For example, the following investigation provides students with another view of the formula for the area of a circle, $A = \pi r^2$. What is the area of the square in Fig. 9.12?

Because the radius of the circle is r, the length of each side of the square is 2r, and the area of the square in the middle of Fig. 9.12 is $(2r)(2r) = 4r^2$. Using the squared paper, the area of the square is 100 square units. The area of the circle is less than 100 square units or, saying it another way, it is less than $4r^2$. A reasonable estimate could be that the area of the circle is a bit more than three fourths of the area of the square. Another way of saying it could be that three fourths of the area of the square is covered by the area of the circle.

An interesting activity for determining the area of a circle involves cutting a circle. A convenient central angle is chosen (30°, for example), creating several pie-shaped wedges. The circle is then "unrolled" and interlaced so you have a shape like that

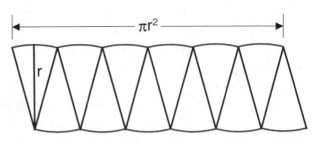

FIG 9.13.

in Fig. 9.13, which approximates a parallelogram. Exploring this leads to the idea that the area of a circle is found by taking the product of half the circumference and the radius, or $\left(\dfrac{\text{circumference}}{2}\right)$ (r), which is $\left(\dfrac{\pi d}{2}\right)$ (r). That can be expressed as $\left(\dfrac{2\pi r}{2}\right)$ (r), or πr^2.

Your Turn

9.11. Rationalize why it would or would not be preferable to use $A = bh$ for the formula for the area of a rectangle rather than $A = lw$.

9.12. Describe how you would help your students understand that the overlap between rectangles ADCJ and AFBH in Fig. 9.7 does not impact the resultant area of triangle ABC.

9.13. Describe your reaction to the average of the "bases times the height" approach for finding areas of so many different figures.

9.14. Why do we use squares as our unit of area measure?

9.15. You are trying to make a decision between buying a large pizza (the diameter is 16 inches) or two small pizzas (the diameter of each is 8 inches). Is one large pizza the same amount as the two small pizzas? (Adapted from Bassarear, 2001.)

VOLUME

We discussed area using a two-dimensional model. Volume can be measured

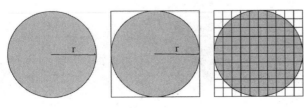

FIG 9.12.

using a three-dimensional model. How many rolls of quarters will it take to exactly fill your sock drawer? You might need to break your unit roll into subunits to completely fill the space but you could get a nonstandard answer. How many cubes will it take to fill a right circular cylinder drink container? You might need to come up with some estimation strategies. As you stuff the cubes in the container, some of them will be out of sight.

Suppose a rectangle is 8 units long and 4 units wide. From the area work, the rectangle would be covered by exactly 32 unit squares. Place a unit cube on each of those squares and a wondrous thing happens. That area rectangle is still visible (the tops of the cubes) but there is now a depth factor. Counting the cubes, rather than the top face of each cube, tells us that the figure has a volume of 32 unit cubes. We have a length of 8 units, a width of 4 units and a height of 1 unit, giving a total of 32 unit cubes. If a second layer of cubes is placed on top of the first, the length is still 8 units, the width is still 4 units, but the height is now 2 units, and we have used 64 unit cubes. A pattern is emerging:

$$32 = 8 \times 4 \times 1$$
$$64 = 8 \times 4 \times 2$$

The model, a right-rectangular-based prism, could be made taller by following this pattern of adding a layer of 32 unit cubes for each unit increase in height. The top faces of the model would still look like the initial rectangle, but the volume would change as a function of the height. A familiar formula may come to mind: $V = l \times w \times h$, where the length times the width is the area of the top face. The terms length, width, and height can be replaced with other terms, such as base, height, and depth, but the idea of three dimensions is the critical issue. You could stand the prism

on the 3×4 side. Now the prism is 8 layers tall, but the volume is still 96 unit cubes. Moving the prism around does not change the measures, so it doesn't matter what we call the three measures. Rather than saying length times width times height, it could be said that the area of the base times the height gives the volume.

Suppose you had a right triangle with a base of 8 and a height of 4. We know its area is half the area of the bounding rectangle. Cover the base squares with cubes and build the figure 3 layers high and you have the right-rectangular-based prism from the preceding paragraph. Now cut that solid with a plane along a major diagonal of the rectangular base, and you end up with a right-triangle-based right prism where the area of the base is half that of the bounding rectangle. But half the area of the bounding rectangular base is the area of the triangular base, so again it could be said that the area of the base times the height gives the volume.

The discussion of area of the base times the height could be developed for other right-polygonal-based prisms. The resultant generalized formula would be $V = Bh$, where the capital B defines the area of the base. Although that is a nice concise formula for a lot of different shapes, the formulas for areas of the respective bases ultimately need to be employed.

All volume problems do not come in right prisms. Figure 9.14 represents the front view of a non-right-rectangular-based prism. The slanted edge is easiest seen at the far left of the figure. The prism

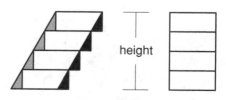

height

FIG 9.14.

is sliced into four congruent pieces that are transformed into rectangles by moving the lighter shaded triangular section to the darker shaded position. The right part of Fig. 9.14, which transforms into a rectangle, is composed of the four slices from the left figure. Thus, the non-right-based prism is transformed into a right-based prism with congruent bases. Because the height is measured perpendicular to the base of both prisms, it is the same. So, using $V = Bh$, the volumes of the two prisms must be equal. This process should convince students that non-right-based prism volume is not too difficult to deal with.

ANGLE MEASURE

About 2000 years ago, the astronomer Claudius Ptolemy divided a full rotation into 360 equal parts, which we now call degrees. Protractors represent only half a rotation and therefore indicate 180°, which is initially sufficient. Later there are discussions of angles with degree measures greater than 180°, and two other units of measure for rotation are introduced: radians and gradients. Also, angles are subdivided into minutes, which are subdivided into seconds. As with any measurement, units are part of the answer so denominate numbers appear in a practical manner.

To use a protractor, such as the one represented in Fig. 9.15, place the wedge of the protractor (the point in the very center on the straight edge) on the vertex of the angle, lining up one leg of the angle with the straight edge of the protractor. The other leg of the angle indicates the number of degrees of rotation. The angle in Fig. 9.15 measures 30°. The arc segments in Fig. 9.15 are 5 apart. Most protractors have 9 smaller segments between each of the 10° segments shown to enable measure of angles to within 1°. Also, many of the straight segments at the bottom of Fig 9.15 are calibrated to function as a ruler.

Right angles are so common in daily life that many people are intrigued when looking at a corner that is not a right angle. Carpenters use an instrument called a square to verify right angles. Mathematics can express the idea as a right angle or by using 90° or perpendicular lines. Acute and obtuse angle definitions depend on knowledge of right angles. A common student error is to read the wrong scale when using a protractor. This tendency is easy to correct with an estimation application. Have the students decide whether an angle appears to be acute, right, obtuse, or straight before measuring. The angle in Fig. 9.15 appears to be acute, but the ray goes through 150° as well as 30°, so which one is correct? Here, 150° does not make sense for an acute angle. In other words, the correct scale is the one that counts up from the initial leg at 0°.

Angles are created by intersecting lines, rays, segments, parallel lines cut by a transversal, and so on. Figure 9.16 shows the eight angles formed when a transversal cuts two parallel lines. Only one measurement provides the information to determine all eight angle sizes. Suppose angle 1 is 35°. Then angles 3, 5, and 7 also measure 35°. Angles 1 and 3 are vertical angles and they have the same measure. Angles 1 and 5 are corresponding angles and they have the same measure. That accounts for four

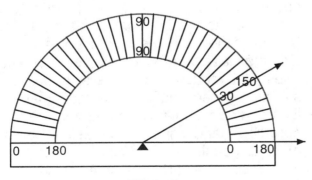

FIG 9.15.

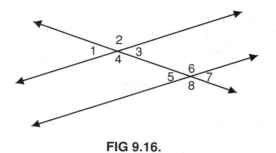

FIG 9.16.

of the eight angles. Angles 1 and 2 are supplementary, making angle 2 measure 145°, which will be the measures of angles 4, 6, and 8.

The sum of the measures of the interior angles of any convex polygon can be determined by sectioning it into triangles. Because the measures of the interior angles of each triangle total 180°, you only need to know how many triangles are involved. For quadrilaterals, which divide into two triangles, the sum of the measure of the interior angles is $2 \times 180° = 360°$. Pentagons divide into three triangles, giving $3 \times 180° = 540°$, for the sum of the measure of the interior angles. Hexagons would give $4 \times 180° = 720°$, and so on. You should notice that, in each case, the multiple of 180° is 2 less than the number of sides in the figure. Thus, a generalization arises out of the pattern: $(n - 2) \times 180°$ = the sum of the measures of the interior angles of an n-gon, where n represents the number of sides in the polygon being considered. Patterning and generalizations can come at you almost anywhere. ☺

DIMENSIONAL ANALYSIS

Sometimes it isn't possible to measure using the units desired for reporting. Using a matchbox car and a ramp, it would not be reasonable to measure speed in miles per hour (mph) because neither the distance traveled nor the time period involved would be great enough for accurate measure. Using dimensional analysis, the average speed of the little car in miles per hour can be determined after measuring the distance in feet and the time in seconds. Dimensional analysis sounds so serious but it is a straightforward application of fraction multiplication and ratios. Here are two formats that are in common usage for determining the mph of the car, assuming it took 0.2 seconds to travel 14 feet of track.

Format A:

$$\frac{14 \text{ ft}}{0.2 \text{ sec}} \times \frac{1 \text{ mi}}{5280 \text{ ft}} \times \frac{60 \text{ sec}}{1 \text{ min}} \times \frac{60 \text{ min}}{1 \text{ hr}}$$

$$= \frac{50400 \text{ mi}}{1056 \text{ hr}} = \frac{47.7 \text{ mi}}{1 \text{ hr}}$$

Format B:

14 ft	1 mi	60 sec	60 min
0.2 sec	5280 ft	1 min	1 hr

$$= \frac{50400 \text{ mi}}{1056 \text{ hr}} = \frac{47.7 \text{ mi}}{1 \text{ hr}}$$

CONCLUSION

We have not covered all measurement topics (time, money, capacity, weight, temperature, and so on). They certainly are a part of your students' lives and deserve consideration. We have opted to leave that as an open-ended opportunity for you as the need arises. Think of life outside the classroom. What are some of the roles that measurement plays in . . . construction? medicine? commerce? manufacturing? accounting? computers? transportation? landscaping? real estate? art? music? cooking? parenting? entertainment? taxes? sports? or other activities? Did you learn to think of measurement in terms of uses as opposed to being a stand-alone concept or skill?

STICKY QUESTIONS

9.1. When is a reasonable time to begin teaching measurement to students?

9.2. If linear measure, area, volume, time, and money are introduced in the elementary school, is there a need to revisit them in the middle school?

9.3. How much measurement is enough?

9.4. Do denominate numbers with measures enhance arithmetic operation understanding? Do they confuse the issue because regroupings are not always based on integral powers of 10 in the inch-foot-pound system?

9.5. Is it reasonable to expect middle school students to be functional in both the metric and inch-foot-pound systems? Why or why not?

9.6. Most people, when asked how far it is from town A to town B, will respond in terms of hours. Why do we do that? Does that kind of a response hinder understanding of linear measure?

TAG

9.1. How do you show 15 minutes with only two hourglasses, one that goes for 7 minutes and one that goes for 11 minutes?

9.2. You have equal volumes of coffee and tea, each in their respective container. A cup of coffee is removed from the coffee container and mixed with the tea. Then, a cup of the mixture is placed in the coffee container, making the volumes equal again. Is there more tea in the coffee or more coffee in the tea?

9.3. There are three sealed envelopes. One contains two $5 bills, one contains a $10 and a $5 bill, and the third contains two $10 bills. Unfortunately, all three envelopes have the wrong amount marked on the outside. How could you correct all three by opening one envelope and looking at only one bill?

9.4. How many 3-cent stamps are there in a dozen?

9.5. A rope ladder hangs over the side of a ship. The rungs are 1 foot apart and the ladder is 12 feet long. The tide is rising at 4 inches an hour. How long will it take before the first 4 rungs of the ladder are underwater?

9.6. Which would you rather have, a trunk full of nickels or a trunk half full of dimes?

9.7. Steve has 3 piles of sand and Mike has 4 piles of sand. All together, how many do they have?

9.8. Given a box with a lid and a 12-inch ruler, how can you measure the distance from a bottom corner to a diagonally opposite top corner, without opening the box? Hint: Do not use mathematical calculations.

9.9. You have 2 ropes and a lighter. Each rope burns in exactly 60 minutes, and not evenly (meaning that some parts of the rope burn faster than other parts). You want to measure 45 minutes—how do you do it?

9.10. Builders spend a lot of time staking out houses. When doing so, they need accurate measurements of lengths and angles. How could you stake out a house that is guaranteed rectangular?

9.11. How can you weigh a car with graph paper and a tire pressure gauge?

9.12. How many lines of symmetry are there for an equilateral triangle, a square, a rectangle, a circle?

9.13. Make a kite. There are all kinds of measurement needs in the production.

9.14. If there are 12 1-cent stamps in a dozen, how many 37-cent stamps are in a dozen?

9.15. How long will it take a mile-long train traveling 40 miles an hour to go through and completely out of a mile-long tunnel?

9.16. Suppose you have 3 bags, 2 of which contain gold weighing 1 ounce per nugget and the third bag containing gold that weighs 1.1 ounce per nugget. How can you determine which bag contains the real gold with only one weighing?

9.17. There is one in every minute, one in each month, two in the next millennium, and yet only one in a million years. What is it?

9.18. What is the next letter in the sequence? S, M, H, D, W, M, _?_

9.19. Two cars travel between two towns that are 200 miles apart. Car A averages 50 mph one way and 40 mph on the return trip. Car B averages 45 mph both ways. Do the cars travel the total distance in the same amount of time?

9.20. A window is a square, one yard on a side. It lets in too much light and so half of it is covered. After the covering, the window is still a yard high and a yard wide but it lets in only half as much light. How can that be?

9.21. How long will it take to cut a 40-yard-long piece of cloth into 40 one-yard-wide pieces if each cut takes a minute?

9.22. You have two U.S. coins that have a total value of $0.35. One of them is not a quarter. How can that be?

9.23. What U.S. coin doubles its value when half is removed?

9.24. How many birthdays does the average person have?

9.25. An XYZ Corp. motorcycle courier was sent from headquarters to pick up a letter at the local airport. The plane was ahead of schedule. An XYZ Corp. bicycle courier started toward headquarters with the letter from the airport. After the bicycle courier had been riding a half hour the two couriers met. The motorcycle courier took the letter and returned to headquarters. The motorcycle courier arrived back at headquarters 20 minutes ahead of the anticipated time. How many minutes early was the plane?

9.26. A simple protractor can be constructed that will help students understand the basic protractor measures. Fold the long edge of a rectangular piece of paper in half. That fold will be a 90° mark. Fold that resultant 90° angle in half by using the midpoint of the initial folded side as a vertex and placing the fold on top of the half-length of the original side of the paper. The ensuing OR subsequent fold will be 45°. The process could continue to 22.5°, but accuracy quickly becomes an issue. Still, a continuance does give an idea of what is happening.

9.27. Congruent circles are cut out of a rectangular piece of metal (see Fig. 9.17) to make lids. What percent of the metal is wasted? Would the answer differ if the size of the circles being used is changed?

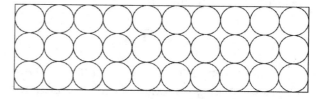

FIG 9.17.

REFERENCES

Bassarear, T. (2001). *Mathematics for elementary school teachers* (2nd ed.). New York: Houghton Mifflin.

Seeley, C. (October, 2004). *NCTM News Bulletin.* Reston, VA: National Council of Teachers of Mathematics.

10
Data Analysis and Probability

Kids know about rolling dice, flipping coins, and drawing cards. They may think they know more than they do about those actions, but they do have a level of familiarity. Thus, students need to see new and different instruments to truly experiment with probability, statistics, and data analysis.

We live in a data-rich world. You encounter opinion polls, statistical reports, and graphs in newspapers, on the radio, and on television. Knowledgeable future citizens for our society must be able to intelligently navigate the sea of information that is put before them. It is likely that you have had a limited exposure to probability, statistics, and data analysis. Furthermore, it is likely that your students will have had little, if any, exposure to much beyond basic flipping coins, rolling dice, drawing cards, and spinners. Thus, the challenge of developing understanding of data analysis, probability, and statistics is a daunting one.

GATHERING DATA

What are data and how are they used? Simply put, data are made up of information. Data are the basis for inferences and generalizations. For projections to be useful, rules need to be followed that ensure the information represents the situation. Faulty assumptions about what the data represent lead to inaccurate, and even worthless, conclusions. Information can be misrepresented accidentally or deliberately. When a sample is used to draw data, sampling bias and size could be other sources of misleading information.

Data can be presented with graphs. However, caution should be exercised when interpreting graphs because information contained therein could also be accidentally or deliberately distorted. Categorical data is presented in a bar graph. This type of data (see Fig. 10.1) places individuals in a category such as boy, girl, blond, brunette, and so on. It makes no sense to average the data and the categories must be kept separated by spaces between bars. What is the average hair color in your class?

Figure 10.2 is a histogram showing numerical data for a group of 20 middle schoolers. There is no space between the bars on a histogram. Numerical data must make sense to average. It would make sense to compute the average height of this group of students. Numbers also represent phone area code, but they are not

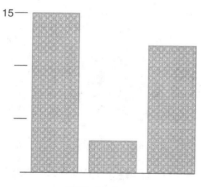

FIG 10.1.

considered numerical data. Does it make sense to find the average area code of U.S. residents?

Figure 10.3 shows a Web site's (http://www.blackholeboards.com) listing of the five most popular selling skateboards. The information is presented in a circle graph, which we made up for this discussion and is not anything constructed or claimed by Blackhole Boards. Exactly what information does the figure provide? Does the size of the sector indicate the proportion of the total sales of these five? Can a number of boards sold be determined from what is provided? For your information, the size of each sector is contrived, essentially saying that the material presented is totally misleading. But, the picture looks realistic, doesn't it?

Suppose you want to know how many middle school students are using each of the five most popular selling complete

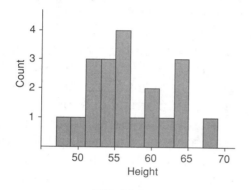

FIG 10.2.

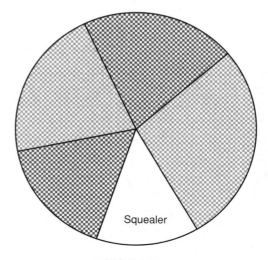

FIG 10.3.

skateboards that Fig. 10.3 shows. How would you determine that? You could not ask all middle school students. First, you need to define a middle school student. Would it be reasonable to survey middle schoolers whose families work for Blackhole Boards? Where and how you gather your information makes a huge difference.

A random sample, which is a representative sample of a population to be used to infer or generalize about the entire population, is one method researchers and statisticians use to gather data. How do you get a random sample? It is not as simple as it sounds because it has to come from the entire population. With the complete skateboards question, we would have to gather all middle school students and then randomly select from that group. However, the information would be outdated each school year. A random sample is not easy to come up with.

Convenience samples are much more common and are often inappropriately defined as random samples because they come from a select group, like all the students at a given school. If we randomly selected from all the middle school students at a given school, we would have a random collection from a convenient population. Although that might give us an idea of how to answer our question, we would not be able to generalize to the entire population. Suppose that the school we used was in an isolated town and the main employer was the company that makes the Blind Slasher skateboard. Is it reasonable to expect many Blackhole Boards products being purchased in that town? More than likely, our convenience sample would give us biased data when it comes to representing the purchasing habits of skateboarders from the entire country.

Data can be gathered by observing your surroundings. How many people in your class wear glasses? Do you count the person with glasses pushed up to the top of their head? What about contact lenses? Maybe that was not so easy. How about observing who is wearing shoes. That sounds simple enough and yet, do you count flip-flops as shoes? How about sandals? It seems like there could be some confusion there, too. Consider long pants and observe who in the class is wearing them. That seems to be something we could gather data on without confusion by what we mean. Oops, what about capri pants? This brings out an important point; when gathering data, be clear on exactly what is wanted. If there are any latitudes for confusion, how useful will the data be?

Four Activities for Gathering Data

These activities are examples of possible investigations that could be done with students. They can work on gathering the data and come up with a report to the whole class (individually or as collaborative groups) about their findings. The instructions and discussions are purposely vague in spots to stimulate flexibility on your part as you work with students. You need to develop the teaching skill of responding spontaneously to unexpected questions. Furthermore, students can be extremely resourceful as they do these activities. Too much instruction and guidance from you hampers that creativity.

1. The Pulse Rate activity (Hynes & Brumbaugh, 1976, pp. 176–177) does exactly what the name suggests. Have the pulse of each student in the class taken by two students of the same gender and two of the opposite gender, recording the gender of the student taking the pulse and the rate obtained. This activity can be used to stimulate discussion in a variety of mathematical topics. Save the data and, when using them, starting the class with a question like, "Remember when we did the pulse rate activity?" will usually create a positive attitude because students traditionally enjoy gathering and analyzing this data.

Most of the time, medical personnel count pulse beats for 15 seconds and multiply by 4 to get the pulse (heartbeats per minute). They could count for 5 seconds and multiply by 12 or 6 seconds and multiply by 10, but that might insert significant error into the results. They could count for a minute, but that takes too much time. So, counting for 15 seconds and multiplying by 4 seems to be a compromise that works well enough. What you just read can be a good set of class discussion points.

After the data are gathered, the results can be used to get things like the average pulse of girls taken by boys, boys taken by girls, girls taken by girls, boys taken by boys, or the entire class. Any of those discussions would have to include what is meant by average pulse rate and whether it makes sense to talk about an average pulse rate for a group. That could lead to comments about normal pulse rates for middle school students and whether there is a different normal pulse rate for girls than for boys. Does physical condition matter? What if soda, coffee, or tea had been ingested not long before the pulse was taken? Would the results vary if the individual had just exercised? What is the pulse rate of your dog, cat, or horse? Do you see where this activity opens a variety of options?

Could any style graph be used to report the data? What statistical information (mean, median, mode, range) would make sense to talk about? Based on the information you gathered, what recommendations would you make to a medical board regarding the pulse-rate-taking practices? Would it be appropriate to do some Internet research into pulse rates? The beat goes on, and on, and on!

2. How Tall (Hynes & Brumbaugh, 1976, pp. 171–173) involves studying the growth rate of beans. In addition to the connection to biology, the opportunity for recording data and developing graphs is extensive. It is best to use 50 to 100 beans to compensate for soil, light, and water conditions and still provide adequate production. Decisions about whether all beans use similar soil, get the same light exposure, get different amounts of water per period of time, and so on all influence the outcome of this activity. Generally three weeks will provide an extensive collection of data and good plant height.

For the sake of this discussion, consider only the height of the plant. How is that measured? Is it read after the longest sprout is stretched as tall as possible, or is it taken only from the highest point as it grows? Would different time intervals between measurements create skewed data? Which graph type (bar graph, circle graph, box plot, and so on) should be used and why? What would you tell a group of farmers about your findings and conclusions on bean planting?

3. Car Pool (Hynes & Brumbaugh, 1976, pp. 177–179) relates to something the stu-

dents may be involved in as they commute between home and school. The media occasionally has commentaries on public transportation and car pools as a means of saving fuel and decreasing traffic. Are individuals changing habits as a result of the urgings to conserve?

Data for this activity can be gathered in a variety of ways. As students are riding on a given day, at a given time, they could be asked to conduct a survey that counts the number of occupants of vehicles. Decisions on what to include or exclude in the survey need to be made. For example, one of the authors of this text drives a Harley Davidson motorcycle, one drives a four-door 1935 Ford Street Rod, and one drives a minivan. Would they all be included? How about pickup trucks (not extended cabs)? How about 18-wheelers? How about buses? As different vehicles are included and excluded, the results could be influenced; that Harley cannot carry as many people as a minivan. Thus, decisions need to be made.

Should you consider the time of day or the location of the survey? What if some students stood by the entrance to the school drop-off zone before school and conducted the survey? Would that generate different results from those gathered at the exit of the school drop-off zone before school? Would rush hour traffic generate results different from those of midday traffic? How about a mall entrance on a Saturday morning as opposed to a factory entrance at shift change time? More decisions! After the decisions have been made, the survey conducted, and the data compiled, how are they presented and reported?

4. Rain Gauge (Hynes & Brumbaugh, 1976, pp. 185–187) uses nature and geography as central events. What does a weather forecast stating a 60% chance of showers mean? Will those showers

blanket the area? Each student should record the rainfall at their home over an established period of time. Perhaps friends in other towns around the country could be convinced to gather data over the same time period. What is the difference in rainfall under a tree and in open ground in the same yard?

Rain gauge results should be recorded daily. After the designated elapsed time, the results for each location can be compiled. Now daily average, time total, location variations, and so on are all available for reporting. More than likely, differences will occur by location, even within the same town, or perhaps within the same part of town. That prompts the ever important, "Why?" If the recording period is lengthened, will the differences between locations decrease? What is the best way to report the data? The options linked to this activity seem to pour in.

INTERPRETING RESULTS

Activities like Pulse Rate, How Tall, Car Pool, and Rain Gauge provide data. Questions were raised about how to report those data. Which measure of central tendency is most appropriate (mean, median, mode)? What graph type is most appealing? Does getting too mathy negatively impact the appeal of the report? How to tell the story of the data is not necessarily an easy decision.

Figure 10.2 shows the height of several middle school students. That same information can be presented in a box plot, shown in Fig. 10.4, which is also called a box and whisker plot. The rectangle in the box plot contains three vertical line segments. The one in the interior of the rectangle represents the median of all the heights. The left vertical side of the rectan-

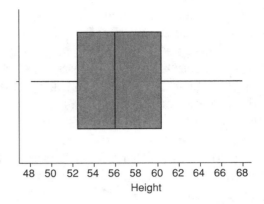

48 50 52 54 56 58 60 62 64 66 68

Height

FIG 10.4.

gle is the first quartile, or the median of the shortest half of the class. The right vertical side of the rectangle is the third quartile and represents the median of the tallest half of the class.

Questions to Help Understand Interpreting Results

How many cards must be drawn from a standard 52-card canasta deck to be certain that at least 2 cards from each of the four suits will be selected? There are 13 cards in each suit. The best-case scenario would have the first 2 cards drawn from one suit, the next 2 from a second suit, the next 2 from a third suit, and the last 2 from the fourth suit, meaning a total of 8 cards would be needed. The worst-case situation would have the first 13 cards drawn from the same suit, the next 13 from a second suit, and the next 13 from a third suit. Therefore, it is possible that, after 39 cards, cards from only 3 suits will have been drawn. Two more cards would be needed to guarantee at least 2 cards from each suit. Scoffing would probably occur with either the worst-case or best-case descriptions. Unlikely as either might be, they are possible and they do provide parameters that need to be considered as information is reported about an activity.

Find the mean of the five-number summary of the data set {2, 4, 6, 7, 11, 22, 24, 26}. The question asks for the mean of the five-number summary, which uses the minimum value, quartile 1, median, quartile 3, and the maximum value. Students may say that the mean is 9, mistaking the median for the mean. The five number summary is as follows: minimum = 2, quartile 1 = 5, median = 9, quartile 3 = 23, and maximum = 26. The mean is $\frac{2 + 5 + 9 + 23 + 26}{5} = \frac{65}{5}$, which is 13.

The first important idea addressed by the five-number summary question is the mathematics language issue. Care must be taken that the question is not misread. The second consideration brought out by this question is things that seem to be too easy to be true might be exactly that; it might be worth re-reading a question to see if the question has been misinterpreted. The last concern is that challenging questions are often designed with basic skills embedded in them.

Here is another question that might seem simple at first. Suppose two years ago you played one third of the game minutes on your basketball team. You made 47 out of 113 foul shots attempted, 42 out of 150 of the 2-point shots attempted, and committed 53 fouls. Last year you played half of all the game minutes and made 92 out of 139 foul shots attempted, 79 out of 140 of the 2-point shots attempted, and committed 41 fouls. What kind of a statistical argument can you make to convince the coach that you should get more playing time in this, your third year? Your data are as follows:

It is not reasonable to expect the coach to accept your statistical argument as the only reason to give you more playing time. The assumption is that, because you have improved from your first to your second year, you would continue improving or at least play at the level of your second year. However, that is an assumption. The coach is watching you in practice and that will be a huge factor in determining whether or not you get more playing time, or even as much as you got last year.

Statistically based extensions like the basketball one are common. Mathematics books often contain problems like, "Speedy runs a 4-minute mile. Given that, how long would Speedy take to run a marathon (26.2 miles)?" One huge assumption is that Speedy can maintain the same pace over the marathon (a distance race) that is run in a mile (a sprint). Sprinting and distance running are entirely different games. What about terrain? Mile runs are usually conducted on quarter-mile flat tracks. Marathons are generally held where the participants traverse 26.2 miles between point A and point B. The bottom line is that data interpretation must include consideration of assumptions.

STATISTICS

With the advent of the Advanced Placement (AP) statistics course in the late 1990s, the mathematical curriculum has changed. Standards 2000 added to the statistics movement with the K-12 content standard "Data Analysis and Probability." The ripple effect of the AP statistics course

	Year 1	Year 2	Improvement in performance	
Foul percentage	41.6	66.2	59.1%	$\left(\frac{66.2 - 41.6}{41.6}\right)$
Shot percentage	28	56.4	101.4%	$\left(\frac{56.4 - 28}{28}\right)$
Fouls committed	53	41	−22.6%	$\left(\frac{41 - 53}{53}\right)$

and the National Council of Teachers of Mathematics call for increased emphasis on data analysis means that you are going to be teaching more and more statistics, probability, and data analysis–related topics. That statement carries some significant implications. Recall the three axioms a teacher of mathematics should possess (Joby M. Anthony, personal communication, May 26, 2004):

1. Know the content being presented.
2. Know more than the content being presented.
3. Teach from the overflow of knowledge.

You need to examine your background in the area of data analysis, probability, and statistics, using the microscope of knowing enough to be able to teach from the overflow. The indicator might be that you need to better prepare yourself. For the sake of discussion, we assume appropriate readiness on your part and also of your students to deal with some statistical topics. Some of the extensions we discuss might be beyond your students' capabilities because of the algebra used in the explanations.

Questions to Help Understand Statistics

Four students are entered in a drawing for a bike. Three names will be drawn and those students will win bikes. How many ways are there for the bikes to be given? There are different ways to solve this problem. One involves labeling the finalists A, B, C, and D. A sample space of possible pairings of winners would be {ABC, ABD, BCD, ACD}. Because the order of the student selection does not matter, something like ADB is not listed because it is already present as ABD. Listing the possible pairings using sample space is a basic way

to solve this problem. If the question had asked for 10 out of 50 students, the sample space would be a tedious way to solve the problem, even though it could be done.

There is another way of looking at this problem, which is significant. If you are picking three out of four students, you are doing the same thing as leaving one out. How many ways are there to leave one of four students out? Now that this idea is in place, creating a list that omits one student is simpler. People do not usually think of this approach. Remember that doing a problem more than one way stimulates divergent thinking. Many assignments do not ask for multiple ways of solving a problem, so that is something to consider as you work with your future students over your career.

Here is a statistical approach to the problem. Combination is the process of finding how many ways to select "r" out of "n" possible individuals when the order of selection does not matter. Permutation is used if the order does matter. Both formulas are available in statistics textbooks. Most graphing calculators have a $_nC_r$ function key for combinations and a $_nP_r$ function key for permutations. The combinations and permutations we will use could be done using sample spaces, without technology. Still, you should be aware of the possibilities of technology as well as the algebraic approach to these problems.

Your Turn

10.1. If 5 students are to be chosen from a class of 20 to represent that class in a competition, in how many ways can it be done if order counts (AB does not equal BA)? Is this a combination or a permutation?

A) 15504
B) 624,882
C) 1,860,480

D) 2,631,944

E) _____ (If your answer is different, put it in the blank.)

10.2. You normally invite 14 friends for a Friday night party. However, this Friday your roommates ask that you only invite 8 of those friends. How many choices do you have as to whom to invite? Is this a combination or a permutation?

A) 3002

B) 3003

C) 3004

D) 3005

E) _____ (If your answer is different, put it in the blank.)

10.3. For the experiment of randomly selecting 1 card from a deck of 52, let

C = event the card selected is a heart

D = event the card selected is a face card

E = event the card selected is an ace

Determine which of the following pairs of events are mutually exclusive:

A) C, D

B) C, E

C) D, E

D) _____ (If your answer is different, put it in the blank.)

Stem-and-Leaf Plots

Stem-and-leaf plots are a graphing, statistical approach for reporting data given or collected in some problems. Suppose you wanted to find the product of the minimum and the maximum values (did you notice the range there?) listed and divide that product by the difference of the median and quartile 1, rounding the final answer to nearest hundredth.

0	1 1 2 5 9
1	0 0 0 2 3 4 5 8 9 9
2	4 5 5 5 6 8 9 9
3	2 2 2 3 7 8
4	1 8 8
5	3 7 9

In stem-and-leaf plots, 4|8 means 48. Think of each entry in this example as a two-digit number (although you are not limited to two digits). The tens digit (stem) is to the left of the vertical segment and the ones digit (leaves) is to the right of that vertical segment. Thus, the fourth row represents 41, 48, and 48.

Depending on the situation, the digit to the left of the vertical segment could be the ones digit of a decimal and the values to the right of the vertical segment could each represent a tenths digit, making the fourth row represent 4.1, 4.8, and 4.8.

Remember we are looking for the product of the minimum and the maximum values listed in the stem-and-leaf plot, and we want to divide that product by the difference of the median and quartile 1. The minimum of the data set is 1 and the maximum is 61 and their product is 61. The median is 26 and quartile 1 is 13. The difference of the median and quartile 1 is 13. So, the answer to the question is $\frac{61}{13} = 4.69$, rounded to the nearest hundredth. This example shows how information can be retrieved from a stem-and-leaf plot.

We have not exhausted the topic of statistics by any stretch of the imagination. Still, we have provided you a few extensions beyond mean, median, and mode, which are typically presented in the middle school setting. As you can see, the situations we provided extend the window a bit. As you go through your teaching career, you should continue to expand your statistical horizons.

Your Turn

10.4. What are some uses for each of the different types of graphs (pictographs, circle or pie graphs, coordinate graphs, histograms, line plots, stem-and-leaf plots, or box plots)? Describe real-life situations in which some types of graphs are more appropriate than others, and explain why.

10.5. What are the three measures of central tendency used in statistics? Describe ways in which teachers can help middle school students understand each measure.

PROBABILITY

The probability of an event is a number between 0 and 1, with 0 meaning that the event will never occur, and 1 meaning that the event always occurs. Probabilities are expressed as decimals, fractions, or percents. So a probability of 1.0 refers to a 100% chance. The probability of all possible nonoverlapping events must add up to 1. In a sixth-grade class, there cannot be a 40% chance of randomly selecting a boy and a 70% chance of randomly selecting a girl. Selecting a boy and selecting a girl are nonoverlapping events because it is possible to fall into only one category.

Probability refers only to a random event (flipping a coin) or something randomly chosen (pulling a name out of a hat). If there is no randomness, there is no probability. What is the probability you wore a red shirt today? If you did not close your eyes and reach in your closet to select a shirt, there is no probability associated with your shirt choice. Relating probability with a nonrandom event is a very common error.

When randomly selecting cards from a deck, it is important to notice whether a selected card is being replaced in the deck before a second selection is made. If the first card is replaced, the probability of the second draw does not change. For example, the probability of selecting a red card the first time is 26 out of 52, $\frac{1}{2}$, or 0.50. The probability of selecting a red card the second time, assuming replacement, is also 26 out of 52, $\frac{1}{2}$, or 0.50. If the first card is

not replaced, the probability changes with the second draw. We know the probability of selecting a red card the first time is 0.50. The probability of selecting a red card the second time is 25 out of 51 if a red card was chosen first and 26 out of 51 if a black card was chosen first.

Probabilities are not always as transparent as they are when coins are flipped or cards are drawn from a deck. A classic problem involves asking a class if they think two people in the group will share a birthday (both month and day of month). Typically, the response is, "no way!" The reasoning is that it would take a large group before it would be very probable to have at least one matching month and day. Start with a simpler problem.

Suppose each of 30 people knew the day of the week on which they were born. How many people would need to report the day of their birth before there would be a guaranteed match? The first two could have both been born on Monday and thus match. However, that may not occur. Consider the worst-case scenario: person 1 is born on Sunday, person 2 on Monday, person 3 on Tuesday, person 4 on Wednesday, person 5 on Thursday, person 6 on Friday, and person 7 on Saturday. Now what? The eighth person will match someone, because all days of the week have been taken. The probability that the eighth person will match one of the prior 7 as far as the day of the week upon which they were born is 1. If you have 13 people in a group, the probability is 1 that there will be a match on the birth month. The first 2 could match, but a worst-case scenario would have the first 12 people using all 12 months on our calendar. The thirteenth person must match someone. It is important to ask this month question after the day of the week question to ensure that students grasp the concept. In addition, it gives the opportunity for someone to successfully ask a question. The mentality could be extended to looking for a match if the individuals know the week of the year of their birth (1 through 52). Here, students might become skeptical about success because of having only 30 out of 52 possibilities covered. The probability of a match in this setting is quite high (0.999976).

Look at the initial question—what is the probability of getting 2 people to match on a month and day of the month in a group of 30. Logic seems to dictate that a very large number of people would be needed to have any level of assurance of a match and, certainly, it would appear to be highly unlikely in a group of 30 people. Use 365 for the number of days in a year. The month and day of birth for the first person is announced. There are then 364 days left that do not match for a second person. The probability of a third person not matching means that this third person has 363 options left. At this stage of development, $\frac{(365)(364)(353)}{365^3}$ expresses the probability of having no match, which in this case happens to be 0.9917958. That means that the probability of a match between three people is about $1 - 0.9918$, or approximately 0.0082, definitely not very high. If 10 people are considered, the probability is close to 0.8831 that none of their birth dates will be the same, and for 20, the probability of no match is almost 0.5886. At 23 people, the probability that no 2 people will have a matching birthday is nearly 0.4927. Another way of saying this is that there is almost a 0.5073 probability that, in a group of 23 people, at least 2 of them will share a birthday (only in terms of day of the month and the month itself).

Preposterous! That just does not seem right! In a group of 23 people, there is about a 0.5 probability that 2 of them will share a birthday. Do the activity with a group and see what happens. Even if the group

used does not have a match, the question still lingers for many—"How or why?" Some middle schoolers were given this problem. They wanted to know how such a seemingly impossible answer could happen. They wanted to prove why it was right or wrong. The "right" environment was created, as was the need for a proof.

They knew that the probability of 3 people not having the same birthday approximates 0.9918. The class developed a general formula for the probability of not having the same birthday $\frac{365!}{(365 - n)!(365^n)}$, where n is the number of people in the group. This would give the probability of n people not having the same birthday. The difficulty was their calculators could not handle 365! But, they concluded that because they knew the probability with 3 people, the rest was trivial. To find 4, multiply the result of 3 by 362 and divide by 365, which can be done on most calculators.

They quickly realized that this approach was effective but still tedious. They turned to a spreadsheet. The first column showed n or the number of people. Using the method for 2 people, the second column showed the probability of not having the same birthday and the third column the probability of having the same birthday. Table 10.1 shows part of the spreadsheet results that the middle school class generated (Brumbaugh & Rock, 2005).

Figure 10.5 includes a graphical representation using the Table 10.1 data points. What is the significance of the point where the two curves intersect? If you continue the graph to the right, what would eventually happen to the curve representing the probability that there are two persons who share the same birthday? (adapted from Jacobs, 1982).

Although we would not advise sharing what we are about to discuss with middle

TABLE 10.1

Number of people	Different birthdays	Matching birthdays
2	0.9973	0.0027
3	0.9918	0.0082
4	0.9836	0.0164
5	0.9729	0.0217
6	0.9595	0.0405
7	0.9438	0.0562
8	0.9225	0.0743
9	0.9054	0.0946
10	0.8831	0.1169
. . .	. . .	. . .
20	0.5886	0.4114
21	0.5563	0.4437
22	0.5243	0.4757
23	0.4927	0.5073
. . .	. . .	. . .
30	0.2937	0.7063
40	0.1088	0.8912
50	0.0342	0.9794
60	0.0058	0.9942

school students, we want you to take a look at how sometimes a situation appears to prove something is most probable. *What follows is an illegal scheme.* A crook sent out 128,000 letters to potential financial advisees. Of those letters, 64,000 said the value of a stock would rise over a given period. The content of the other 64,000 letters said the value of that same stock would stay the same or fall over the same period of time.

A second round of letters was sent, but only to individuals who had received an original letter containing a prediction that had been correct. The contents of the second letter would be the same as the first one, with the possible exception of different stock. This time, of the letters sent, 32,000 individuals got one predicting the stock would rise in value and 32,000 other letters stated it would not. At the end of the second prediction period, a quarter of the original 128,000 people, or 32,000 had received two letters with correct predictions. The scenario was repeated three more times and the original group of 128,000 was reduced to 4,000 individuals, each of whom had received five letters correctly predicting the movement of the stock market.

A sixth letter was sent, but this one did not contain a prognostication. Instead, it carried a reminder that the correct movement of the stock market had been demonstrated in the last five letters the individual

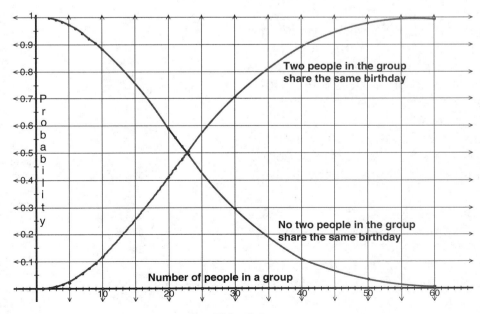

FIG 10.5.

had received. That succession of correct forecasts proved that a certain system for foretelling the path stocks take was available. The letter carefully explained that the service would be made available only to a select few individuals for a modest annual fee. The implication was that no matter what amount was charged for the service, the client would easily recoup the expenses from profits.

Suppose the letter, including letterhead, envelope, software, hardware, and postage required to produce it, was sent for $0.50. The payment for the producer's time (not jail time here, but the time spent bringing this scheme to fruition) will be computed later. The 128,000 letters sent generated an expense of $64,000. Suppose each potential client was charged an annual fee of $500 for the services. If each individual joins, $1,936,000 is generated after the $64,000 cost is taken out. That is a significant profit. Even if only half of the potential clients sign up, after taking out the costs, the profit is over $900,000. Only 128 people paying $500 cover the expenses. Do you think there would be more than 128 takers on a scheme like this? Do you see why it is illegal? If you were to do it, you would be classified as doing business with the intent of defrauding people. This is one of the classic con games that have been used on unsuspecting victims who are duped into believing probability can be removed from a setting and they can get rich quick. Knowing probability helps create wise consumers and connects the mathematical curriculum with the real world.

Simulations and integration of graphing and statistics with probability should happen at the middle school level. The emphasis should start shifting to developing understanding of theoretical probability, including work with theoretical values for simple events such as tossing coins or rolling a die or a couple of dice. How-

ever, the experimental aspect of probability should not be neglected. Rolling a pair of dice is an example of this type of activity that can involve comparisons of experimental and theoretical probabilities and distributions (see Your Turn 10.11).

Your Turn

10.6. The birthdays of 42 of the U.S. presidents are included in Table 10.2.

TABLE 10.2

#	President	Birthday
1	Washington	February 22
2	J. Adams	October 30
3	Jefferson	April 13
4	Madison	March 16
5	Monroe	April 28
6	J. Q. Adams	July 11
7	Jackson	March 15
8	Van Buren	December 5
9	W. H. Harrison	February 9
10	Tyler	March 29
11	Polk	November 2
12	Taylor	November 24
13	Fillmore	January 7
14	Pierce	November 23
15	Buchanan	April 23
16	Lincoln	February 12
17	A. Johnson	December 29
18	Grant	April 27
19	Hayes	October 4
20	Garfield	November 19
21	Arthur	October 5
22	Cleveland	March 18
23	B. Harrison	August 20
24	McKinley	January 29
25	T. Roosevelt	October 27
26	Taft	September 15
27	Wilson	December 28
28	Harding	November 2
29	Coolidge	July 4
30	Hoover	August 10
31	F. D. Roosevelt	January 30
32	Truman	May 8
33	Eisenhower	October 14
34	J. F. Kennedy	August 29
35	L. B. Johnson	August 27
36	Nixon	January 9
37	Ford	July 14
38	Carter	October 1
39	Regan	February 6
40	G. Bush	June 12
41	Clinton	August 19
42	G. W. Bush	July 6

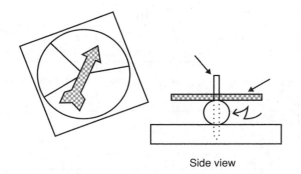

Side view

FIG 10.6.

Before looking at the table, what do you think is the probability that two of them have the same birthday? What about you having the same birthday as one of the presidents? What about one of the students in your group having the same birthday as one of the presidents? Explain your answers (adapted from Jacobs, 1982).

10.7. Using a spinner, how could you establish a discussion about bias?

It is easy to construct a spinner using a board, nail, bead with a hole in it, stiff paper, and some circles made out of paper. Make an arrow out of the stiff paper, punching a hole at its center of gravity. Figure 10.6 shows an example of the spinner.

10.8. If you made a template for the spinner in Fig. 10.6 that equally spaced the digits around a circle, letting the odd digits represent the head of a coin and the even digits represent the tail of a coin, would the generated results parallel the expected results of flipping an honest coin? Why or why not?

One of the difficulties with activities involving probability is novelty. Most students have been exposed to flipping coins and rolling dice. Finding novel instruments can add interest to the learning atmosphere and avoid the attitude of, "I know that" or "Not that, again!" (Check out TAG activities 3 and 4 at the end of this chapter for novel ideas.) Another idea involves stick spaghetti. Give each student 4 sticks. Your instructions to them should be: "Please do as I instruct with a piece of spaghetti. Do not ask questions of anyone, including me. Do not look at what someone else is doing. Simply do what I ask." Then you should instruct them to break the stick into 3 pieces. Most people attempt to break their stick into three equal pieces.

At this point, you should have a discussion with the class, elaborating on how many reflexively attempted to break their spaghetti into equal pieces. This does provide an opportunity to talk about normal and the bell curve, even if only at an informal level. At the conclusion of the discussion, ask that the set of 3 pieces that came from that first stick be set aside. Now you provide a different set of instructions: Take each of your remaining 3 sticks and break them into 3 pieces, keeping each set separate. The desire here is that the piece not be broken into equal segments. At the end of this part of the activity, each person should have 4 sets of 3 segments of stick spaghetti.

The follow-up question is, "Can you make a triangle with a set of 3 segments?" The ends of the segments must touch to make a vertex. Scene 1 of Fig. 10.7 shows a set of 3 that does form a triangle, whereas scenes 2 and 3 show sets that do not. Then survey the class, asking how many of their sets formed triangles. Typically, about 25% of the sets will make triangles. This then becomes the probability of making a triangle under the instructions of this activity. Notice that the need for randomness applies, as long as the students do not know your ultimate goal for the activity.

Scene 1   Scene 2   Scene 3

FIG 10.7.

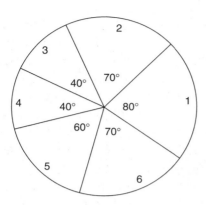

FIG 10.8.

Your Turn

10.9. Given the game board in Fig. 10.8, you need to spin either a 3 or a 5 to stay in a game. What is the probability that your spin entitles you to stay in the game?

10.10. The numbers 1 to 200 (inclusive) are put into a hat. What is the probability that the first three numbers chosen at random are prime numbers? (As the numbers are chosen, they are not placed in the hat again.)

10.11. Unequally likely outcomes: You roll a pair of dice and find the sum of the dots (called pips) on the dice.

a. How many possible outcomes are there for this experiment?

b. Suppose you have one red and one white die. What are the possible outcomes from rolling the red die? What are the possible outcomes from rolling the white die? What possible sums are there? For each of these sums, show all the possible ways in which the sum might be obtained. Use ordered pairs such as (3, 4) where 3 represents the outcome of rolling the red die and 4 is the outcome for rolling the white die. Based on this information, answer the following questions: How many ways can you roll each one of the outcomes and what is the theoretical probability for each one?

c. Find the theoretical probabilities for each of the following, based on 36 tosses: What is the theoretical probability that the sum is even? What is the theoret-

TABLE 10.3

Sum	Tally (for 72 rolls)	Frequency	Experimental Probability
Total:		72	$\frac{72}{72}$

ical probability that the sum is greater than 6? What is the theoretical probability that the sum is prime? What is the theoretical probability that the sum is prime or greater than 6? What is the theoretical probability that the sum is less than 5?

d. Now roll a pair of dice 72 times, recording the information in Table 10.3, and answer the following questions. What is the expected number of occurrences for each outcome (sum)? Remember that the expected (theoretical) number of outcomes is based on 72 rolls, not 36. How closely do your obtained results compare to the expected results?

10.12. If you toss three coins, which probability is larger: getting at least one head or getting at least one tail?

10.13. A spinner for a game is arranged so it may point to any of 7 numbers with equal probability. The numbers on the spinner are 1, 2, 3, 4, 5, 6, and 7. If you spin once, what is the probability it points to a prime number?

10.14. Basketball simulation: free throw shooting. In basketball, a personal foul is committed by player A on player B from the other team because of illegal contact while the ball is in play. For 1 point each, player B takes 2 free throws.

a. Assume that player B has 60% accuracy from the free throw line, and has to 2 free throws. What is the expected percent for 2 points (made both shots), 1 point (made one of the 2 shots), and zero points (missed both shots)?

b. If this player tries 10 2-free-throw trips (2 free throws each) for a game, what is the expected frequency for the different point combinations (2, 1, or zero points) of these 10 trips? Using a spinner (see Fig. 10.6), simulate this experiment. Show your work.

10.15. Visit a middle school mathematics classroom and informally assess several students' understanding and misconceptions of data analysis, statistics, and probability. You can also interview a teacher regarding the students' understanding of these ideas.

10.16. Examine a middle school textbook's section on data analysis, statistics, and probability in terms of concepts and activities included.

10.17. A parent of one of the students in your middle school classroom feels that you are expending too much instructional time on data analysis, statistics, and probability concepts in your classroom. How would you respond to this parent's concern?

TECHNOLOGY AND DATA ANALYSIS, PROBABILITY, AND STATISTICS

Technology makes working with any mathematics so much easier because it eliminates a lot of the arithmetic-intensive segments. There is no question that students need to know how to do basic computations that relate to all areas, including data analysis, probability, and statistics. Once the concept is understood, then technology should be available.

Graphing calculators designed for middle schoolers (Casio FX-7400G PLUS, HP 9G, and TI 73) do combinations, permutations, factorials, and some basic statistic maneuvers. This technology provides the opportunity to discuss some fundamental concepts much sooner by removing the arithmetic hurdles. Earlier in this chapter we discussed 4 students in a drawing to win a bike. Three of those students would win bikes. We used a sample space to show possible pairings of winners and then concluded by saying that, if the question had asked for 10 out of 50 students, sample space would be a tedious way to solve the problem. The concept is explained and demonstrated with the bike drawing and, once understood, the discussion could shift to how to compute the number of ways winners could be grouped, or the combination possibilities. At that point, assuming a level of comprehension for the students, the arithmetic could be discarded in favor of the use of technology.

Introduction of technology in all areas of the curriculum should follow the description given in the last paragraph—once the students understand the concept and the basics of computing the desired results, technology becomes a viable option for solving problems. At this point, the emphasis should shift from computational questions to ones of analysis, interpretation, and application. That is, once students can use technology to compute how many different combinations there are of selecting 10 students out of a total of 50, the accent should shift to problems where the student would need to decide if this is a combination or permutation problem.

Whereas calculators are one source of technology that can be used with probability, statistics, and data analysis, software is a different avenue that should be explored. There are several powerful statistics software packages available that you may have heard of, seen, or even used. Focusing on utility for middle schoolers, we will use Fathom (www.keypress.com).

Figures 10.2 and 10.4 were done in Fathom. Students are given the opportunity to explore, analyze, and communicate conclusions based on their work using Fathom. The software is dynamic and any changes in the data are reflected in all aspects of the related links or applications within the software.

Your Turn

10.18. How would you use technology to assist with the organization and interpretation of data?

10.19. Have students collect data on any topic of their choice. Using the data collected, have students create a histogram and/or box plot using Fathom software.

CONCLUSION

There you have it. Well, actually, no you do not have it. We did not cover all possible related topics (Did you read about odds?) and they too deserve consideration. We have opted to leave that as an open-ended opportunity for you to investigate as the need arises. Because we live in such a data-frich environment, you are standing at the beginning of a long and complex journey with your students. It is imperative that they comprehend the magnitude of, and the potential impact of, data analysis, probability, and statistics on their lives. From deciding whether or not to play the lottery games, select a variable or fixed-rate loan, buy a car at 0% financing and no rebate as opposed to getting a rebate and paying on a three-year 6% loan, and on and on, your students will be faced with an ever-increasing number of decisions to be made. Chances are that the advantages of understanding the basics of data analysis, probability, and statistics should be obvious to you (we worded that sentence that way on purpose). It is imperative that all students understand the impact of this section of their studies on their daily lives,

starting now, and growing ever more complex. Conveying that message is your responsibility. Get ready; get set; GO!

STICKY QUESTIONS

10.1. Forty-two students took a mathematics exam in school in which the passing score was 70. The mean score of the 42 students *who took the exam* was 75.5 whereas the mean score of the students who *passed the exam* was 81, and the mean score of the students who *failed* was 60. How many students failed the exam?

10.2. You are going to ride to a town exactly 70 miles from your house and then back. The car you are in averages 35 miles per hour (mph) going one way and 63 mph going the other way. What is the average speed of the car for the entire journey?

10.3. Suppose there are two jars, one containing 100 red and the other containing 100 blue marbles. Assume 10 blues are removed from the blue jar and placed in the red jar. The jar with 110 marbles is stirred. Then 10 marbles are randomly removed (color unknown) from the jar with 110 marbles in it and placed in the blue jar. Both jars have 100 marbles in them again. How many reds are in the blue jar? How many blues are in the red jar?

10.4. The vertices of a rectangle lie on the coordinate plane at the coordinates (1,1), (5,1), (1,7), and (5,7). If a point is randomly selected within the rectangle, what is the probability that the x coordinate of the point is greater than the y coordinate?

TAG

10.1. Create parallel line segments that are a toothpick length apart on a sheet of paper (where the toothpick is perpendicular to the segments). Hold a toothpick at least a foot above the center of the paper and drop it. Record the number of times the toothpick touches one

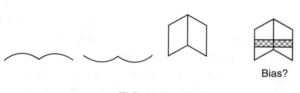

FIG 10.9.

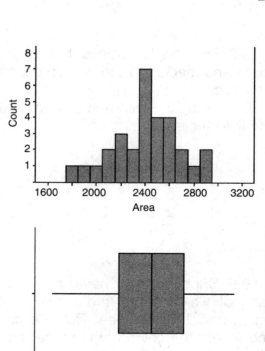

of the segments you created. If you drop more than one toothpick at a time, and if one toothpick leans on another, but passes over one of the created segments, that counts as a touch. The larger the number of drops, the better the results. Compute $\frac{2\ (total\ number\ of\ drops)}{number\ of\ hits}$.

10.2. Pair the students. Have one student hide a coin in one hand and have the other student guess which hand holds the coin. Repeat the activity 10 times, recording the total number of correct guesses. Then switch places. Which of the two students is the best guesser? Is this an example of a random event? If you say this is not a random event, explain why it is not. If you say this is a random event, explain why it is.

10.3. Fold a rectangular piece of paper (2 inches by 4 inches is a good size) in half so the fold is parallel to the shorter side. That paper can land one of three ways, fold up, fold down, or on edge, as shown in Fig. 10.9. What is the probability for each of the three cases? Would placing tape on the paper bias the results? Would the placement of the tape matter? Would the tape use matter?

10.4. When a paper cup is dropped, there are three realistic ways it can land: on its top, bottom, or side, as shown in Fig. 10.10. What is the probability of each occurrence?

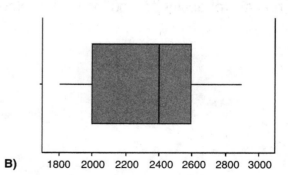

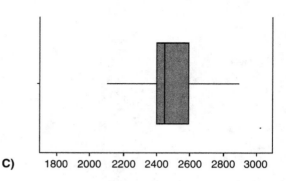

FIG 10.11.

FIG 10.10.

10.5. Which box plot (A, B, or C) displays the same data as the histogram (see Fig. 10.11)? Explain how you know the data are the same.

10.6. Find the difference between the mean and median of the first 20 counting numbers.

10.7. Using the following stem-and-leaf, find the median.

```
0 | 1 1 2 5 9
1 | 0 0 0 2 3 4 5 8 9 9
2 | 4 5 5 5 6 8 9 9
3 | 2 2 2 3 7 8
4 | 1 8 8
5 | 3
```

10.8. Suppose you have two cubes, each of which has 3 red faces, 2 blue faces, and 1 green face. Roll the cubes and record the color that lands facing up. What is the most likely event? To answer this question, you must construct a theoretical probability distribution for this experiment. Comment on your results. Does this theoretical distribution surprise you?

10.9. Drop balls of different shapes and sizes. Drop each ball 3 times from 10 different dropping heights. Record the bounce height for each trial on a data table.

REFERENCES

Abbott, E. A. a Square. (1884). *Flatland: A romance of many dimensions*. Copyright expired. Dover Thrift Publications Mineola, NJ.

Brumbaugh, D. K., & Rock, D. (2005). *Teaching secondary mathematics* (3rd ed.). Mahwah, NJ: Lawrence Erlbaum Associates.

Hynes, M. C., & Brumbaugh, D. K. (1976). *Mathematics activities handbook for grades 5–12*. West Nyack, NY: Parker.

Jacobs, H. R. (1982). *Mathematics, human endeavor* (2nd ed.). New York: W. H. Freeman.

11

Algebra in the Middle School Classroom

FOCAL POINTS

- Generalization of arithmetic patterns
- Using algebra to solve problems
- Understanding of patterns, relations, and functions
- Study of structures
- Planning
- Assessment
- Technology
- Conclusion
- Sticky questions
- TAG
- References

In middle school, algebraic concepts developed informally earlier need to be formalized and expanded using patterns, functions, and generalizations. These same concepts need to be integrated with other topics in the curriculum. Students should have opportunities to work with symbols while becoming more comfortable relating expressions containing variables to verbal, tabular, and graphical representations of numerical and quantitative representations (NCTM, 2000).

Algebra is an important component in middle school mathematics. Students' algebraic background and success could stimulate or detract from their progress and development in future mathematics courses and career selection. Students should have foundational experiences in numerical, visual, and abstract algebra when they enter middle school.

Within the numerical model, investigation might focus on a problem where a pattern could be analyzed using numerical methods resulting in hypotheses and generalizations. Visualizations can grow through the use of graphing calculators, manipulatives, or software. A problem investigated with a numerical model might be represented in a visual mode, facilitating connections among topics. The abstract model appears through problems that can be solved symbolically using more standard algebraic procedures, promoting appreciation of the efficiency and elegance of algebraic solutions. Students should have plenty of educational opportunities to explore, experiment, and interconnect these algebraic models.

GENERALIZATION OF ARITHMETIC PATTERNS

Usiskin (1997) describes algebra as generalized arithmetic, where students conceptualize algebraic ideas without the use of unknowns. For example, "$6 \cdot 12 = 12 \cdot 6$" projects the idea that the order of factors can be reversed and the product is still the same. The $6 \cdot 12$ example can be generalized to, "You can multiply two numbers in either order, and the answer is the same," which could also be stated as, "For any numbers a and b, a • b = b • a." The students will have seen at least some of this developmental sequence as they worked with the commutative property of multiplication on different sets of numbers. Which is easier to understand from a beginning standpoint: "The product of any number and zero is zero" or "For all n, n • 0 = 0"? The ultimate desire is that the algebraic version is understood to be superior to the description in words. Why would we say that? When you deal with n • 0 = 0, you first must define n and then come up with the idea that any number, whole, natural, rational, real, complex, and so on, could be represented by n. That is a more abstract level of thinking. And, mathematically, it is easier to visualize and manipulate the statement with variables rather than words.

Early in their development of algebraic thinking, students should use generalizations such as "add zero to a number and the answer is the same number," or "add a number to itself and the result is two times the number." Later, they should also use the language of algebra to generalize: $0 + n = n = n + 0$, and $t + t = 2t$, respectively. Some important number properties for the set of real numbers at the middle school level are as follows:

Commutative property of addition:
$a + b = b + a$
Commutative property of multiplication:
$a • b = b • a$
Associative property of addition:
$(a + b) + c = a + (b + c)$
Associative property of multiplication:
$(ab)c = a(bc)$
Distributive property of multiplication over addition: $a(b + c) = ab + ac$
Additive identity: $a + 0 = a = 0 + a$
Multiplicative identity: $a • 1 = a = 1 • a$

The arithmetic background developed in elementary school is an important readiness element for middle and high school mathematics in general, and algebra in particular. Computation skills with whole numbers, fractions, decimals, and integers are essential. The students should have prior work with the meaning of the operations and proper use of symbols. Number sense and estimation are also important prerequisites for algebra fundamentals. All of these are arithmetic topics that will be generalized into basic algebraic maneuvers.

Your Turn

11.1. Find and describe three examples of "algebra as generalized arithmetic" presented in a middle school mathematics textbook.

11.2. Describe three examples of verbal descriptions used in middle school that may be translated or generalized into algebraic notation.

11.3. Find sample activities in a middle school mathematics textbook for the major number properties.

USING ALGEBRA TO SOLVE PROBLEMS

Generalized arithmetic is an important view of algebra. The study of procedures for solving certain types of problems is a popular and appropriate conception of algebra in middle school grades. Usiskin (1997) provides a glimpse of a developmental sequence leading from arithmetic to algebraic expressions of the problem, "What number, when added to 3, gives 7?":

Fill in the blank: $3 + \_ = 7$
Put a number in the square to make this sentence true: $3 + \square = 7$
Find the ?: $3 + ? = 7$
Solve: $3 + x = 7$

Some might argue that only $3 + x = 7$ is algebra because conventionally we use a letter to represent an unknown. However, the formative stages for $3 + x = 7$ are established earlier and, arguably, could also be called algebra. For example, "How different from the letter x is the □?" Another example is, "When 4 is added to 2 times a certain number, the sum is 10. Find the number" (Usiskin, 1988). This problem would be $2x + 4 = 10$ in the language of algebra. This is not the end though, because we need to solve for the variable by subtracting four from both sides of the equation and then divide both sides of the resultant equation by two. These two examples should amplify the advantages of algebraic abstractions in expressions. Still, it is important not to overlook the readiness events that facilitate expressing things algebraically.

Your Turn

11.4. Find other examples of algebra as the study of procedures for solving problems in a middle school textbook.

11.5. What prerequisites are necessary for proper mastery of algebra as the study of procedures for solving problems?

Properties of Equality

When using algebra to solve problems, students need to express situations as equations and solve and simplify them. The property of equality is an important prerequisite for this task. Elementary and middle school students should have the opportunity to experiment with double pan balances in both mathematics and science as they do experiments. The following activity is an example.

The scale in Fig. 11.1 is balanced. We know it will stay balanced if you subtract or add the same amount to both sides. What

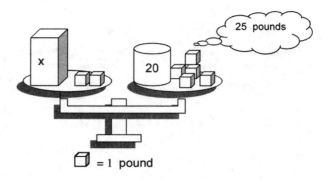

FIG 11.1.

algebraic expression shows the amount on the left side of the scale? The answer in this case is $x + 2$. What amount would you have to take away from the left side of the scale to have the variable (box named x) alone? We need to take away 2 pounds from the left side. But, is the balance still there when you do that? No! So, 2 pounds must be removed from the right side to maintain balance. In this case, we will have 23 pounds on the right side of the scale. Since the scale is balanced, it must be that $x = 23$ pounds, or 23 pounds + 2 pounds = 25 pounds or $x - 2$ pounds equals 25 pounds − 2 pounds, all different ways of saying the same thing, which is another valuable algebraic skill.

Your Turn

11.6. Working this problem in a semi-concrete form is an important step toward dealing with the abstractions upon which algebra is built. Not purposefully moving students to the semiconcrete and ultimately to the symbolic would be a disservice to them. Ask middle school students to solve the following problems and make annotations of their answers given that scales A and B in Fig. 11.2 are balanced. The objects are the same in all the pictures.

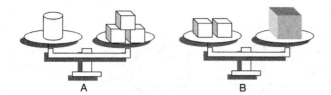

FIG 11.2.

a.

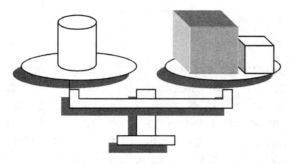

FIG 11.3.

b.

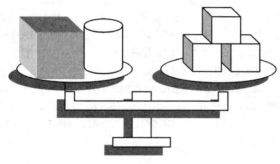

FIG 11.4.

c.

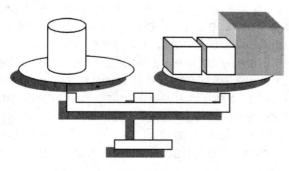

FIG 11.5.

d.

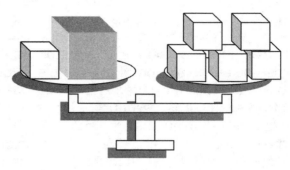

FIG 11.6.

Decide which of the following scales are balanced and write an equality or inequality to describe the situation (see Figs. 11.3–11.6).

11.7. Ask middle school students to write an algebraic equation that summarizes what Fig. 11.7 shows. Jumps the same size are the same distance, depicting whole numbers between zero and ten. Big jumps represent distances that are greater than the smaller jumps.

11.8. Using two variables to represent the different-sized jumps shown in Fig. 11.8, ask middle school students to write an algebraic equation that summarizes the situation. Jumps of the same size are the same distance. All jumps are whole numbers. All jumps are greater than zero and less than ten. Big jumps represent distances that are greater than the smaller jumps.

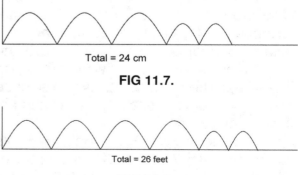

Total = 24 cm

FIG 11.7.

Total = 26 feet

FIG 11.8.

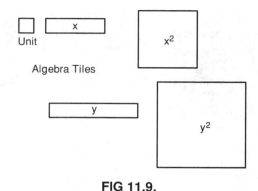

FIG 11.9.

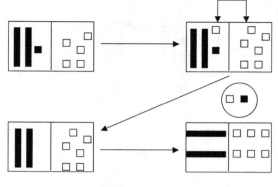

FIG 11.11.

Algebra Manipulatives

Algebra Tiles and Algebra Lab Gear help students solve or simplify equations. Figure 11.9 shows the typical pieces used for Algebra Tiles. The lengths of the x and y pieces are not multiples of the unit dimensions, which avoids making trades as would be done with base 10 blocks. Shading or nonshading could be used to represent positive or negative, respectively. A cube could be used to represent x^3 or y^3.

In Fig. 11.10, the small squares represent units and the rectangles are variables. The number represented by the pieces to the left side of the middle line segment in Fig. 11.10 equals the same as the number represented by the pieces to the right side of the middle line segment. Figure 11.10 shows $x - 2 = 4$. We can solve this equation by solving for x and removing the white squares ($^-2$) from the left side. But, we cannot remove them and maintain balance. If we add 2 black squares to the left side and 2 more to the right side, things stay the same. Note that a white square and a black square combined on the same

side cancel each other since $^+1 + \ ^-1 = 0$, or they add to zero. Now we can remove 2 white squares and 2 black squares from the left side and solve the equation because together they equal zero, giving $x = 6$ (see Fig. 11.10).

Figure 11.11 shows $2x + 1 = \ ^-5$. We need to find the value of x. To solve this equation, add one white square to each side as shown in Fig. 11.11. By doing this, the one unit on the left side of the middle line segment is eliminated and we are left with the $2x = \ ^-6$. Finally, rearrange the pieces to show that $x = \ ^-3$.

Partial products dissect problems into simpler information while connecting with previous work. If the partial product process is developed from the beginning of instruction in multiplication after concrete exposures, it is a simple matter for the partial product to be abandoned in favor of the standard algorithm, and eventually algebraic expressions. Doing 23 • 85 via partial product would appear as follows:

$$
\begin{array}{rl}
20 + 3 & \\
\underline{80 + 5} & \\
15 & (3 \cdot 5) \\
100 & (5 \cdot 20) \\
240 & (80 \cdot 3) \\
\underline{1600} & (80 \cdot 20) \\
1955 &
\end{array}
$$

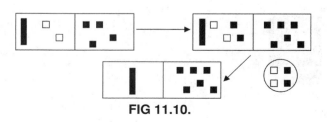

FIG 11.10.

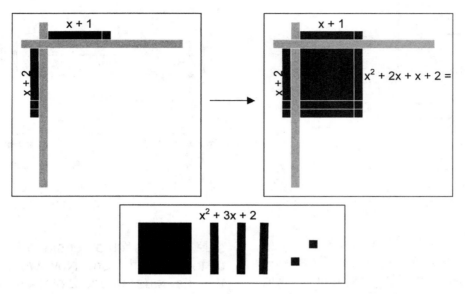

FIG 11.12.

Figure 11.12 illustrates $(x + 1)(x + 2)$, which yields: $1 \cdot 2$, $1 \cdot x$, $x \cdot 2$, and $x \cdot x$. Did you notice the connection between this algebra discussion and finding the partial product of two whole numbers?

Figure 11.13 shows $(2x + {}^-2)({}^-x + 3)$, giving the partial products: $3 \cdot {}^-2$, $3 \cdot 2x$, ${}^-x \cdot {}^-2$, and ${}^-x \cdot 2x$.

Hands-On Equations

Hands-On Equations is another manipulative that helps develop algebraic concepts. These materials may be used to solve equations like the ones discussed earlier. They are more abstract than the Algebra Tiles or Algebra Lab Gear because

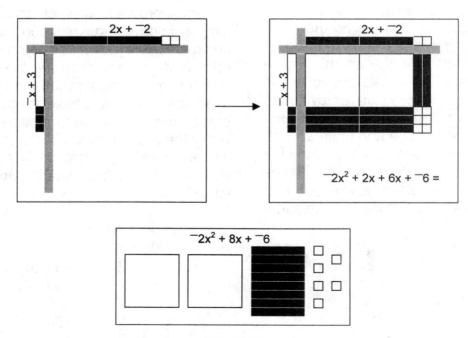

FIG 11.13.

A Sample Problem Using Hands-On Equations®
(this method of solution is protected by U.S. Patent #4,713,009)

Let's consider the equation **4x + 5 = 2x + 13**. The student first represents this equation on the flat laminated balance scale using the game pieces. The blue pawns represent the x's, and the numbered cubes represent the constant. The student is then ready to perform the **legal moves** in order to simplify and solve the equation. The procedure is illustrated below:

Ex. 4x + 5 = 2x + 13

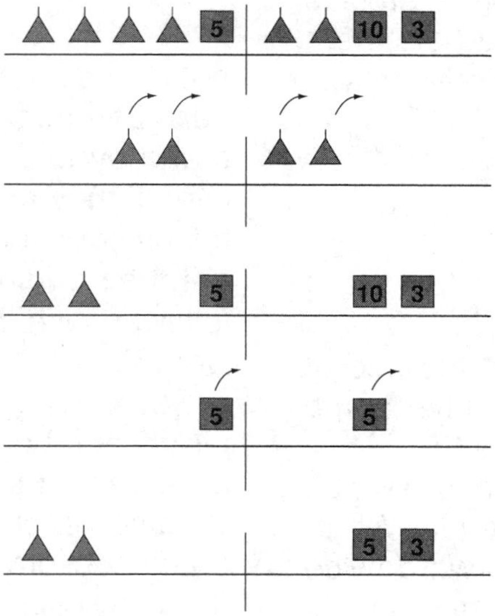

From this we see that **x = 4**. The check, in the **original physical setup**, reveals that 21 = 21.

[Note : The above example is taken from Lesson #4 of the program. The three previous lessons help the student to arrive at, and understand, the above solution. Later on in the program, the student will also work with white pawns, which represent the opposite of x, and with green cubes, which represent negative constants. No previous fromal algebraic experience is assumed for success with the program.]

FIG 11.14.

numerals are used instead of squares or circles to represent units. The example shown in Fig. 11.14 is from http://www.borenson.com/html/sample.html.

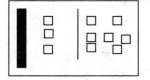

FIG 11.15.

Your Turn

11.9–11.11 Help middle school students use Algebra Tiles, Algebra Lab Gear, Hands-On Equations, or drawings of the manipulatives to find what x represents in terms of the equations in Figs. 11.15–11.17:

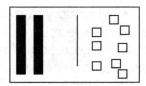

FIG 11.16.

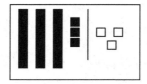

FIG 11.17.

11.12. Present the following exercises to middle school students, and help them solve the equations using manipulatives:

a. $(x + 2)(x + {}^-2)$
b. $({}^-2x + {}^-3)({}^-x + {}^-2)$

Variable as a Placeholder

The following are examples of the use of variables as placeholders to solve some algebra problems (Usiskin, 1997):

Monopoly or other board games in which the following is given—Roll the die. Whatever number you get, move forward twice that number of spaces. Ask students to translate that rule into algebraic language, which becomes, "If you roll d on the die, then move forward 2d."

Spreadsheets use algebra. Take the number in one cell of an array (for example, cell A1), subtract it from a number in a different cell (for example, cell A2), and put the missing addend in another cell (for example, cell A3 = A2 − A1). As in the die situation, we do not need to know what number we have to understand the directions. If the number in cell A1 is x and the number in the cell A2 is y, the number in cell A3 is y − x.

Consider the number trick: pick any counting number, double it, add 6, divide by 2, subtract 3, what do you get? Do that with a class and the reaction is generally one of surprise. The question that usually follows the expressions of amazement often is, "Does that always work?" The appropriate teacher response to that is, "I do

TABLE 11.1

Instruction	Algebraic interpretation
Pick a number	n
Double it	2n
Add 6	2n + 6
Divide by 2	$\frac{2n + 6}{2} = n + 3$
Subtract 3	(n + 3) - 3
What did you get?	n

not know, try it again with a different number." Eventually it will dawn on the class that they are all using different numbers, even if they are not counting numbers, yet things continue to work out so they always get their original number. That is typically followed with the question, "How does this work?"

Several things are going on with the pick-a-number discussion in the preceding paragraph. First, each student is involved. Second, each student is getting needed arithmetic practice. Third, most students (hopefully all) are thinking. Fourth, a generalization is being discovered. Finally, when they ask, "How does this work?" the opportunity for proof enters and the concept of variable plays an important role as shown in the summary in Table 11.1.

Your Turn

11.13. Describe at least three examples of variables being used as a placeholder in a middle school textbook.

11.14. Describe a board game that involves algebraic thinking and explain how middle school students could apply algebra as they play it.

11.15. Draw a picture or visual model that could be used with middle school students, and write an algebraic expression for each of the following situations:

a. weight of a box plus five,
b. three years less than a certain age.

11.16. Try the following exercises with middle school students, and analyze their attempts to solve the problems:

Each letter represents one of the following numbers: 12, 18, or 21. Tell what each letter represents.

a. $p \cdot (q - r) = 162$
b. $(2 \cdot g) - (h + i) = 12$

A Sequence of Equation-Solving Skills

Middle school students need to start by solving one-question equations. The following are some examples and related questions:

$x + 9 = 16$:	What number plus nine equals 16?
$10 \cdot x = 80$:	Ten times what number is equal to 80?
$p - 48 = 38$:	What number minus 48 is equal to 38?
$12 = 120 \div a$:	Twelve is equal to 120 divided by what number?

The emphasis is placed on reading the equation as a question to be answered with a number. The magic squares in Your Turn 11.17, cross-number arrays in Your Turn 11.18, and function machines with input–output boxes in Your Turn 11.25 could be used to help students work questions to be answered with numbers. These should be followed by a discussion of how to read the equations and the techniques used to solve them.

Equations involving more than one unknown require student understanding of a set of rules. For $x + x = 12$, students need to realize that x has to represent the same number ($6 + 6 = 12$, where $x = 6$). We cannot say that $x = 9$ and $x = 3$, even though $9 + 3 = 12$. If we have $x + y = 12$, x and y could represent the same value or different values: $9 + 3 = 12$, where $x = 9$ and $y = 3$; $12 + 0 = 12$, where $x = 12$ and $y = 0$; or $6 + 6 = 12$, where $x = y = 6$.

Equations involving two operations and one variable (two-question equations)

could be introduced next. The following examples show equations and related questions.

$5 \cdot y + 2 = 42$: The first question is, "What number plus 2 equals 42?" The answer is 40. The second question is, "Five times what number is 40?" The answer is 8: $5 \cdot 8 + 2 = 42$.

$3 \cdot b - 8 = 31$: The first question is, "What number minus 8 is equal to 31?" The answer is 39. The second question is, "Three times what number is 39?" The answer is 13: $3 \cdot 13 - 8 = 31$.

$51 - 15 \cdot m = 6$: The first question is, "Fifty-one minus what number is 6?" The answer is 45. The second question is, "15 times what number is 45?" The answer is 3: $51 - 15 \cdot 3 = 6$. This problem requires the appropriate use of the order of operations. The students need to think about $15 \cdot m$ as a single number first. The cover-up technique illustrated in Fig. 11.18 could be used to help students visualize the steps in solving the equation. In this case, $15 \cdot m$ would need to be covered first in the equation. Then the students should

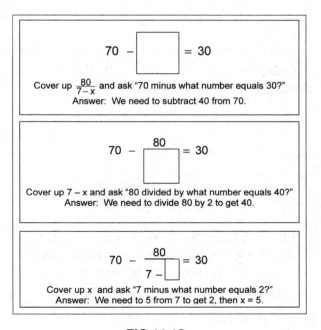

FIG 11.18.

be able to state the first question more readily.

The cover-up technique is an intuitive approach to teach and solve equations (Whitman, 1982). These intuitive skills help students read mathematical symbols and solve equations with understanding. A three-step equation like $70 - \dfrac{80}{7-x} = 30$ may be solved by using this approach, as illustrated in Fig. 11.18.

Your Turn

Try the next few exercises with your middle schoolers and analyze their solutions.

11.17. Magic Square: Place the numbers 1, 2, 3, 4, 5, 6, 7, 8, and 9 in the little squares in Fig. 11.19 to form sums equal to 15 in all directions (up, down, and diagonally).

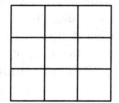

FIG 11.19.

11.18. Cross-number array: Make the sum 30 in each direction (up, down, and diagonally) using Fig. 11.20.

8		
6		
16	2	

FIG 11.20.

11.19. State the question in words before solving the equation. For example, in $d + t = 5$ the question is, "what number plus another number equals 5?"

a. $p + p = 16$
b. $t + t = 15$
c. $1 = g + g + g$

d. $16 = x \cdot x$
e. $n \cdot n \cdot n = 8$
f. $x + x = x$
g. $5 + n = 2 + n + 3$
h. $g + 3 = g$
i. $r \cdot r = r$

11.20. State the question or questions in words before solving the equation:

a. $5 \cdot m + 3 = 2$
b. $4 - 2 \cdot t = -(2 \cdot t - 4)$
c. $100 = 4 \cdot n^2$
d. $\dfrac{3}{5} \cdot b = 6$
e. $\dfrac{2 \square b + 7}{3} = 5$

UNDERSTANDING PATTERNS, RELATIONS, AND FUNCTIONS

Algebra includes the study of patterns, relationships among quantities, and functions. An important distinction related to this conceptualization of algebra is that the variables change within a given set of numbers. This approach provides a more dynamic view of variables. An example of this is the following:

Using whole numbers, which one is larger, $2n$ or $n + 2$ (Kücheman, 1978)? This example involves the use of a variable to represent a range of numbers, not just an unknown or specific amount. The pattern to be generalized is algebraic. Rather than describing a single relationship, it is necessary to explain how one relationship depends on another (Kücheman, 1978). The answer depends on whether n was greater than or less than 2. If students treat the variable as an unknown, then they will find one possible solution and will not consider the complex relationship involved in this situation. A more dynamic view of variables is needed. If the students just substitute for one value, then no generalization will be possible. They might say that $2n$ is the larger one because $2 \cdot 3 = 6$ and $2 + 3 = 5$,

TABLE 11.2

Number of Minutes	0	10	20	30	40	50	60
First Company	$20.00	$21.00	$22.00	$23.00	$24.00	$25.00	$26.00
Second Company	$0.00	$4.50	$9.00	$13.50	$18.00	$22.50	$27.00

and since $6 > 5$, then $2n > n + 2$. A good follow-up would involve asking if their conclusion is always true.

Another example for this conception of variable is the following:

What happens to the value of $\frac{1}{x}$ as x gets larger and larger (Usiskin, 1988)?

This idea of variable confuses many middle school students. We are not asking for one specific value of x, so x does not represent an unknown here. Also, we are not asking to translate a problem or generalize an arithmetic pattern. We are trying to generalize an algebraic pattern. Here, variables are used as arguments (a domain value of a function) or parameters (a number in which other numbers depend).

The study of patterns also requires the use of variables to represent a range of values. NCTM (2000) indicates that the study of patterns and quantity relationships in the middle school should focus on associations that connect to linear functions, which arise when there is a constant rate of change. The representation and examination of patterns should include the use of different models: numeric (tables), visual (graphs), and abstract (words and symbolic expressions). Consider the following problem:

Two cellular telephone companies are offering the following monthly rates. The first company offers phone services for a basic fee of $20.00 plus $0.10 for each minute of use. The second company has no monthly fee but charges $0.45 for each minute of use. Both companies charge for the exact number of minutes, or part thereof, the service is used. Compare these two companies' charges for specific amounts of minutes for a month. Start-

ing with zero, use intervals of 10 minutes to make the comparisons: 0, 10, 20, 30, 40, 50, and 60. Which of these companies would you select for cellular telephone service and why (adapted from NCTM, 2000)?

Table 11.2 shows how students might attack the cell phone problem. Making a table, including the labels and information needed in the table, is a skill that needs to be practiced. Figure 11.21 shows the plotted points for minutes and costs. The graphing model will help students visualize the relation between minutes and costs. The students could describe the relationship using words: The first company charges $20.00 plus $0.10 more per minute and the second company just charges $0.45 per minute. Students might use a formula to describe the relationship among these quantities: $y = \$20.00 + \$0.10x$ for the first company and $y = \$0.45x$ for the second company, where $y =$ final cost in dollars and $x =$ any number of minutes (other forms could be: $y = \$0.10x + \$20$, $\$20 + \$0.10x = y$, or $\$0.10x + \$20 = y$ for the first one). The students will then use these equations to find the values for different situations.

The use of different models helps students have a better grasp of the whole situation and make better sense of the possibilities. After carefully examining the table and graph involving information from both companies, students might notice that the selection of the company could depend on the number of minutes the service is used and that a closer look at the charges provides some hidden issues and concerns. It might also be noticed that the first company will charge $20.00 even if the service is not used. They could also see the

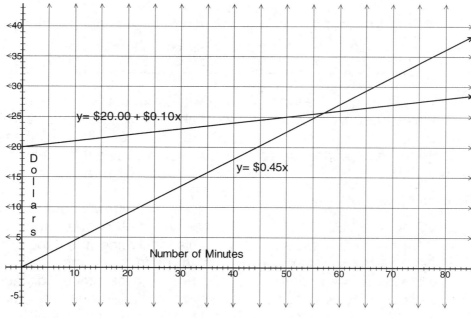

FIG 11.21.

linear relationship among the quantities for each company. For example, which company is a better choice if you only have $50.00 to spend every month, or when does it become more expensive to use the second company and why (adapted from NCTM, 2000)?

Students should have the opportunity to discuss the ways data are modeled. What are the strengths and limitations of graphical, tabular, and symbolic models? When should one be used over the other? How do you read the information from each model? Are there major differences? On one hand, graphs give a picture or visual representation of the relationship between the quantities and allow the quick recognition of linearity when change is constant. On the other hand, algebraic equations could offer a compact, easily interpreted description of the relationship between variables.

As middle school students study algebra and encounter questions that focus on quantities that change, they should analyze different graphs that provide different representations of the situation. The prob-

lem with the two cellular telephone companies provides an example for analyzing different relationships within the same set of data. Consider the second company that charged $0.45 per minute for phone calls. In this case, the cost per minute is constant, but the total cost changes as the telephone is used more. Middle school students need to differentiate between these relationships.

Your Turn

Analyze the responses middle school students give for the following exercises.

11.21. This problem involves using objects, and looking for patterns, but no verbal rule is required: Two cellular telephone companies are offering the following rates per minute every month. The first company offers phone services for a basic fee of $20.00 plus $0.20 for each minute of use. The second company has a monthly fee of $15.00 and charges $0.45 for each minute of use. Both companies charge for the exact amount of minutes the cellular telephone service is used, counting any partial minute as a full minute. Compare these two companies' charges for specific amounts of minutes for a month.

11.22. Use objects to build the designs shown in Fig. 11.22. Look for patterns to help. Copy and complete Table 11.3.

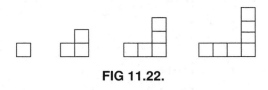

FIG 11.22.

TABLE 11.3

Area	1	3	5	7	9	11
Perimeter	4	8	12			

11.23. It takes 2 hexagons to flank 2 triangles in Fig. 11.23. It takes 3 hexagons to flank 4 triangles. How many hexagons are needed to flank 20 triangles? What is the total number of blocks that would be used? Copy and complete Table 11.4.

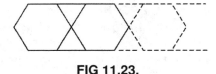

FIG 11.23.

TABLE 11.4

Number of Hexagons	2
Number of Triangles	2
Total number of blocks	4

11.24. These problems involve using objects, looking for patterns, and forming a verbal rule:

a. Which is larger $2n$ or $n + 2$? Explain your answer.

b. What happens to the value of $\frac{1}{x}$ as x gets larger and larger? Explain your answer.

c. Fill in the blank: Part of the shape is hidden behind the black rectangle in Fig. 11.24 and all of the sides of this

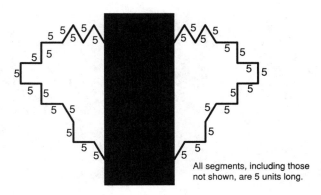

All segments, including those not shown, are 5 units long.

FIG 11.24.

shape are the same length. There are n sides, each 5 units long (adapted from Booth, 1988). The perimeter of this shape is _____ units.

11.25. Devise questions that could be used to teach the middle school students about substitution in an algebraic expression. Using the function machines in Figs. 11.25 and 11.26, find possible missing whole number inputs or outputs.

a.

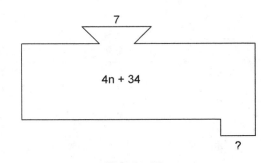

FIG 11.25.

b.

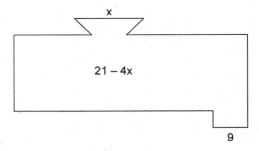

FIG 11.26.

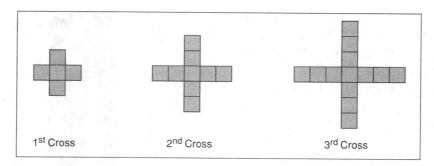

1st Cross   2nd Cross   3rd Cross

FIG 11.27.

11.26. The rules for this exercise are as follows:

> The same shape must have the same value.
>
> Different shapes could have different or the same value.
>
> Only whole numbers are involved: 0, 1, 2, 3, ...

Given the rules described above, ask middle school students to examine the following equations. They are to find the values for $\bigcirc$ and $\triangle$, explain how they got their answer, and why their answer makes sense. If $\bigcirc + \bigcirc + \bigcirc = 72$ and $(\bigcirc - \triangle) + 10 = 25$ then $\triangle = \underline{\quad}$ and $\bigcirc = \underline{\quad}$.

11.27. What rule will be developed from the following?

In Fig. 11.27, the first cross takes 5 squares to build, the second takes 9, and the third takes 13. How many squares will it take for the fourth, tenth, thirtieth, and the nth cross? Find and continue the pattern, and describe the rule for the general pattern in the space provided in Table 11.5.

Nonlinear Functions

Students in middle school should have experiences modeling situations and relationships with nonlinear functions. A problem dealing with amoebas could provide an interesting and challenging context for exploring a nonlinear function. Amoebas have the property that they split in two over time intervals. Table 11.6 lists first several ordered pairs of the quantities for this relationship. Figure 11.28 represents the graph for this relationship. Students could be asked if the relation between the number of splits and the number of amoebas graph as a straight line? Why or why not?

This example and the exercises that follow provide a readiness for the study of functions.

For middle school students, the emphasis should be on students' reasoning and justification, and their involvement with questions like "Why is that true (or false)?" "What is it about the situation that makes this possible (or impossible)? What is your

TABLE 11.5

Cross	Number of Squares
1st	5
2nd	9
3rd	13
4th	
10th	
30th	
nth	Rule: _____

TABLE 11.6

Number of Splits	Number of Amoebas	
0	1	
1	2	2^1
2	4	2^2
3	8	2^3
4	16	2^4
5	32	2^5

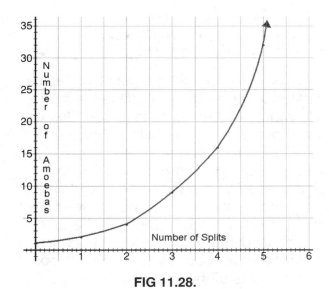

FIG 11.28.

a.

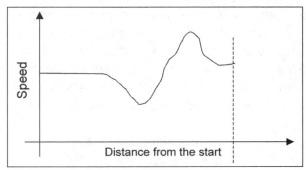

FIG 11.30.

b.

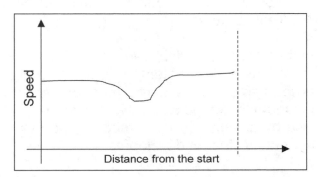

FIG 11.31.

c.

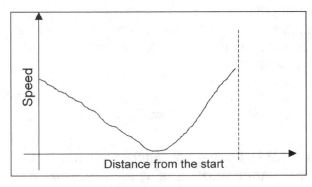

FIG 11.32.

argument in favor (or against) this step or solution?" (Jones & Bush, 1996).

Your Turn

11.28. Ask middle school students to find how long it would take to double an amount of money when the interest rate is 6% compounded annually? Assume that savings are in a tax-sheltered account so that you do not have to pay taxes until the money is withdrawn.

11.29. Peter jogs along a route that is essentially flat except for one hill. Figure 11.29 shows the route. Which of the following graphs (Figs. 11.30, 11.31, or 11.32) best describes what happens to the speed of Peter as he jogs along the route?

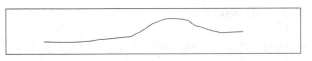

FIG 11.29.

STUDY OF STRUCTURES

The study of structures involves situations like the following:

Factor $3x^2 + 4a - 132a^2$.

The answer is $(3x + 22a)(x - 6a)$. Here, the variables are treated as arbitrary marks on paper (without having to go back to specific numbers). The variables are manipulated and their use is justified out of the overview of number properties developed when working with algebra as generalized arithmetic. Two more examples would be:

- $(1 + b) + a$ is equivalent to $1 + (b + a)$ by using the associative property of addition on the set of real numbers,
- $3(3a + 1)$ is equivalent to $9a + 3$ by using the distributive property of multiplication over addition on the set of real numbers.

In these items, students are to manipulate the mathematical statements according to properties on the set of real numbers. Asking them to defend steps made in an exercise by stating correct number properties enhances student development.

Your Turn

11.30. Try the following item with middle school students and analyze their responses. What specific justification were they able to give? What property could be used to justify the following mathematical statement?

$$a(cx + cy) = a(cx) + a(cy)$$

11.31. Try the following item with middle school students and analyze their responses. What specific justification were they able to give?

Which of the statements are true? Choose an appropriate calculation method to help you decide. Also, you need to justify or explain why you think the statement is true or false.

a. $(6 + 14) \cdot 7 = 6 + (14 \cdot 7)$
b. $78 \cdot 37 = (78 \cdot 7) + (78 \cdot 30)$
c. $587 \cdot 0 \cdot 963 = 2874 + 5 - 2879$

11.32. Find or adapt algebra problems related to the study of structures in a middle school mathematics textbook, like the ones presented previously in Figs. 11.30 and 11.31. Describe their use.

11.33. Using a pre-algebra textbook, find at least five examples of each of the different conceptions of algebra. Do you think there is a fair representation of the different conceptions of algebra in the chosen pre-algebra textbook? What are some positive aspects of the textbook? What could be done to make it better?

PLANNING

When planning for teaching algebra, you should take into account the students' readiness for learning algebra. This includes their background with the different conceptions of algebra and required prerequisites: generalized arithmetic, study of procedures for solving certain kind of problems, study of relationships among quantities, and study of structures. All the different conceptions of algebra should be presented using different models (numerical, visual, and abstract). As you plan activities, look for, and use, contexts that are motivational, meaningful, and challenging for the students.

Your Turn

11.34. Explain in writing why it is important for a teacher to take into account the different conceptions of algebra when planning teaching activities.

11.35. Develop a lesson plan that involves and integrates at least two of the different conceptions of algebra.

Planning Quickie

What follows in this section is a set of procedures for a series of lessons on solving two equations in two unknowns, which took several days to cover. Except for the initial one, the activities should be done using technology. The intent is to deal with one frequent question about using technology to teach mathematics, which is whether or not the material being covered transfers to paper/pencil tasks. The answer is a resounding YES.

For homework, the students graph pairs of equations and determine the coordinates of the point of intersection. Their results are sketched on paper for the next day. In the class following the homework assignment, technology should be used to project $y = x + 3$ and $y = ^-x + 7$ and students give the coordinates of the point of intersection.

> By inspection, they should see the common point (2, 5).
>
> They are now ready to proceed to the next topic.
>
> Using technology, adding the two equations gives $y + y = x + 3 - x + 7$.
>
> Observe that all the ys are on the left and all the xs and constants are on the right.
>
> Simplifying using technology gives $2y = 10$.
>
> Note this is one equation with one unknown, the y value would be 5.
>
> Note that 5 is the y value obtained when graphing.

Now, students summarize what transpired, and continue.

Experiment with a group of equations (all coefficients of variables ±1).

Arrive at some conclusions like the following:

> Adding two equations where the respective signs of the variables are the same result in one equation with two unknowns.
>
> Subtracting two equations where the respective signs of the variables are the same results in a nonsense situation like $0 = 6$.
>
> When the signs of the respective variables are opposite and the equations are added, something like $0 = 6$ appears.
>
> If the signs of the respective variables are opposite and the two equations are subtracted, one equation with two unknowns appears.
>
> If one of the variables has the same sign and the other has the opposite sign, either addition or subtraction yields a solveable equation with one unknown.

Ask students how to deal with $y = x + 3$ and $2y = 3x + 4$. Expect statements like the following:

> It will not do any good to add or subtract them because you will get one equation with two unknowns.
>
> If we had 2y we could subtract.
>
> That means we have to multiply that one equation.
>
> Yes, but do not forget to multiply both sides.
>
> Then we can subtract one equation from the other and get one equation with one unknown.
>
> Maybe we should multiply by a negative 2 because we make fewer sign mistakes when adding as opposed to subtracting.

ASSESSMENT

As part of the planning process, you should integrate all possible conceptions of algebra and different uses of variables at appropriate times within your assessment tasks for students. The following are some examples of common student misconceptions when using variables:

- Belief that letters have order: thinking that $a < b$ because of the order of letter in the alphabet;
- Thinking that variables are labels for objects, not number representations: $a \neq$ apples; $a =$ number of apples;
- Tendency to mix letters and numbers: rewriting $3a + 4$ as $7a$, or $2x + 3y$ as $5xy$ (Students need to understand that the expression $4ab$ conventionally means $4 \cdot a \cdot b$ and that $4 \cdot 5$ is not 45. Even though we express the commutative property of multiplication on the whole numbers as $ab = ba$, that does not work with 45 because it is not equal to 54.);
- Tendency to ignore operations in generalizations: incorrectly assuming that, since $7a \div a = 7$, then $7a - a = 7$;
- Lack of understanding of notation: $5a = 5 \cdot a$, or $ab = a \cdot b$;
- Writing 5 times n as 5n leads to 56 when $n = 6$;
- Changing the value in an equation changes the problem (Wagner, 1981). Given the equations $7 \cdot w + 22 = 100$, and $7 \cdot n + 22 = 100$, students were asked whether w or n would have a larger value (Some indicated that they could not tell without solving the equation. Others believed that order of the letter alphabetically must correspond to the order of the size of the numbers represented by w and n, so w would be larger because it comes after n in the alphabet.);
- Thinking that the equal sign means they should carry out the calculation that precedes it, and that the number after the equal sign is always the answer to the calculation. (In a study involving understanding of equality, Falkner, Levi, and Carpenter (1999) asked 145 sixth-grade students to identify the number that should go in the box in $8 + 4 = \square + 5$. All the students thought that the answer was either 12 or 17. This is an indication of the type of misconception students have when dealing with equality. The equal sign is not seen as a symbol that expresses the relationship "is the same as." See the property of equality for some ideas on how to help students develop the idea of equality.)

Assessment Quickie

Consider a multiple-choice diagnostic test. The questions should be similar for each concept (numbers or letters change but that is all) and the concepts do not have to be related. Each distracter should follow a given error pattern for the concept being tested. For example, if you ask a student to solve $2x + 3 = 19$,

- $2x = 19 - 3$ or $2x = 16$ or $x = 8$ would be correct;
- $2x = 19 + 3$ or $2x = 22$ or $x = 11$, the student added rather than subtracted;
- $2x = 19 - 3$ or $2x = 16$ or $x = 32$, the student multiplied not divided; and so on. Each error pattern would be duplicated in the questions concerning a concept. That way, when the test is assessed, if a consistent error shows up, the necessary adjustments can be made with the student.

Your Turn

11.36. Describe three possible examples of student misconceptions in algebra. (You could search for error patterns in student work or interview a middle school teacher for possible examples.)

11.37. What could be the reasons for student misconceptions you identified in problem 11.36?

11.38. What type of remediation would be appropriate for the student misconceptions you identified in exercise 11.36?

TECHNOLOGY

The use of technology to teach algebraic concepts provides avenues that will save time and offer better representation of the data (as opposed to paper and pencil methods). For example, using technology to graph $y = 2x + 6$, $y = 2x + 3$, and $y = 2x - 1$ helps students arrive at the conclusion that the number at the end of the equation tells where the line crosses the y axis, as shown in Fig. 11.33. You can discuss comparing the first and second graphs and first and second equations. Then throw in the third,

repeating the comparison. Eventually the students conclude that the constant in the equation is the y intercept.

The use of technology provides room for more explorations, in a faster manner, of different versions of tables or graphs. For example, using the cellular phone problem discussed with Table 11.2 and Fig. 11.21, the students could explore and manipulate how increasing or decreasing the basic fee for each company could affect the values and graphs. What happens to the graph if the second company starts charging a basic fee each month and the other company stays the same? What happens to the graphs if the first company increases its cost per minute from $0.10 to $0.15 or $0.20? Special attention could be drawn to the y intercept. It is important that middle school students develop a general understanding of, and facility with, slope and y intercept and their manifestations in tables, graphs, and equations.

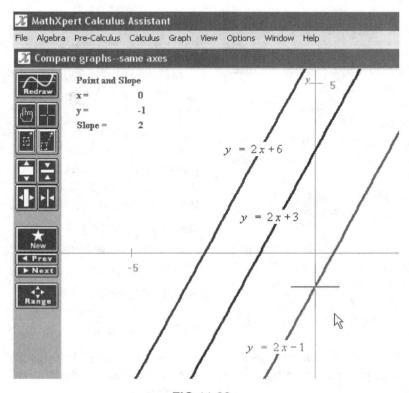

FIG 11.33.

Other variations of the cell phone problem that could be handled with technology involve extension to nonlinear relationships or addition of a nonlinear pricing plan for a third company. For example, what if the companies did not charge proportionally for portions of minutes used? If the companies rounded the cost to the nearest minute, then the monthly cost for each company would be graphed as a step function rather than a linear function (NCTM, 2000).

Technology Quickie

We now describe a series of procedures for developing and using the distance formula. Assume students know and can use the Pythagorean theorem.

- Put the axis on the screen using snap to grid.
- Plot two points using whole number coordinates.
- Connect the points with a thick colored segment.
- Create dashed lines parallel to the x axis through each point.
- Create dashed lines parallel to the y axis through each point.
- What kind of triangle has been formed?
- The thick segment is the hypotenuse of the triangle.
- Given two points on the x axis, how do we find the distance between them?
- How can we find the length of the leg parallel to the x axis?
- How can we find the length of the leg parallel to the y axis?
- How do we find the length of the thick segment?
- Do the same thing for a new triangle.
- Generalize how to find the length of the thick segment.

- Create a formula that represents the generalization.
- You just developed the distance formula.

You have never told them the distance formula—they told you.

Site Quickies

For ideas and examples of virtual manipulatives from the National Council of Teachers of Mathematics visit the following Web site: http://nctm.org

Online Version of the Principles and Standards for School Mathematics: http://standards.nctm.org

Electronic Examples—Interactive Activities that Support Principles and Standards: http://standards.nctm.org/document/eexamples/index.htm

Illuminations: Internet resources to improve the teaching and learning of mathematics for all students: http://illuminations.nctm.org/

For Virtual Manipulatives visit the following Web sites.

National Library for Virtual Manipulatives: http://nlvm.usu.edu/en/nav/index.html

Educational Java Programs: This Web site contains Java™ applets whose purpose is to be used as tools to help and enhance the education of children: http://arcytech.org/java/java.shtml

Pattern blocks:
http://www.arcytech.org/java/patterns/patterns_j.shtml

Base 10 blocks:
http://www.arcytech.org/java/b10blocks/b10blocks.html

Cuisenaire rods (Integers Rods):
http://www.arcytech.org/java/integers/integers.html

Fraction bars:
http://www.arcytech.org/java/fractions/fractions.html

For activities and other links visit the following Web site: http://mason.gmu.edu/~mmankus

Other Web sites:
Buffon's Principle demo
http://www.mste.uiuc.edu/reese/buffon/buffon.html

Matrix Multiplication of vector animation
http://www2.gasou.edu/facstaff/lroberts/demos/browser/matvec/matvec.html

3 by 3 Matrix Multiplication:
http://www.sci.wsu.edu/math/faculty/genz/220v/lessons/kentler/FullMult/break fullMatrixMultiply.html

Office for Mathematics, Science and Technology Education (University of Illinois):
http://www.mste.uiuc.edu/java/default.xml?category=Geometry

Your Turn

11.39. Find a middle school mathematics textbook and analyze the different uses of technology within this textbook. Are these uses appropriate?

11.40. Develop a lesson plan for middle school grades involving technology.

CONCLUSION

We have not covered all the middle school algebra topics, but we have started you along the desirable trail. As a professional, your responsibility is to blaze your own trail. Table 11.7 presents a summary of the conceptions of algebra and uses of variables presented in this chapter.

Middle schoolers should have many opportunities to develop, explore, and understand each of the conceptions of algebra in rich and motivational contextual settings.

TABLE 11.7

Conception of Algebra	Use of Variables
Generalized arithmetic	Pattern generalizers (translate arithmetic pattern, generalize). Example: $a + b = b + a$.
Means to solve problems	Unknown, constants (solve, simply). Example: What number, when added to 3, gives 7?
Study of relationships	Arguments, parameters (relate, graph). Example: Which one is larger $2n$ or $n + 2$?
Study of structures	Arbitrary marks on paper (manipulate, justify). Example: What property could be used to justify the following mathematical statement? $a(cx + cy) = a (cx) + a (cy)$

The proper use of manipulative materials and technology to enrich, enhance, and facilitate student learning is crucial.

STICKY QUESTIONS

11.1. Is it reasonable to expect that schools will have appropriate calculators, dynamic geometry software, dynamic data analysis software, and dynamic algebra software available for students and teachers? Defend your response.

11.2. Should you be required to teach using manipulatives like Algebra Lab Gear and Algebra Tiles? Defend your response.

11.3. Is it reasonable to expect that you keep current with teaching techniques that involve manipulatives and technology? Defend your response.

11.4. Should students be expected to have exposures to proof prior to taking algebra 1? Defend your response.

11.5. Should geometry be presented in algebra 1? If you say yes, what topics should be included? If you say no, defend your response.

11.6. As an investigative reporter, you are to interview a system of two equations with two unknowns. List five questions you would ask.

11.7. Write responses to the following:

Why should I learn algebra?
What should be taught in algebra 1?
Should the focus in algebra 1 be on mechanics, concepts, or applications?

TAG

11.1. Pick a number.

Double it.
Add 4 to the proct.
Divide the sum by 2.
Subtract the original number.
What do you get?

EXTENSION: How could the instructions be altered to get a different final response?

11.2. Pick any prime number greater than 3.

Square it.
Add 15.
Divide by 12.
What is the remainder?

EXTENSION: Prove why this is so.

11.3. $(36)(42) = 1512 = (63)(24)$
$(26)(93) = 2418 = (62)(39)$

In the two preceding examples, reversing the order of the digits in both factors gives the same product. Find other examples where this is true.

EXTENSION: Find other examples. Show when this will be true.

11.4. Two objects have a combined price of $6.80. One of the objects sells for $6.00 more than the other. What is the cost of the less expensive object (it is not $0.80)?

EXTENSION: Create a similar problem. Explain the similarities and differences between your problem and this one, and how they both work.

11.5. Pick a counting number.

Square it.
Find the square of the next largest counting number.
Find a fast way to find the second square.

EXTENSION: Will this work for integers? Fractions? Decimals?

11.6. Given a quadratic expression $ax^2 + bx + c$, a, b, and c can always be determined by the following process:

Substitute 0 into the expression. Record the result (call it R).
Substitute 1 into the expression. Record the result (call it S).
Substitute 2 into the expression. Record the result (call it T).
Record the result of S − R (call it U).
Record the result of T − S (call it V).
Record the result of V − U (call it W).

$a = 0.5W$
$b = U - 0.5W$
$c = R$

Ask someone to use a quadratic expression and give you R, S, and T. You can then identify the expression used.

EXTENSION: How does this work?

11.7. Pick any counting number.
Add the next highest counting number.
Add 9 to the sum.
Divide this new sum by 2.
Subtract the original number.
What do you get?
How does this work?

EXTENSION: Will this work for integers? Rational numbers?

11.8. Pick any counting number.

Multiply it by 6.
Add 12 to that product.
Divide the new sum by 3.

Subtract 2 from the new missing factor (quotient).

Divide this missing addend (difference) by 2.

Subtract the original number from this missing factor.

Add 9 to the missing addend.

What is the sum? Why will the sum always be the same?

EXTENSION: Does this work for integers? Rational numbers?

11.9. When Johann Friederich Carl Gauss was 10, he was asked by his teacher to find the sum of the "... following sort, 81297 + 81495 + 81693 + ⋯ + 100899, where the step from one number to the next is the same all along (here 198) and a given number of terms (here 100) ..." Gauss had the sum almost as quickly as the problem was finished being stated whereas the rest of the class took over an hour to do it. A similar problem like 1 + 2 + 3 + ⋯ + 100 can be used to show the basics of what Gauss did to solve the problem.

$$
\begin{array}{cccccccc}
1 + & 2 + & 3 + & 4 + \cdots + & 98 + & 99 + & 100 \\
\underline{100} + & \underline{99} + & \underline{98} + & \underline{97} + \cdots + & \underline{3} + & \underline{2} + & \underline{1} \\
101 + & 101 + & 101 + & 101 + \cdots + & 101 + & 101 + & 101
\end{array}
$$

The sum would be (100)(101) or the number of terms times the sum of the first and last term. However this sum is twice what it should be to answer the problem because of using each addend twice. So, the final answer of 10,100 should be divided by 2, giving 5050, the sum of the first 100 consecutive counting numbers. Do a similar problem where the constant difference between terms is not one, trying to determine a rule for the solution.

EXTENSION: Give a generalization showing how to do the sum of the first "n" consecutive counting numbers. Develop a generalization that would work for the type problem Gauss did.

11.10. Pick any counting number.

Square it.

Square the counting number that is one larger than your initial selection.

Find the difference between the two squares.

Subtract one from that missing addend (difference).

Divide the new missing addend by two.

What do you get? Why will this work every time?

EXTENSION: Does this work with integers? Rational numbers?

11.11. Using a standard rummy deck of cards, let ace = 1, jack = 11, queen = 12, and king = 13. Also, clubs = 4, diamonds = 5, hearts = 6, and spades = 7.

A volunteer should do each of the following:

Select a card, show it to the class (not you) and return the card to the deck.

Add the card value and the next highest counting number.

Multiply the sum by 5.

Add the value of the suit to this product.

Tell the answer.

At this point, you look through the deck and find the initial card. How does this work?

11.12. Use a software program that does symbolic manipulations and graphs to do the following:

Graph $y = x^2$.

What are the coordinates of the lowest point?

Graph $y = x^2 + 3$.

What are the coordinates of the lowest point?

Graph $y = x^2 + 4$.

What are the coordinates of the lowest point? If you need to do more examples, make up your own. Predict what $y = x^2 + 6$ will look like.

What are the coordinates of the lowest point?

Describe what the graph and coordinates of the lowest point of any equation like $y = x^2 + a$ (where a is any counting number) will be.

EXTENSION: Do the same activity where a is any integer.

What happens if $y = {}^-x^2 + a$ (where a is any integer)?

11.13. Use a software program that does symbolic manipulations and graphs to do the following:

Graph $y = x^2$. What are the coordinates of the lowest point?

Graph $y = (x + 3)^2$. What are the coordinates of the lowest point?

Graph $y = (x + 5)^2$. What are the coordinates of the lowest point?

If you need to do more examples, make up your own.

Predict what $y = (x + 7)^2$ will look like.

What are the coordinates of the lowest point?

Describe what the graph and coordinates of the lowest point of any equation like $y = (x + a)^2$ (where a is any counting number) will be.

EXTENSION: Do the same activity where a is any integer. What happens if $y = {}^-(x + a)^2$ (where a is any integer)?

REFERENCES

Booth, L. (1988). Children's difficulties in learning algebra. In A. F. Coxford and A. P. Shulte (Eds.), *The ideas of algebra K-12: NCTM yearbook*. Reston, VA: National Council of Teachers of Mathematics.

Falkner, K. P., Levi, L., & Carpenter, T. P. (1999). Children's understanding of equality: A foundation for algebra. *Teaching Children Mathematics, 5*, 232–236.

Jones, D., & Bush, W. S. (1996). Mathematical structure: Answering the "why" questions. *Mathematics Teacher, 89*, 716–722.

Kücheman, D. E. (1978). Children's understanding of numerical variables. *Math in Schools, 7*, 23–26.

National Council of Teachers of Mathematics. (2000). *Principles and standards for school mathematics*. Reston, VA: Author.

Usiskin, Z. (1988). Conceptions of school algebra and uses of variables. In A. F. Coxford and A. P. Shulte (Eds.), *The ideas of algebra K-12, 1988 yearbook*. Reston, VA: NCTM.

Usiskin, Z. (1997). Doing algebra in grades K-4. *Teaching Children Mathematics, 3*, 346–348.

Wagner, S. (1981). Conservation of equation and function under transformation of variable. *Journal for Research in Mathematics Education, 12*(2), 107–118.

Whitman, B. S. (1982). Intuitive equation-solving skills. In L. Silvey and J. R. Smart (Eds.), *Mathematics for middle grade (5–9), 1988 yearbook*. Reston, VA: NCTM.

12
Geometry in the Middle School Classroom

What geometry is taught and where or when in middle school? Geometry is scattered throughout the middle school curriculum. There is no specific course, and as the trend moves toward integrated topics, even if the course existed, it would be blended into a set of topics covered over the middle school years. The topics broached in the elementary grades are revisited. Why? If the concepts were taught well, understood by the students, and so on, why would they be repeated in the middle school? One reason sometimes put forward is that we have always done it that way. That is not a good reason. If the students know the topic being covered, why go over it again? That only serves to stimulate their dislike of mathematics in general, and geometry in particular. At the same time, if the students do not know the necessary information, it is im-

perative that they be properly introduced to the topics. A delicate balance, isn't it? How do you learn what to do? For the most part, you need to be aware of your students, their needs, where they have been, prior exposures, and where they are going mathematically. That coupled with the experience you will gain as you teach will provide you with guidance in your decision-making process.

DEVELOPMENTAL STAGES OF GEOMETRIC UNDERSTANDING

As decisions are made regarding what, and when or where, different geometric topics should be included, student developmental stages of geometric understanding should be taken into account. Diane van Hiele-Geldof and her husband Pierre van Hiele concluded that individuals pass through five stages of geometric understanding: Visualization (level 0), Analysis (level 1), Informal Deduction (level 2), Formal Deduction (level 3), and Rigor (level 4) (van Hiele, 1986). Middle school students should concentrate on working with activities at the Formal Deduction stage as they deal with geometric concepts and forms, assuming appropriate readiness. For example, they could discuss quadrilaterals being called squares, rectangles, rhombi, trapezoids, and parallelograms, along with things like all squares are rectangles, but

235

not all rectangles are squares. In addition, they can move beyond quadrilaterals to polygons and discuss which quadrilaterals would be in the set of regular n-gons. To develop geometry activities and accommodate instruction, consider the following (Cathcart, Pothier, Vance, & Bezuk, 2003):

1. The van Hiele stages are not age dependent; students who lack exposure to appropriate experiences will be developmentally stunted in their ability to comprehend the interdependence of geometric topics.

2. Each student must pass through each of the sequential stages in order as their understanding increases. For example, a student operating at the Visualization stage will be unable to understand an activity at the Analysis or higher stages because of inappropriate background. Developmentally, even gifted students who appear to skip levels pass through the sequential stages; they just do it quickly.

3. Students need to experience a variety of activities involving exploring, experiment, and communicating about shapes, properties, and relationships.

4. Language must match the student's geometric stage. Otherwise, the student might only be able to learn procedures and memorize relationships without real understanding. The teacher is responsible for ensuring that all (teacher and students) are speaking the same language, and students understand what is being discussed, modeled, and reasoned about. Even words that one would ordinarily assume to be commonly understood and used might not be understood in the intended way.

5. It will be difficult for students at different stages to communicate effectively with each other. A student at the Informal Deduction stage might think that a square has four congruent sides and angles, opposite parallel sides, and diagonals that are perpendicular bisectors of each other. A student at the Visualization stage might think about a compact disk case, and that is all.

Your Turn

12.1. Visit a middle school mathematics classroom and informally assess two or three students' understanding of geometry. You should look for strengths and weaknesses. Where would you place their thinking related to the developmental stages of geometric understanding?

12.2. Examine a middle school mathematics textbook's section on geometry and describe it in relation to the developmental stages of geometric understanding.

12.3. Write a lesson plan to introduce a geometry topic of your choice to middle school students at developmental stage 2 (Informal Deduction) of geometric understanding. Then write a lesson to introduce a related topic to middle school students at developmental stage 3 (Formal Deduction) of geometric understanding.

EXTENDING GEOMETRIC IDEAS IN MIDDLE SCHOOL

Topics introduced in the elementary curriculum can be revisited and extended in middle school geometry. Triangles, for example, can be reinvestigated, this time discovering that the sum of the measures of all interior angles is 180°. Topics are extended two ways: providing opportunities to investigate ideas and establishing an intuitive background for a variety of concepts. These are two very important factors in students' development of geometric understanding and moving through the van Hiele levels.

Investigations could focus on the sum of the measures of all the exterior angles of a triangle. Thus, geometry is blended with algebra, discovery, and generalization. The crucial ingredient is that you

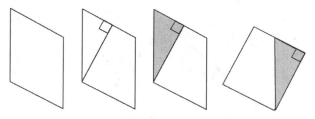

FIG 12.1.

must be willing to investigate geometry. Too many times, teachers make the decision to bypass geometry because of the lack of time, thinking students will get it next year! When does this stop? Where should it start? Geometry should not be an unfamiliar topic in the tenth grade.

Figure 12.1 shows a standard set of steps for showing that a parallelogram can be transformed to a rectangle, leading to the conclusion that the area of a parallelogram is base times height. This should, at the same time, establish a connection between two shapes and how to find area. It should also raise a question. Because the new figure looks like a rectangle, why don't we use length and width as elements of the formula for the area of a parallelogram? Or reverse the wording and use base times height for the area of the rectangle? It may appear as no big concern for us because we know, but students now have two more vocabulary words to learn and are identifying the same thing by two different names, each of which is to be used in a given setting (length with rectangle and base with parallelogram). Does that make sense? Does it really matter? Could we be more consistent in our discussion with students?

Your Turn

12.4. Research the naming of terms in the formulas for finding the area of rectangles and parallelograms in the middle school curriculum. When did the different names occur and is there any logical reason for them?

Establishing a connection between two shapes and finding area should not be abandoned too quickly. Revisit finding the area of a trapezoid: $\left(\dfrac{b_1 + b_2}{2}\right)$ (h). This formula can be written in a variety of formats and, depending on the algebraic skills of the students, confusion can exist as teachers attempt to shift from one form to another. For this discussion, use the form shown here and state it as the average of the bases, times the height. Using that, look at finding the area for a rectangle, parallelogram, square, trapezoid, triangle, and circle as shown in Fig. 12.2. Even though the figures are not in standard position, you can see that the area for each of them can be found by taking the average of the bases times the height.

The rectangle and parallelogram transformations are relatively straightforward. For a square, the area is usually given as $A = s^2$. Using that idea and the trapezoid formula of the average of the bases, the area of a square becomes $\left(\dfrac{\text{side} + \text{side}}{2}\right)(\text{side}) = \left(\dfrac{2\,(\text{side})}{2}\right)(\text{side}) = (\text{side})^2 = s^2$. The triangle seems a little confusing at first, but the lower base is the side to which the altitude is drawn. The upper base is the vertex, which is the top of the altitude, and has a length of zero. So for the triangle area, using the average of the bases gives $\left(\dfrac{\text{side} + \text{zero}}{2}\right)(\text{height}) = \left(\dfrac{\text{base}}{2}\right)(\text{height})$.

The circle seems strange initially, and it does require some editorial liberty to discuss. We normally think of bases as being straight-line segments. For this discussion, the base is a curved line segment, the length of which is one fourth of the circumference of the circle. That is, for this example, arc AB = arc CD = $0.5\pi r$. The diameter, or height in this case, will be 2r. Using the average of the bases formula,

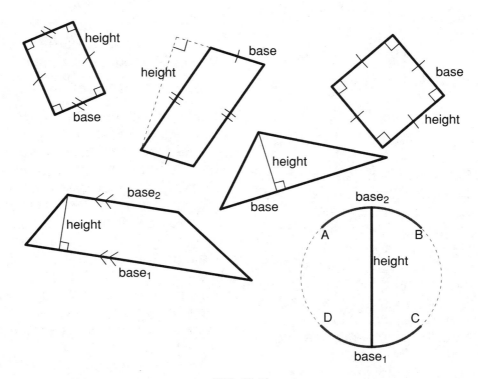

FIG 12.2.

$A = \left(\dfrac{0.5\pi r + 0.5\pi r}{2}\right)(2r) = \left(\dfrac{\pi r}{2}\right)(2r) = (\pi r)(r) = \pi r^2$.

You might be saying, "Why didn't someone show me this before?" "Why don't we teach this method in the schools?" Those are legitimate questions that can be partially answered, but not totally. The easy part of the answer involves preparation to get to the level where a student understands the average of the bases formula. Some students are confused by the algebra involved and are unable to readily relate average of the bases to $\left(\dfrac{b_1 + b_2}{2}\right)\left(\dfrac{h}{2}\right)$ or $\left(\dfrac{1}{2}\right)(b_1 + b_2)(h)$.

Given that algebraic confusion, it would be difficult for some students to understand applying that formula to a variety of shapes. In addition, before applying the formula, areas of rectangles and parallelograms, at least, have to be considered. Once those are done, some would question the reasonableness of returning to

them to give a different formula. It seems that this approach would be a wonderful extension for those students who have mastered the formulas for area of the shapes mentioned.

Middle school provides the setting for presenting a multitude of topics at an intuitive level that can be investigated in greater depth and more formally later in the secondary curriculum. Joining the midpoints of the sides of a triangle to form four smaller triangles, all of which are congruent and similar to the initial triangle, is one example as shown in Fig. 12.3.

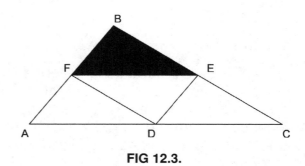

FIG 12.3.

Here, triangles ADF, FEB, DCE, and EFD are congruent and similar to triangle ABC. Software now available will measure the area of each of the triangles, as well as slopes and lengths of sides. These tools provide students with the opportunity to investigate and develop insight into relations that exist in triangles. For example, they could conclude that the area of triangle ADF is 0.25 times the area of triangle ABC. Some students might say they know that the area of triangle ABC is four times that of triangle ADF because of the measures they see. They need to learn of the inaccuracies that are inherent in measuring. They should also be conscious that segments AB and DE are parallel, and that the length of segment BC is twice that of segment DF. All of these intuitive feelings would spring from simple investigations and discoveries using the technology now available. Later, in formal geometry, where such things are proven (van Hiele levels 3 and 4), the groundwork laid via the technology should establish valuable background information, and perhaps even a realization for the need for a more formal authentication of the intuitive feelings. Perhaps the side-side-side congruence theorem would be used to establish that the four smaller triangles are, in fact, congruent.

Another interesting extension involving the initial triangle ABC in Fig. 12.3 can be developed. Segment DE joins the midpoints of sides AC and BC, respectively. Rather than using the midpoint, establish D on AC somewhere. Construct a line parallel to AB through D and create E as the intersection of the new line and side BC. Measure the length of segments AC and CD and the area of triangles CDE and CAB. Establish a ratio between the long and short length and the large and small area. When the length ratio is 2:1, the area ratio will be 4:1. When the length ratio is 3:1, the area ratio will be 9:1. Before long,

the students should be able to generalize the pattern. At the same time, many students will become aware of the differences between linear changes and those of areas.

Extending the idea of similar triangles that stimulated the last two ideas, it is important that students not only gain a feel for the existence of such things, but also that they see uses of them. In either an informal or formal geometry course, use of similar triangles to measure heights is common, but typically they occur in the form of pictures in the text. There are some activities that can be used to stimulate development and see applications at the same time. One of the most intriguing ways of measuring heights of inaccessible objects involves the use of a mirror, marble, and linear measuring device, shown in Fig. 12.4 (Kidd, Myers, & Cilley, 1970, p. 248). Assume the ground is horizontal and that the flagpole is perpendicular to the ground. The marble is used to ensure that the mirror lies in the plane parallel to the ground. If the marble rolls off one edge of the mirror, objects would be used to level the mirror before any measurements are made. An individual is positioned so that the top of the flagpole can be seen in the mirror. That mirror spot is marked mentally or physically and measurements are taken. The distance in Fig. 12.4 from the point on the

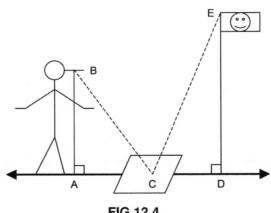

FIG 12.4.

mirror to a point below the person's eye (AC) is measured. The height of the person's eye above the ground (AB) can be determined. The distance from the point on the mirror to a point below the top of the object being used (CD) can also be found. Precision can be impacted by measuring accuracy, but the similar triangles are observed and used to find the missing height. Triangle ABC is similar to triangle CED. Knowing that the ratio AB:AC is the same as CD:CE and being able to measure AB, AC, and CD permits calculation of DE.

The height of that same triangle can be measured using a statia tube, which is a long cylinder (used like a telescope) with two parallel strings a known distance from where the eye would be placed at one end of the tube. The top of the pole is aligned with the top string, and the bottom of the pole with the bottom string, as shown in Fig. 12.5. Segments BG and AF represent the strings, which are 1 centimeter apart. The distance from the eyeball, C, to the plane determined by BG and AF is 1 meter. Because the ratio of length of tube to height of strings is 100:1, when the top and bottom of the pole can be seen, the viewer will be 100 times the height of the pole away from the base of the pole. Only the distance from below the eye of the viewer to the base of the pole needs to be measured.

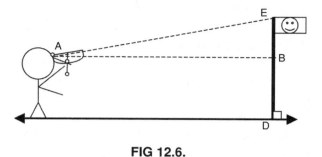

FIG 12.6.

Your Turn

12.5. Give a geometric explanation of why the statia tube will provide the height of the flagpole. (This activity involves van Hiele levels 2 and 3.)

A hypsometer can be fashioned using a protractor, string, weight, drinking straw, and tape. The string, with the weight at one end, is attached to the wedge of the protractor. The straw is taped to the straight edge of the protractor and is used as a sighting mechanism as shown in Fig. 12.6. Assuming horizontal ground, sight the top of the pole through the straw and mark the angle of elevation on the protractor. Knowing the height from the eyeball to the ground (same as segment BD), the distance from the person to the flagpole (same as segment AB), and the angle of elevation, the height of the pole can be calculated as $\overline{BD} + \overline{BE}$. A variation could involve attaching the hypsometer to a clipboard that has a piece of graph paper on it. The sight straw would be collinear with one of the graph segments. The weighted string becomes the hypotenuse of a right triangle, and similar triangles could be used to calculate the height of the object once the distance from it is measured.

Another interesting topic available for investigation and extension in the middle school geometry program is the Pythagorean theorem. Different proofs can be examined, depending on the students'

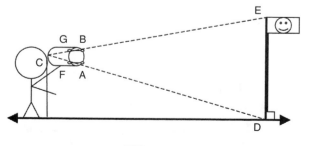

FIG 12.5.

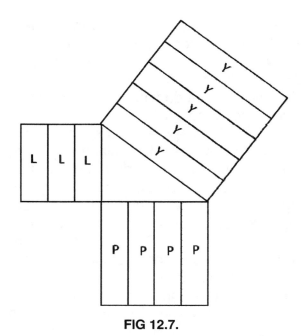

FIG 12.7.

mathematical strengths. One example of proof is shown in Fig. 12.7 using Cuisenaire rods. Figure 12.8 shows how equilateral triangles can be used to establish the Pythagorean theorem. Note: When White is the unit, Lime = 3, Purple = 4, and Yellow = 5.

Your Turn

12.6. There are three other ways the lime and purple Cuisenaire rods can be arranged to build the yellow square and show that $3^2 + 4^2 = 5^2$. Sketch them,

remembering that a rod may not be split into parts. (This activity involves van Hiele level 2.)

12.7. Determine whether or not "proofs" like that shown in Fig. 12.8 are limited to regular polygons. Show an example to support your position.

12.8. Do the Pythagorean theorem "proof" shown in Fig. 12.8 using semicircles. (This activity could involve van Hiele levels 3 and 4.)

12.9. One U.S. president did a couple proofs of the Pythagorean theorem. Name the president and show examples of his proofs.

Discussions about locus can provide attention-grabbing objectives for some students. With dynamic software, students can be enticed to conjecture what will happen as the locus of a point or line is investigated. For example, given two points, what is the locus of all points equidistant from them? In Fig. 12.9, segment CD is the radius of the circles centered at A and B. E and F are equidistant from A and B. Tracing the locus of E and F as CD changes quickly reveals that the desired result is the perpendicular bisector of segment AB. Students could be asked to develop the construction and conjecture the results before the actual trace. One difficulty with this approach is that the students will know the power of the software, and there is a temptation to use it to answer

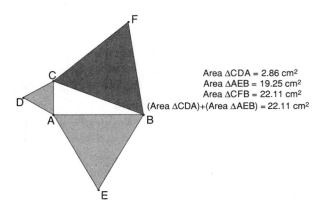

Area ΔCDA = 2.86 cm²
Area ΔAEB = 19.25 cm²
Area ΔCFB = 22.11 cm²
(Area ΔCDA)+(Area ΔAEB) = 22.11 cm²

FIG 12.8.

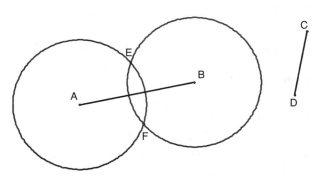

FIG 12.9.

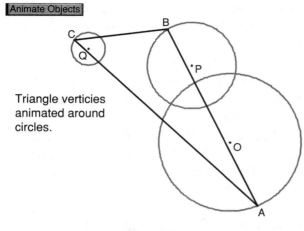

Triangle verticies
animated around
circles.

FIG 12.10.

the question without giving the question much thought. It is your responsibility to sell the students on the advantages of thinking about a situation where the answer can be quickly derived so the patterns and habits necessary for resolving more complex issues can be established. Part of your sales presentation should include the need to more formally prove the things being established. The proof may come later in a formal geometry class, and it may even be in the classic two-column format. The students who possess this intuitive "feel" for what the situation encompasses should be better equipped to deal with establishing an advanced-level proof.

The trace function of dynamic software permits an early approach to the topic of locus. At the same time, it can raise the curiosity level of students enough that they will investigate traces of a variety of things.

Figure 12.10 shows a triangle that was constructed and shown to a group of seventh graders. Each vertex was located on a circle of random radius length. After construction, each vertex was animated around its respective circle. An animation button was created and then the circles and their centers were hidden. As motion was started, the students were to deter-

mine how the construction was created. They were to create a similar situation to show the idea had been mastered. They did, and the objective was accomplished. However, one student traced the locus of a side of the triangle as the action was taking place. The idea spread and soon a multitude of traces was taking place. The variety of designs created and the discussion about what could be done were invigorating. Several students created similar designs for other polygons and did traces with them as well. Given the tools, encouragement, and some latitude, students will investigate and discover many things. Perhaps, more important, questions are raised and background is laid for the need for more formal proof, which could be approached at the time, or later, depending on student readiness as well as other factors.

For scaled drawings, you often see grids drawn on a cartoon character and then a greater scale grid used to produce an enlarged version. That method certainly works, but there is another way to accomplishing the objective. Tie a number of rubber bands together by looping one inside the end of another. Suppose you have three rubber bands connected in this manner as shown in Fig. 12.11. Fix one end of the string beyond one side of the figure to be enlarged so there is a slight stretching of the string of rubber bands to get the

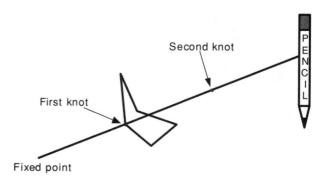

FIG 12.11.

first knot to be over the closest point of the sketch. Place a pencil inside the other end of the rubber band chain. Visually trace the first knot of the rubber band chain along the figure. The pencil at the end of the chain will enlarge the figure.

Historically, students have constructed perpendicular lines using a straightedge and compass. It is a way to help students see and gain a "feel for" right angles. Another method of accomplishing the task is to fold a piece of paper. Open the paper and then refold it so that part of the initial fold lies on top of itself. Opening reveals perpendicular line segments. Repeating the process of folding part of one segment onto itself at a different point will yield parallel line segments. The third segment, perpendicular to the other two, serves as a transversal. A fourth fold could be created to establish an oblique transversal. Folding with waxed paper is advantageous because of its translucence. Other classic folding activities involve bisecting an angle and constructing a parabola. Patty Paper geometry (Serra, 1994) has come onto the scene as a distinct topic in the study of geometry.

Your Turn

12.10. Describe the sequence of steps necessary to bisect an angle using paper folding. Give your instructions to a novice to determine if they are clear enough to produce the desired results. (This activity involves van Hiele levels 2 and 3.)

12.11. Describe the sequence of steps necessary to produce a parabola using paper folding. Give your instructions to a novice to determine if they are clear enough to produce the desired results. (This activity involves van Hiele levels 2 and 3.)

12.12. Do a Patty Paper construction. This should be different from the ones de-

scribed or assigned in this text. Cite the reference used to obtain the problem. Describe the sequence of steps used to complete the construction. (This activity involves van Hiele levels 2 and 3.)

Finally comes the question of how we study informal geometry. In most instances, it is inserted into the middle school curriculum as separate features in the textbook. As the trend to integrate topics grows, the likelihood is that there will be more informal geometry. An informal geometry text that covers the topics of a classic geometry course would not focus on formal proofs. Proofs would be basically given as facts and the students would work exercises using the theorems given. At first glance this may not seem like a good thing to do. However, if the students gain insight and an intuitive feel for what the theorems project, that background can be used later when there is a need for more formal coverage of the topic. Geometer's Sketchpad, Cabri, TI 92, Casiopia A22, Peanut Software (http://math.exeter.edu/rparris/), and so on could be used to generate this intuitive feel by manipulation of constructed figures.

Your Turn

12.13. Is the figure created in Fig. 12.11 an exact duplicate or distorted? Give a geometric defense of your response. (This activity could involve van Hiele levels 2, 3, and 4.)

12.14. Is there a need for an informal geometry course in the curriculum that precedes the typical high school geometry course? Why or why not?

12.15. Rather than a separate informal geometry course, should the topics be intertwined into the current preformal geometry curriculum as it is now done in most districts? Why or why not?

CHARACTERISTICS AND PROPERTIES OF TWO- AND THREE-DIMENSIONAL SHAPES

Middle school students should have investigation opportunities that involve precisely describing, classifying, and understanding relationships among types of two- and three-dimensional objects (e.g., angles, triangles, quadrilaterals, cubes, and cones) and using the defining properties and similar attributes of these objects (including their angles, side lengths, perimeters, areas, and volumes; NCTM, 2000). This section provides some discussion and examples of this type of investigations, first using two-dimensional shapes and second using three-dimensional shapes. The investigations for two-dimensional shapes involve convex (interior angles are less than 180°) and concave (nonconvex) polygons. Polygons are named according to the number of sides (quadrilateral [4], pentagon [5], hexagon [6], and so on, or n-gon in general, where n represents the number of sides of the polygon). The following are some possible activities involving two-dimensional figures.

Your Turn

12.16. Ask middle school students to make different triangles on a geoboard using rubber bands and then draw a picture of their triangle on dot paper (see Fig. 12.12), describing each triangle, incorporating precise geometric language (equilateral, isosceles, scalene, acute, right, or obtuse). (This activity involves van Hiele levels 0, 1, and 2.)

12.17. Ask middle school students to make different squares on a geoboard and sketch them on dot paper (see Fig. 12.12). Ask them to find as many squares as possible (limited to a 5-pin by 5-pin section of

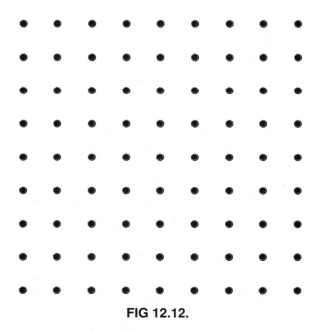

FIG 12.12.

the geoboard) and to answer the following questions:

How many squares did you find?

How do you know if you have found all possible squares?

(This activity involves van Hiele levels 0, 1, and 2.)

12.18. Ask middle school students to find as many different rectangles as possible on a geoboard (limited to a 5-pin by 5-pin section of the geoboard). (This activity involves van Hiele level 3.)

Two-dimensional shapes can also be investigated using transformational geometry. Transformational geometry could be used to describe sizes, positions, and orientation of shapes through flips, turns, slides, and scaling, also including examination of the congruence, similarity, and line or rotational symmetry of objects (NCTM, 2000).

Translations, rotations, reflections, and glide reflections preserve shape and size and can create images that have symmetry. Compare your left hand with your right hand. They are an approximate (we know there are slight differences in the hands)

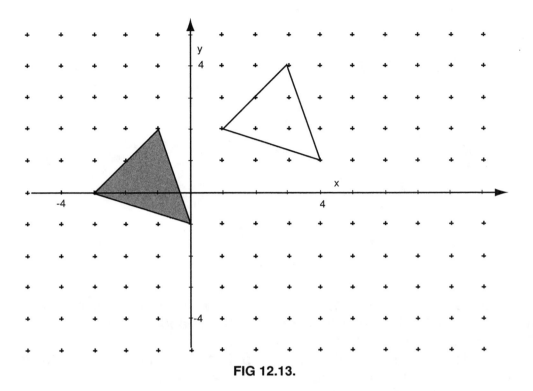

FIG 12.13.

example of symmetry created by reflection. For translation or sliding symmetry, consider a wallpaper pattern that repeats. Cut out a piece of the wallpaper and slide it up or down. It matches a new section exactly. Rotation or turning symmetry can be seen on fancy car wheels. We recommend that you read about the work of M. C. Escher and review some of his famous images using transformations. (Information can be found at http://www.mcescher.com.)

Translations preserve not only size and shape but also orientation. When we translate (or slide) a triangle with vertices at (3,4), (4,1), and (1,2) four steps to the left and two steps down, we have a triangle that appears identical, except that it has vertices at (⁻1, 2), (0, ⁻1), and (⁻3, 0), as shown in Fig. 12.13. The two triangles, the original and the shaded copy, demonstrate translation symmetry.

Rotations preserve size and shape, but the orientation changes as the figure is turned about the center of rotation. The tri-

angle in Fig. 12.14 has been rotated 130° clockwise. The two dashed figures indicate the rotation. The image, or copy, has been shaded. The center of rotation may be near or far from the figure; it may even be on or inside the figure as it is in the quadrilateral in Fig. 12.14, which shows a rotation of 80° counterclockwise about a vertex of the figure (the image has been shaded).

An axis of symmetry, reflection line, or mirror is required to reflect a figure. As with the point of rotation, this axis may be far from the figure, near the figure, on the figure, or even inside the figure. In Fig. 12.15, the mirror is indicated by a thick line segment, over which the figure on the left has been flipped to create a congruent, but reversed, image on the right. You can see that, although the orientation of the shaded image is different from that of the original figure, size and shape have been preserved. Additionally, the original hexagon and its image are equally distant from the line of reflection.

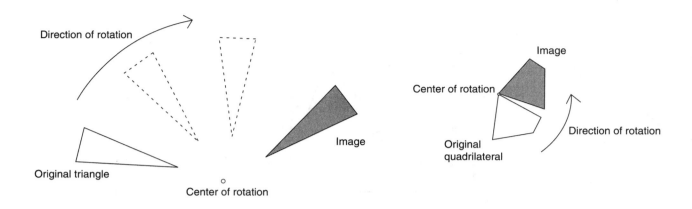

FIG 12.14.

The last transformation, and perhaps the most fun one, is the glide reflection. In Fig. 12.16, a pattern of footprints was created from a single original sketch. For each image, the original is either translated or both translated and reflected. Can you figure out which is the original sketch? Do you think each of the images is congruent to the original? Can you find the mirror line?

Your Turn

12.19. Consider the following capital letters of our alphabet.
A B C D E F G H I J K L M N O P Q R S T U V W X Y Z

a. Determine which have reflectional symmetry about a vertical mirror within the letter.
b. Determine which have reflectional symmetry about a horizontal mirror within the letter.
c. Determine which have rotational symmetry within the letter.
d. Which letters have more than one type of symmetry within the letter?
e. Which letters have all three types of symmetry within the letter?
f. Which letters have no symmetry within the letter? (This activity involves van Hiele levels 1 and 2.)

The investigation of three-dimensional shapes is very important at the middle school level. This includes the study of polyhedra, which are three-dimensional shapes with polygon faces (triangles, squares, and so on), edges, and vertices. A regular polyhedron is one whose faces

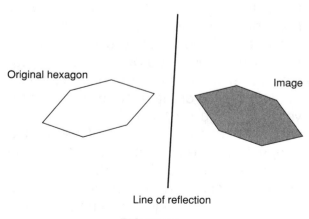

FIG 12.15.

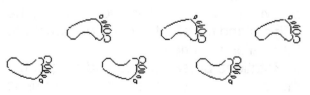

FIG 12.16.

consist of the same type of regular congruent polygons. There are five regular polyhedra: tetrahedron (4 equilateral triangles), octahedron (8 equilateral triangles), icosahedron (20 equilateral triangles), hexahedron (6 squares), and dodecahedron (12 regular pentagons). Pythagoras (582–500 B.C.) is thought to have begun the study of polyhedra. Plato (427–347 B.C.) studied these polyhedra, and subsequently they became known as the Platonic Solids. There is another set of polyhedra, studied by Archimedes (287–212 B.C.), known as the Archimedean Solids. They are 13 semiregular shapes composed of more than one type of regular polygon. Soccer balls are made up of regular pentagons and hexagons with the same side length. If the faces of the polygons were not on a curved surface, the soccer ball would be an Archimedean Solid. Other three-dimensional shapes are prisms, pyramids, cylinders, and cones.

Your Turn

12.20. Using an assortment of three-dimensional shapes, ask students to classify and describe the geometric shapes (how they are different or the same). You should also ask students to verbalize what they notice about the shapes. For example, some shapes can roll and others cannot. (This activity involves van Hiele levels 1 and 2.)

12.21. Using a set of three-dimensional shapes, organize the shapes in two different groups, and ask students to tell why the shapes in each group belong together. (This activity involves van Hiele levels 1 and 2.)

12.22. Using a set of three-dimensional shapes, ask students to choose two shapes and tell how they are alike or dif-

TABLE 12.1

Polyhedron	Faces	Vertices	Edges
Tetrahedron			
Cube			
Octahedron			
Triangular prism			
Square pyramid			

ferent. (This activity involves van Hiele levels 1 and 2.)

12.23. Using a set of three-dimensional shapes, ask students to examine a shape and write several statements about its characteristics. (This activity involves van Hiele levels 1 and 2.)

12.24. Ask students to find and record the number of faces, vertices, and edges for a set of polyhedrons: tetrahedron, cube, octahedron, triangular prism, and square pyramid (see Table 12.1). Ask students to find relationships among the shapes and to look for patterns. (This activity involves van Hiele levels 1 and 2.)

12.25. Ask students to make a replica of a cube using modeling clay. Then ask them to tell what various polygons occur when a plane cuts through a cube (a knife could be used to cut the cube and experiment). Figure 12.17 presents two possible cuts. Ask students to predict responses for the following questions and then verify their predictions, recording their results in Table 12.1:

Are all cross sections of a cube bounded by quadrilaterals?

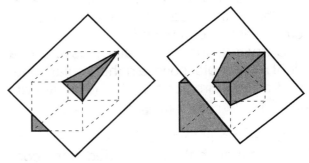

FIG 12.17.

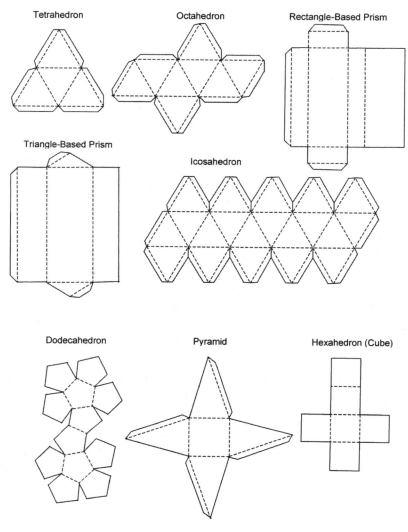

FIG 12.18.

What kinds of polygonal regions could be cross sections of a cube? (Find as many cross sections as you can.)

What is the least number of edges a cross section can have?

What is the greatest number of edges a cross section can have?

Carry out the same activities using a right rectangular solid, a right circular cone, and a right circular cylinder. (This activity involves van Hiele level 3.)

A net is a flat version of a three-dimensional shape that can be folded along connecting edges of the faces to form a solid with all faces connected edge to edge and having no overlapping faces or open gaps. Figure 12.18 provides nets (with flaps for connecting) for tetrahedrons, hexahedrons, octahedrons, rectangular solids, dodecahedrons, icosahedrons, pyramids, and right triangular prisms. The students should have opportunities to construct similar polygons to make nets of their own.

Your Turn

12.26. Can you construct a three-dimensional shape with parallelograms?

Describe the shape and compare it with a rectangular-based prism. (This activity involves van Hiele levels 2 and 3.)

Middle school students should have many opportunities to explore geometric situations and develop an intuitive background by using visualization, spatial reasoning, and geometric modeling to solve problems. This should also include opportunities for students to use two-dimensional representations of three-dimensional objects (NCTM, 2000). Murray (2004) asked middle school students to explore the relationship between the surface area and volume of right-rectangular-based and right-non-rectangular-based prisms using eight cubes and a constant volume. One student's written reflection was:

In these two investigations, we worked with rectangular and non-rectangular prisms. First, we arranged cubes into shapes of rectangular prisms. While doing this, we found that we could reduce the surface area of a prism but still have the same amount of volume. We found that the more cube-like the prism was, the less surface area there was. This is because the cubes are not showing many faces. If you had a long, skinny, and short prism (one cube high and wide), you would have a lot of surface area because every cube would show at least four sides. Here is an example. If you have 2 prisms, both with a volume of 8, you could have two different surface areas. You could have a cube $= 2 \times 2 \times 2$, or a long, skinny, and short prism $= 1 \times 1 \times 8$. To find the surface area of them, it will help to draw them. Here they are. (p. 6)

(See Fig. 12.19.)

Another student reflected after the same activity in the following manner:

I will start with the $2 \times 2 \times 2$ prism. I know that all of sides are the same, so all that I have to do is figure out one side and multiply it by 6. To find the surface area of one face, I will multiply its two dimensions together to

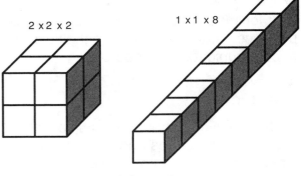

FIG 12.19.

get 4 units square, which I then multiply by 6 to get to 24 square units. That is the surface area of the $2 \times 2 \times 2$ prism.

The $1 \times 1 \times 8$ prism is not as easy. There are two different size faces: two 1×1s, and four 1×8s. The 1×1 faces are easy because $1 \times 1 = 1 \times 2$ (because there are two) $= 2$ units square. The four 1×8 are harder $1 \times 8 = 8 \times 4$ (because there are four 1×8 faces) $= 32$ square units. $32 + 2 = $ a total surface area of 34 square units. Its surface area is 10 square units larger than the $2 \times 2 \times 2$ prism, but has the same volume.

Next, we developed strategies for finding the volume of both rectangular and non-rectangular prism. While we were making these strategies, we found that the number of unit cubes that are needed to fill a prism, and the volume are the same.

We also made a strategy to find the volume of any prism. First, you have to find the surface area of the bottom. Next, you have to find the height. Then you multiply them together to get the volume. The surface area of the bottom will tell you how many cubes will fit on the bottom, then the height will tell you ho many cubes will fit. (p. 7).

Both students demonstrated some understanding and acceptable use of vocabulary. The first student's reflection shows a deeper understanding of prisms, surface area, and maximum and minimum surface area when volume is held constant. The other student offers no convincing evidence of understanding. Related vocabulary is used to analyze the relationship, but there is no connection to problem solutions or examples (Murray, 2004). As students look for meaning, we need to provide experiences that will allow them the flexibility to communicate their ideas.

Your Turn

12.27. Give a group of middle school students eight cubes and ask them to explore the relationship between the surface area and volume of right-rectangular-based and right-non-rectangular-based prisms using eight cubes and a constant volume. At the end, ask them to write a reflection about their findings.

CREATING AND CRITIQUING INDUCTIVE AND DEDUCTIVE ARGUMENTS

The middle school students should continue studying, creating, and critiquing inductive and deductive arguments concerning geometric ideas and relationships, such as congruence, similarity, and the Pythagorean theorem. For example, students should be asked to create symmetrical designs using pattern blocks, geoboards, or draw some on graph paper. Having done that, they should develop the skill of discussing their creation. As they converse about their work, they should learn to describe their thought processes and why what they have come up with is correct. Their arguments need to be well developed, coherent, and mathematically sound.

Your Turn

12.28. Ask students to draw three-by-three squares on graph paper, and shade three of the small squares so that the figure created has one line of symmetry. Explain the two examples illustrated in

FIG 12.20.

Fig. 12.20. Present students with the following questions:
- How many different patterns with one line of symmetry can you make by shading in three small squares?
- Can you make patterns with two lines of symmetry?
- Shade in four small squares and make figures with one line of symmetry; with two lines of symmetry.
- Can you make figures with more than two lines of symmetry when four small squares are shaded? Ask students to compare their findings. (This activity involves van Hiele levels 2 and 3 and was adapted from Eperson, 1982.)

CONCLUSION

The study of geometry at the middle school level should focus on students' development of informal deduction (van Hiele level 2) and formal deduction (van Hiele level 3) involving concrete and pictorial experiences. When students have opportunities to investigate and work with scale drawings, tessellations, coordinate geometry, and expand appropriate mathematical language, they are developing spatial reasoning and spatial visualization. The activities presented in this chapter have overlapping benefits. As students work with these different activities, you should also look for information about their geometric thinking level. This is an informal but powerful way of assessing understanding, and will help you comprehend students' geometric development.

STICKY QUESTIONS

12.1. Herodotus (484?–425 B.C.) was a Greek historian who described the building of a tunnel through Mount Castro to bring water to the capital city Samos, on the Greek island of Samos. Archaeologists rediscovered the tunnel in 1882. The tunnel was about 1 kilometer long and about 2 meters high. The floor of the tunnel contained a deep ditch (2 meters in width at top and 8 meters in width at bottom of the ditch), probably to allow for more pipes. There were vertical vents for changing air and cleaning away rubble. The tunnel was dug from opposite ends with the digging teams meeting at the center, which is verifiable because there is a 10-meter horizontal and 3-meter vertical jog at the center.

How the tunnel was dug without benefit of guiding shafts was not told, but the assumption is that similar triangles were used. See Fig. 12.21 (which is not drawn to scale) for measurements related to this discussion (Steen, 1994, pp. 576–578). Assume the tunnel entrances are at A and B.

Construct a rectangle with a notched-out corner as shown in Fig. 12.21. Mark off a convenient distance, BE (750 meters). Construct a right angle at each corner of the figure. Make EF = 1000 meters, FG = 2000 meters, and GH = 800 meters, which

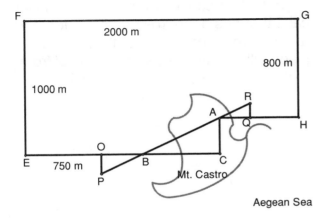

FIG 12.21.

forces AC to be 200 meters. Suppose AH is 250 meters, which forces BC to be 1000 meters. So, in triangle ABC, AC = 200 meters and BC = 1000 meters.

Construct similar triangle OBP with OB = 50 meters and OP = 10 meters, which makes corresponding angles ABC and OBP congruent. Sight from P through B toward A. Do the same thing at A with triangle RAQ and sight from R through A toward B. Dig it?

Duplicate the sketch for Fig. 12.21 using a dynamic geometry software. Perform the calculations in detail for this problem. Does it seem reasonable that this complex construction could be done almost 2600 years ago? Why or why not?

12.2. Eratosthenes measured the earth's circumference to within 1% of what we now have it to be. He did it in the late part of the 3rd century B.C. Eratosthenes knew that at summer solstice (about June 21) the sun would be directly over the city of Syene in Egypt. He could tell this because the sun's rays were reflected from the water in a deep well with no well wall shadows. He put a vertical rod in the ground at Syene and also at Alexandria. The Syene stick cast no shadow at noon and the Alexandrea one did. From that, Eratosthenes calculated the angle of elevation of the sun to be 82.8° (see Fig. 12.22). He knew the distance between the two sticks was about 500 miles. He used the alternate interior angle theorem to conclude that the central angle between the two sticks was 7.2°. But, because 7.2° is of the circumference of a circle, he deduced that the circumference was about 25,000 miles. Note: He computed in stadia (10 stadia = 1 mile; Rosskopf, 1970, p. 381). Figure 12.22, which is not drawn to scale, shows the idea behind what Eratosthenes did. Find another example of measurement in the history of mathematics. Describe how the

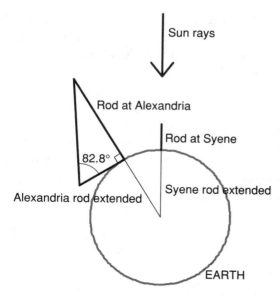

FIG 12.22.

measurements were done and create a sketch using dynamic software that will show what was done.

12.3. Should we teach inductive, deductive, formal, or informal geometry in middle school? Why or why not?

12.4. Should we teach topics from transformational geometry in middle school? Why or why not?

12.5. We name polygons as triangles, quadrilaterals, pentagons, and so on. Perhaps you have seen some of the larger sided ones called 14-gons, 15-gons, and so on. Why not call them all n-gons and insert the appropriate value for n; like 3-gon, 4-gon, 5-gon, and so on?

TAG

12.1. Break the code: A = 2, B = 0, C = 2, D = 0, E = 3, F = 3, G = 2, H = 4, I = 2, J = 2, K = 4, L = 2.

12.2. How many pennies can you arrange so each penny touches every other penny?

12.3. Arrange 6 pennies in the form of a cross (see Fig. 12.23). Move the coins and form two straight rows with 4 pennies in each.

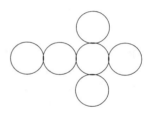

FIG 12.23.

12.4. Design a single piece that will fit into all three of these holes (see Fig. 12.24).

12.5. Start with a square piece of paper. Draw the largest circle possible inside the square, cut it out and discard the trimmings. Draw the largest square possible inside the circle, cut the square out, and discard the trimmings. What fraction of the original square piece of paper has been cut off and thrown away?

12.6. Given a circle, use 3 line segments (curved, straight, open, or closed) to divide the circle into 8 sections.
EXTENSION: How can this be done so that all 8 sections have the same area?

12.7. Use 9 toothpicks to form 3 squares, each side of which is a complete toothpick length.

12.8. One person holds a ball representing the earth. A second person holds a ball representing the moon. How far apart do the two people need to stand to show the distance between the earth and moon?

12.9. How can you cut a square layer cake that has been frosted on the top and all sides (but not the bottom) so that each piece will contain the same amount of frosting and the same volume of cake?

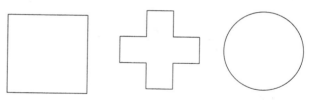

FIG 12.24.

12.10. Make 2 squares and 4 triangles from 8 toothpicks without breaking, overlapping, or bending them.

12.11. How can a nursery person plant 10 trees in 5 rows, having 4 trees in each row?

12.12. A kid is full after eating a 6-inch round pizza. Assuming there are 2 kids with the same eating capacity, what size pizza (only one) should they order so they will both be full and there will be no leftovers?

12.13. Arrange 6 toothpicks to form 4 congruent equilateral triangles. The side length of each triangle must equal the total toothpick length.

12.14. Using 24 toothpicks, how many squares can be made using 6 toothpick lengths on a side? Five toothpick lengths on a side? Four toothpick lengths on a side? three toothpick lengths on a side? Two toothpick lengths on a side? One toothpick length on a side? For some of these, you may not be able to use all the toothpicks.

12.15. A 9 by 12 rectangular rug has a 1 by 8 hole in its center, the hole being 4 feet from either long side and 2 feet from either short side. The sides of the hole are parallel to the sides of the rug. Cut the rug into exactly 2 pieces, which can be sewn together to make one 10 by 10 square rug.

12.16. How many squares are there on a checkerboard?

12.17. Draw a line segment on a piece of paper. Subdivide that segment into 3 segments. Using the 3 segments as side lengths, construct a triangle. NOTE: Geometry software helps.

12.18. A rhombus is formed by 2 congruent equilateral triangles sharing a common side. The midpoints of each of the sides of the equilateral triangles are formed, creating 8 smaller congruent equilateral triangles. Remove 4 seg-

ments from this figure and leave exactly 4 triangles. NOTE: A toothpick is easily used to represent one side of the smaller triangle.

12.19. Use a circle of a given radius and circumscribe a regular triangle, square, pentagon, hexagon, and decagon. What conclusion can be made about the areas of each of the circumscribed figures?

12.20. Use a circle of a given radius and inscribe a regular triangle, square, pentagon, hexagon, and decagon. What conclusion can be made about the respective areas of each of the inscribed figures?

12.21. Why are manhole covers round? EXTENSION: Is there any other shape that will work? Assumptions with this question are: the cover and the hole are the same shape; the hole is at least a meter across at the narrowest point; if the hole and lid were concentric figures, the lid would be slightly larger (1.02 m across at the narrowest point) than the hole.

12.22. Each of the 6 figures in Fig. 12.25 is made up of 5 congruent squares. All 30 of the squares are congruent. What is the question?

12.23. Out of construction paper, make small boxes that are 2 × 1 × 2.5 units on a side. How many of these boxes can be fit in a larger box that is 4 × 6 × 5 units? The assumption is that the maximum number of small boxes possible will be placed in the large box. Describe your solution. Is your solution unique?

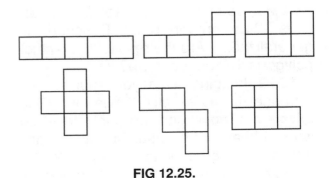

FIG 12.25.

12.24. Cut a scalene triangle out of a piece of construction paper. Label the 3 vertices and tear them off the triangle. Place the 3 vertices together with each vertex being at a common point and adjacent to some existing piece after the first one is placed. Describe your result. EXTENSION: Do this activity using a piece of software.

12.25. Cut a quadrilateral out of a piece of construction paper. Label the 4 vertices and tear them off the quadrilateral. Place the 4 vertices together with each vertex being at a common point and adjacent to some existing piece after the first one is placed. Describe your result. EXTENSION: Do this activity using a piece of software.

12.26. Cut a pentagon out of a piece of construction paper. Label the 5 vertices and tear them off the pentagon. Place the 5 vertices together with each vertex being at a common point and adjacent to some existing piece after the first one is placed. Describe your result. EXTENSION: Do this activity using a piece of software.

12.27. Cut a hexagon out of a piece of construction paper. Label the 6 vertices and tear them off the hexagon. Place the 6 vertices together with each vertex being at a common point and adjacent to some existing piece after the first one is placed. Describe your result. EXTENSION: Do this activity using a piece of software.

12.28. Compare the results from problems 12.25 through 12.27. Describe the generalization. Are the results different for polygons that are concave?

12.29. Imagine a canyon spanned by a bridge that is exactly 1 mile long. The bridge has no expansion joints in it, so when it heats, it bows up. On one hot day the bridge lengthened to 1 mile plus 2 feet. Approximately how high above its original

position before the bridge heated is the midpoint of the bridge?

12.30. Describe a roller blade. In your description, use appropriate geometry terminology.

12.31. Use a piece of software to perform the following constructions: bisect an angle; bisect a line segment; equilateral triangle; rhombus. The assumption is that you will not use any automatic capabilities to do these tasks if the software possesses it.

12.32. Create a large scalene triangle. In that triangle construct the 3 medians. Write a conclusion about the medians. Measure each median part and write a conclusion about the ratio of the lengths. NOTE: This activity is much more meaningful to the student if software that allows the triangle and medians to be altered is used.

12.33. Create a large scalene triangle. In that triangle construct the 3 angle bisectors. Write a conclusion about the angle bisectors. NOTE: This activity is much more meaningful to the student if software that allows the triangle and medians to be altered is used.

12.34. Create a large scalene triangle. In that triangle construct the 3 altitudes. Write a conclusion about the altitudes. NOTE: This activity is much more meaningful to the student if software that allows the triangle and medians to be altered is used.

12.35. Create a large scalene triangle. In that triangle construct the perpendicular bisector for each side. Write a conclusion about the perpendicular bisectors. NOTE: This activity is much more meaningful to the student if software that allows the triangle and medians to be altered is used.

12.36. Create a large scalene triangle. In that triangle construct the angle bisector for each angle, the altitude to each side, the perpendicular bisector for each side, and the median for each side, marking the point of concurrence for each set. Which 1 of the 4 points of concurrence is not always collinear with the other 3? The line through the 3 collinear points is called the Euler Line, named after Leonard Euler (1707–1783), who was the first to prove the 3 points concurrent. NOTE: This activity is much more meaningful to the student if software that allows the triangle and medians to be altered is used.

EXTENSION: Do the same construction with an isosceles triangle and an equilateral triangle. In each case describe conclusions you reach.

12.37. Create a scalene triangle with exterior angles. Measure the exterior angles. Write a conclusion about the sum of the measures of the exterior angles. NOTE: Geometer's Sketchpad is particularly useful for this activity because it permits changing of the triangle. The calculator feature can be used to show the measurements changing in real time.

12.38. Create a quadrilateral with exterior angles. Measure the exterior angles. Write a conclusion about the sum of the measures of the exterior angles. NOTE: Geometer's Sketchpad is particularly useful for this activity because it permits changing of the triangle. The calculator feature can be used to show the measurements changing in real time.

12.39. Given a point, 6 equilateral triangles can be placed adjacent to each other so that all space about that point is occupied. Because each angle of the equilateral triangle is 60°, the sum of all the angles about the point is 360°. Can this be done with any triangle? That is, given any triangle, can it be arranged so that 6 of them are placed so the sum of the angles about a point is 360°?

12.40. Create a pentagon with exterior angles. Measure the exterior angles. Write a conclusion about the sum of the measures of the exterior angles. NOTE: Geometer's Sketchpad is particularly useful for this activity because it permits changing of the triangle. The calculator feature can be used to show the measurements changing in real time. Write a conjecture dealing with the exterior angles of a polygon. Does it matter if the polygon is concave?

12.41. The 9-point circle, formed with any scalene triangle, passes through the point at the base of each altitude, the midpoints of each side, and the midpoint of each segment joining a vertex to the point shared by the 3 altitudes. Do the construction. NOTE: Software is particularly useful with this problem.

12.42. Triangles can be shown congruent by a variety of methods. Which of the following constructions can always be used to give a triangle congruent to a given triangle? Show a construction to demonstrate any that will not always yield a triangle congruent to the given triangle: SSS, SSA, AAA, ASA, SAS, SAA.

12.43. Construct a circle with center G. Mark points M, N, and H on the circle, connecting M and N with G, and M and N with H. Measure angle MHN and angle MGN. Move the points on the circle or change the radius of the circle. Write a conjecture describing this situation. NOTE: Software that permits moving points and changing radii of circles is particularly useful with this problem.

12.44. Gather several cylinders, and a tape measure or calipers. A calculator will be useful for this activity. Measure the circumference and diameter of each of the cylinders. Divide the circumference by the diameter. Arrange the results in a table and write a conjecture to accompany the information shown in the table.

12.45. Create a nonregular pentagon (ABCDE). Locate a point F and predict what the rotated view of ABCDE will be.

After the figure is rotated, create a line segment and predict what the reflected view of the rotated figure will be.

EXTENSION: Would the end result be the same if the initial figure was reflected then rotated about a point? Do similar activities increasing the complexity of the initially used figure.

12.46. Squares can be used to cover a plane with no overlaps and no gaps or spaces. (This is called a pure tessellation of a plane.) An example would be a piece of graph paper. Equilateral triangles can be used to tessellate a plane as well. Squares and equilateral triangles are regular polygons. Name another regular polygon that can be used to tessellate a plane. Other shapes that are not regular can be used to tessellate a plane. A rectangle would be an example. Create an n-gon that will tessellate a plane where n > 4 and sketch your result. If more than one shape is used, the shapes are said to tessellate the plane, but because more than one shape is used, it is not a pure tessellation. A flattened version of a soccer ball is an example. Use two or more shapes to tessellate the plane and sketch your result.

12.47. Cut a circle into an even number (8 or more) congruent "pie-shaped" pieces with the length of each straight side being equal to the length of the radius of the circle. Put the pieces together. Notice that the shape looks like a parallelogram. Assume the edges made up of curves are straight (the more pieces used, the straighter the long side appears). What is the length of the "parallelogram"? What is its height? What is its area? Because the "parallelogram" was made from a circle, what is the area of the circle?

12.48. The Golden Ratio is $\frac{1 + \sqrt{5}}{2}$ or 1.618034. A segment divided into two parts where the ratio of the entire seg-

ment length is to the longer segment as the longer segment is to the shorter is divided satisfies the requirements for being a Golden Ratio. The Fibonacci sequence (1, 1, 2, 3, 5, 8, 13, 21, 34, 55, 89, 144, 233, 377, 610, . . . , where each new term is defined by adding the two preceding terms) can be used to provide approximations that approach the Golden Ratio. Provide at least 4 decimal equivalents from different adjacent number pairs in the Fibonacci sequence. Describe a conclusion about adjacent pairs of Fibonacci numbers and the Golden Ratio.

REFERENCES

Cathcart, W. G., Pothier, Y. M., Vance, J. H., & Bezuk, N. S. (2003). *Learning mathematics in elementary and middle schools*. Upper Saddle River, NJ: Preston Education.

Eperson, C. B. (1982). Puzzles, pastimes, problems. *Mathematics in School, 12*(2), 20–21.

Kidd, K. P., Myers, S. S., & Cilley, D. M. (1970). *The laboratory approach to mathematics*. Chicago: Science Research Associates.

Murray, M. (2004). *Teaching mathematics vocabulary in context: Windows, doors, and secret passageways*. Portsmouth, NH: Heinemann.

National Council of Teachers of Mathematics. (2000). *Principles and standards for school mathematics*. Reston, VA: Author.

Rosskopf, M. F. (1970). *The teaching of secondary school mathematics*. Reston, VA: National Council of Teachers of Mathematics.

Serra, M. (1994). *Patty Paper geometry*. Berkeley, CA: Key Curriculum.

Smith, A. S., Nelson, C. W., Koss, R. K., Keedy, M. L., & Bittinger, M. L. (1992). *Informal geometry*. Reading, MA: Addison Wesley.

Steen, L. A. (Ed.). (1994). *For all practical purposes: Introduction to contemporary mathematics* (3rd ed.). New York: Freeman.

van Hiele, P. M. (1986). *Structure and insight: A theory of mathematics education*. Orlando, FL: Academic Press.

Solution Manual

1.1. Determine how the answer to any 10-term Lucas sequence problem can be found quickly.

Solution: One easy answer would be to multiply the seventh term by 11 using a calculator.

Suppose you want to multiply XYZ, where X, Y, and Z are digits, by 11. Write X. To its left put the sum of X and Y. If the sum is greater than 9, write the units digit of the sum only. Then write the sum of Y and Z, plus the regrouped tens digit from X + Y if necessary. If that sum is greater than 9, write only the units digit of the sum. Finally write Z plus the regrouped tens digit from the sum of Y + Z if necessary.

For example, 234 × 11: write the 4. To its left, write 7 (sum of 3 and 4). To its left write 5 (sum of 2 and 3). To its left, write 2. The product is 2574.

968 × 11: write the 8. 8 + 6 = 14. Write the 4 and regroup the 1. 6 + 9 = 15 + the regrouped 1 is 16. Write the 6 and regroup the 1. 9 + 0 = 9 plus the regrouped 1 is 10. The product is 10648.

Another way to think of this in Trachtenberg language is to keep adding a digit to its left neighbor (and also add a regrouped value if necessary) until there are no more left neighbors. The leftmost digit in the factor always has a left neighbor of zero, which was used in the explanation in the preceding 968 × 11 example.

See Cutler, A. (1960). *The Trachtenberg speed system of basic mathematics.* Garden City, NY: Doubleday.

1.2. Locate some specific applications in nature of the Fibonacci sequence.

Solution: Answers will vary. While we realize listing Web addresses is risky because of changes, deletions, etc., here are some to consider:

http://www.mcs.surrey.ac.uk/Personal/ R.Knott/Fibonacci/fibnat.html

http://www.mcs.surrey.ac.uk/Personal/ R.Knott/Fibonacci/fib.html

http://www.sdstate.edu/~wcsc/ http/fibhome.html

http://www.world-mysteries.com/ sci_17.htm

http://encarta.msn.com/encnet/ refpages/refarticle.aspx?refid= 761579463

1.3. Is there any quick way to find the sum of the first 20 terms of a Lucas sequence? Defend your response.

Solution: Answers will vary here. Students could come up with some schemes or patterns to find the sum of the first 20 terms of a Lucas sequence. Whether or not they are easier than just doing the adding is debatable.

1.4. If the first two terms of a Lucas sequence are 9 and 4, will the same sum be derived from a sequence starting with a 4, followed by a 9? Why or why not? Develop a series of questions you would use to assist a student in learning this result.

Solution: No.

9, 4 gives 9 + 4 = 13, the third term. Then 4 + 13 = 17, the fourth term.

4, 9 gives $4 + 9 = 13$, the third term. Then $9 + 13 = 22$, the fourth term. After the fourth term, the addends will be different (and essentially unique), thus giving different sums.

The question used to assist a student could be similar to the example given. You could also just ask them to find the sum for the first 10 terms in either case. Generally they will realize the discrepancy at the fourth or fifth term. This is a wonderful opportunity for some small group work during class.

1.5. Is there any set of numbers that could not be used as terms for a Lucas sequence? Defend your answer.

Solution: No. Because the original development was done with X and Y as the initial terms, X and Y can belong to the real numbers. Fractions can get pretty messy, but they work. Even picking additive inverse integers will work because, even though the third term will be zero, the fourth will not be. A good thought question to ask the students relates the integers to the idea developed in exercise 1.4.

1.6. If the length of one side of a rectangle is doubled and the other tripled, what is the impact on the area of the rectangle? Does it matter if the roles are reversed as to which side is doubled and which is tripled? Why or why not?

Solution: Area is multiplied by 6. No. $3 \times 2 = 2 \times 3$.

1.7. If the base of a triangle is doubled and the height is quadrupled, what factor is the area multiplied by?

Solution:

$$A_{\text{original}} = \frac{bh}{2}; \; A_{\text{new}} = \frac{(2b)(4h)}{2} \text{ which is } 8\left(\frac{bh}{2}\right).$$

1.8. In a triangle, what factors can be used with the base and height as multiples and still keep the area the same? State a generalization for this situation.

Solution: Any pair of multiplicative inverses.

For example,

$$A_{\text{original}} = \frac{bh}{2}; \; A_{\text{new}} = \frac{(3b)\left(\frac{1}{3}\right)h}{2} \text{ which is } \frac{bh}{2}.$$

1.9. Given a trapezoid with height h, upper base b_1, and lower base b_2, what is the impact on the area if only the height is doubled? What is the impact on the area if only the length of b_2 is halved? Write a generalization about changing only one of the dimensions of a trapezoid. Don't forget the slant height.

Solution: Doubling h.

$$A_{\text{original}} = \left(\frac{b_1 + b_2}{2}\right)h; \; A_{\text{new}} = \left(\frac{b_1 + b_2}{2}\right)2h,$$

$$\text{which is } \left\{\left(\frac{b_1 + b_2}{2}\right)h\right\}2.$$

Halving b_2,

$$A_{\text{original}} = \left(\frac{b_1 + b_2}{2}\right)h; \; A_{\text{new}} = \left(\frac{b_1 + \frac{b_2}{2}}{2}\right)h,$$

$$\text{which is } \left(\frac{2b_1 + b_2}{4}\right)h.$$

Changing one dimension. Answers will vary, depending on which dimension is changed. Note that doubling a slant height will double the height.

1.10. Describe at least two different real-world applications that involve the mathematics covered in the middle school curriculum.

Solution: Answers will vary. Arc radii in a skateboard park would be an example. The cost of pirating music over the Internet could be another one.

1.11. Use a source like Newman's *The World of Mathematics* (1956), the *VNR Concise Encyclopedia of Mathematics* (Gellert, Kustner, Hellwich, & Kastner,

1977), or Eves' *History of Mathematics* (1967) to investigate a mathematical topic found in the middle school setting. You are to learn a new way of working with the topic. Present your conclusions in written form, giving appropriate bibliographic credit.

Solution: Answers will vary.

1.12. Duplicate sketch 1.3 in Sketchpad. Move the vertices and sides. Move vertex F so that $\overline{AB}$ appears to coincide with $\overline{CD}$. Do you think this could be another way to informally establish that ABCD is a parallelogram? Why or why not?

Solution: Yes, this is another way. Rationale will vary.

1.13. Create a situation in Sketchpad that includes animation to establish the idea for students that respective alternate interior, alternate exterior, and corresponding angles are congruent.

Solution: Answers will vary but should look something like Fig. 1.16.

1.14. The problem $x + 4 = 7$ can be done using online sources. One example is algebra.help which is found at http://www.algebrahelp.com. Click on calculators under the Students heading and select the Equation Calculator. Using it, you will see the following.

Equation as entered:

$$x + 4 = 7$$

Subtract 4 from each side:

$$+x + 4 = +7$$
$$-4 - 4$$
$$x = 3$$
$$1x = 3$$

Use this online source to develop a lesson that would use the technology to lead students to generalize a set of rules for solving equations like $5x + 9 = 17$.

Solution: Answers will vary depending on lesson selected. The lesson should include example(s) formatted something like what is shown here to indicate that the software gives reasons for steps that are made. Those examples should be combined with questions and a discussion that leads the student to the appropriate generalization, where the emphasis is not teacher telling.

1.15. Develop a lesson similar to the one for adding unit fractions for subtracting unit fractions using a calculator that operates with fractions, giving results as fraction.

Solution: Answers will vary.

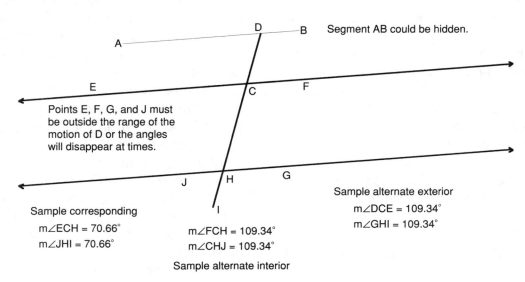

FIG 1.16.

1.16. Develop a lesson that would have students show results of some collection of data as a histogram on a graphing calculator.

Solution: Solution: Answers will vary.

1.17. Measure the height and wrist size of the members of your class in centimeters. Record the information in a table in interactive statistics software and graph it. What is the equation generated to predict height from wrist circumference or vice versa? Would the results be different if the measurements were taken in inches?

Solution: Answers will vary. The equations will differ when centimeters or inches are used, but the predictability should be the same.

1.18. Describe mathematical applications or extensions related to a hobby or personal interest you have.

Solution: Answers will vary.

1.19. Select something from the history of mathematics and describe how mathematics was created or refined to meet a need. Your description should be in a form that could be used to attract the attention of a middle school student.

Solution: Answers will vary.

1.20. Make a set of cards like those described for the values less than 32, but make your set for all values less than 64.

Solution: Directions are given in the text. One additional card will need to be added and the patterns on the other five cards will need to be extended to include 63. The new cards will contain all values from 32 through and including 63.

1.21. Make a set of "hole" cards for values less than 32 and demonstrate the trick to a middle school class. Write a summary of the class reaction.

Solution: The cards are shown in the text. The easy way to make a set is to copy the text cards and enlarge them to the desired dimensions.

2.1. Explain when and how technology should be inserted into the addition continuum, or should it?

Answers will vary. At this stage of their development, it is likely that students will espouse uninformed opinions. It would be desirable that eventually they develop informed opinions. For example, some consider technology to be an acceptable tool to learn number facts, reasoning that, if a student enters a fact into a calculator, the correct answer is generated each time. Consider 7×8, which can be a dilemma for some. Is the product 54 or 56? Technology resolves the matter. There is another way to answer this particular question that students find interesting and amusing— $56 = 7 \times 8$. They notice that the digits are in sequence. So, do we teach a bunch of mnemonics like this, or do we insert technology?

2.2. Describe an equitable solution to the dilemma posed about no technology or the same technology for all that is mentioned in the preceding paragraph.

Answers will vary.

2.3. Textbooks will be a part of your world from now on. You need to be familiar with the things done in them. Select one topic and see how the publisher presented it in a series (like pre-algebra and algebra I or seventh and eighth grade). The texts should be published about the same time. How are the presentations the same (for example, some series have actually used the same pictures in three different sequential texts)? How are the presentations different? When the topic is treated the second (or third) time, what is done to stimulate new interest?

Answers will vary. One response could be that the second in a series does not provide any extension of the topic and gives a more basic approach to learning the information.

2.4. We said in the text, "Even today, after the extensive effort put forth by mathematics educators and organizations to stem the tide, arithmetic holds center-stage in many classrooms." Assuming that is a true statement, rationalize why that is the case.

Answers will vary. There should be a realization that we tend to teach as we were taught and, because most of us experienced an emphasis on arithmetic, the cycle continues.

2.5. Describe how you will convince your students that assessment is done *for* them, not *to* them.

Answers will vary.

2.6. Realizing that we are spending your money, rationalize why it is or is not appropriate for each future teacher to own interactive software and calculators.

Answers will vary. Students should realize these are tools they need to be effective teachers of mathematics in the 21st century.

2.7. Understanding the magnitude of this statement, we strongly recommend that you read, summarize, and discuss all four of NCTM's basic standards books:

Curriculum and Evaluation
Professional Standards
Assessment Standards
Principles and Standards

Answers will vary. Perhaps executive summaries could be used rather than the entire documents.

3.1. Make your own representation to illustrate what ratio of the surfboard sales are black.

Solution: Students can see that in every set of 20 surfboards sold at the surf shop 12 are black, 3 are red, and 5 are blue. They can conclude that $\frac{12}{120}$ or $\frac{6}{10}$, $\frac{3}{5}$, or 0.6 of the surfboard sales are black. Representation models may vary.

3.2. Make a model to show what percent of the surfboard sales are blue.

Solution: Replicate a set of 20 five times to see that the print shop uses 25 blue cartridges in every 100 used. Therefore, 25% of the printing is blue. Representation models may vary.

3.3. If 60 black surfboards were sold in a month, what is the total number of red and blue surfboards sold in that month, assuming the described ratios hold? Make a representation to show this number.

Solution: A set of 60 black surfboards comprises 5 sets of 12 cartridges and that a total of 8 red and blue cartridges are used in the time that 12 black cartridges are used. Thus, it follows that 40 red and blue cartridges—15 red and 25 blue—are used in the time that it takes to use 60 black cartridges.

Models may vary.

3.4. Write the descriptions in the empty cells in Fig. 3.6.

Solution: Answers may vary.

3.5. Make a mathematical representation for as many groupings of 18 as you can. Examples could include $17 + 1$, $16 + 2$, and $16 + 1 + 1$,

Solution: Other examples include $15 + 3$, $15 + 2 + 1$, $15 + 1 + 1 + 1$, $14 + 4$, $14 + 3 + 1$, $14 + 2 + 2$, $14 + 2 + 1 + 1$, and $14 + 1 + 1 + 1 + 1$.

3.6. Figure 3.10 represents a pool with a one-ceramic-tile-wide border (Ferrini-Mundy, Lappan, & Phillips, 1997). Explain in words, with numbers or tables, visually, and with symbols the number of tiles that will be needed for pools of various lengths and widths (NCTM, 2000).

Solution: The formula for the number of tiles is $T = 2(L + W) + 4$. Make a table with columns for L, W, and T. Count the tiles for the pictures, fill in the numbers in the table, and look for a pattern. You always add the length to the width, double that answer, and then add 4. Your table and visual representation may look like Table 3.1 and Fig. 3.13, respectively.

TABLE 3.1

L	W	T
1	1	8
2	1	10
3	1	12
3	2	14
3	3	16
3	4	18

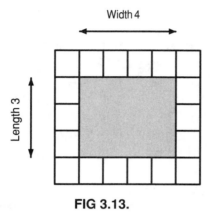

FIG 3.13.

4.1. List at least three careers requiring mathematics beyond the courses taken by a college-bound high school graduate.

Solution: Answers will vary. Entries could be: middle school teacher of mathematics, secondary teacher of mathematics, mathematician, statistician, business major, science education majors, elementary education majors, medical doctor, forest ranger, nursing major, software technician, computer engineer, chemist, pharmacist, computer science major, aerospace engineer, economist, chemical engineer, accountant, appraiser, realtor, bank dfficer/business management, financial planner, investment banker, venture capitalist/investor, and on and on.

5.1. Should your lessons follow the structure of the text? Why or why not?

Solution: Answers will vary. We would hope that there would be variation to include manipulatives, technology, supplemental materials, applications, enrichment, and so on.

5.2. Should two teachers in the same grade, with students of the same ability, in the same school, follow the same lesson plans? Why or why not?

Solution: Answers will vary. It is very difficult to follow someone else's lesson plan totally. Each individual will have strengths, preferences, biases, and so on that will surface and probably conflict with the literal plan prepared by another individual.

5.3. If you can't finish the curriculum, how do you decide what to sacrifice?

Solution: Answers will vary. One factor would be any mandated assessments from a school, district, state, or national level.

5.4. What are the ramifications of eliminating some topics in the curriculum? Is there a way this dilemma can be resolved?

Solution: Answers will vary. One huge ramification is if a topic is eliminated and it is an emphasis point on a high-stakes test. Alignment among the needs of students, curricular emphasis, and assessment goals is critical.

6.1. Describe how you would get your students to not draw polygons in standard position.

Solution: Answers will vary. This is a wonderful place to use interactive geometry software. Create a rectangle in nonstandard position and then rotate it, showing that it maintains all of its qualities: all angles are right angles, opposite sides are parallel and congruent, diagonals are congruent, diagonals bisect each other, a diagonal divides the rectangle into congruent right triangles, and so on.

6.2. Describe how you would convince your students that coloring the polygon means coloring the segments that make up that polygon, not the interior.

Solution: Answers will vary. Discussion about a polygon dividing a plane into three regions—points that are inside the polygon, points that are outside the polygon, and points that make up the polygon—would be appropriate here.

6.3. Did you notice that the addend denominators in each problem from the set just discussed in the text are relatively prime? Will the process work for unit fractions with denominators that are not relatively prime?

Solution: The students probably will not notice that the denominators of the addends are relatively prime. $\frac{1}{2}+\frac{1}{4}=\frac{6}{8}$ shows that the process works for that example, but it is true in general. The one issue is whether or not the answer must have common factors divided out, and, if it does, does that fault the process? We say it does not.

7.1. The Seven Bridges of Konigsberg, a discussion of Gauss, and the Egyptians using geometry to measure flooded ground were given as examples of historical topics that could be inserted into the middle grades classroom. Find a different historical topic appropriate for middle schoolers. Give all pertinent bibliographic information and create a lesson plan that would incorporate your topic.

Answers will vary according to historical topics chosen. A beginning source of information to start with is http://aleph0.clarku.edu/~djoyce/mathhist/webresources.html.

7.2. Read the parts in NCTM's *Curriculum and Evaluation Standards for School Mathematics* pertaining to problem solving in the middle school. Reflect on what the publication says and write your feelings about their position on problem solving in the elementary curriculum.

Answers will vary. The assumption is that the comments will be positive and include statements about not having thought about problem solving that way.

7.3. "You have been contracted to use gold to guild the page numbers in a reproduction of an ancient manuscript, starting with page 1. Because of the expense and time required for this process, you will be paid by the number of digits you guild. If you guild a total of 642 digits, how many pages did you number in the manuscript?" Try your hand at using the working-backwards strategy to come up with a solution.

Solution: 642 digits were written;

$642 - 9 = 633$ (first nine pages took nine digits),
$633 - 180 = 453$ (the next 90 pages used 2 digits each),
$\frac{453}{3} = 151$ (each new page will have 3 digits each),
9 pages + 90 pages + 151 pages = 250 pages.

7.4. Consider the following problem: "In the early days of movie making, a villain might do things that cannot be done in real life. In today's movie making, directors often use consultants to avoid this type of blunder. A director has asked you to determine if it is reasonable for the villain to grab a $1,000,000 ransom, in one-dollar bills, and run. You know a dollar bill weighs about one gram. Is the scene reasonable?"

Solution: If every dollar weighs a gram, then $1,000,000 weighs 1,000,000 grams. There are 1000 grams in a kilogram, thus there are 1000 kilograms in 1,000,000 grams. You can either recall or look up that one kilogram is about 2.2 pounds. Then 1000 kilograms is approximately equivalent to 2200 pounds or about one ton. You should advise the producer that no ordinary person would be able to pick up $1,000,000 in one-dollar bills because they would weigh about one ton!

7.5. Find a list different from the four steps Polya presents for problem solving. Describe the similarities and differences between the list you found and Polya's.

Solution: Answers will vary. Read, reread, restate; list information; plan solution; work out solution; check; generalize.

7.6. List the four components for problem solving. Explain how these components will help you in preparing for instruction.
Solution: The four components for problem solving are understand the problem, make a plan, carry out a plan, and look back. Answers for helping you prepare for instruction may vary.

7.7. Provide examples of different types of problems. How can you use them in the classroom to teach problem solving to middle schoolers?
Solution: Answers may vary.

7.8. Identify two topics that would be of interest to middle school students and the mathematics related to those topics. Determine the grade level or subject in which each topic could be used to introduce the defined mathematical concept(s).
Solution: Answers may vary according to interests.

8.1. Give three examples of subtraction facts and 1 counterexample.
Solution: Answers will vary.

8.2. Give three examples of multiplication facts and one counterexample.
Solution: Answers will vary.

8.3. Give three examples of division facts and one counterexample.
Solution: Answers will vary.

8.4. Write a definition that will describe a number fact, no matter what operation is used.
Solution: Three numbers are involved for a given operation $(+, -, \times, \div)$ and at least two of them must be digits.

8.5. You might see texts where the commutative property of addition on the set of counting numbers is initially listed as $a + b = b + a$. Explain why that is, or is not, the best way to do things.
Solution: Answers will vary. One could argue that the students have seen this information in elementary school and, thus, they should be familiar with the generalized expression. On the other hand, even

if they have seen it, it could be the case that they have never had basic conceptualization developed. Thus, it would be advisable to start with the union of disjoint sets, progress to different sets of numbers, and finally generalize the idea of commutativity of addition on the whole numbers. The idea of universal generalizability must be delayed because there are so many sets of numbers beyond the wholes that these students have not experienced yet.

8.6. If there are examples beyond $2 + 2 = 2 + 2$ and $2 \times 2 = 2 \times 2$, list one. If there are not, explain why this is a unique example.
Solution: Zero will work the same, if substituted for the 2s.

8.7. Provide an example where the commutative property of subtraction on the set of integers is true.
Solution: $2 - 2 = 2 - 2$.

8.8. Provide an example where the commutative property of division on the set of reals is true.
Solution: $5 \div 5 = 5 \div 5$.

8.9. Is there any example of adding two counting numbers where the sum is not a counting number?
Solution: No.

8.10. True or false—the digits are closed for multiplication?
Solution: False. $5 \times 7 = 35$, and 35 is not a digit.

8.11. Develop a continuum for helping students arrive at a generalized conceptualization of each of the 11 field axioms.
Solution: Answers will vary. Each case should start with simple examples from the smallest set where the property holds true and spiral up through the different sets. Subtleties like needing the commutative property for an operation's identity element should be present, as should discussion about the possible existence of special cases (like whole number subtraction commuting if the numbers are the same).

8.12. Is there a right distributive property of division over addition?
Solution: Yes.
$(6 + 8) \div 5 = 6 \div 5 + 8 \div 5$
$\qquad = 14 \div 5$, for example.

8.13. Is there a left distributive property of division over addition?
Solution: No.
$12 \div (6 + 4) = 12 \div 6 + 12 \div 4$
$\qquad = 2 + 3$
$\qquad = 5$, but $12 \div (6 + 4)$
$\qquad = 12 \div 10$, which is not 5.

8.14. Do $967 + 579 + 418$ using the partial sum method.
Solution:

$$
\begin{array}{r}
967 \\
579 \\
+\ 418 \\
\hline
1800 \\
140 \\
24 \\
\hline
1964
\end{array}
$$

8.15. Do $967 + 579 + 418$ using the scratch method.
Solution:

$$
\begin{array}{r}
9\ 6\ 7 \\
5\ 7\ 9 \\
+\ 4\ 1\ 8 \\
\hline
1\ 8\ 4\ 4 \\
9\ 6
\end{array}
$$

8.16. Do $967 + 579 + 418$ using the low-stress method.
Solution:

```
  1    2
  9    6    7
  5    7    9
 14   13   16
+ 4    1    8
      8    4    1
---------------
 19    6    4
```

8.17. Explain the scratch method to someone who does not know how to add that way.
Solution: Answers will vary.

8.18. Explain the low-stress method to someone who does not know how to add that way.
Solution: Answers will vary.

8.19. Provide an analytical discussion of $7436 - 2518$, where you discuss regroupings, place value, and so on.
Solution: Answers will vary. The idea is that one of the 3 tens in the tens place of 7436 is regrouped to form 16 ones, which will allow the initial subtraction to be performed. They should include the idea that no regrouping is needed from the hundreds to the tens in this particular problem. Not to be overlooked is the idea that 7 thousands is regrouped to 6 thousands, giving 10 hundreds to the already existing 4 hundreds in 7436, thus permitting that place subtraction to be done.

8.20. Do $67953 - 18476$ using the borrow-payback method. Describe your thought process as you do it.
Solution: Descriptions will vary.

```
          17    15   13
    6     7 9   5 3
    2     5 8
 -  1     8 4   7 6
 ---------------------
    4     9 4   7 7
```

8.21. Do $67953 - 18476$ using integer subtraction. Describe your thought process as you do it.
Solution: Descriptions will vary.

$$
\begin{array}{r}
67953 \\
-18476 \\
\hline
-3 \\
-20 \\
+500 \\
-1000 \\
+50000 \\
\hline
49477
\end{array}
$$

8.22. Do $5007 - 2345$ by renaming 5007 as $4999 + 8$. Do you think this is a good method to show students? Explain why or why not.
Solution: Answers will vary.

8.23. Do 5007 − 2345 using the scratch method for subtraction. Do you think this is a good method to show students? Explain why or why not.
Solution: Answers will vary.

8.24. In the "simple halving doubling" routine for multiplying two numbers, one situation exists where the halving factor will always be even except for one. Describe the situation and how it occurs.
Solution: If the halving number is accounting number power of 2, all the remainders will be zero, except for the last halving value.

8.25. Compare the Russian peasant method with the lattice multiplication approach. Which do you prefer and why?
Solution: Answers will vary.

8.26. Compare lattice multiplication with the partial product method. Which do you prefer and why?
Solution: Answers will vary.

8.27. Multiply a two-digit number by a two-digit number. Use the product and the two-digit factor to create a division problem, making the other two-digit factor become the missing factor. Now, do the division problem using the repeated subtraction approach. *You may not estimate accurately!* Give a low estimate for both the ones value and the tens value as shown in the example in the text.
Solution: Answers will vary.

8.28. Write a summary of your impressions on the advantages and disadvantages of repeated subtraction division.
Solution: Answers will vary.

8.29. Show someone who is not in your class how to "reduce" a fraction and describe their reaction.
Solution: Answers will vary.

8.30. Should students be expected to express fractions where the greatest common factor between the numerator and denominator is one? Explain your reasoning.
Solution: Answers will vary.

8.31. Describe how you would help a student see the advantage of dividing out common factors first in problems like $\frac{2}{3} \times \frac{3}{4} \times \frac{4}{5} \times \frac{6}{7} \times \frac{7}{8}$.
Solution: Answers will vary. The discussion should include ideas from dividing out common factors with equivalent fractions and the greater risk of errors when larger numbers are involved.

8.32. Create a model for explaining $2\frac{1}{4} \times 3\frac{1}{3}$.
Solution: Answers will vary. One way would be to create a figure similar to Fig. 8.11 in the text. An alternate figure could be:

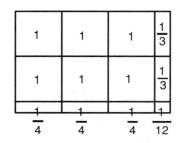

FIG 8.32.

8.33. Do $\frac{4}{5} \div \frac{7}{8}$ using the equivalent fraction process. Make up at least two more fraction division problems where the denominators are unrelated and do them using the equivalent fraction process. After you have done at least those three problems, describe your feelings of the equivalent fraction division process.
Solution: Answers will vary for the reactions.

$$\frac{4}{5} \div \frac{7}{8} = \frac{32}{40} \div \frac{35}{40}$$
$$= \frac{32 \div 35}{40 \div 40}$$
$$= \frac{32 \div 35}{1}$$
$$= \frac{32}{35}$$

8.34. Find a student (or adult not in your class) with the appropriate background to be dividing fractions and demonstrate equivalent fraction division. Describe their reaction to what you show them.
Solution: Answers will vary.

8.35. Find an example of a fraction divided by a fraction, something like $3 \div \frac{1}{2}$. For this assignment, dividing something in half would be like dividing by $\frac{2}{1}$ and is not acceptable.
Solution: Answers will vary. If you have a yard of material and you want to cut it into 6-inch strips, you divide the material into $\frac{1}{2}$ foot sections. Thus, you would have $3 \div \frac{1}{2}$, yielding 6 strips.

8.36. Has all of this discussion caused you to rethink technology? There are calculators that work directly with fractions in pretty print, divide out common factors, present equivalent fractions, and so on. Should we just use them and forget all of this development stuff? Explain your thoughts.
Solution: Answers will vary. Certainly the technology is tempting. However, there is a need for the development of understanding what is going on with addition of fractions. The process provides essential background information for future mathematical study.

8.37. Suppose a student says $\frac{2}{3} + \frac{1}{8} = \frac{3}{11}$. Describe how you would help the student understand that the sum is $\frac{19}{24}$.
Solution: Answers will vary. The response could include a discussion about building a sequence, perhaps starting with manipulatives.

8.38. Define an error pattern for adding fractions that is different from placing the sum of the numerators over the sum of the denominators of the addends. De-

scribe how you would help a student making such an error correct it.
Solution: Answers will vary.

8.39. Create a sequence for student development for subtracting fractions starting with two unit fractions with the same denominator and ending with mixed numbers with quasi-related denominators.
Solution: Answers will vary.

8.40. As the addition sequence for fractions was developed, some discussion focused on providing steps that were not listed in the table. For example, $\frac{1}{7} + \frac{2}{7}$ was listed as a potential entry between $\frac{1}{7} + \frac{1}{7}$ and $\frac{2}{7} + \frac{3}{7}$. Does the sequence you created in exercise 8.39 allow for such detail or would this detail need to be added?
Solution: Answers will vary. There will probably be a need to add some intermediate steps, particularly at the beginning.

8.41. Suppose you asked your students to do a series of problems like $\frac{1}{4} - \frac{1}{12}, \frac{1}{5} - \frac{1}{15}, \frac{1}{6} - \frac{1}{18}$, and so on. What generalization could they be expected to develop?
Solution: The numerator of the missing addend is always 2.

8.42. If the problems from exercise 8.41 were followed by sets of problems like $\frac{1}{4} - \frac{1}{16}$, which would be followed by problems like $\frac{1}{4} - \frac{1}{20}$, which would be followed by problems like $\frac{1}{4} - \frac{1}{24}$, and so on for as long as necessary, what generalization could students be expected to develop?
Solution: The numerator of the missing addend is always one less than what the denominator and numerator of the sum must be multiplied by to get an equivalent fraction so both denominators in the problem are the same.

8.43. Create a lesson plan using the calculator to help students discover that $\frac{3}{10} = 0.3$.

Solution: Answers will vary. The lesson should have students using the F<->D key on the calculator. Preferably, the calculator produces fractions in pretty print.

8.44. What happens when you enter 0.700 in your calculator and touch =, enter, or EXE? Do this activity with a friend and explain the result.

Solution: Answers will vary. Generally the result will be either 0.7 or .7.

8.45. Create a lesson plan to help students realize that $0.32 = 0.320 = 0.3200. \ldots$

Solution: Answers will vary. Base 10 blocks would be a good way to build this concept.

8.46. Suppose a student consistently shows: $3.2 + 0.98 + 4.657 = 47.87$, $2.178 + 4.6 + 0.35 = 22.59$, and $0.46 + 1.3 + 5.278 = 53.37$. Describe how the decimal is being placed in the answer. Outline how you would correct the error.

Solution: Answers will vary. The student submitting this work said that there were 6 decimal places in the problem and 3 addends, so the average was 2 decimal places. Interestingly, the student said it did matter whether you count from the left or from the right.

8.47. Create a three-digit (hundredths) times a two-digit problem (tenths) and do it using partial product, lattice, and Russian peasant multiplication.

Solution: Answers will vary. The procedures for each problem should parallel those done with whole numbers, with the exception of decimal point placement.

8.48. Provide a written defense for when it is appropriate to permit students to use technology when doing decimal division problems.

Solution: Answers will vary.

8.49. Assume your position for permitting the use of technology in decimal division differs from that of your department, school, district, or state standards. What do you do and why?

Solution: Answers will vary.

8.50. Make up a problem involving a whole number divided by a decimal. Explain how to convert your problem to one where it is a whole number divided by a whole number.

Solution: Answers will vary.

8.51. Make up a problem involving a decimal divided by a decimal. Explain how to convert your problem to one where it is a whole number divided by a whole number.

Solution: Answers will vary.

8.52. A student consistently moves the decimal point the correct number of places when converting a decimal to a percent or vice versa, but always in the wrong direction. Describe what you would do to help stimulate understanding of the error.

Solution: Answers will vary. The discussion should refer back to work with decimals and how the point location concept was developed.

8.53. When values are greater than 100%, a student consistently omits the hundreds (237% is shown as 37%). Describe what you would do to help stimulate understanding of the error.

Solution: Answers will vary. This should include points about using base 10 blocks to show the situation.

8.54. When values are less than 1%, a student consistently omits the necessary zeros (like 0.05% would be expressed as 5%). Describe what you would do to help stimulate understanding of the error.

Solution: Answers will vary. This should include points about using base 10 blocks to show the situation.

8.55. Describe your opinion of having students add positive numbers without signs, then insisting that they insert the signs, and later telling them not to worry about the signs?

Solution: Answers will vary. The discussion should include points about the need to include the signs to provide background for work with negative addends.

8.56. How could absolute value be explained to your students?

Solution: Answers will vary. A number line focusing on distance from zero on either side is one way to have the discussion. With the colored chips, the idea of how many, ignoring the color, and then adding or subtracting the set cardinalities, would be another.

8.57. Describe how technology could be used to help develop generalizations about adding signed numbers.

Solution: Answers will vary. Writing the problems and answers generated with the technology, where the problems are all grouped by format, should help.

8.58. Describe how you would lead a class to the generalization for changing the sign of the second number and following the rules for addition when dealing with the subtraction of integers.

Solution: Answers will vary. The discussion should evolve out of use of chips, technology, or some other medium that can be used to establish the answers to the different problem types.

8.59. Create a lesson plan covering each of the four problem types for subtracting integers represented by colored chips. Be sure to include detailed examples and questions that would lead to the desired generalizations.

Solution: Answers will vary. This should be an extension of the presentation in the text where $^{+}2 - {}^{+}5$ and $^{+}2 - {}^{-}6$ are developed.

8.60. Do the sequence of problems that started with $^{-}6 \times {}^{+}6 = {}^{-}36$ and ended with $^{-}6 \times {}^{-}1 = {}^{+}6$ with someone not in the class

using this text. As you do it, focus on their reaction to the comments as a problem is compared with the preceding one. Write your reflections to their responses and actions.

Solution: Answers will vary. The report should include boredom with repeating the same thing over and over. There should also be some surprise when the final step reveals they have a negative times a negative giving a positive.

8.61. Describe how you would convince students that the product of two factors with the same sign is positive.

Solution: Answers will vary. The positive times positive part should focus on technology, repeated addition, or perhaps something like colored chips. The negative times negative will probably come from technology or a pattern similar to the one used in the text.

8.62. Describe how you would convince students that the product of two factors with opposite signs is negative.

Solution: Answers will vary. Technology or colored chips would work here, or even a number line could be used for a positive times a negative. The negative times a positive is limited to technology or use of the suspected commutativity of multiplication on the set of integers.

8.63. Can the GCF of two numbers be greater than both numbers? How would you explain this to a student?

Solution: No. Explanations will vary.

8.64. Will the GCF of two numbers always be less than both numbers? How would you explain this to a student?

Solution: No. One of the numbers could be a multiple of the other like with 15 and 45 in the text. Explanations will vary.

8.65. Can the LCM of two numbers be less than both numbers? How would you explain this to a student?

Solution: No. Assuming the two numbers are different, it must be greater than at least one of them. The example with 15 and 45 would show it. Explanations will vary.

8.66. Should students be required to prove a divisibility rule? Why or why not?
Solution: Yes. It develops the need for proof and applies a plethora of basics that need regular reinforcement.

9.1. Describe how you would help students understand angle measure that exceeds 180°.
Solution: Answers will vary. One way could be to place two same-sized protractors so the wedges (center of arc) are on top of each other and the straight segments are collinear. That will show a complete circle and can be interpreted as 180° and 180° more. That argument could be extended to go beyond 360°, or for values between 180° and 360°.

9.2. If you had the power to determine what measurement concepts would be focal points in the middle school curriculum, what would you list and why?
Solution: Answers will vary. Length, area, volume, time, and money will probably be listed.

9.3. Investigate the inch-foot-pound system of measure. List at least three units of measure you had not heard of, along with their definitions.
Solution: Answers will vary.

9.4. What is the connection between pace, rod, furlong, and stadium (stadia)?
Solution: A pace is 5 feet. A rod is 5.5 yards. A furlong is 40 rods. A furlong is 660 English feet. A stadium is 625 Roman feet.

9.5. Describe the historical development of 16-ounce and 12-ounce pounds.
Solution: Answers will vary. Most think the 16-ounce pound was preferred because it could be divided into halves, quarters, eights, and sixteenths. Initially things were defined in terms of a grain, defined as the weight of a single barleycorn. The 12-ounce pound (troy pound) came from the Saxons. An ounce was

480 grains. Jewelers and druggists used the troy pound until the 19th century. The troy ounce is still used in financial markets everywhere to quote gold and silver prices.

9.6. Describe the history of the long and short ton and the connection with the metric ton, which is used as the standard for most shipping today.
Solution: The avoirdupois ounce is 437.5 grains. The troy ounce is 480 grains. The troy system was used only for precious metals and for pharmaceuticals, whereas the avoirdupois pound was used for everything else. Since 1400 A.D. a standard weight unit in Britain has been the hundredweight, ironically 112 avoirdupois pounds rather than 100. The 112 pounds made the hundredweight equivalent to the German and French units. The ton was originally a unit of wine measure, equaling 2240 pounds. In the 1800s, Americans redefined the hundredweight to be 100 pounds, rather than 112. The definition of the ton as 20 hundredweight created the long ton (2240 pounds in England) and the short ton (2000 pounds in the United States). Today, most international shipments are in metric tons, which is close to the long ton.

9.7. Describe the history of the defining of a gallon.
Solution: Before the 1900s, it was hard to measure the capacity in cubic units, and so the standards were defined as the weight of something like wheat or beer. The gallon was originally the volume of eight pounds of wheat.

9.8. Investigate SI and present at least 3 rules that you did not know.
Solution: Answers will vary. It could be that 12,345 is written with no comma, as 12 345, with a space between the 2 and 3 rather than the comma. It could be that 6789 is acceptable written without a comma, rather than 6,789. It could be that "L" is used for liter and is the only capital

letters used in units unless a proper name is the unit (like Celsius). It could be that 27 cg has period after cg because cg is a symbol.

9.9. Rationalize the need for several different formulas for finding the perimeter of a rectangle.

Solution: Answers will vary. Application of different number properties, like distributive property of multiplication over addition on the real numbers for 2(L + W), or commutative and associative properties of addition to get from L + L + W + W to L + W + L + W, should be a part of the discussion.

9.10. Does $\frac{22}{7} = \pi$? Explain your reasoning.

Solution: Solution: No. It is an approximation, as is the other common value 3.14, an irrational number.

9.11. Rationalize why it would, or would, not be preferable to use A = bh for the formula for the area of a rectangle rather than A = lw.

Solution: Answers will vary. Discussion should include the connection between lw and length and width, common reference terms for side lengths of a rectangle. The dialogue should also include the idea that base and height are used with other figures when computing area, with the exception of squares.

9.12. Describe how you would help your students understand that the overlap between rectangles ADCJ and AFBH in Fig. 9.7 does not impact the resultant area of triangle ABC.

Solution: Answers will vary. The main point is that the overlap region is inside the triangle and the parts subtracted from the area of the bounding rectangle were outside that rectangle.

9.13. Describe your reaction to the average of the bases times the height approach for finding areas of so many different figures.

Solution: Answers will vary. More than likely part of the discussion will include the concept that this was new information.

9.14. Why do we use squares as our unit of area measure?

Solution: Answers will vary. Why change will be a dominant theme.

9.15. You are trying to make a decision about buying a large pizza (the diameter is 16 inches), or two small pizzas (the diameter of each is 8 inches). Is one large pizza the same amount as the two small pizzas? (adapted from Bassarear, 2001)

Solution: We can use the area formula to find the area of each situation: area for one large pizza (d = 16 inches; r = 8 inches) is equal to $\pi r^2 = \pi(8)^2 = 64\pi \approx 201$ square inches; area of one small pizza (d + 8 inches; r = 4 inches) is equal to $\pi r^2 = \pi(4)^2 = 16\pi$; area of two small pizzas is 32 $\pi \approx 100.5$ square inches. Amazingly, they are not the same area; furthermore, it takes four small pizzas to have the same area as a large pizza. Figure 9.16 illustrates a way to show the relationship between the large and small pizzas.

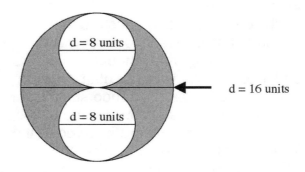

FIG 9.16.

10.1. If 5 students are to be chosen from a class of 20 to represent that class in a competition, in how many ways can it be done if order counts (AB does not equal BA)? Is this a combination or a permutation?

A) 15504   B) 624,882   C) 1,860,480
D) 2,631,944 E)_____

Solution: C) 1,860,480. Permutation since order does matter.

10.2. You normally invite 14 friends for a Friday night party. However, this Friday your roommates ask that you only invite 8 of those friends. How many choices do you have as to whom to invite? Is this a combination or a permutation?
A) 3002   B) 3003   C) 3004   D) 3005
E)____
Solution: B) 3003. Combination since order does not matter.

10.3. For the experiment of randomly selecting one card from a deck of 52, let

C = event the card selected is a heart

D = event the card selected is a face card

E = event the card selected is an ace
Determine which of the following pairs of events are mutually exclusive.
A) C, D   B) C, E   C) D, E   D)____
Solution: C) D, E since you could not draw a face card, which is also an ace.

10.4. What are some uses for each of the different types of graphs (pictographs, circle or pie graphs, coordinate graphs, histograms, line plots, stem-and-leaf plots, or box plots)? Describe real-life situations in which some types of graphs are more appropriate than others, and explain why.
Solution: Pictographs should be used to read, interpret, and discuss data. The students should have a good understanding of the representations used. In some cases, fractions and percents are involved in the development of pictographs.

Circle or pie graphs can be seen frequently in newspapers, magazines, and brochures. This type of graph is useful to show how a whole has been divided into parts, such as data from surveys, time expended in different activities, budget, revenue, or breakdown of expenses. They are not as appropriate to represent temperatures. Line plots are more appropriate for this purpose. The reading, construction, and meaningful understanding of circle or pie graphs are usually delayed until middle school because these require an understanding of fractions, percents, and angular measures.

Coordinate graphs could be integrated with other subject areas like social studies. For example, a map can be superimposed on a map and use coordinates to locate buildings on the map.

Histograms are graphical representations of the frequency with which scores happen. Line plots can substitute and have been substituted for histograms in many cases Stem-and-leaf plots bear some resemblance to the histograms, but in the stem-and-leaf plots all the data values are retained, easily identified, and easily ordered; categories are not arbitrary; construction is easier; and other descriptive statistics can be calculated from the display.

Box plots include the median and chart the dispersion of data in a way that adds information about the spread of scores, which are not directly available in other types of graphs like stem-and-leaf pots Two or more box plots could be superimposed on the same reference line to make comparisons between groups, like gender or economical status

10.5. What are the three measures of central tendency used in statistics? Describe ways in which teachers can help middle school students understand each measure.
Solution: Mode, median, and mean (arithmetic average or average) are the three measures of central tendency used in statistics. Use line and stem-and-leaf plots to provide very visual representations of the mode to students. The median is usually introduced in the middle school grades. The computational procedures should be left until these grades, but the concept should be introduced earlier than that. The mean is the most frequently used measure of central tendency. It is a good

idea to start by asking students what they believe this term stands for in different real-life situations. What does it mean to be average? Is it good to be average? In what situations are you average? Use a set of blocks of different heights to show how to make these sets the same height, and demonstrate the process of concretely determining the mean of the quantities represented by the sets.

10.6. The birthdays of 42 of the U.S. presidents are included in Table 10.2. Before looking at the table, what do you think is the probability that two of them have the same birthday? What about you having the same birthday as one of the presidents? What about one of the students in your group having the same birthday as one of the presidents? Explain your answers (adapted from Jacobs, 1982).

Solution: The probability that two of the presidents have the same birthday is about 0.91 (or 91%). Presidents Harding (28th) and Polk (11th) have the same birthday. The probability that you will have the same birthday as one of the presidents is the same because the number of different birthdays is still 41. The probability for your class will depend on how many students are in your class.

Other lists of names could be used for this purpose, such as famous authors or inventors.

10.7. Using a spinner, how could you establish a discussion about bias?

It is easy to construct a spinner using a board, nail, bead with a hole in it, stiff paper, and some circles made out of paper. Make an arrow out of the stiff paper, punching a hole at its center of gravity. Figure 10.6 shows an example of the spinner.

Solution: Because one color section of the template is almost half of the region the spinner sweeps, it should be the dominant result. If the desire is to have the three colors be equally likely, then the template is biased in favor of one color. To get all three

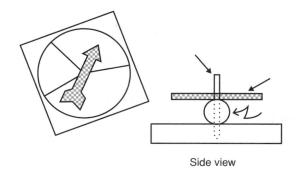

Side view

FIG 10.6.

colors to be equally likely, each would need to occupy a third of the template.

10.8. If you made a template for the spinner in Fig. 10.6 that equally spaced the digits around a circle, letting the odd digits represent the head of a coin and the even digits represent the tail of a coin, would the generated results parallel the expected results of flipping an honest coin? Why or why not?

Solution: The results should parallel those of a flipped honest coin because there are five odd digits that occupy half of the area of the template and five even digits that occupy the other half of the template. It is possible that some will say that the template favors the odds because it is often forgotten that zero is even, too. The definition of an even number says that, when divided by 2, the division remainder is zero. $\frac{0}{2} = 0$ with a remainder of zero.

10.9. Given the game board in Fig. 10.8, you need to spin either a 3 or a 5 to stay in a game. What is the probability that your spin entitles you to stay in the game?

Solution: The probability of staying in the game is

$$\frac{\text{Area 3} + \text{Area 5}}{\text{Total Area}}.$$

Use $\frac{n\pi r^2}{360}$, where the radius is 6, area 3 is 40 degrees, and area 5 is 60 degrees.

That gives $\dfrac{(40)(36)\pi}{360} + \dfrac{(60)(36)\pi}{360} = \dfrac{(100)(36)\pi}{360}$ or 10π. The area of the whole thing is 36π. The odds of staying in the game are 5 to 18. Note that the radius could be any value.

10.10. The numbers 1 to 200 (inclusive) are put into a hat. What is the probability that the first three numbers chosen at random are prime numbers? As the numbers are chosen, they are not replaced in the hat.

Solution: There are 46 prime numbers between 1 and 200 (2, 3, 5, 7, 11, 13, 17, 19, 23, 29, 31, 37, 41, 43, 47, 53, 59, 61, 67, 71, 73, 79, 83, 89, 97, 101, 103, 107, 109, 113, 127, 131, 137, 139, 149, 151, 157, 163, 167, 173, 179, 181, 191, 193, 197, and 199). The probability of selecting the first number prime is $\dfrac{46}{200}$. The probability of selecting the second number prime is $\dfrac{45}{199}$, given that the first selection is not put back in the hat. That means that, with the second drawing, there are only 45 possible prime numbers left in the hat out of a new total of 199. The probability of selecting a third number prime, after two have been removed, is $\dfrac{44}{198}$ since there are now only 44 prime numbers left out of a total of 198 numbers still in the hat. In this situa-

tion, the probability is $\dfrac{46}{200} \times \dfrac{45}{199} \times \dfrac{44}{198} = \dfrac{23}{1990}$ because P(A and B and C) = P(A) × P(B) × P(C).

10.11. Unequally likely outcomes: You roll a pair of dice and find the sum of the dots (called pips) on the dice.

Solution:

a. How many possible outcomes are there for this experiment? 36.

b. What are the possible outcomes from rolling the red die? 6.
   What are the possible outcomes from rolling the white die? 6. What possible sums and ways in which the sum might be obtained are there? See Table 10.4.

c. What is the theoretical probability that the sum is even? 1/2 or a 50% chance that the sum is even. There are 4 outcomes, each of which is equally likely:

Die 1 + Die 2 = Sum
Even + Even = Even
Odd + Odd = Even
Even + Odd = Odd
Odd + Even = Odd

Half of the sums are even and half are odd.

What is the probability that the sum is greater than 6? $\dfrac{7}{12}$

TABLE 10.4

Sums	Ways in which the sum might be obtained	Total Ways	Theoretical Probability
2	(1, 1)	1	1/36
3	(1, 2), (2, 1)	2	1/8
4	(1, 3), (3, 1), (2, 2)	3	1/12
5	(1, 4), (4, 1), (2, 3), (3, 2)	4	1/4
6	(1, 5), (5, 1), (2, 4), (4, 2), (3, 3)	5	5/36
7	(1, 6), (6, 1), (2, 5), (5, 2), (3, 4), (4, 3)	6	1/6
8	(2, 6), (6, 2), (3, 5), (5, 3), (4, 4)	5	5/36
9	(3, 6), (6, 3), (4, 5), (5, 4)	4	1/4
10	(4, 6), (6, 4), (5, 5)	3	1/12
11	(5, 6), (6, 5)	2	1/8
12	(6, 6)	1	1/36

TABLE 10.3

Sum	Tally (for 72 rolls)	Frequency	Experimental Probability
	Total:	72	$\frac{72}{72}$

What is the probability that the sum is prime? $\frac{5}{12}$

What is the probability that the sum is prime or greater than 6? $\frac{7}{9}$

What is the probability that the sum is less than 5? $\frac{1}{6}$

d. Now roll a pair of dice 72 times, recording the information in Table 10.3, and answer the following questions. What is the expected number of occurrences for each outcome (sum)? Remember that the expected (theoretical) number of outcomes is based on 72 rolls, not 36. How closely do your obtained results compare to the expected results?

10.12. If you toss three coins, which probability is larger: getting at least one head or getting at least one tail?

Solution: They are both equally likely at 0.875. The chance of getting at least one head is $\frac{7}{8}$, as is the probability of getting at least one tail {HHH, HHT, HTH, HTT, THH, THT, TTH, TTT}.

10.13. A spinner for a game is arranged so it may point to any of 7 numbers with equal probability. The numbers on the spinner are 1, 2, 3, 4, 5, 6, and 7. If you spin once, what is the probability it points to a prime number?

Solution: $\frac{4}{7}$. This is a tricky question. Many people forget that 1 is not a prime.

10.14. Basketball simulation: free throw shooting.

In basketball, a personal foul is committed by player A on player B in the other team because of illegal contact while the ball is in play. For 1 point each, player B takes 2 free throws.

Solution:

a. Assume that a player B has a 60% accuracy from the free throw line and has 2 free throws, what do you think is the expected percent for 2 points (made both shots), 1 point (made one of the two shots), and zero points (missed both shots)?

Two points (made both shots): 36%

One point (made 1 of the 2 shots): 48%

Zero points (missed both shots): 16%

b. If this player tries 10 two-free-throw trips (2 free throws each) for a game, what is the expected frequency for the different point combinations (1, 2, or 0 points) of the 10 trips? Using a spinner (see Fig. 10.6), simulate this experiment. Show your work.

Two points = 3 or 4 out of 10 free throw trips.

One point = 5 out of 10 free throw trips.

Zero points = 1 or 2 out of 10 free throw trips.

The answers for the experiment will vary but are expected to be close to the theoretical distribution.

10.15. Visit a middle school mathematics classroom and informally assess several students' understanding and misconceptions of data analysis, statistics, and probability. You can also interview a teacher regarding the students' understanding of these ideas.

Solution: Answers will vary.

10.16. Examine a middle school textbook's section on data analysis, statistics, and probability in terms of concepts and activities included.

Solution: Answers will vary. This will depend a lot on the grade level and textbook and resources you select to examine.

10.17. A parent of one of the students in your middle school classroom feels that you are expending too much instructional time on data analysis, statistics, and probability concepts in your classroom. How would you respond to this parent's concern?

Solution: Answers will vary. However, the main thing to keep in mind is to keep students' parents and/or guardians informed of the teaching practices you are implementing in your classroom from beginning to end. A letter at the beginning of the academic year, regular meetings with parents, family nights, a Web site with information, and/or any other open and honest channels of communication might help with this aspect of instruction.

10.18. How would you use technology to assist with the organization and interpretation of data?

Solution: Some examples are given in the technology section of this chapter.

10.19. Have students collect data on any topic of their choice. Using the data collected, have students create a histogram and/or box plot using Fathom software.

Solution: Answers will vary according to data collected but histogram and box plot may look like the ones below.

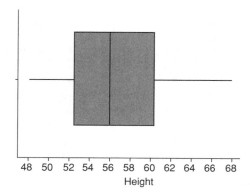

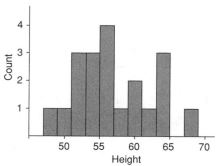

11.1. Find and describe three examples of "algebra as generalized arithmetic" presented in a middle school mathematics textbook.

Solution: Answers will vary.

11.2. Describe three examples of verbal descriptions used in middle school that may be translated or generalized into algebraic notation.

Solution: Answers will vary.

11.3. Find sample activities found in a middle school mathematics textbook for the major number properties.

Solution: Answers will vary.

11.4. Find other examples of algebra as the study of procedures for solving certain types of problems in a middle school textbook.

Solution: Answers will vary. The problem-solving section of the textbook you have selected should have some examples of algebra as the study of procedures for solving certain types of problems.

11.5. What prerequisites are necessary for proper mastery of algebra as the study of procedures for solving problems?
Solution: Among other prerequisites, the students should have knowledge of algebra as generalized arithmetic, problem-solving skills, number sense, and place value and computation skills.

11.6. Working this problem in a semi-concrete form is an important step toward dealing with the abstractions upon which algebra is built. Not purposefully moving students to the semiconcrete and ultimately to the symbolic would be a disservice to them. Ask middle school students to solve the following problems and make annotations of their answers given that scales A and B in Fig. 11.2 are balanced. The objects are the same in all the pictures.

Decide which of the scales are balanced and write an equality or inequality to describe the situation (see Figs. 11.3–11.6).
Solution:
   a. Yes.
   b. No.
   c. No.
   d. No.

11.7. Ask middle school students to write an algebraic equation that summarizes what Fig. 11.7 shows. Jumps the same size are the same distance, depicting whole numbers between zero and ten. Big jumps represent distances that are greater than the smaller jumps.
Solution: Let A represent the short jumps and N the large jumps. What do we know about A and N? They are both whole numbers. They are not equal to zero and are less than 10. $A < N$ or $N > A$, and $A \neq N$. N could be equal to 2, 3, 4, 5, 6, 7, 8, or 9, and A could be equal to 1, 2, 3, 4, or 5. The possible equation is the following: $3N + 2A = 24$ cm. The possible combina-

tions that meet these requirements are the following:

N = 5 and A = 3; 3(5) + 2 (3) = 15 + 6 = 21: No.

N = 6 and A = 3; 3(6) + 2(3) = 18 + 6 = 23: Yes.

N = 7 and A = 2; 3(7) + 2(2) = 21 + 4 = 25: No.

11.8. Ask middle school students to write an algebraic equation that summarizes the Fig 11.8 situation. Jumps the same size are the same distance, depicting whole numbers between zero and ten. Big jumps represent distances that are greater than the smaller jumps.
Solution: The new equation is $4N + 2A = 26$ feet. The possible combinations that meet these requirements are the following:

N = 6 and A = 1; 4(6) + 2(1) = 24 + 2 = 26: Yes.

N = 5 and A = 3; 4(5) + 2(3) = 20 + 6 = 26: Yes.

11.9. Use Algebra Tiles, Algebra Lab Gear, or drawings of the manipulatives to find what x represents in terms of the equations (see Fig. 11.15).
Solution: See Fig. 11.34.

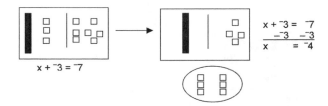

FIG 11.34.

11.10. Use Algebra Tiles, Algebra Lab Gear, or drawings of the manipulatives to find what x represents in terms of the equations (see Fig. 11.16).
Solution: See Fig. 11.35.

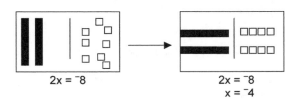

FIG 11.35.

11.11. Use Algebra Tiles, Algebra Lab Gear, or drawings of the manipulatives to find what x represents in terms of the equations (see Fig. 11.17).
Solution: See Fig. 11.36.

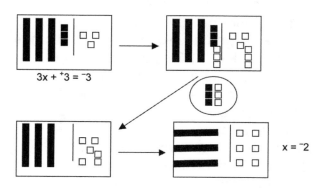

$3x + {}^+3 = {}^-3$

$x = {}^-2$

FIG 11.36.

11.12. Use Algebra Tiles, Algebra Lab Gear, or drawings of the manipulatives to find what x represents in terms of the equations.
Solution: See Figs. 11.37 and 11.38.

a.

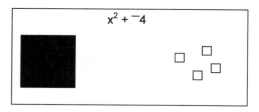

$x^2 + {}^-4$

FIG 11.37.

b.

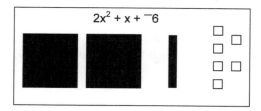

$2x^2 + x + {}^-6$

FIG 11.38.

11.13. Describe at least three examples of variables being used as a placeholder in a middle school textbook.
Solution: Answers will vary.

11.14. Describe a board game that involves algebraic thinking, and explain how middle school students could apply algebra as they play it.
Solution: Possible examples are Clue, The Game of Life, Guess Who?: The Mystery Face Game, and Risk.

11.15. Draw a picture or visual model that could be used with middle school students, and write an algebraic expression for each of the following situations.
Solution: Possible algebraic expression and visual representation (see Figs. 11.39 and 11.40).

a. weight of box plus 5 units: w + 5

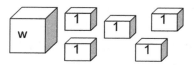

FIG 11.39.

b. three years less than a certain age: A–3

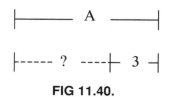

FIG 11.40.

11.16. Try the following exercises with middle school students, and analyze their attempts to solve the problems. Each letter represents one of the following numbers: 12, 18, or 21. Tell what each letter represents.

a. p • (q − r) = 162
Solution: Account for all possibilities for p • (q − r) = 162.

p = 21, q = 18 and r = 12 : 21 • (18 − 12) = 21 • 6 = 126. Not a solution.

p = 18, q = 21 and r = 12 : 18 • (21 − 12) = 18 • 9 = 162. Yes.

p = 12, q = 21 and r = 18 : 12 • (21 − 18) = 12 • 3 = 36. Not a solution.

b. $(2 \cdot g) - (h + i) = 12$
Solution: Account for all possibilities for $(2 \cdot g) - (h + i) + 12$.

$g = 18$, $h = 21$, $i = 12$: $(2 \cdot 18) - (21 + 12) = 36 - 33 = 3$. Not a solution.

$g = 21$, $h = 18$, $I = 12$: $(2 \cdot 21) - (18 + 12) = 42 - 30 = 12$, or

$g = 21$, $h = 12$, $I = 1\ 8$: $(2 \cdot 21) - (12 + 18) = 42 - 30 = 12$. Yes.

$g = 12$, $h = 21$, $I = 12$: $(2 \cdot 18) - (21 + 12) = 24 - 33 = {}^{-}9$. Not a solution.

11.17. Magic square: Place the numbers 1, 2, 3, 4, 5, 6, 7, 8, and 9 in the little squares in Fig. 11.19 to form sums equal to 15 in all directions (up, down, and diagonally).

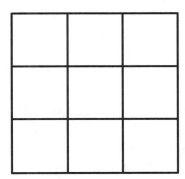

FIG 11.19.

Solution: See Fig. 11.41.

2	9	4
7	5	3
6	1	8

FIG 11.41.

11.18. Cross-number array: Make the sum 30 in each direction (up, down, and diagonally) using Fig. 11.20.

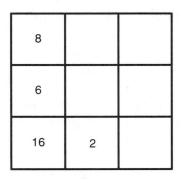

FIG 11.20.

Solution: See Fig. 11.42.

8	18	4
6	10	14
16	2	12

FIG 11.42.

11.19. State the question in words before solving the equation. For example, in $d + t = 5$ the question is "A number plus another number equals 5?"

The wording of the questions may vary:

a. $p + p = 16$
Solution: What number plus itself equals 16? $p = 8$.

b. $t + t = 15$
Solution: What number plus itself equals 15? $t = \dfrac{15}{2}$ or $7\dfrac{1}{2}$.

c. $1 = g + g + g$
Solution: One is equal to what number plus itself, plus itself? $g = \dfrac{1}{3}$.

d. $16 = x \cdot x$
Solution: Sixteen is equal to what number times itself? $x = 4$ or ${}^{-}4$.

e. $n \cdot n \cdot n = 8$
Solution: What number times itself, times itself equals 8? $n = 2$.

f. $x + x = x$
Solution: What number plus itself equals itself? $x = 0$.

g. $5 + n = 2 + n + 3$
Solution: Five plus what number is the same as 2 plus that number plus 3? Any number works.

h. $g + 3 = g$
Solution: What number plus 3 equals that same number? No number works.

i. $r \cdot r = r$
Solution: What number times itself equals itself? $r = 0$ or 1.

11.20. State the question or questions in words before solving the equation
The wording of the questions may vary:

a. $5 \cdot m + 3 = 2$
Solution: What number plus three equals 2? $^{-}1$. Five times what number equals $^{-}1$? $\dfrac{-1}{5}$, then $5 \cdot \dfrac{-1}{5} + 3 = 2$.

b. $4 - 2 \cdot t = ^{-}(2 \cdot t - 4)$
Solution: Four minus 2 times what number is the same as the negative of 2 times that number plus minus 4? Answer: any number works.

c. $100 = 4 \cdot n^2$
Solution: One hundred equals 4 times what number? Answer: 25. What times itself equals 25? Answer: 5, and $^{-}5$, then $100 = 4 \cdot 5^2$.

d. $\dfrac{3}{5} \cdot b = 6$
Solution: Three fifths times what number equals 6? 10.

e. $\dfrac{2 \square b + 7}{3} = 5$
Solution: What number plus $\dfrac{7}{3}$ equals 5? Answer: $\dfrac{8}{3}$. Two times what number equals $\dfrac{8}{3}$? Answer: $\dfrac{8}{6}$. What number divided by 3 equals $\dfrac{8}{6}$? 4.

11.21. This problem involves using objects, and looking for patterns, but no verbal rule is required: Two cellular telephone companies are offering the following rates per minute every month. The first company offers phone services for a basic fee of $20.00 plus $0.20 for each minute of use within a month. The second company has a monthly fee of $15.00 and charges $0.45 for each minute of use within a month. Both companies charge for the exact amount of minutes the cellular telephone service is used, counting any partial minute as a full minute. Compare these two companies' charges for specific amounts of minutes for a month.
Solution: First company: $y = \$20.00 + \$0.20x$. Second company: $y = \$15 + 0.45x$.

Number of Minutes	0	10	20	30	40	50	60
First Company	$21.00	$22.00	$24.00	$26.00	$28.00	$30.00	$32.00
Second Company	$17.25	$19.50	$24.00	$28.50	$33.00	$37.50	$42.00

11.22. Use objects to build the designs shown in Fig. 11.22. Look for patterns to help. Copy and complete Table 11.3.

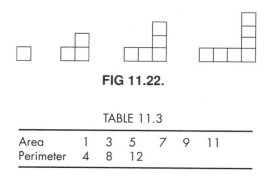

FIG 11.22.

TABLE 11.3

Area	1	3	5	7	9	11
Perimeter	4	8	12			

Solution: See Table 11.8 for solution.

TABLE 11.8

Area	1	3	5	7	9	11	**13**	**15**
Perimeter	4	8	12	**16**	**20**	**24**	**28**	**32**

11.23. It takes 2 hexagons to flank 2 triangles in Fig. 11.23. It takes 3 hexagons to flank 4 triangles. How many hexagons are needed to flank 20 triangles? What is the total number of blocks that would be used? Copy and complete Table 11.4.

FIG 11.23.

TABLE 11.4

Number of Hexagons	2
Number of Triangles	2
Total number of blocks	4

Solution: See Table 11.9.

TABLE 11.9

Number of Hexagons	2	3	4	5	6
Number of Triangles	2	4	6	8	10
Total number of blocks	4	7	10	13	16

11.24. These problems involve using objects, looking for patterns, and forming a verbal rule:

a. Which is larger, 2n or n + 2? Explain your answer.

Solution: The expected correct answer was "it depends on whether n was greater or less than 2." If n = 2, then they are equal. If n < 2, then 2n < n + 2. If n > 2, then 2n > n + 2.

b. What happens to the value of $\frac{1}{x}$ as x gets larger and larger? Explain your answer.

Solution: The expected correct answer was that "the value decreases as x gets larger."

c. Fill in the blank: Part of the shape is hidden behind the black rectangle in Fig. 11.24 and all of the sides of this shape are the same length. There are n sides, each 5 units long (adapted from Booth, 1988). The perimeter of this shape is _____ units.

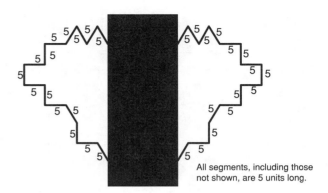

All segments, including those not shown, are 5 units long.

FIG 11.24.

Solution: This item involves the use of variables as arguments or parameters, as indicated in the use of algebra as the study of relationships. Here, the variable was used to describe and generalize the mathematical relationship between quantities. The variable was thought of as representing several values rather than just one value. Some students might count the sides actually drawn and give the answer accordingly by multiplying by five (5). In this case, the students were using the variable as an unknown or constant. The expected correct answer is 5n.

11.25. Devise questions that could be used to teach middle school students about substitution in an algebraic expression. Using the function machines in Figs. 11.25 and 11.26, find possible missing whole number inputs or outputs.

a.

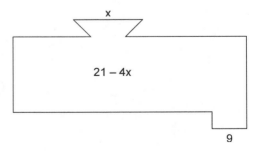

FIG 11.25.

Solution: x = 3.

b.

7

4n + 34

?

FIG 11.26.

Solution: n = 62.

11.26. The rules for this exercise are:

The same shape must have the same value.

Different shapes could have different or the same value.

Only whole numbers are involved: 0, 1, 2, 3, ...

Given the rules described above, ask middle school students to examine the following equations. They are to find the values for $\bigcirc$ and $\triangle$, and explain how they got their answer, and why their answer makes sense.

If $\bigcirc + \bigcirc + \bigcirc = 72$ and $(\bigcirc - \triangle) + 10 = 25$ then $\triangle = \_$, and $\bigcirc = \_$.
Solution: $\triangle = 9$, and $\bigcirc = 24$.

11.27. What rule will be developed from the following?
In Fig. 11.27, the first cross takes 5 squares to build, the second takes 9, and the third takes 13. How many squares will it take for

the fourth, 10th, 30th, and the nth cross? Find and continue the pattern, and describe the rule for the general pattern in the space provided in Table 1.5.

TABLE 11.5

Cross	Number of Squares
1st	5
2nd	9
3rd	13
4th	
10th	
30th	
nth	Rule: ____

Solution: See Table 11.10.

TABLE 11.10

Cross	Number of Squares
1st	5
2nd	9
3rd	13
4th	**17**
10th	**4(10) + 1 = 41**
30th	**4(30) + 1 = 121**
nth	**Rule: 4N + 1**

11.28. Ask middle school students to find how long would it take to double an amount of money when the interest rate is 6% compounded annually. Assume that savings are in a tax-sheltered account so that you don't have to pay taxes until the money is withdrawn.
Solution: If we start with $100 dollars, from the graph (see Fig. 11.43) we can

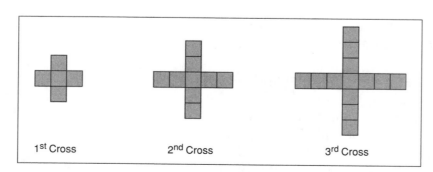

1ˢᵗ Cross   2ⁿᵈ Cross   3ʳᵈ Cross

FIG 11.27.

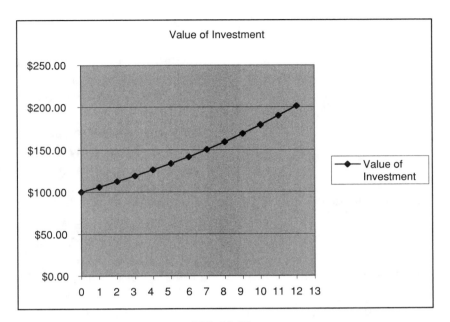

FIG 11.43.

estimate that we will reach $200 (double $100) in about 12 years. Values from the table could be used too (see Table 11.11).

TABLE 11.11. Table for Values

Year	Value of Investment	
0	$100.00	
1	$106.00	$100 \cdot 1.06^1$
2	$112.36	$100 \cdot 1.06^2$
3	$119.10	$100 \cdot 1.06^3$
4	$126.25	$100 \cdot 1.06^4$
5	$133.82	$100 \cdot 1.06^5$
6	$141.85	$100 \cdot 1.06^6$
7	$150.36	$100 \cdot 1.06^7$
8	$159.38	$100 \cdot 1.06^8$
9	$168.95	$100 \cdot 1.06^9$
10	$179.08	$100 \cdot 1.06^{10}$
11	$189.83	$100 \cdot 1.06^{11}$
12	$201.22	$100 \cdot 1.06^{12}$

11.29. Peter jogs along a route that is essentially flat except for one hill. Figure 11.29 shows the route.
Which of the following graphs (Figs. 11.30, 11.31, or 11.32) best describes what happens to the speed of Peter as he jogs along the route?

FIG 11.29.

a.
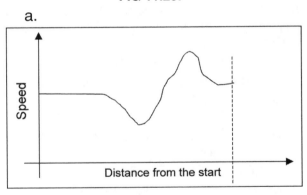

FIG 11.30.

b.
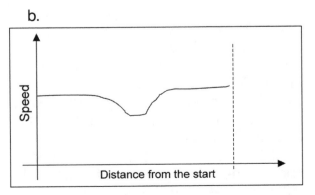

FIG 11.31.

c.

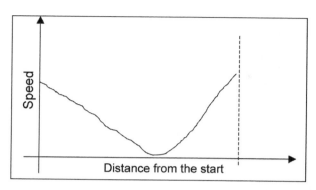

FIG 11.32.

Solution: The correct selection is "a".

11.30. Try the following item with middle school students and analyze their responses. What specific justification were they able to give?

$a(cx + cy) = a(cx) + a(cy)$.

Solution: Distributive property.

11.31. Which of the statements are true? Choose an appropriate calculation method to help you decide. Also, you need to justify or explain why you think the statement is true or false.

a. $(6 + 14) \cdot 7 = 6 + (14 \cdot 7)$

Solution: False. This is a misuse of the associative property.

b. $78 \cdot 37 = (78 \cdot 7) + (78 \cdot 30)$

Solution: True. This is true because of the distributive property.

c. $587 \cdot 0 \cdot 963 = 2874 + 5 - 2879$

Solution: True. Multiplying by zero is involved in this case.

11.32. Find or adapt algebra problems related to the study of structures in a middle school mathematics textbook, like the ones presented previously in Figs. 11.30 and 11.31. Describe their use.

Solution: Answers will vary. Some examples might be found in a section of the textbook dealing with proof.

11.33. Using a pre-algebra textbook, find at least five examples of each of the different uses of conceptions of algebra.

Do you think that there is a fair representation of the different uses or conceptions of algebra in the chosen pre-algebra textbook? What are some positive aspects of the textbook? What could be done to make it better?

Solution: Answers will vary.

11.34. Write why it is important for a teacher to take into account the different conceptions of algebra when planning teaching activities.

Solution: Answers will vary.

11.35. Develop a lesson plan that involves and integrates at least two of the different conceptions of algebra.

Solution: Answers will vary.

11.36. Describe three possible examples of student misconceptions in algebra. (You could search for error patterns in student work or interview a middle school teacher for possible examples.)

Solution: Answers will vary.

11.37. What could be the reasons for student misconceptions you identified in problem 11.36?

Solution: Answers will vary.

11.38. What type of remediation would be appropriate for the student misconceptions you identified in exercise 11.36?

Solution: Answers will vary.

11.39. Find a middle school mathematics textbook and analyze the different uses of technology within this textbook. Are these uses appropriate?

Solution: Answers will vary.

11.40. Develop a lesson plan for middle school grades involving technology.

Solution: Answers will vary.

12.1. Visit a middle school mathematics classroom and informally assess two or three students' understanding of geometry.

Solution: It is important that you look for both strengths and weaknesses. This will give a more complete picture of the students' understanding of geometry and where they should be placed within the developmental stages of geometric understanding.

12.2. Examine a middle school mathematics textbook's section on geometry and describe it in relation to the developmental stages of geometric understanding.

Solution: Answers will vary. If possible, you should also take a look at the teacher's edition of the textbook and any supporting materials they might have available.

12.3. Write a lesson plan to introduce a geometry topic of your choice to middle school students at developmental stage 2 (Informal Deduction) of geometric understanding. Then write a lesson to introduce a related topic to middle school students at developmental stage 3 (Formal Deduction) of geometric understanding.

Solution: Answers will vary. This activity will give an opportunity to adapt instruction and develop a feel for different geometry developmental stages.

12.4. Research the naming of terms in the formulas for finding the area of rectangles and parallelograms in the middle school curriculum. When did the different names occur and is there any logical reason for them?

Solution: Answers will vary.

12.5. Give a geometric explanation of why the statia tube will provide the height of the flagpole. (This activity involves van Hiele levels 2 and 3.)

Solution: You have similar triangles. The distance between the two segments in the tube is known. The distance from your eye at one end of the tube to the two segments at the other end of the tube is known. In the other triangle, the distance from you to the flagpole is known. Using ratio, the height can be found.

12.6. There are three other ways the lime and purple Cuisenaire rods can be arranged to show that $3^2 + 4^2 = 5^2$. Sketch them, remembering that a rod may not be split into parts. (This activity involves van Hiele level 2.)

Solution: See Fig. 12.25.

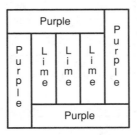
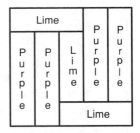
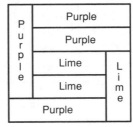

FIG 12.25.

12.7. Determine whether or not "proofs" like that shown in Fig. 12.8 are limited to regular polygons. Show an example to support your position.

Solution: They are not. The shapes do need to be similar.

12.8. Do the Pythagorean theorem "proof" shown in Fig. 12.8 using semicircles. (This activity involves van Hiele levels 3 and 4.)

Solution: See Fig. 12.26.

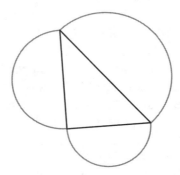

FIG 12.26.

12.9. One U.S. president did a couple proofs of the Pythagorean theorem. Name the President and show examples of his proofs.

Solution: James A. Garfield developed a proof of the Pythagorean theorem based on the construction of a trapezoid containing a right triangle that was published in the *New England Journal of Education*. Later in 1881, he became the 20th U.S. president.

12.10. Describe the sequence of steps necessary to bisect an angle using paper folding. Give your instructions to a novice to determine if they are clear enough to produce the desired results. (This activity involves van Hiele levels 2 and 3.)

Solution: Fold the paper to form the angle. Then, fold so that one side of the angle lies on top of the other.

12.11. Describe the sequence of steps necessary to produce a parabola using paper folding. Give your instructions to a novice to determine if they are clear enough to produce the desired results. (This activity involves van Hiele levels 2 and 3.)

Solution: Create a line segment on the paper and a point not on the segment. Fold the paper so the point lands on the segment. Move the point to a different location on the segment and fold again. Repeat the process several times and the segments produced by the folds will outline a parabola.

12.12. Do a Patty Paper construction. This should be different from the ones described or assigned in this text. Cite the reference used to obtain the problem. Describe the sequence of steps used to complete the construction. (This activity involves van Hiele levels 2 and 3.)

Solution: Answers will vary. Michael Serra's *Discovering Geometry* (Key Curriculum Press) is a wonderful resource, as are several other KeyPress publications. There are some articles in different NCTM publications as well.

12.13. Is the figure created in Fig. 12.11 an exact duplicate or distorted? Give a geometric defense of your response. (This activity could involve van Hiele levels 2, 3, and 4.)

Solution: It will be distorted. The point where the enlarger is centered is like a vanishing point, giving the figure a perspective.

12.14. Is there a need for an informal geometry course in the curriculum that precedes the typical high school geometry course? Why or why not?

Solution: Yes. Without it, the students are going to be expected to function logically and abstractly about topics they have little feeling for. The informal geometry provides essential background information.

12.15. Rather than a separate informal geometry course, should the topics be intertwined into the current preformal geometry curriculum as it is now done in most districts? Why or why not?

Solution: Answers will vary. The problem with intertwining the topics is that many times geometry is one of the last chapters in many books (just like this one) and if time gets short, the chapter is skipped, or covered too quickly.

12.16. Ask middle school students to make different triangles on a geoboard using rubber band, and then draw a picture of their triangle on dot paper (see Fig. 12.12), describing each triangle, incorporating precise geometric language (equilateral, isosceles, scalene, acute, right, or obtuse). (This activity could involve van Hiele levels 0, 1, and 2.)

Solution: Figure 12.27 includes three examples of possible answers. Triangle A is isosceles in terms of the sides and right in terms of angles. Triangle B is isosceles in terms of the sides and acute in terms of angles. Triangle C is scalene in terms of the sides and obtuse in terms of angles.

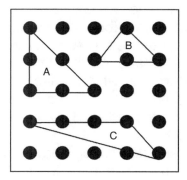

FIG 12.27.

12.17. Ask middle school students to make different squares on a geoboard, and sketch them on dot paper (see Fig. 12.12). Ask them to find as many squares as possible (limited to a 5-pin by 5-pin section of the geoboard), and to answer the following questions:

- How many squares did you find?
- How do you know if you have found all possible squares? (This activity could involve van Hiele levels 0, 1, and 2.)

Solution: There are squares with parallel sides to the sides of the geoboard, which will be more apparent to the students (see Fig. 12.28). You could specify this idea in the instructions of the problem. There are 16 one-by-one, 9 two-by-two (some of them overlap over each other), 4 three-by-three (some of them overlap over each other), and 1 four-by-four squares, for a total of 30 squares with sides parallel to the sides of the geoboard.

Figure 12.29 presents other possible types of squares that the students might find on the geoboard with sides that are not parallel to the sides of the geoboard. It is good for the students to visualize a different orientation of the sides of the squares. The

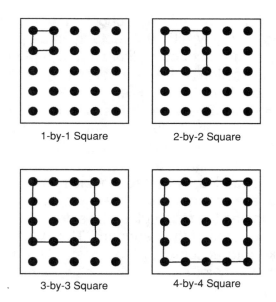

1-by-1 Square   2-by-2 Square

3-by-3 Square   4-by-4 Square

FIG 12.28.

length of each side of the squares is calculated by using the Pythagorean theorem. There is a total of 16 of this type of squares (notice that some of these squares overlap on the geoboard). Then the total for all squares (with sides parallel or not parallel to the sides of the geoboard) is 46 altogether.

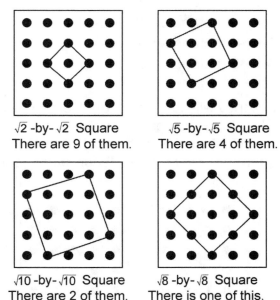

$\sqrt{2}$ -by- $\sqrt{2}$ Square
There are 9 of them.

$\sqrt{5}$ -by- $\sqrt{5}$ Square
There are 4 of them.

$\sqrt{10}$ -by- $\sqrt{10}$ Square
There are 2 of them.

$\sqrt{8}$ -by- $\sqrt{8}$ Square
There is one of this.

FIG 12.29.

12.18. Ask middle school students to find as many different rectangles as possible on a geoboard (limited to a 5-pin by 5-pin section of the geoboard). (This activity could involve van Hiele level 3.)

Solution: This problem is similar to the one with squares. If students have solved the problems using only squares, they might notice that squares are a subset of the set of rectangles. They need to find rectangles that are not squares. They could also start by finding the rectangles with sides parallel to the sides of the geoboard. They have to take into account all the possibilities and how many for each. In this case, there are 63 possibilities:

1-by-2 rectangles: 12

1-by-3 rectangles: 8

1-by-4 rectangles: 4

2-by-1 rectangles: 12

3-by-1 rectangles: 8

4-by-1 rectangles: 4

2-by-3 rectangles: 6

2-by-4 rectangles: 3

3-by-2 rectangles: 6

4-by-2 rectangles: 3

3-by-4 rectangles: 2

4-by-3 rectangles: 2

4-by-4 rectangles: 1

Then, they will need to account for the rectangles (nonsquares) with sides that are parallel to the sides of the geoboard. Some of them will overlap over each other (see Fig. 12.30).

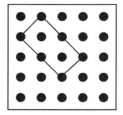 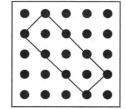

$\sqrt{2}$ -by- $\sqrt{8}$ Square
There are 8 of them.

FIG 12.30.

12.19. Consider the following capital letters of our alphabet.

A B C D E F G H I J K L M N O P Q R S T U V W X Y Z

a) Determine which have reflectional symmetry about a vertical mirror within the letter: A, H, I, M, O, T, U, V, W, X, and Y.

b) Determine which have reflectional symmetry about a horizontal mirror within the letter: B, C, D, E, H, I, O, and X.

c) Determine which have rotational symmetry within the letter: A, H, I, M, O, T, U, V, and X.

d) Which letters have more than one type of symmetry within the letter? A, H, I, M, O, T, U, V, and X.

e) Which letters have all three types of symmetry within the letter? H, I, O, and X.

f) Which letters have no symmetry within the letter? (This activity could involve van Hiele levels 1 and 2.) F, G, J, K, L, P, Q, R, S, and Z.

12.20. Using an assortment of three-dimensional shapes, ask students to classify and describe the geometric shapes (how the shapes are different or the same). You should also ask students to verbalize what they notice about the shapes. For example, some shapes can roll and others cannot. (This activity could involve van Hiele levels 1 and 2.)

Solution: This activity is mainly to allow students to develop and use vocabulary skills related to geometry.

12.21. Using a set of three-dimensional shapes, organize the shapes in two different groups, and ask students to tell why the shapes in each group belong together. (This activity could involve van Hiele levels 1 and 2.)

Solution: The answers will vary depending on the attributes used to sort and classify the shapes.

12.22. Using a set of three-dimensional shapes, ask students to choose two shapes and tell how they are alike or different. (This activity could involve van Hiele levels 1 and 2.)
Solution: The answers will vary depending on the attributes used to sort and classify the shapes.

12.23. Using a set of three-dimensional shapes, ask students to examine a shape and write several statements about its characteristics. (This activity could involve van Hiele levels 1 and 2.)
Solution: The answers will vary.

12.24. Ask students to find and record the number of faces, vertices and edges for a set of polyhedrons: tetrahedron, cube, octahedron, triangular prism, and square pyramid (see Fig. 12.17). Ask students to find relationships among the shapes and to look for patterns. (This activity could involve van Hiele levels 1 and 2.)
Solution: The special relationship exists among the number of faces (F), vertices (V), and edges (E) of polyhedra, which is known as the Euler's rule. In 1752, the Swiss mathematician Leonard Euler stated a formula representing the relationship between the number of faces, vertices (corners), and edges:

$$F + C = E + 2$$

The rule states that given the value of two of the three variables (F, V, and E), you can calculate the value of the third variable.
The completed table is presented in Table 12.2

TABLE 12.2

Polyhedron	Faces	Vertices	Edges
Tetrahedron	4	4	6
Cube	6	8	12
Octahedron	8	6	12
Triangular prism	5	6	9
Square pyramid	5	5	8

12.25. Ask students to make a replica of a cube using modeling clay. Then, ask them to tell what various polygons occur when a plane cuts through a cube (a knife could be used to cut the cube and experiment). Figure 12.17 presents two possible cuts. Ask students to predict responses for the following questions, and then, verify their predictions, recording their results in Table 12.1:

Are all cross sections of a cube bounded by quadrilaterals? No, some are triangular.

What kinds of polygonal regions could be cross sections of a cube? (Find as many cross sections as you can.) Rectangles, and triangles.

What is the least number of edges a cross section can have? Six edges (the tetrahedron is the simplest polyhedron).

What is the greatest number of edges a cross section can have? Twelve edges is the greatest number of edges.

Carry out the same activities using a right rectangular solid, a right circular cone, and a right circular cylinder. (This activity could involve van Hiele level 3.)

Solution: Answers will vary.

12.26. Can you construct a three-dimensional shape with parallelograms? Describe the shape and compare it with a rectangular based prism. (This activity could involve van Hiele levels 2 and 3.)
Solution: Yes, you can construct a three-dimensional shape with parallelograms.

12.27. Give a group of middle school students eight cubes and ask them to explore the relationship between the surface area and volume of right-rectangular-based and right-non-rectangular-based prisms using eight cubes and a constant volume. At the end, ask them to write a reflection about their findings.

Solution: Answers will vary.

12.28. Ask students to draw three-by-three squares on graph paper, and shade three of the small squares so that the figure created has one line of symmetry. Explain the two examples illustrated in Fig. 12.20. Present students with the following questions:

> How many different patterns with one line of symmetry can you make by shading in three small squares?
>
> Can you make patterns with two lines of symmetry?
>
> Shade in four small squares and make figures with one line of symmetry; with two lines of symmetry.
>
> Can you make figures with more than two lines of symmetry when four small squares are shaded? Ask students to compare their findings.

Solution: Start by explaining the two examples with three shaded squares, and one line of symmetry in Fig. 12.20 (see Fig. 12.31 for lines of symmetry).

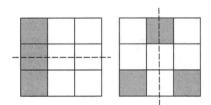

FIG 12.31.

Other possible answers with three shaded squares, and one or two lines of symmetry are represented in Fig. 12.32 (similar answers could be developed by transforming the shapes using flips, slides, and/or turns).

Possible answers with four shaded squares, and one or four lines of symmetry are represented in Fig. 12.33 (similar an-

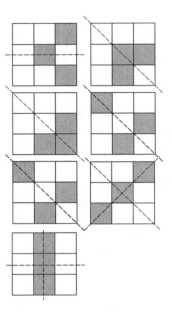

FIG 12.32.

swers could be developed by transforming the shapes using flips, slides and/or turns).

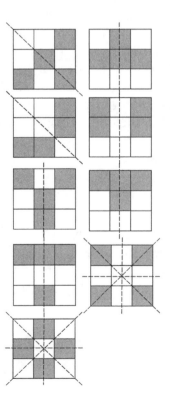

FIG 12.33.

TAG Solutions

1.1. What symbol comes next in the sequence?

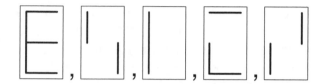

Solution: Look at the digital display of a calculator. The "E" is the segments of the digit that are not lit when the numeral 1 is typed. The next one is the two segments not lit when the numeral 2 is typed.

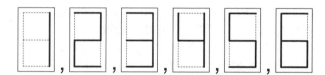

1.2. How do you multiply any two numbers whose ones digits sum to 10 and the rest of the digits are the same in both factors (143 × 147, 52 × 58) the fast way (excluding calculators)?

Solution: Take the product of the ones digits to be the ones and tens digits of the final product. Square the common part of the numbers. Add the common part to the square and place that sum to the left of the ones and tens digits to make the rest of the product of the original two factors. In 58 × 52, 8 × 2 = 16. $5^2 = 25$.
25 + 5 = 30. Product = 3016.
How it works. 10A + B = first number.
10A + (10 − B) = second number.
$(10A + B)(10A + (10 − B)) = 100A^2 + 100A − 10AB + 10AB + B(10 − B)$

NOTE: Could also do the Common part (C)(C + 1) rather than doing $C^2 + C$.

1.3. How do you square a number ending in 3 fast (excluding calculator)?
Solution: Last digit is a 9.
+ 60 times the rest of the number (left of the 3)
+ 100 times the rest of the number (left of 3 squared followed by 00)

$73^2 = 9 + 60(7) + 100(7^2)$
$= 9 + 420 + 4900$
$= 5329$

$123^2 = 9 + 60(12) + 100(12^2)$
$= 9 + 720 + 14400$
$= 15129$

Why? Suppose the number is "Nty"-three.

$(N3)^2 = (10N + 3)^2 = 100N^2 + 60N + 9$

1.4. Place the first 10 counting numbers, one each on a card. Arrange the cards so that when you start with the top card and spell the number word "one," moving a card to the bottom of the stack for each letter said, after the card for "e" is moved to the bottom of the stack, the numeral 1 is showing. Remove the 1. Spell "two," and after the third card is placed on the bottom of the stack, the numeral card 2 is showing. Remove it. Continue through all 10 counting numbers, spelling each and removing the card associated with the word spelled. What is the original sequence of cards that makes this work?
Solution: 4, 9, 10, 1, 3, 6, 8, 2, 5, 7.

1.5. How can the following be done? From 6 take away 9; from 9 take away 10; from 40 take away 50 and when you are done, have 6 left.

291

Solution:

$$\begin{array}{ccc} \text{SIX} & \text{IX} & \text{XL} \\ \underline{\text{IX}} & \underline{\text{X}} & \underline{\text{L}} \\ \text{S} & \text{I} & \text{X} \end{array}$$

1.6. Why does a piece of bread with peanut butter and jelly on one side land bread side up when it slides off a kitchen counter?

Solution: The height of a typical kitchen counter allows for a half spin on the piece of bread. Move the height of the shelf to about 10 feet and it will land bread side down.

1.7. When does $10 + 4 = 2$?

Solution: Think time.

2.1. Use three 9s and one minus sign to make 1.

Solution: (9^{9-9})

2.2. A customer at a 7-11 store selected four items to buy, and was told that the cost was $7.11. He was curious that the cost was the same as the store name, so he inquired as to how the figure was derived. The clerk said that he had simply multiplied the prices of the four individual items. The customer protested that the four prices should have been ADDED, not MULTIPLIED. The clerk said that that was OK with him, but the result was still the same: $7.11. What were the exact prices of the four items (no rounding or use of mils)?

Answer: $1.20, $1.25, $1.50, $3.16 Email brumbad@pegasus.cc.ucf.edu, ortiz @mail.ucf.edu, or ggresham@mail.ucf. edu for a proof of this problem (it is several pages long).

2.3. How do you show 15 minutes with only two hour glasses, one that goes for 7 minutes and one that goes for 11 minutes?

Solution: Start them both. When 7 minutes is over, turn the 7-minute glass over. When the 11-minute glass runs out, turn the 7 back over.

2.4. Do the following and see what you get: From 6 take away 9; from 9 take away 10; from 40 take away 50 and when you are done, have 6 left.

Solution:

$$\begin{array}{ccc} \text{SIX} & \text{IX} & \text{XL} \\ \underline{\text{IX}} & \underline{\text{X}} & \underline{\text{L}} \\ \text{S} & \text{I} & \text{X} \end{array}$$

2.5. Take ace through king of any suit from a bridge deck of cards. Stack the cards so that when you spell "ACE" by taking a card and without looking at it say the letter "A," a second card saying "C" and a third saying "E," the next card will be the ace. Then do the same thing spelling "two", etc. As a card is viewed, it is removed from the stack. Continue until all cards are shown and the resultant removal stack is in the proper order.

Solution: Arrange 13 rectangular boxes vertically. Starting with the top box, spell ace with one letter in each of the top 3 boxes. The fourth box down would have the full word "ACE" put in it and will not be used any more because it represents the card to be removed. Boxes 5, 6, and 7 would be used to spell out "two, with box 8 being used for the word "TWO" and then it would not be used again. Boxes 9, 10, 11, 12, and 13 would be used to spell out "Three." Looping back to the beginning, Box 1 would hold the word "THREE" and would not be used again. Boxes 2, 3, 5, and 6 would be used to spell "FOUR," etc. The boxes will show you how to arrange the deck initially.

2.6. Did you know that 86,400 equals 1,440 and that 1,440 equals 24 and that 24 equals 1? How is this possible?

Solution: They are all equal to one day. 1 day = 24 hours = 1,440 minutes = 84,600 seconds.

2.7. A fish had to swim 1,010 feet to reach the other fish. Every 5 minutes the fish swam 30 feet upstream, but then in the next 2 minutes, the rushing current pushed the fish back 10 feet downstream. The fish continued swimming for 5 minutes, then resting for 2 minutes until reaching its destination. How long did it take the fish to swim the entire 1,010 feet?

Solution: It will take the fish 348 minutes or 5 hours and 48 minutes to swim 1,010 feet. For each 7 minute cycle of swimming and resting the fish made 20 feet of progress (30 feet upstream minus 10 feet downstream) so it will take 50 (1,010 divided by 20) 7 minute cycles to reach its destination. $50 \times 7 = 350$ minutes. However, in the last cycle, the fish reached the destination before the usual 2 minute rest, so it actually reached it in 348 minutes.

2.8. Madison injured her leg surfboarding and while absent from school, received 31 get-well cards from her friends. There were 5 more cards from girls than boys. She got a card from each classmate and 6 other cards from girls in other classes. How many boys and how many girls are there in Madison's class?

Solution: The class has a total of 13 girls and 13 boys. First add up to 31 and have a difference of 5. She got 18 cards from girls and 13 cards from boys. Next, to find the number of girls in her class, subtract 6 from 18 and you get 12. Then add 1 girl for Madison and you have 13 girls altogether. Therefore, her class must have 13 boys since you have total of 26 students.

3.1. A person likes 225 but not 224; 900 but not 800; 144 but not 145. Which would be preferred; 1600 or 1700? Why?

Solution: 1600 (perfect squares).

3.2. Take any number. Subtract the sum of the digits. That missing addend will always be a multiple of nine. Example $736 - 16 = 720$.

Solution: Other examples include $800 - 8 = 792$, and $1092 - 12 = 1080$.

3.3. Place digits 1 through 6 in the circles so the value inside the triangle is the sum of the digits at its vertices (see Fig. 3.11).

Solution: See Fig. 3.14.

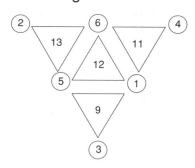

FIG 3.14.

3.4. Arrange three 6s in a configuration that equals 20.

Solution:

$$\frac{(6 + 6)}{0.6}$$

3.5. How many pennies can you arrange so each penny touches every other penny?

Solution: 4.

3.6. Arrange 6 pennies in the form of a cross (see Fig. 3.12). Move the coins and form two straight rows with 4 pennies in each.

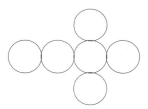

FIG 3.12.

Solution: Move the leftmost penny on top of the center one in the vertical row (see Fig. 3.15).

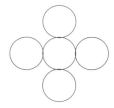

FIG 3.15.

3.7. In the pattern O T T F F S S , what comes next?

Solution: Answer: E. These are the first letters of the counting numbers: One, Two, Three, Four,. . . .

4.1. 1729 is the smallest number that can be expressed two different ways as the sum of two cubes. What are the two ways? The story behind this problem relates that the mathematician G. H. Hardy arrived in a taxi numbered 1729 when visiting the mathematician Srinivasa Ramanvjan and the question was posed.
Solution: $1^3 + 12^3 = 1729$ and $10^3 + 9^3 = 1729$.

4.2. Sum the consecutive counting numbers from 1 through N. This is a great place to relate the Gauss story about discovering how to do this.

1	2	3		N−2	N−1	N
N	N−1	N−2	...	3	2	1
N+1	N+1	N+1		N+1	N+1	N+1

Solution: The sum is $\dfrac{N(N+1)}{2}$.

4.3. Divide the 4×4 grid into 2 congruent shapes, each resulting in the same sum when the elements in the cells are added.

5	5	1	25
5	25	10	10
1	5	5	10
10	10	25	10

Solution:

5	5	1	25
5	25	10	10
1	5	5	10
10	10	25	10

Use the top two elements of the first column from the left, the top three elements of the second column from the left, the top one element from the third column from the left, and the top two elements of the rightmost column for one sum.

4.4. If you have 142 Hatfields and 154 McCoys fighting for 69 oil wells over 5 years, who won? Type 14215469 × 5 on your calculator. Turn it upside down to read the answer.
Solution: "Shelloil"

4.5. A person likes 225 but not 224; 900 but not 800; 144 but not 145. Which would be preferred; 1600 or 1700? Why?
Solution: 1600 (perfect squares).

4.6. You are given a choice of two payment options: One cent on the first day, two cents on the second day, and double your salary every day thereafter for the thirty days; or Exactly $1,000,000. (That's one million dollars!) It should be noted that this problem is posed in many forms, one of which is connected to the legend that this kind of payment arose from an ancient king of the Middle East. The king promised to pay a poor and unworthy suitor of the king's daughter to go away. The agreement was that the king would pay 1 grain of rice on the first square of a chessboard, 2 on the 2nd, 4 on the 3rd, and so on for all 64 squares. Alas, the king became the pauper and the suitor possessed all of the wealth. The suitor and the daughter married and lived happily ever after. What is the better option to take? Why?
Solution: The better option is to take the first option. Your money will double as each day passes with a total of $10, 737,418.23 at the end of 30 days.

4.7. If you add 9 and 9 you get 18, and if you multiply 9 by 9 you get 81 (the reverse of 18). There are 2 more pairs of numbers with the same characteristics and where the result is two-digit: $24 + 3 = 27$ and $24 \times 3 = 72$ and $47 + 2 = 49$ and

$47 \times 2 = 94$ However, there is only one pair of numbers with a triple digit result and its reverse. What are the numbers?

Solution: The numbers are 497 and 2: $497 + 2 = 499$ and $497 \times 2 = 994$.

4.8. Arrange four nine's to equal 100.

Solution: $99 + \frac{9}{9} = 100$.

5.1. A mouse will gain 2 grams of weight every day eating as much cheese as possible. Not eating results in losing 3 grams of weight per day. If the mouse gained 5 grams over 20 days, how many days were spent not eating for the mouse?

Solution: X = number of days spent eating $(20 - X)$ = number of days not eating. So,

$2X - 3(20 - X) = 5$
$2X - 60 + 3X = 5$
$5X = 65$
$X = 13$

$20 - 13 = 7$ He did not eat for 7 days.

5.2. If n is a real number, find the smallest possible real value for the expression: $n^2 - 3n + \sqrt{n-3} - \sqrt{n+3}$.

Solution: Since the solution must be real, $\sqrt{n-3}$ must be real. Therefore, n must be greater than or equal to 3. If $n = 3$, then $n^2 - 3n + \sqrt{n-3} - \sqrt{n+3} = {}^-\sqrt{6}$ because $n^2 - 3n = 0$ and $\sqrt{n-3} = 0$ leaving $-\sqrt{n+3}$ which is $-\sqrt{3+3}$. If n is greater than 3, then $n^2 - 3n > 0$ and $\sqrt{n-3} > 0$. Therefore, the sum of $n^2 - 3n$ and $\sqrt{n-3}$ will increase the value of $-\sqrt{n+3}$. Therefore, the least value will occur when $n = 3$.

5.3. When you divide your favorite number by 7, you get a remainder of 5. What is the remainder if you multiply your favorite number by 5 and then divide by 7?

Solution: The number is of the form $7k + 5$, for some integer k. If you multiply the number by 5, you get $5(7k + 5) = 35k + 25$. Because 35 is a multiple of 7, then 35k is also a multiple of 7, and the remainder when 35k is divided by 7 is 0. When 25 is divided by 7, the remainder is 4. Hence, the remainder when $35k + 25$ is divided by 7 is 4.

5.4. The pattern ABBCCCDDDDEEEE E...ZZZ...Z repeats continuously such that after the final Z the letters ABBCCCD DDDEEEE...begin again. What will be the 3000th letter in the pattern?

Solution: The pattern ABBCCCDDDDEE EEE...has 351 letters which can be found by finding the sum of the first 26 counting numbers. $\frac{3000}{351} = 8$ with a remainder of 192. Find the 192nd letter in the pattern. The last S represents the 190th letter. Therefore, T represents the 3000th letter in the pattern.

5.5. You drive to and from school over the same route each day. On Friday, you drive at an average rate of 52 kph and are 1 minute late. On Monday, you drive at an average rate of 60 kph and are 1 minute early. If you left home at the same time each day, how far do you travel from home (one way) to school?

Solution: Use distance = rate × time. Be sure time is in the same units throughout the problem.

Friday $d = 52 \left(t + \frac{1}{60} \right)$, where t is the time it would take to arrive on time and $\frac{1}{60}$ represents 1 minute.

Monday $d = 60 \left(t - \frac{1}{60} \right)$, where t is the time it would take to arrive on time and $\frac{1}{60}$ represents 1 minute.

Since d is the same distance for Friday and Monday $52 \left(t + \frac{1}{60} \right) = 60 \left(t - \frac{1}{60} \right)$

$$52t + \frac{52}{60} = 60t - \frac{60}{60}$$

$$\frac{52}{60} = 8t - \frac{60}{60}$$

$$\frac{112}{60} = 8t$$

$$t = \frac{7}{30}$$

Substituting t in for either equation

$$d = 60\left(\frac{7}{30} - \frac{1}{60}\right)$$

$$d = 60\left(\frac{14}{60} - \frac{1}{60}\right) \text{ or } 13$$

5.6. The counting numbers 1–500 inclusive are placed in a hat. What is the probability that the first randomly chosen number from the hat is a multiple of 6 or 19?

Solution: There are 83 multiples of 6 contained in 1–500 while there are 26 multiples of 19. The key is to find the numbers that are both multiples of 6 and 19 because you do not want to count these twice. 6×19, 12×19, 18×19, and 24×19. Therefore $83 + 26 - 4 = 105$. $\frac{105}{500} = \frac{21}{100}$.

5.7. Determine the exact sum of all ten-digit numbers.

Solution: The 10-digit numbers range from 1000000000 to 9999999999 and we want the sum. To find the sum of all of these numbers, we will sum from 1 to 9999999999 (1 to the last 10-digit number) as well as 1 to 999999999 (1 to the last 9 digit number). The difference between these values will be the solution.

Sum of n from 1 to 9999999999 is $\frac{(9999999999)(10000000000)}{2}$

Sum of n from 1 to 999999999 is $\frac{(999999999)(1000000000)}{2}$

$$\frac{(9999999999)(10000000000)}{2} - \frac{(999999999)(1000000000)}{2}$$

$$= 49\ 499\ 999\ 995\ 500\ 000\ 000.$$

5.8. The average of two four-digit positive integers is found by placing a decimal point between the two numbers. Find the sum of the two four-digit numbers.

Solution: Let abcd and efgh be the two numbers.

$$\frac{abcd + efgh}{2} = abcd.efgh \text{ or } efgh.abcd$$

Looking at abcd.efgh will suffice. The decimal portion when dividing by 2 is either 0 or 0.5. Therefore, efgh must be either 0000 or 5000. Since efgh must be a four-digit number, it must be 5000. Therefore

$$\frac{abcd + 5000}{2} = abcd.5000$$

abcd + 5000 = 2(abcd.5000)
abcd + 5000 = 2(abcd + 0.5000)
abcd + 5000 = 2(abcd) + 2(0.5000)
abcd + 5000 = 2(abcd) + 1
2abcd + 1 = 5000 + abcd
abcd + 1 = 5000
abcd = 4999 and the sum of 4999 + 5000 = 9999

5.9. The game of passing a saying around a group and determining how it changes because of communication can be used in the classroom. Start with the statement, "A square is a polygon that is a regular quadrilateral, parallelogram, rectangle, and rhombus." Was that the expression the last participant gave?

Solution: Answers will vary.

5.10. Pair the students. Have one person create a simple collection of geometric figures like the one shown in Fig. 5.6. That person describes the work to the partner (who does not see the finished product that was created), who is to create a duplicate from the description. Compare results.

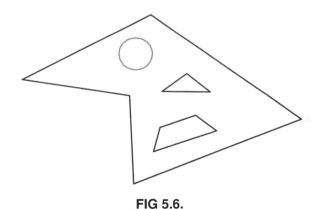

FIG 5.6.

Solution: Answers will vary.

6.1. Determine the values of a, b, and c given that $a^3 + b^3 + c^3 = 6396$, $(a)(b)(c) = 935$, and $a + b + c = 33$.

Solution: Begin with the prime factorization of $935 = 5 \times 11 \times 17$. Checking, these values, $5 + 11 + 17 = 33$. Substituting them into $a^3 + b^3 + c^3$ gives $5^3 + 11^3 + 17^3 = 6369$.

6.2. A five-digit number is represented by ABCDE. If we affix the digit 1 at the left end of ABCDE, giving 1ABCDE, then the product of 1ABCDE and 3 will be the six-digit number ABCDE1. What is the original five-digit number ABCDE?

$$
\begin{array}{r}
1ABCDE \\
\times \quad\quad 3 \\
\hline
ABCDE1
\end{array}
$$

Solution: Let X represent ABCDE. The number 1ABCDE can be represented by $100000 + X$, where X represents ABCDE. At the same time ABCDE1 can be represented by $10X + 1$.

$(1ABCDE)(3) = ABCDE1$	Given
$(100000 + X)(3) = 10X + 1$	Substitution
$300000 + 3X = 10X + 1$	Dist. of multiplication over addition on reals
$299999 = 7X$	Simplification
$42857 = X$	Division

6.3. Sometimes problems that appear complex can be approached from a surprising direction. Looking at the following problem, calculators and most interactive algebra software will struggle to work the problem because of the magnitude of the numbers involved. What is $\dfrac{1000! - 996!}{997!}$?

Solution: Rewrite $\dfrac{1000! - 996!}{997!}$ as $\dfrac{1000!}{997!} - \dfrac{996!}{997!}$

$\dfrac{1000!}{997!}$ can be expressed as $(1000)(999)(998)\left(\dfrac{997!}{997!}\right)$

$(1000)(999)(998)\left(\dfrac{997!}{997!}\right) = (1000)(999)(998)$.

$(1000)(999)(998) = 997002000$.

$\dfrac{996!}{997!}$ can be expressed as $\dfrac{996!}{(996!)(997)}$.

$\dfrac{996!}{(996!)(997)} = \dfrac{1}{997}$.

$\dfrac{1000!}{997!} - \dfrac{996!}{997!} = 997002000 - \dfrac{1}{997}$

$\quad\quad\quad = 997001999\dfrac{996}{997}$.

6.4. A right triangle with integral side lengths has an area of 756 square units. What is the hypotenuse of this right triangle?

Solution: A right triangle with area 756 square units must have a hypotenuse that is the major diagonal of a rectangle with area 1512 square units. Thus, the legs or base and a height of the triangle must be factors of 1512. The possible factor pairs are: 1, 1512; 2, 756; 3, 504; 4, 378; 6, 252; 7, 216; 8, 189; 9, 168; 12,126; 14, 108; 18, 84; 21, 72; 24, 63; 28, 54; 36, 42. Of all of these factor pairs, only 21 and 72 provide a hypotenuse that is also an integer: 75. The hypotenuse of any of the other listed pairs of factors will not be an integer.

6.5. A 44-foot rope is attached to the top of a vertical 20-foot flagpole. When the other end of the rope stretched tight and touched to the ground, a right triangle is formed. What is the area of the largest circle that can be drawn using this rope attached to the top of the pole, assuming the rope does not wrap around the pole at all as the circle is drawn?

Solution: The rope is the hypotenuse of a right triangle. Using the Pythagorean theorem,

$$20^2 + b^2 = 44^2$$
$$400 + b^2 = 1936$$
$$b^2 = 1536$$
$$b = \sqrt{1536} \text{ feet.}$$

This would also be the radius of the circle made by the rope. The area of the circle would be $\pi(\sqrt{1536})^2$ or $\pi(1536)$ square feet.

6.6. It is known that 40% of boys and 28% of girls in a school are soccer players. If the school contained an equal number of boys and girls, what is the probability that a randomly selected person in that school is a soccer player?

Solution: Consider the school to have 100 boys and 100 girls. Of the 100 boys, 40 must be soccer players. Of the 100 girls, 28 must be soccer players. That is a total of 68 soccer players of the 200 students.

The overall percentage of soccer players is 34% (68 out of 200). Therefore, the probability of randomly selecting a soccer player is 34%.

Another solution: Since there is an equal amount of boys and girls at the school, the percentage of soccer players at the school is just the average of the two percentages:
$$\frac{0.40 + 0.28}{2} = 0.34.$$

Still another solution:

$$P(\text{Soccer}) = P(\text{Soccer and Boy})$$
$$+ P(\text{Soccer and Girl})$$

$$P(A) = P(A \text{ and } B) + P(A \text{ and } B)$$

$$P(\text{Soccer and Boy}) = [P(\text{Soccer}|\text{Boy}) \times [\,[P(\text{Boy})]$$

$$P(\text{Soccer and Girl}) = [P(\text{Soccer}|\text{Girl}) \times [\,[P(\text{Girl})]$$

$$P(A \mid B) = \frac{P(A \text{ and } B)}{P(B)}$$

This leads to $(0.40)(0.5) + (0.28)(0.5) = 0.34$.

6.7. To square any two-digit number starting with 5, add 25 to the ones digit and you will have the thousands and hundreds digits of the product. Then square the ones digit and that result becomes the tens and ones digits of the product. Note, you might need 0 for the tens digit of the final product if the ones digit of the number being squared is 0, 1, 2, or 3.

Solution: Let the number be 5x, where x is any digit.

$(5x)^2 = (50 + x)^2$ Expanded notation
$= 2500 + 100x + x^2$ Squaring a binomial

But, 100x is 100 times the ones digit of the number being squared so it could be written x00. Then $2500 + x00 = (25 + x)00$, which is 25 plus the ones digit of the number being squared. Since x is a digit, its square will be, at most, a two-digit number. Those two digits will be added to zeros in their respective places.

6.8. Using 3 different digits, form all possible 2-digit numbers (including repeating the digits). Add all 9 of the 2-digit numbers you form. Divide this sum by the sum of the original 3 digits. The answer will be 33.

Solution: Let a, b, and c be the digits. Written in expanded notation, the 2-digit forms would be: 10a + a, 10a + b, 10a + c, 10b + a, 10b + b, 10b + c, 10c + a, 10c + b, and 10c + c. The sum of these 9 addends is $30(a + b + c) + 3(a + b + c) = 33(a + b + c)$. But $(a + b + c)$ is the sum of the digits and when the sum of all nine 2-digit numbers formed $(33(a + b + c))$ is divided by $(a + b + c)$, the answer will be 33.

6.9. How can these products be done quickly in your head?

$$(36)(34) = 1224$$
$$(53)(57) = 3021$$
$$(62)(68) = 4216$$
$$(41)(49) = 2009$$

Solution: Multiply the ones digits of the factors. That answer becomes the ones and tens digits of the final product. The rest of the final product is found by multiplying all values to the left of the ones digit (they must be the same in both factors) by itself plus one; in (62)(68), (6)(7) = 42.

Proof: The original factors can be expressed as m5 + n and m5 − n, where m is any counting number and $0 > n < 4$. In expanded notation, m5 is expressed as 10m + 5, so:

$$(m5 + n)(m5 - n) = (10m + 5 + n) \leq (10m + 5 - n)$$
$$= 100m^2 + 100m + 25 - n^2.$$

But, $100m^2 + 100m = (m^2 + m)(100)$
$$= (m)(m + 1)(100),$$

where m all that is to the left of the ones digit of the original factors (remember, m is not limited to digits). But, (m)(m + 1) is the same as saying you are multiplying all values to the left of the ones digit (they must be the same in both factors) by itself plus one. Multiplying by 100 allows for the rest of the answer to be added with no regrouping concerns.

The rest of the product is reflected by $25 - n^2$, which is shown in the example (62)(68). Here, n would be 3 and the product would be expressed as $(65 - 3)(65 + 3)$. Using $25 - n^2$, you would have $25 - 9$, or 16, which is also the product of 2 and 8.

6.10. What is wrong with the following calculations that seem to prove that 2 equals 1?

$a = b$	Let $a = b$
$aa = ab$	Multiply both sides by a
$aa - bb = ab - bb$	Subtract bb from both sides
$(a + b)(a - b) = b(a - b)$	Factor
$a + b = b$	Divide both sides by $(a - b)$
$2a = a$	Substitute a for b
$2 = 1$	Divide both sides by a

Solution:
$a = b$ means that $aa = bb = ab$, so when we have
$aa - bb = ab - bb$ we actually end up with
$0 = 0$.

Another way of looking at it is that when both sides are divided by $(a - b)$ we are actually dividing by zero, which cannot be done. Yet, $(a - b)$ does not clearly show as zero for many people until it is called to their attention.

6.11. $23 \times 96 = 2208 = 32 \times 69$. Notice that the product of left side of the equation is equal to the product of the digits reversed on the right side. Find another pair of 2-digit numbers that share the same product when their digits are reversed. Repeated-digit factors are not permitted (like 33×33). Prove why this is possible.

Solution: $12 \times 63 = 21 \times 36$ (and others). Consider a, b, c, and d to be the digits so that (ab)(cd) = (ba)(dc).

$(a\,b)(c\,d) = (b\,a)(d\,c)$	Given
$(10a + b)(10c + d) = (10b + a)(10d + c)$	Expanded notation
$100ac + 10ad + 10bc + bd = 100bd + 10bc + 10ad + ac$	Distributive of x over + on reals
$100ac + \cancel{10ad} + \cancel{10bc} + bd = 100bd + \cancel{10bc} + \cancel{10ad} + ac$	$= - - = \rightarrow =$
$100ac - ac = 100bd - bd$	Like terms on same side($= - - = \rightarrow =$)
$99ac = 99bd$	Collect like terms
$ac = bd$	$= \div = \rightarrow =$

$(a\,b)(c\,d) = (b\,a)(d\,c)$ is true as long as $ac = bd$.

7.1. A farmer had 26 cows. All but 9 died. How many lived?
Solution: 17 cows died and 9 cows lived.

7.2. A uniform log can be cut into 3 pieces in 12 seconds. Assuming the same rate of cutting, how long will it take for a similar log to be cut into 4 pieces?
Solution: 2 cuts divide the log into 3 pieces; then 3 cuts divide the log into four pieces. If 2 cuts take 12 seconds; then 3 cuts will take 18 seconds. Another way of looking at this is to make one cut parallel to the long sides of the log and then a second cut perpendicular to it. That will give 4 pieces. Granted, the length of the log could be such that the time required would differ, but you have to admit that this is a pretty creative solution, and it was proposed by a third grader.

7.3. How many different ways can you add four odd counting numbers to get a sum of 10?
Solution: {1, 1, 1, 7}, {3, 3, 3, 1}, and {1, 1, 3, 5} are the sets of four odd counting numbers that total 10.

$\{1, 1, 1, 7\} : 1+1+1+7, 1+1+7+1, 1+7+1+1, 7+1+1+1$

$\{3, 3, 3, 1\} : 3+3+3+1, 3+3+1+3, 3+1+3+3, 1+3+3+3$

$\{1, 1, 3, 5\} : 1+1+3+5, 1+3+1+5, 3+1+1+5, 1+1+5+3, 1+5+1+3, 5+1+1+3, 5+3+1+1, 5+1+1+3, 1+5+3+1, 3+1+5+1, 3+5+1+1, 1+3+5+1$

7.4. What is the sum of the first 100 consecutive counting numbers?
Solution: $100+1 = 101$; $99+2 = 101$; $98+3 = 101$; etc. down to $50+51 = 101$
$50 \times 101 = 5050$ OR

$$1+ \quad 2+ \quad 3+ \cdots + \quad 98+ \quad 99+100$$
$$\underline{100+ \quad 99+ \quad 98+ \cdots + \quad 3+ \quad 2+ \quad 1}$$
$$101+101+101+\cdots+101+101+101$$

This gives 100 pairs of addends, each with a sum of 101, for a total of 10100. That is twice as much as needed, because each number is used twice. Divide by two, getting 5050.

7.5. How many cubic inches of dirt are there in a hole that is 1 foot deep, 2 feet wide, and 6 feet long?
Solution: The hole is 12 in. × 24 in. × 72 in.; there are 0 cubic inches of dirt in it or it wouldn't be a hole.

7.6. How many squares are there in a 5 by 5 square grid?
Solution: 1—5 × 5 square; 4—4 × 4 squares; 9—3 × 3 squares; 16—2 × 2 squares; 25—1 × 1 squares
$1+4+9+16+25 = 55$.

7.7. A little green frog is sitting at the bottom of the stairs. She wants to get to the tenth step, so she leaps up 2 steps and then slides back 1. How many leaps will she have to take if she follows this pattern until she reaches the tenth step?
Solution: 9 leaps. Ground to **2** to 1 to **3** to 2 to **4** to 3 to **5** to 4 to **6** to 5 to **7** to 6 to

8 to 7 to **9** to 8 to **10**. The bold indicates leaps up.

7.8. If there are 7 months that have 31 days in them and 11 months that have 30 days in them, how many months have 28 days in them?
Solution: All of the months have 28 days.

7.9. TTTTTTT9 What number does this represent?
Solution: sevenT-nine.

7.10. You are given 5 beans and 4 bowls. Place an odd number of beans in each bowl. Use all beans.
Solution: Visualize 4 bowls arranged from smallest to largest and stack the bowls one inside the other. You could place all 5 beans in the smallest bowl and be done. There are other solutions.

7.11. You are to take a pill every half hour. You have 18 pills to take. How long will you be taking pills?
Solution: 3 are taken the first hour, then two each hour after—8.5 hours

7.12. If you got a 40% discount on a $150.00 pair of sport shoes and 20% off a $200 set of roller blades, what was the percent discount on the total purchase (assuming no taxes are involved)?
Solution: $\frac{100}{350} = 28.57\%$

7.13. Where should the Z be placed and why?

A		E F	HI	K L M N		T	V W X Y
B C D			G	J		O P Q R S	U

Solution: Z goes in the top because it doesn't have any curved parts.

7.14. Estimate how old will you be in years if you live 1,000,000 hours?
Solution: $\frac{1000000}{(24)(365.25)} \approx 114.39$ years

7.15. A child has $3.15 in U.S. coins, but only has dimes and quarters. There are more quarters than dimes. How many of each coin does the child have?

Solution:
$3.15 − $0.10 = $3.05
$3.05 − $0.10 = $2.95
$2.95 − $0.10 = $2.85
$2.85 − $0.10 = $2.75 : $2.75 is a multiple of 25 so 11 quarters and 4 dimes is a solution. Continuing this thinking, $2.25 is the next possible answer for quarters but that is 9 quarters and that demands 9 dimes.

7.16. There are 3 children in a family. The oldest is 15. The average of their ages is 11. The median age is 10. How old is the youngest child?

Solution: 8, 10, and 15 are the ages. You are given 2 of the ages. One of them is directly shown as 15. Median, since there are 3 kids, must be the middle age. So, $10 + 15 + n$ must equal 33, if the average is 11. $33 − (10 + 15) = 8$.

7.17. A famous mathematician was born on March 14, which could be written 3.14. This date is the start of a representation for pi. It is interesting that this mathematician was born on "pi day." Give his name.

Solution: Albert Einstein.

8.1. Square a number ending in 3.
Last digit is a 9.

+ 60 times the rest of the number (left of the 3)

+ 100 times the rest of the number (left of 3 squared followed by 00)

$73^2 = 9 + 60(7) + 100(7^2)$ $123^2 = 9 + 60(12) + 100(12^2)$

$= 9 + 420 + 4900$ $= 9 + 720 + 14400$

$= 5329$ $= 15129$

Why does this work? Suppose the number is "Nty"-three.

$$(N3)^2 = (10N + 3)^2 = 100N^2 + 60N + 9$$

8.2. Place the first 10 counting numbers, one each on a card. Arrange the cards so that when you start with the top card and spell the number word "one," moving a card to the bottom of the stack for each letter said, after the card for "e" is moved to the bottom of the stack, the numeral 1 is showing. Remove the 1. Spell "two," and after the third card is placed on the bottom of the stack, the numeral card 2 is showing. Remove it. Continue through all 10 counting numbers, spelling each and removing the card associated with the word spelled. What is the original sequence of cards that makes this work?

Solution: 4, 9, 10, 1, 3, 6, 8, 2, 5, 7. Arrange 10 rectangular boxes vertically. Starting with the top row, spell "one" with a single letter in each of the top 3 rows. The fourth row down would have the full word "ONE" in it and will not be used any more because it represents the card to be removed. Rows 5, 6, and 7 would be used to spell out "TWO", with row 8 being used for the word "TWO" and then it would not be used again. Looping to a new column, rows 9, 10, 1, 2, and 3 would be used to spell out "THREE". Since row 4 is not to be used again, row 5 will hold the word "THREE." Rows 6, 7, 9, and 10 would be used to spell "FOUR," etc. The rows will show you how to arrange the deck initially.

1	o	r	FOUR								
2	n	e	f	i	v	e	h	n	n	NINE	
3	e	e	i	x	e	i	t	i	e		TEN
4	ONE										
5	t	THREE									
6	w	f	v	SIX							
7	o	o	e	s	n	g	EIGHT				
8	TWO										
9	t	u	FIVE								
10	h	r	s	e	SEVEN						

8.3. Tell someone you will race their calculator skills in multiplying a two-digit number by 55.
Ask for a two-digit number.
Divide the selected number by 2.
Move the decimal point one place to the right (call this number A).
$B = 10A$
Find $A + B$

Examples	
Pick 28.	51
$28 \div 2 = 14$	$51 \div 2 = 25.5$
Decimal one to right 140 (=A)	$255 = A$
$B = 10(140) = 1400$	$B = 2550$
$A + B = 140 + 1400 = 1540$	$A + B = 255 + 2550$
So $28 \times 55 = 1540$.	So $51 \times 55 = 2805$

(Source: BEATCALC@aol.com)

Solution: Suppose the original number is CD where C is the tens digit and D is the units digit. The initial problem would be (CD)(55). But $55 = \frac{110}{2}$, and the problem becomes $(CD)\left(\frac{110}{2}\right)$, which could be expressed as $\left(\frac{CD}{2}\right)(110)$. But $110 = 100 + 10$, making $\left(\frac{CD}{2}\right)(10) + \left(\frac{CD}{2}\right)(100)$.

Note: BEATCALC is great source of number oddities. A new one is produced each week and it is free!

8.4. A person likes 225 but not 224; 900 but not 800; 144 but not 145. Which would be preferred; 1600 or 1700? Why?
Solution: 1600 (perfect squares).

8.5. Place digits 1 through 6 in the circles so each triangle is a correct sum.

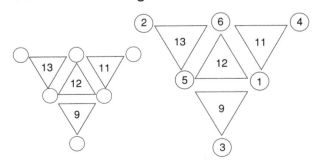

8.6. Use three 6s and addition, subtraction, multiplication, and division to get 20. HINT: You will need a decimal.
Solution: $\dfrac{6 + 6}{0.6}$

8.7. Use three 9s and a minus sign to make 1.
Solution: $9^{(9-9)}$

8.8. Which number becomes larger when it is turned upside down? The number of correct answers is infinite.
Solution: 6 becomes 9. Any proper fraction becomes larger when the numerator and denominator are interchanged (0 and ∞ excluded).

8.9. A farmer threw 9 ears of corn in the barn. A rat came in and left with 3 ears each day. It took the rat 9 days to take all the corn. Why?
Solution: When the rat leaves, it has an ear of corn and its own two ears.

8.10. Ask for a 3-digit number comprised of the same digit. Ask that the number be doubled and then divided by 37. The answer will be 6 times the selected digit. How does it work?
Solution: Let x be the selected digit. The number, $xxx = x(111)$. Two times $x(111) = x(111)(2)$. But $111 = (37)(3)$, so $x(111)(2) = x(37)(3)(2)$, which is $x(37)(6)$. However, dividing by 37 leaves 6x.

8.11. How can you quickly square numbers made up of 9s up to 9 digits long?
Solution: Consider 9999 to be squared. Square has: 1 less 9 than the number has (999), one 8, the same number of zeros as 9's (000), and a final 1. $9999 \times 9999 = 99980001$.

999999 squared has 1 less 9 than the number (99999), one 8, the same number of zeros as 9's (00000), and a final 1. $999999 \times 999999 = 999998000001$.

8.12. In the pattern O T T F F S S, what comes next?

Solution: E. This is the first letter of the counting numbers: One, Two, Three, Four, Five, Six, Seven, Eight . . .

8.13. What is two times a half of 456,789?

Solution: $(2)\left(\frac{1}{2}\right)(456{,}789) = 456{,}789$

8.14. Take a bus between two towns. The bus travels at an average speed of 30 miles per hour. How fast would the bus have to travel on the return trip for the average speed of the round trip to be 60 miles per hour?

Solution: The answer to the problem is the same no matter what the distance is. Suppose the distance between the towns is 120 miles. Then the round trip would be a total distance of 240 miles. If the average speed of the round trip is to be 60 miles per hour, then it should take 4 hours for the bus to make the entire trip. But, if the first 120 miles are traveled at an average speed of 30 mph, then this trip alone uses up the entire 4 hours, and there is no time left for the bus to make the return trip. Therefore, the bus would have to make the return trip in no time at all, which is impossible. There is no speed for the return trip that can make the average speed for the round trip 60 miles per hour.

8.15. The people on a certain island are divided into two groups—the truth-tellers and the liars. The truth-tellers always tell the truth. The liars always lie. There are no half-truths or half-lies.

A stranger comes to the island one day and sees three of the natives standing together. The first native says, "I am not a liar." The second native says, "He's lying." The third native says, "They are both lying."

What is the third native—a truth-teller or a liar?

Solution: If the first native told the truth, then the second native lied. If the first native lied, then the second native told the truth. Either way, one of them told the truth and the other lied, so the third native has to be a liar.

8.16. Did you know that the Hindu Arabic number system was illegal for years in Europe? The thinking was that since it came from Hindus and Arabs, it had to be unclean. By using the system, it was assumed that the individual was doing the work of the devil.

8.17. Ask an individual to give a 3-digit number. Have the individual duplicate the digits in the order given, yielding a 6-digit number. Divide that 6-digit number by 7; divide that answer by 11; divide that answer by 13. The result will be the original 3-digit number. How does that work?

Solution: Let the digits be x, y, and z. The 6-digit number would be xyzxyz, which is $1000(xyz) + xyz$; but that is $xyz(1000 + 1)$ or $xyz(1001)$. $(7)(11)(13) = 1001$.

8.18. Mnemonic to remember division by zero: $\frac{O}{K}$ and $\frac{N}{O}$.

8.19. Try the Fraction Squares Game (adapted from Ortiz, 2000) with middle school students using the game board (Fig. 8.20) and game rules for addition version. Make some annotations of the students' work as they use the game.

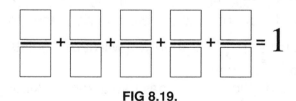

FIG 8.19.

a. Number of Players: Two to four individual players, or teams of two to three players.

b. Materials: 40 game pieces (see Fig. 8.20) and fraction kit (optional). This provides game pieces for halves, fourths, and eighths, and enough game pieces for four players or teams. You need 10 game pieces per player or team. Copy and enlarge this page on cardboard and cut each.

1	1	2	2	4	4	8	8
1	1	2	2	4	4	8	8
1	1	2	2	4	4	8	8
1	1	2	2	4	4	8	8
1	1	2	2	4	4	8	8
1	1	2	2	4	4	8	8

FIG 8.20.

c. Place the game pieces face down in front of the players for round 1 of the game.

d. Each player (or team of players) takes turns selecting randomly 10 game pieces each.

e. After selecting the game pieces, use as many of your game pieces to form fractions that add up to one (1) on the game board (see Fig. 8.19). You will earn one point for each game piece that you use correctly. The more game pieces you use the more points you earn. There may be many possible correct combinations that can be played during a given round, but you may only play one of the possible combinations of the game pieces to add up to one whole. For example, if you use 1, 1, 2, and 2 out of your selected game pieces to form $\frac{1}{2} + \frac{1}{2} = 1$, then you will earn 4 points for this round.

f. (Optional) You may use a fraction kit or Cuisenaire Rods to represent one whole, halves, fourths, and eighths, to help you find the best possible answer.

g. After, deciding your choice for the first round, count the number of game pieces that you were able to use, and record your points for round 1 of the game in the scoring table (see Table 8.3). Every player or team should have a turn.

h. After every player or team has had a chance to play, place the game pieces face

down, scramble them, and select randomly 10 new game pieces.

i. Record the score for each player or team at the end of the round (see Table 8.3). Repeat the preceding steps for the other three rounds of the game.

TABLE 8.3

Name/ Team	Round 1	Round 2	Round 3	Round 4	Final Scores
1.					
2.					
3.					
4.					

j. The player or team with the most points at the end of four rounds wins the game!

EXTENSION: Alternative game pieces for thirds, sixths, and twelfths (see Fig. 8.21) could be used instead of or in combination with the game pieces illustrated in Fig. 8.20, and game board for subtraction (see Fig. 8.22).

1	1	3	3	6	6	1	1
1	1	3	3	6	6	1	1
1	1	3	3	6	6	1	1
1	1	3	3	6	6	1	1
1	1	3	3	6	6	1	1
1	1	3	3	6	6	1	1

FIG 8.21.

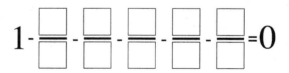

FIG 8.22.

Solution: Answers will vary.

8.20. Each of the following set of problems involving whole numbers is done incorrectly the same way. Determine the error pattern, solve the fourth and fifth problems using that pattern, describe it in your own words, indicate possible reasons for the error, and describe ways to help the student overcome the misconception (for more information on error patterns, see Ashlock, 1998).

a.

```
  23    64    27    82    34
 + 4   + 5   + 4   + 9   + 6
 ───   ───   ───
   9    15    13
```

Solution: 19, 13. The student is adding digits and disregarding place value. Among other reasons, it is possible that student is confusing this exercise with column addition. Remediation in the areas of place value and regrouping at the concrete level is needed.

b.

```
  38    52    27    64    81
 +47   +83   +39   +59   +28
 ───   ───   ───
 715   135   516
```

Solution: 1113, 109. The student is disregarding regrouping. The second problem is correct because no regrouping is involved. Among other reasons, student might have some misunderstanding of the concept of place value. The use of base 10 blocks could help.

c.

```
              1     4
 342    74   385   282   279
+631   +43  +667  +723  +836
────   ──   ────
 973    18  9116
```

Solution: 915, 1115. The student is adding from left to right and regrouping the incorrect digit. This might be because this is the way we read. The first exercise is correct because no regrouping is involved. Estimating the answer might help in developing better number sense.

d.

```
  32   245   524   458   241
 -16  -137  -298  -372   -96
 ───  ────  ────
  24   112   374         255
```

Solution: 126, 255. Always subtracting the smaller number from the larger number.

The first problem involving two digit numbers was correct. Some mental computation comparing the two numbers might have been done. Either correcting the steps to following for a left to right algorithm needs to be developed properly or the development of another correct type of subtraction algorithm should be provided. The borrow-payback or the decomposition methods could be alternatives.

e.

```
 578   479   554   195   355
+179  +578  +256  +589  +256
────  ────  ────
 647   947   700
```

Solution: 674, 501. The student is disregarding the regrouping from ones to tens. The student might need help with understanding place value and how it is used in the regrouping process.

f.

```
 8 17   6 16   7 14
 1̶9̶ 7̶   1̶7̶ 6̶   3̶8̶ 4̶   273   385
 - 4 3  - 2 3  - 5 9   - 51  - 39
 ─────  ─────  ─────
 14 14  14 13  32 5
```

Solution: 2112, 346 The student is regrouping when it is not needed. The third problem is correct because regrouping was necessary. The student might have overgeneralized the regrouping process.

g.

```
  8       2     5 12 16
 1̶9̶1     3̶2̶5   7̶ 2̶ 6̶    638   638
 - 43   - 151  - 3 4 9  - 349  - 129
 ────   ─────  ───────
  148    174    2 8 7   199    509
```

Solution: 199, 509. The student has no difficulties solving exercises involving regrouping only one regrouping (from tens to ones or from hundreds to tens). The student does not correctly perform exercises involving regrouping from tens to ones and hundreds to tens at the same time. In this case, the student will take two hundreds and incorrectly distribute them as tens and ones.

h.

$$\begin{array}{c} 2 \\ 23 \\ +\ 39 \\ \hline 71 \end{array} \quad \begin{array}{c} \\ 53 \\ +\ 26 \\ \hline 79 \end{array} \quad \begin{array}{c} 3 \\ 28 \\ +\ 45 \\ \hline 91 \end{array} \quad \begin{array}{c} \\ 45 \\ +\ 35 \\ \hline \end{array} \quad \begin{array}{c} \\ 48 \\ +\ 36 \\ \hline \end{array}$$

Solution: 71, 111. The student is reversing the proper order of the place value for regrouping purposes. The student might have mismemorized the steps of the algorithm. Understanding of place value is a major concern.

i.

$$\begin{array}{c} 313 \\ \times\ \ \ 4 \\ \hline 1252 \end{array} \quad \begin{array}{c} 210 \\ \times\ 15 \\ \hline 210 \end{array} \quad \begin{array}{c} 524 \\ \times\ 34 \\ \hline 1576 \end{array} \quad \begin{array}{c} 135 \\ \times\ 463 \\ \hline \end{array} \quad \begin{array}{c} 345 \\ \times\ 36 \\ \hline \end{array}$$

Solution: 485, 920. The student is disregarding the regrouping process and partial products. They might be thinking about the addition computation algorithm and made the improper generalizations.

j.

$$\begin{array}{c} 32 \\ \times\ 3 \\ \hline 6 \\ 9 \\ \hline 15 \end{array} \quad \begin{array}{c} 42 \\ \times\ 4 \\ \hline 8 \\ 16 \\ \hline 24 \end{array} \quad \begin{array}{c} 31 \\ \times\ 8 \\ \hline 8 \\ 24 \\ \hline 32 \end{array} \quad \begin{array}{c} 23 \\ \times\ 3 \\ \hline \end{array} \quad \begin{array}{c} 42 \\ \times\ 3 \\ \hline \end{array}$$

Solution: 15, 18. The student is treating the numbers as single digits and disregarding place value and partial products.

k.

$$\begin{array}{c} 34 \\ \times\ 2 \\ \hline 68 \end{array} \quad \begin{array}{c} 27 \\ \times\ 4 \\ \hline 88 \end{array} \quad \begin{array}{c} 18 \\ \times\ 3 \\ \hline 34 \end{array} \quad \begin{array}{c} 24 \\ \times\ 4 \\ \hline \end{array} \quad \begin{array}{c} 35 \\ \times\ 3 \\ \hline \end{array}$$

Solution: 86, 95. The student might be forgetting to add the regrouped tens to the second partial product. The exercises not requiring regrouping are correct. Demonstrations using base 10 blocks and repeated addition model could be used here.

l.

$$\begin{array}{c} 27 \\ \times\ 5 \\ \hline 255 \end{array} \quad \begin{array}{c} 43 \\ \times\ 6 \\ \hline 308 \end{array} \quad \begin{array}{c} 62 \\ \times\ 7 \\ \hline 494 \end{array} \quad \begin{array}{c} 38 \\ \times\ 6 \\ \hline \end{array} \quad \begin{array}{c} 28 \\ \times\ 5 \\ \hline \end{array}$$

Solution: 428, 300. The student is incorrectly adding the regrouped tens and multiplying this sum. The student might have mismemorized the step required in the algorithm. Demonstrations using base 10 blocks and repeated addition model could be used here.

m.

$$\begin{array}{c} 233 \\ 2\overline{)176} \end{array} \quad \begin{array}{c} 221 \\ 4\overline{)824} \end{array} \quad \begin{array}{c} 231 \\ 3\overline{)713} \end{array} \quad 3\overline{)639} \quad 4\overline{)518}$$

Solution: 213, 142. The student is always dividing the smaller number into the larger number and disregarding the remainders. The fourth problem is correct.

n.

$$\begin{array}{c} 33 \\ 3\overline{)99} \\ \underline{90} \\ 9 \\ \underline{9} \\ 0 \end{array} \quad \begin{array}{c} 25 \\ 7\overline{)364} \\ \underline{35} \\ 14 \\ \underline{14} \\ 0 \end{array} \quad \begin{array}{c} 78 \\ 8\overline{)696} \\ \underline{64} \\ 56 \\ \underline{56} \\ 0 \end{array} \quad 4\overline{)192} \quad 6\overline{)528}$$

Solution: 84 (instead of 48), 88 (apparently correct). Improperly placing the digits of the final answer by reversing the ten and one places. This is an improper implementation of the algorithm. The student might have mismemorized the steps of the algorithm.

8.21. Each of the following set of problems involving fractions is done incorrectly the same way. Determine the error pattern, solve the fourth and fifth problems using that pattern, describe it in your own words, indicate possible reasons for the error, and describe ways to help the student overcome the misconception (for more information on error patterns, see Ashlock, 1998).

a.

$$\frac{4}{5} + \frac{1}{2} = \frac{5}{7} \quad \frac{1}{4} + \frac{1}{4} = \frac{2}{8} \quad \frac{1}{6} + \frac{3}{4} = \frac{4}{10} \quad \frac{3}{4} + \frac{1}{3} = \quad \frac{5}{8} + \frac{1}{9} =$$

Solution: $\dfrac{4}{7}, \dfrac{6}{17}$. The student is not finding the common denominators and equivalent fractions before adding them.

b.

$$\begin{array}{c} \frac{1}{2}=\frac{2}{4} \\ +\frac{1}{4}=\frac{2}{4} \\ \hline \frac{4}{4}=1 \end{array} \qquad \begin{array}{c} \frac{1}{3}=\frac{3}{9} \\ +\frac{2}{3}=\frac{6}{9} \\ \hline \frac{9}{9}=1 \end{array} \qquad \begin{array}{c} \frac{3}{5}=\frac{6}{10} \\ +\frac{1}{10}=\frac{2}{10} \\ \hline \frac{8}{10}=\frac{2}{5} \end{array} \qquad \begin{array}{c} \frac{1}{7}= \\ +\frac{3}{14}= \end{array} \quad \begin{array}{c} \frac{1}{5}= \\ +\frac{5}{6}= \end{array}$$

Solution: $\dfrac{8}{14}=\dfrac{4}{7}, \dfrac{18}{3}=6$ The student is converting fractions improperly and when it is not necessary. The student might need to work with equivalent fractions at the concrete level.

c.

$$\begin{array}{c} 3\frac{1}{2}=\frac{3}{6} \\ +2\frac{1}{3}=\frac{2}{6} \\ \hline \frac{5}{6} \end{array} \quad \begin{array}{c} 2\frac{2}{5}=\frac{4}{10} \\ +8\frac{2}{10}=\frac{2}{10} \\ \hline \frac{6}{10} \end{array} \quad \begin{array}{c} 8\frac{1}{4}=\frac{5}{20} \\ +7\frac{3}{5}=\frac{12}{20} \\ \hline \frac{17}{20} \end{array} \quad \begin{array}{c} 5\frac{1}{6} \\ +3\frac{3}{12} \end{array} \quad \begin{array}{c} 3\frac{1}{5} \\ +2\frac{3}{6} \end{array}$$

Solution: $\dfrac{5}{12}, \dfrac{21}{30}=\dfrac{7}{10}$. The student is disregarding the whole number part of the mixed number and adding the fractions only. The student needs to work with converting mixed numbers into improper fractions before adding the fractions.

d.

$$\frac{1}{8}\times 1=\frac{1}{8} \qquad \frac{2}{3}\times 3=\frac{6}{9} \qquad \frac{4}{5}\times 2=\frac{8}{10} \qquad \frac{3}{9}\times 4= \qquad \frac{1}{9}\times 5=$$

Solution: $\dfrac{12}{36}, \dfrac{5}{45}$. The student is multiplying the fraction numerator and denominator by the whole number (1, 3, 2, 4 or 5, respectively) and will essentially get an equivalent fraction. The student is multiplying the fraction by one instead of using the fraction form of the whole number (which is the whole number over one). The first exercise is correct because we happen to be multiplying by one. The student needs

to work on converting whole numbers to a fraction and what this implies.

e.

$$\frac{2}{3}\times\frac{3}{5}=90 \quad \frac{1}{5}\times\frac{3}{4}=60 \quad \frac{2}{3}\times\frac{2}{5}=60 \quad \frac{3}{6}\times\frac{1}{7}= \quad \frac{5}{6}\times\frac{3}{7}=$$

Solution: 126, 630. The student is multiplying all the fraction numerators and denominators as single factors to get the final product. The student needs to work with the meaning of multiplying fractions, and the difference between multiplying whole numbers and proper fractions.

8.22. Each of the following set of problems involving decimals is done incorrectly the same way. Determine the error pattern, solve the fourth and fifth problems using that pattern, describe it in your own words, indicate possible reasons for the error, and describe ways to help the student overcome the misconception (for more information on error patterns, see Ashlock, 1998).

a.

$$\begin{array}{c} 0.3 \\ +\,0.9 \\ \hline 0.12 \end{array} \quad \begin{array}{c} 0.4 \\ +\,0.7 \\ \hline 0.11 \end{array} \quad \begin{array}{c} 0.4 \\ +\,0.8 \\ \hline 0.12 \end{array} \quad \begin{array}{c} 0.5 \\ +\,0.6 \end{array} \quad \begin{array}{c} 0.9 \\ +\,0.9 \end{array}$$

Solution: 0.11, 0.18. The student might be using the incorrect algorithm when placing the decimal point for the sum. The student might be counting the number of decimal places as you do in multiplication of decimals.

b.

$$\begin{array}{c} 3.69 \\ -\,2.8 \\ \hline 1.1 \end{array} \quad \begin{array}{c} 5.32 \\ -\,4.3 \\ \hline 1.9 \end{array} \quad \begin{array}{c} 7.18 \\ -\,3.5 \\ \hline 4.3 \end{array} \quad \begin{array}{c} 8.97 \\ -\,5.8 \end{array} \quad \begin{array}{c} 6.34 \\ -\,4.3 \end{array}$$

Solution: 3.9, 2.1. The student is disregarding the tenths place in the decimal number and subtracting across the tenths from the hundredths. When needed, the student seems to be regrouping from the tenths to the hundredths before subtracting.

c.

4 12	6 12	4 14		
5.32	7.22	5.34	7.67	9.85
− 0.08	− 0.06	− 0.09	− 0.08	− 0.08
4.34	6.26	4.35		

Solution: 6.69, 8.87. The student is regrouping from the ones to the hundredths, skipping the tenth place value altogether. The student has probably mismemorized the steps for the algorithm.

d.

2.7	8.36	0.765	4.64	5.65
× 0.6	× 6	× 2.6	× 0.5	× 7
16.2	50.16	4590		
		1530		
		19.890		

Solution: 23.20, 39.55. The student is making an incorrect placement of the decimal point for the final product. The student is probably bringing down the decimal point as you do with addition of decimals. In some cases, the answer is correct.

e.

```
       0.543        9.062       27.871
    6)3.27       4)36.26      3)83.62       4)78.65      5)78.68
      30            36            6
      27            26           23
      24            24           21
       3             2           26
                                 24
                                 22
                                 21
                                  1
```

Solution: 19.661, 15.733. The student is incorrectly placing the remainder as part of the final answer (quotient).

9.1. How do you show 15 minutes with only two-hour glasses, one that goes for 7-minutes and one that goes for 11 minutes?

Solution: Start them both. When 7 minutes is over, turn the 7-minute glass over. When the 11-minute glass runs out, turn the 7 back over.

9.2. You have equal volumes of coffee and tea, each in their respective container. A cup of coffee is removed from the coffee container and mixed with the tea. Then, a cup of the mixture is placed in the coffee container, making the volumes equal again. Is there more tea in the coffee or more coffee in the tea?

Solution: Suppose after the mixing, there is a tablespoon of coffee in the cup to be placed in the coffee container. The coffee container gains that 1 tablespoon of coffee back and a cup minus that tablespoon of tea. At the same time, the tea container has lost a tablespoon of coffee and a cup minus 1 tablespoon of tea (which along with that tablespoon of coffee made the cup of mixture). So, a cup minus 1 tablespoon of coffee was blended with the tea, and a cup minus 1 tablespoon of tea was blended with the coffee. Thus, both containers hold the same amount of the other brew.

9.3. There are three sealed envelopes. One contains two $5 bills, one contains a $10 and a $5 bill, and the third contains two $10 bills. Unfortunately, all three envelopes have the wrong amount marked on the outside. How could you correct all three by opening one envelope and looking at only one bill?

Solution: Open the envelope marked $15. Since it is marked incorrectly it has to contain either two $5 bills or two $10 bills. If you open the $15 envelope and pull out a $10 bill then you know that envelope actually contains $20. Given this fact, you are left with two remaining envelopes one with $15 and one with $10. Both are labeled incorrectly as either $10 or $20 on the outside. Again since all three are marked incorrectly you deduce that the one marked $10 must contain $15 (and not $10 because then it would be marked correctly). Finally, the remaining $20 envelope must contain the $10.

9.4. How many 3-cent stamps are there in a dozen?

Solution: 12

9.5. A rope ladder hangs over the side of a ship. The rungs are one foot apart and the ladder is 12 feet long. The tide is rising at four inches an hour. How long will it take before the first four rungs of the ladder are underwater?

Solution: Ship will rise and fall with the tide so the rungs stay the same level with the water.

9.6. Which would you rather have, a trunk full of nickels or a trunk half full of dimes?

Solution: Dimes are smaller in volume so pick them.

9.7. Steve has three piles of sand and Mike has four piles of sand. All together, how many do they have?

Solution: When they put them together, there will be one pile.

9.8. Given a box with a lid and a 12-inch ruler, how can you measure the distance from a bottom corner to a diagonally opposite top corner, without opening the box? Hint: Do no use mathematical calculations.

Solution: Put the box on the corner of the desk and measure one width of the tin. Move the box down that amount, keeping a side on the box along the desk. Now take the ruler and measure from the corner of the desk to the appropriate corner of the box. That's the measure of the diagonal.

9.9. You have two ropes and a lighter, each rope burns in exactly 60 minutes, and not evenly (meaning that some parts of the rope burn faster than another part), you want to measure 45 minutes, how do you do it?

Solution: Light one rope at both ends, and the other rope from one end. When the first rope has completely burned, exactly 30 minutes have passed! Then light the other end of the second rope (while the other end is still burning). When the second rope is burned completely, 45 minutes have passed.

9.10. Builders spend a lot of time staking out houses. When doing so, they need accurate measurements of lengths and angles. How could you stake out a house that is guaranteed rectangular?

Solution: This will vary with available equipment. A surveyor's transit makes this easier. Another way—put a stake in the ground. Measure the long side and put a second stake. Tie a string from the first to the second stake but do not cut it. Make a 3, 4, 5 right triangle beyond the second stake and a right angle is established. Measure the short side length along the perpendicular string and drive a third stake. Run a string on the diagonal between the first and third stake, marking the midpoint (fold it in half). Use a string the same length as the diagonal, starting from the second stake (where you made the right angle), passing it over the midpoint of the other diagonal. The endpoint of the second diagonal string determines the location of the fourth stake, establishing a rectangle.

9.11. How can you weigh a car with graph paper and a tire pressure gauge?

Solution: Each wheel of the car must be on a piece of graph paper. Mark the sheets so you know which tire was on which sheet of paper. The sides and the front or back edge of the tire will be marked by the dirt from the tire. Mark the remaining edge of the tire on the paper using a pencil, pen, etc. Move the car off the paper. Compute the area of the marked region on each sheet of graph paper. Measure the air pressure in each tire and mark it on the respective piece of graph paper. Air pressure is measured in pounds per square inch. You have the area in terms of square inches and the product of the two values will give you the weight supported by that tire. The sum of the four products will be the weight of the car. There are many sources of error in this activity. If someone is in the car when it is moved onto the graph paper, that weight will be a part of the car. Accuracy in marking the tire print will influence the resultant area. The tread grooves are not supporting weight.

9.12. How many lines of symmetry are there for: equilateral triangle, square, rectangle, circle?
Solution: An equilateral triangle has 3 lines of symmetry. A square and rectangle each have 4. A circle has an infinite number.

9.13. Make a kite. There are all kinds of measurement needs in the production.

9.14. If there are 12 1-cent stamps in a dozen, how many 37-cent stamps are in a dozen?
Solution: 12.

9.15. How long will it take a mile-long train traveling 40 miles an hour to go through and completely out of a mile-long tunnel?
Solution: 40 miles an hour means a mile is covered every 1.5 minutes. It will take 1.5 minutes for the train to be completely in the tunnel and another 1.5 for it to get completely out. Thus, it takes 3 minutes.

9.16. Suppose you have 3 bags, 2 of which contain gold weighing 1 ounce per nugget and the third bag contains gold, which weighs 1.1 ounce per nugget. How can you determine which bag contains the real gold with only one weighing?
Solution: Take 1 nugget from the first bag, 2 from the second, and 3 from the third. If the total weight is 6.1 ounces, the real gold is in the first bag. 6.2 ounces puts it in the second bag. 6.3 ounces means it is in the third bag.

9.17. There is one in every minute, one in each month, two in the next millennium, and yet only one in a million years. What is it?
Solution: M. Some people will claim N, but there are 3 of them in Next milleNNium and the problem called for 2.

9.18. What is the next letter in the sequence? S, M, H, D, W, M, _?_
Solution: Y You are telling time. Seconds, Minutes, Hours, Days, Weeks, Months, *Years.*

9.19. Two cars travel between two towns that are 200 miles apart. Car A averages 50 mph one way and 40 mph on the return trip. Car B averages 45 mph both ways. Do the cars travel the total distance in the same amount of time?
Solution: No. A takes 4 hours one way and 5 the other for a total of 9 hours. B takes about 8.8 hours.

9.20. A window is a square, one yard on a side. It lets in too much light so half of it is covered. After the covering, the window is still a yard high and a yard wide but it lets in only half as much light. How can that be?
Solution: Join the midpoints of the sides of the original window. You now have another square, half the area of the original. But, the height and width are now the diagonals of the square, which will be a yard each.

9.21. How long will it take to cut a 40-yard-long piece of cloth into 40 one-yard-wide pieces if each cut takes a minute?
Solution: 39 minutes. The after 38 cuts, there will be one piece that is 2 yards long. The 39th cut will create pieces 39 and 40. Note that if, after the first cut, the fabric pieces are placed on top of each other, the second cut would create four

10-yard-long pieces. There are a variety of ways to go from there, by continuing the doubling process, cutting what is there in pairs, and so on. However, accuracy would suffer.

9.22. You have two U.S. coins that have a total value of $0.35. One of them is not a quarter. How can that be?

Solution: The other one is the quarter.

9.23. What U.S. coin doubles its value when it half is removed?

Solution: Half-dollar.

9.24. How many birthdays does the average person have?

Solution: One.

9.25. An XYZ Corp. motorcycle courier was sent from headquarters to pick up a letter at the local airport.

The plane was ahead of schedule. An XYZ Corp. bicycle courier started toward headquarters with the letter from the airport. After the bicycle courier had been riding a half hour the two couriers met. The motorcycle courier took the letter and returned to headquarters.

The motorcycle courier arrived back at headquarters 20 minutes ahead of the anticipated time.

How many minutes early was the plane?

Solution: The motorcycle courier would have taken 20 minutes to go from where they met to the airport and back (remember, arrival back at headquarters was 20 minutes ahead of schedule). So, the motorcycle courier was 10 minutes from the airport when the two couriers met. These 10 minutes plus the 30 minutes the bicycle courier had been riding makes the plane 40 minutes ahead of schedule.

9.26. A simple protractor can be constructed that will help students understand the basic protractor measures. Fold the long edge of a rectangular piece of paper in half. That fold will be a 90° mark. Fold that resultant 90° angle in half by using the midpoint of the initial folded side as a vertex and placing the fold on top of the half-length of the original side of the paper. The ensuing OR subsequent fold will be 45°. The process could continue to 22.5°, but accuracy quickly becomes an issue. Still, a continuance does give an idea of what is happening.

Solution: See discussion in text.

9.27. Congruent circles are cut out of a rectangular piece of metal (see Fig. 9.15) to make lids. What percent of the metal is wasted? Would the answer differ if the size of the circles being used is changed?

Solution: Using the diameter of the circle as the linear unit, the dimensions of the rectangle are 3 units by 10 units, and the total area 30 square units. The area of each circle is $\pi r^2 = 3.14 \left(\frac{1}{2}\right)^2 \approx 0.785$ square units, and we have 30 of them for a total of approximately 23.55 square units used for the lids. We need to subtract this quantity from the total area of the rectangle: $30 - 23.55 \approx 6.45$. This is how much metal was wasted. The percent of metal wasted is $\frac{6.45}{30} \approx 21.5\%$.

On the changing circles, yes, the answer would differ. This could lead to a discussion of limits. If the diameter of the circle decreases, the number of circles increases. As the diameter goes to zero, the circle becomes a point. When that happens, there is no waste.

10.1. Create parallel line segments that are a toothpick length apart on a sheet of paper (where the toothpick is perpendicular to the segments). Hold a toothpick at least a foot above the center of the paper and drop it. Record the number of times the toothpick touches one of the segments you created. If you drop more than one toothpick at a time, and if one toothpick leans on another, but passes over one of the created segments, that counts as a touch. The larger the number of drops, the better the results. Compute

$$\frac{2(\text{total number of drops})}{\text{number of hits}}.$$

Solution: This is called Buffon's Principle and a simulation of it can be found at: http://www.mste.uiuc.edu/reese/buffon/buffon.html. The computation should approximate π_.

10.2. Pair the students. Have one student hide a coin in one hand and have the other student guess which hand holds the coin. Repeat the activity 10 times, recording the total number of correct guesses. Then switch places. Which of the two students is the best guesser? Is this an example of a random event? If you say this is not a random event, explain why it is not. If you say this is a random event, explain why it is.

Solution: Results will vary. No, this is not random. The student holding the coin could be using a scheme and the one guessing could be influenced by prior guesses as a choice is made.

10.3. Fold a rectangular piece of paper (2 inches by 4 inches is a good size) in half so the fold is parallel to the shorter side. That paper can land one of three ways, fold up, fold down, or on edge, as shown in Fig. 10.9. What is the probability for each of the three cases? Would placing tape on the paper bias the results? Would the placement of the tape matter? Would the tape use matter?

Bias?

FIG 10.9.

Solution: Answers will vary.

10.4. When a paper cup is dropped, there are three realistic ways it can land: on its top, bottom, or side, as shown in Fig.10.10. What is the probability of each occurrence?

Side

FIG 10.10.

Solution: Answers will vary. It is interesting to get students to bring cups from different fast food establishments.

10.5. Which box plot (A, B, or C) displays the same data as the histogram (see Fig. 10.11)? Explain how you know the data are the same.

Solution: {1800, 1900, 2000, 2100, 2100, 2200, 2200, 2200, 2300, 2300, 2400, 2400, 2400, 2400, 2400, 2400, 2400, 2500, 2500, 2500, 2500, 2600, 2600, 2600, 2600, 2700, 2700, 2800, 2900, 2900}. The middle of this data, the median, is 2400. Answers A and B both have a median of 2400. That eliminates answer C as a correct answer because its median is over 2400. The first quartile is the median of the first half of the data, which is 2200 in this example. The first quartile is at 2200 in A and 2000 in B. Thus B is ruled out as a correct response. The third quartile is the median of the upper 50% of the data. Quartile 3 is 2600, which is confirmed in box plot A.

10.6. Find the difference between the mean and median of the first 20 counting numbers.

Solution: The first 20 counting numbers are 1, 2, 3, 4, 5, 6, 7, 8, 9, 10, 11, 12, 13, 14, 15, 16, 17, 18, 19, and 20. The mean is

$$\frac{1+2+3+4+5+6+7+8+9+10+11+12+13+14+15+16+17+18+19+20}{20}$$

$= 10.5$ while the median is $\dfrac{10 + 11}{2}$ or 10.5. Therefore, the difference is zero.

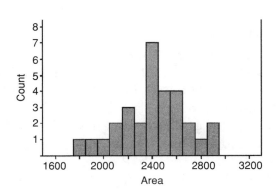

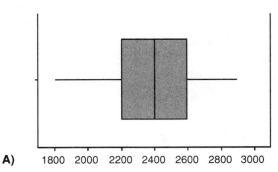

A)

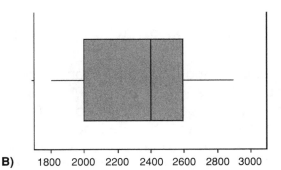

B)

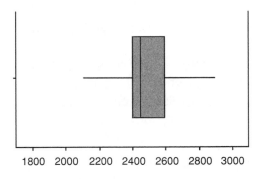

C)

FIG 10.12.

10.7. Using the following stem-and-leaf plot, find the median.

```
0 | 1 1 2 5 9
1 | 0 0 0 2 3 4 5 8 9 9
2 | 4 5 5 5 6 8 9 9
3 | 2 2 2 3 7 8
4 | 1 8 8
5 | 3
```

Solution: Think of each entry in this example as a 2-digit number. The tens digit is to the left of the vertical segment and the ones digit is to the right of that vertical segment. Thus, the fourth row represents 41, 48, and 48. There are 33 numbers in the data set. The 17th number is 25, and it is exactly in the middle, so it is the median.

10.8. Suppose you have two cubes, each of which has 3 red faces, 2 blue faces, and 1 green face. Roll the cubes and record the color that lands facing up. What is the most likely event? In order to answer this question, you must construct a theoretical probability distribution for this experiment.
Comment on your results. Does this theoretical distribution surprises you?
Solution: Solution: the theoretical distribution is the following:

		Die 1				
		R	R	R	B	B	G
Die 2	R	(R, R)	(R, R)	(R, R)	(R, B)	(R, B)	(R, G)
	R	(R, R)	(R, R)	(R, R)	(R, B)	(R, B)	(R, G)
	R	(R, R)	(R, R)	(R, R)	(R, B)	(R, B)	(R, G)
	B	(B, R)	(B, R)	(B, R)	(B, B)	(B, B)	(B, G)
	B	(B, R)	(B, R)	(B, R)	(B, B)	(B, B)	(B, G)
	G	(G, R)	(G, R)	(G, R)	(G, B)	(G, B)	(G, G)

Probability of (R, R) $= 9/36 = \dfrac{1}{4}$

Probability of (R, B) $= 12/36 = \dfrac{1}{3}$

Probability of (R, G) $= 6/36 = \frac{1}{6}$

Probability of (B, B) $= 4/36 = \frac{1}{9}$

Probability of (G, B) $= 4/36 = \frac{1}{9}$

Probability of (G, G) $= \frac{1}{36}$

It might be surprising to see that the probability of (R, B) (remember that order is not important; R, B and B, R, counts as the same) is the highest, not the one for (R, R), which at first impression seems to be the highest.

10.9. Drop balls of different shapes and sizes. Drop each ball 3 times from 10 different dropping heights. Record the bounce height in centimeters for each trial on a data table.

Solution: Answers will vary according to ball size and shape. Table may look like Table 10.5.

TABLE 10.5

Height of Drop (cm)										
Height of Bounce (cm)										
Bounce divided by Height										

11.1. Pick a number.

- Double it.
- Add 4 to the product.
- Divide the sum by 2.
- Subtract the original number.
- What do you get?

Solution: x. 2x. 2x + 4. (2x + 4)/2 = x + 2. x + 2 − x = 2. The statement "Subtract the original number" can be changed to "Subtract 2" and the final result will be the number selected by the student initially. Similarly, rather than multiplying by 2 and adding 4, multiply by 3, add 12 and divide by 3. Getting students to this stage of flexibility is a big help in many classroom algebraic procedures.

11.2. Pick any prime number greater than 3.

Square it.

Add 15.

Divide by 12.

What is the remainder?

Solution: Remainder = 4. Primes greater than 3 are of the form $6n + 1$, n is a counting number. $(6n + 1)^2 = 36n^2 + 12n + 1$. Add 15 and get $36n^2 + 12n + 16$. Divide by 12 and get a remainder of 4.

11.3. (36)(42) = 1512 = (63)(24)
(26)(93) = 2418 = (62)(39)
In the two examples above, reversing the order of the digits in both factors gives the same product. Find other examples where this is true.

Solution: Let a, b, c, and d be the digits involved.

$$(ab)(cd) = (10a + b)(10c + d)$$
$$= 100ac + 10bc + 10ad + bd.$$
$$(ba)(dc) = (10b + a)(10d + c)$$
$$= 100bd + 10bc + 10ac + ac.$$

Setting the two expressions equal to each other and subtracting 10bc and 10ad from both sides, $100ac + bd = 100bd + ac$. This can only be true if $ac = bd$.

11.4. Two objects have a combined price of $6.80. One of the objects sells for $6.00 more than the other. What is the cost of the less expensive object (it is not $0.80)?

Solution: c = cost of less expensive. c + $6.00 is cost of other. c + c + $6.00 = $6.80. 2c = $0.80. c = $0.40.

11.5. Pick a counting number.

Square it.

Find the square of the next largest counting number.

Find a fast way to find the second square.

Solution: If x is the first number, its square is x^2. The next counting number is $x + 1$. $(x + 1)^2 = x^2 + 2x + 1$. So, take the initial square and add twice the original number plus one.

11.6. Given a quadratic expression $ax^2 + bx + c$, a, b, and c can always be determined by the following process:

Substitute 0 into the expression. Record the result (call it R).

Substitute 1 into the expression. Record the result (call it S).

Substitute 2 into the expression. Record the result (call it T).

Record the result of $S - R$ (call it U).

Record the result of $T - S$ (call it V).

Record the result of $V - U$ (call it W).

$a = 0.5W$

$b = U - 0.5W$

$c = R$

Ask someone to use a quadratic expression and give you R, S, and T. You can then identify the expression used.

Solution: $x = 0$ gives C or R. $x = 1$ gives $a + b + c$ or S.

$x = 2$ gives $4a + 2b + c$ or T. $S - R$ gives $(a + b + c) - c = A + B$ or U.

$T - S$ gives $(4a + 2b + c) - (a + b + c) = 3a + b$ or V.

$V - U$ gives $(3a + b) - (a + b) = 2a$ or W.

11.7. Pick any counting number

Add the next highest counting number.

Add 9 to the sum.

Divide this new sum by 2.

Subtract the original number.

What do you get?

How does this work?

Solution: Let n be the selected number. $n + (n + 1)$. $n + (n + 1) + 9 = 2n + 10$.

$(2n + 10)/2 = n + 5$. $(n + 5) - 5 = n$. It works for integers.

Rational numbers will work in special cases, but not in general.

11.8. Pick any counting number.

Multiply it by 6.

Add 12 to that product.

Divide the new sum by 3.

Subtract 2 from the new missing factor (quotient).

Divide this missing addend (difference) by 2.

Subtract the original number from this missing factor.

Add 9 to the missing addend.

What is the sum? Why will the sum always be the same?

Solution: Let a be the selected number. $6a$. $6a + 12$. $\dfrac{6a + 12}{3} = 2a + 4$.

$2a + 4 - 2 = 2a + 2$. $(2a + 2)/2 = a + 1$. $a + 1 - a = 1$. $1 + 9 = 10$.

Integers and rational numbers give a sum of 10.

11.9. A similar problem like $1 + 2 + 3 + \cdots + 100$ can be used to show the basics of what Gauss did to solve the problem.

$$1 + \quad 2 + \quad 3 + \quad 4 + \cdots + \quad 98 + \quad 99 + 100$$
$$100 + \quad 99 + \quad 98 + \quad 97 + \cdots + \quad 3 + \quad 2 + \quad 1$$
$$\overline{101} + \overline{101} + \overline{101} + \overline{101} + \cdots + \overline{101} + \overline{101} + \overline{101}$$

The sum would be $(100)(101)$ or the number of terms times the sum of the first and last term. However this sum is twice what it should be to answer the problem because of using each addend twice. So, the final answer of 10,100 should be divided by two, giving 5050, the sum of the first 100 consecutive counting numbers. Do a similar problem where the constant difference between terms is not one, trying to determine a rule for the solution.

Solution: N terms and a sum of $(n + 1)$ for each term gives $[(n)(n + 1)]/2$. In the extension, using $3 + 6 + 9 + \cdots + 300$ would give $3(1 + 2 + 3 + \cdots + 100)$. Starting with other than one means the sum of the values prior to the starting point would need to be subtracted.

11.10. Pick any counting number.

Square it.

Square the counting number that is one larger than your initial selection.

Find the difference between the two squares.

Subtract one from that missing addend (difference).

Divide the new missing addend by two.

What do you get? Why will this work every time?

Solution: Let the selection be x.

$$x^2(x + 1)^2 = x^2 + 2x + 1 - x^2.$$

$$x^2 + 2x + 1 - x^2 = 2x + 1.$$

$$2x + 1 - 1 = 2x.$$

$$\frac{2x}{2} = x.$$

This does work with integers and rational numbers. When dealing with negatives, be careful with the signs. For example, select $^-7$ as the initial number. $^-6$ is the next highest. The problem then is $(^-6)^2 - (^-7)^2 = {^-13}$. Subtracting 1 gives $^-14$. $\frac{-14}{2} = {^-7}$.

11.11. Using a standard rummy deck of cards, let ace = 1, jack = 11, queen = 12, and king = 13. Also, clubs = 4, diamonds = 5, hearts = 6, and spades = 7.

A volunteer should do each of the following:

Select a card, show it to the class (not you) and return the card to the deck.

Add the card value and the next highest counting number.

Multiply the sum by 5.

Add the value of the suit to this product.

Tell the answer.

At this point, you look through the deck and find the initial card. How does this work?

Solution: x = selected card. x + 1 = next counting number. k = suit value.

$x + (x + 1) = 2x + 1$. $5(2x + 1) = 10x + 5$. $10x + 5 + k$ is the value given you. Subtract 5. The ones digit gives the suit and the tens or hundreds and tens gives the card.

11.12. Use a software program that does symbolic manipulations and graphs to do the following:

Graph $y = x^2$.

What are the coordinates of the lowest point?

Graph $y = x^2 + 3$.

What are the coordinates of the lowest point?

Graph $y = x^2 + 4$.

What are the coordinates of the lowest point? If you need to do more examples, make up your own. Predict what $y = x^2 + 6$ will look like.

What are the coordinates of the lowest point?

Describe what the graph and coordinates of the lowest point of any equation like $y = x^2 + a$ (where a is any counting number) will be.

Solution: Responses will vary.

11.13. Use a software piece that does symbolic manipulations and graphs to do the following:

Graph $y = x^2$. What are the coordinates of the lowest point?

Graph $y = (x + 3)^2$. What are the coordinates of the lowest point?

Graph $y = (x + 5)^2$. What are the coordinates of the lowest point?

If you need to do more examples, make up your own.

Predict what $y = (x + 7)^2$ will look like.

What are the coordinates of the lowest point?

Describe what the graph and coordinates of the lowest point of any equation like $y = (x + a)^2$ (where a is any counting number) will be.

Solution: Responses will vary.

12.1. Break the code: $A = 2$, $B = 0$, $C = 2$, $D = 0$, $E = 3$, $F = 3$, $G = 2$, $H = 4$, $I = 2$, $J = 2$, $K = 4$, $L = 2$.

Solution: You need to find the number of endpoints of each of the letters. That is, A has two endpoints, B has none because it can be made continuously and closed, etc.

12.2. How many pennies can you arrange so each penny touches every other penny?

Solution: See Fig. 12.34 for solution.

FIG 12.34.

12.3. Arrange 6 pennies in the form of a cross (see Fig. 12.23). Move the coins and form two straight rows with 4 pennies in each.

Solution: Put the left most penny on top of the one in the vertical center. That puts 4 per row (assuming thickness is not a factor).

12.4. Design a single piece that will fit into all 3 of these holes (see Fig. 12.24).

Solution: See Fig. 12.35 for possible solution.

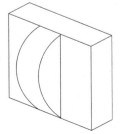

FIG 12.35.

12.5. Start with a square piece of paper. Draw the largest circle possible inside the square, cut it out and discard the trimmings. Draw the largest square possible inside the circle, cut the square out and discard the trimmings. What fraction of the original square piece of paper has been cut off and thrown away?

Solution: The shaded triangular regions in Fig. 12.36 represent the cast off regions and they total half of the original figure.

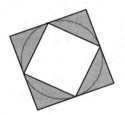

FIG 12.36.

12.6. Given a circle, use 3 line segments (curved, straight, open, or closed) to divide the circle into 8 sections.

EXTENSION: How can this be done so that all 8 sections have the same area?

Solution: 2 of the segments are diameters. The third is another circle.

12.7. Use 9 toothpicks to form 3 squares, each side of which is a complete toothpick length.

Solution: See Fig. 12.37 for possible solution.

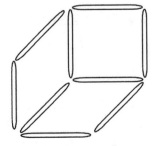

FIG 12.37.

12.8. One person holds a ball representing the earth. A second person holds a ball representing the moon. How far apart do the two people need to stand to show the distance between the earth and moon?

Solution: About 10 times the circumference of the earth ball.

12.9. How can you cut a square layer cake that has been frosted on the top and all sides (but not the bottom) so that each piece will contain the same amount of frosting and the same volume of cake?

Solution: Locate the center of the cake. Divide the cake by drawing segments from the center to each corner. Each side could be subdivided, as long as the lengths of the subdivisions are all the same. Each triangle has the same base and height so they all have the same area. Assuming the layer cake is flat, the volume of cake will also be the same for each piece.

12.10. Make two squares and four triangles from 8 toothpicks without breaking, overlapping, or bending them.

Solution: See Fig. 12.38 for possible solution.

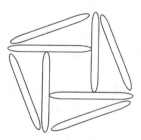

FIG 12.38.

12.11. How can a nursery person plant ten trees in five rows, having four trees in each row?

Solution: See Fig. 12.39 for solution.

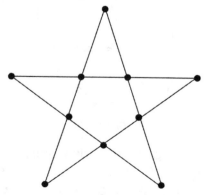

FIG 12.39.

12.12. A kid is full after eating a six-inch round pizza. Assuming there are two kids with the same eating capacity, what size pizza (only one) should they order so they will both be full and there will be no leftovers?

Solution: They will need to order an 8½-inch round pizza. This will give them approximately double the area of the 6-inch round pizza.

12.13. Arrange 6 toothpicks to form 4 congruent equilateral triangles. The side length of each triangle must equal the total toothpick length.

Solution: The shape will look like a tetrahedron.

12.14. Using 24 toothpicks, how many squares can be made using 6 toothpick lengths on a side? Five toothpick lengths on a side? Four toothpick lengths on a side? Three toothpick length on a side? Two toothpick lengths on a side? One toothpick length on a side? For some of these, you may not be able to use all the toothpicks.

Solution: Six, 1. Five, 1. Four, 1. Three, 2 or 3. Two, 3, 6, or 7. One, 6 or 7. Note that it was not said the squares had to be congruent.

12.15. A 9 by 12 rectangular rug has 1 by 8 hole in its center, the hole being 4 feet from either long side and 2 feet from either short side. The sides of the hole are parallel to the sides of the rug. Cut the rug into exactly 2 pieces, which can be sewn together to make one 10 by 10 square rug.

Solution: Starting 2 from the bottom and top of opposite long sides of the original rug, cut 1 wide and 2 high until the hole is reached from each side. Move the bottom piece over one and up two to fit the pieces together.

12.16. How many squares are there on a checker board?

Solution: 204. There is one 8 × 8 square; four 7 × 7 squares, nine 6 × 6 squares, ..., and sixty-four 1 × 1 squares.
$1 + 4 + 9 + 16 + 25 + 36 + 49 + 64 = 204$.

12.17. Draw a line segment on a piece of paper. Sub-divide that segment into 3 segments. Using the 3 segments as side lengths, construct a triangle. NOTE: Geometry software helps.

Solution: It is likely that, unless the students know the sum of the lengths of any 2 sides of a triangle must be greater than the third, some students will not be able to construct a triangle. This can also be used to develop a probability discussion: "How many students were able to construct a triangle?" NOTE: This assumes the students are not aware of the theorem about the statement dealing with the idea that the sum of the lengths of any 2 sides of a triangle must exceed that of the third.

12.18. A rhombus is formed by 2 congruent equilateral triangles sharing a common side. The midpoints of each of the sides of the equilateral triangles are formed, creating 8 smaller congruent equilateral triangles. Remove 4 segments from this figure and leave exactly 4 triangles. NOTE: A toothpick is easily used to represent one side of the smaller triangle.

Solution: There is more than one solution.

12.19. Use a circle of a given radius and circumscribe a regular triangle, square, pentagon and hexagon and decagon. What conclusion can be made about the areas of each of the circumscribed figures?

Solution: As the number of sides increases, the area of the regular polygon decreases, approaching the area of the circle.

12.20. Why are manhole covers round? EXTENSION: Is there any other shape that will work? Assumptions with this question are: the cover and the hole are the same shape; the hole is at least a meter across at the narrowest point; if the hole and lid were concentric figures, the lid would be slightly larger (1.02 m across at the narrowest point) than the hole.

Solution: Manhole covers are round to prevent the lid from falling down the hole. As the number of sides of a regular polygon increases, the situation will begin to react like a circle. An equilateral triangle will not work because the altitude is less than the length of a side and, if the altitude line were held parallel to the plane of the hole, the lid would fall through the hole when the lid was held sufficiently close to the side of the hole. Rouleau-figures with an odd number of sides will work.

12.21. Each of the 6 figures is made up of 5 congruent squares. All 30 of the squares are congruent. What is the question?

Solution: Responses may vary: What is the area? What is the perimeter? What is the maximum perimeter? What is the minimum perimeter? How many squares in all? Which shapes, when folded, form a box with no lid?

12.22. Out of construction paper, make small boxes that are 2 × 1 × 2.5 units on a side. How many of these boxes can be fit in a larger box that is 4 × 6 × 5 units? The assumption is that the maximum number of small boxes possible will be placed in the large box. Describe your solution. Is your solution unique?

Solution: 24. The answer is unique.

12.23. Cut a scalene triangle out of a piece of construction paper. Label the 3 vertices and tear them off the triangle. Place the 3 vertices together with each vertex being at a common point and adjacent to some existing piece after the first one is placed. Describe your result. EXTENSION: Do this activity using a piece of software.

Solution: The 3 vertices form a straight angle. Using the software forces the student to become conversant with the use of computer technology and requires a greater command of geometry that doing it concretely. (IBM's Geodraw [found on Geometry One or Geometry Two], Sunburst's Supposers, Geometer's Sketchpad). Make a tool like the one shown (see Fig. 12.36). The piece with the circular hole in it is made from cardboard. Make similar pieces with holes: square, equilateral triangle, isosceles trapezoid, and parallelogram. Predict what the projection of each hole will be. Use the tool to check your prediction. Explain your result.

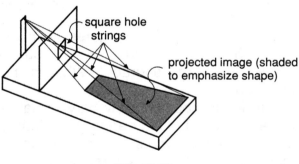

FIG 12.36.

12.24. Cut a quadrilateral out of a piece of construction paper. Label the four vertices and tear them off the quadrilateral. Place the four vertices together with each vertex being at a common point and adjacent to some existing piece after the first one is placed. Describe your result.
EXTENSION: Do this activity using a piece of software.
Solution: The 4 vertices form a 360-degree angle. Using the software forces the student to become conversant with the use of computer technology and requires a greater command of geometry that doing it concretely. (IBM's Geodraw [found on Geometry One or Geometry Two], Sunburst's Supposers, Geometer's Sketchpad).

12.25. Cut a pentagon out of a piece of construction paper. Label the 5 vertices and tear them off the pentagon. Place the 5 vertices together with each vertex being

at a common point and adjacent to some existing piece after the first one is placed. Describe your result.
EXTENSION: Do this activity using a piece of software.
Solution: The 5 vertices form a 540-degree angle. Using the software forces the student to become conversant with the use of computer technology and requires a greater command of geometry that doing it concretely. (IBM's Geodraw [found on Geometry One or Geometry Two], Sunburst's Supposers, Geometer's Sketchpad).

12.26. Cut a hexagon out of a piece of construction paper. Label the 6 vertices and tear them off the hexagon. Place the 6 vertices together with each vertex being at a common point and adjacent to some existing piece after the first one is placed. Describe your result.
EXTENSION: Do this activity using a piece of software.
Solution: The 6 vertices form a 720 degrees angle. Using the software forces the student to become conversant with the use of computer technology and requires a greater command of geometry that doing it concretely. (IBM's Geodraw [found on Geometry One or Geometry Two], Sunburst's Supposers, Geometer's Sketchpad).

12.27. Compare the results from problems 12.25 through 12.27. Describe the generalization. Are the results different for polygons that are concave?
Solution: $(N - 2)180$ degrees where $N =$ the number of sides in the polygon.

12.28. Imagine a canyon spanned by a bridge that is exactly 1 mile long. The bridge has no expansion joints in it, so when it heats, it bows up. On one hot day the bridge lengthened to 1 mile plus 2 feet. Approximately how high above its original position before the bridge heated is the midpoint of the bridge?

Solution: 72.67 feet. Join the midpoint of the flat bridge with the midpoint of the bowed bridge with one endpoint to form a right triangle. The hypotenuse is 2641 feet and one leg is 2640 feet. The remaining leg is the height and can be calculated by using the Pythagorean theorem.

12.29. Describe a roller blade. In your description, use appropriate geometry terminology.

Solution: Answers will vary.

12.30. Use a piece of software to perform the following constructions: bisect an angle; bisect a line segment; equilateral triangle; rhombus. The assumption is that you will not use any automatic capabilities to do these tasks if the software possesses it. NOTE: this is a good one because of the NCTM objectives, which include use of technology.

Solution: Answers will vary.

12.31. Create a large scalene triangle. In that triangle construct the 3 medians. Write a conclusion about the medians. Measure each median part and write a conclusion about the ratio of the lengths. NOTE: This activity is much more meaningful to the student if software that allows the triangle and medians to be altered is used.

Solution: The software allows students to conclude that the 3 medians are always concurrent and the point of concurrence divides each median in a ratio of 2:1.

12.32. Create a large scalene triangle. In that triangle construct the 3 angle bisectors. Write a conclusion about the angle bisectors. NOTE: This activity is much more meaningful to the student if software that allows the triangle and medians to be altered is used.

Solution: The 3 are concurrent.

12.33. Create a large scalene triangle. In that triangle construct the 3 altitudes. Write a conclusion about the altitudes.

NOTE: This activity is much more meaningful to the student if software that allows the triangle and medians to be altered is used.

Solution: The 3 are concurrent.

12.34. Create a large scalene triangle. In that triangle construct the perpendicular bisector for each side. Write a conclusion about the perpendicular bisectors. NOTE: This activity is much more meaningful to the student if software that allows the triangle and medians to be altered is used.

Solution: The three are concurrent.

12.35. Create a large scalene triangle. In that triangle construct the angle bisector for each angle, the altitude to each side, the perpendicular bisector for each side, and the median for each side, marking the point of concurrence for each set. Which 1 of the 4 points of concurrence is not always collinear with the other 3? The line through the 3 collinear points is called the Euler Line, named after Leonard Euler (1707–1783) who was the first to prove the 3 points concurrent. NOTE: This activity is much more meaningful to the student if software that allows the triangle and medians to be altered is used.

EXTENSION: Do the same construction with an isosceles triangle and an equilateral triangle. In each case describe conclusions you reach.

Solution: The angle bisector will not be on the Euler line.

12.36. Create a scalene triangle with exterior angles. Measure the exterior angles. Write a conclusion about the sum of the measures of the exterior angles.

NOTE: Geometer's Sketchpad is particularly useful for this activity because it permits changing of the triangle. The calculator feature can be used to show the measurements changing in real time.

Solution: Sum of exterior angles is 360°.

12.37. Create a quadrilateral with exterior angles. Measure the exterior angles.

Write a conclusion about the sum of the measures of the exterior angles.
NOTE: Geometer's Sketchpad is particularly useful for this activity because it permits changing of the triangle. The calculator feature can be used to show the measurements changing in real time.
Solution: Sum of exterior angles is 360°?

12.38. Given a point, 6 equilateral triangles can be placed adjacent to each other so all space about that point is occupied. Since each angle of the equilateral triangle is 60°, the sum of all the angles about the point is 360°. Can this be done with any triangle? That is, given any triangle, can it be arranged so that 6 of them are placed so the sum of the angles about a point is 360°?
Solution: This can be done many ways. For example,

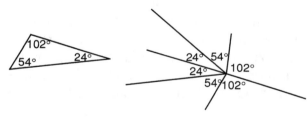

FIG 12.37.

12.39. Create a pentagon with exterior angles. Measure the exterior angles. Write a conclusion about the sum of the measures of the exterior angles.
NOTE: Geometer's Sketchpad is particularly useful for this activity because it permits changing of the triangle. The calculator feature can be used to show the measurements changing in real time. Write a conjecture dealing with the exterior angles of a polygon. Does it matter if the polygon is concave?
Solution: Sum of exterior angles is 360°.

12.40. The 9-point circle, formed with any scalene triangle, passes through the point at the base of each altitude, the midpoints of each side, and the midpoint of each segment joining a vertex to the point shared by the 3 altitudes. Do the construction. NOTE: Software is particularly useful with this problem.
Solution: Answers will vary.

12.41. Triangles can be shown congruent by a variety of methods. Which of the following constructions can always be used to give a triangle congruent to a given triangle? Show a construction to demonstrate any that will not always yield a triangle congruent to the given triangle. SSS, SSA, AAA, ASA, SAS, SAA.
Solution: Answers will vary.

12.42. Construct a circle with center G. Mark points M, N, and H on the circle, connecting M and N with G, and M and N with H. Measure angle MHN and angle MGN. Move the points on the circle or change the radius of the circle. Write a conjecture describing this situation.
NOTE: Software that permits moving points and changing radii of circles is particularly useful with this problem.
Solution: Answers will vary.

12.43. Gather several cylinders, and a tape measure or calipers. A calculator will be useful for this activity. Measure the circumference and diameter of each of the cylinders. Divide the circumference by the diameter. Arrange the results in a table and write a conjecture to accompany the information shown in the table.
Solution: $\dfrac{C}{d} = \pi$.

12.44. Create a nonregular pentagon (ABCDE). Locate a point F and predict what the rotated view of ABCDE will be. After the figure is rotated, create a line segment and predict what the reflected view of the rotated figure will be.
EXTENSION: Would the end result be the same if the initial figure was reflected then rotated about a point? Do similar activities increasing the complexity of the initially used figure.

Solution: Answers will vary.

12.45. Squares can be used to cover a plane with no overlaps and no gaps or spaces. (This is called a pure tessellation of a plane). An example would be a piece of graph paper. Equilateral triangles can be used to tessellate a plane as well. Squares and equilateral triangles are regular polygons. Name another regular polygon that can be used to tessellate a plane. Other shapes, that are not regular, can be used to tessellate a plane. A rectangle would be an example. Create an n-gon that will tessellate a plane where N > 4 and sketch your result. If more than one shape is used, the shapes are said to tessellate the plane, but because more than one shape is used, it is not a pure tessellation. A flattened version of a soccer ball is an example. Use two or more shapes to tessellate the plane and sketch your result.

Solution: Regular hexagon tessellates the plane. Other responses will vary.

12.46. Cut a circle into an even number (8 or more) congruent "pie shaped" pieces with the length of each straight side being equal to the length of the radius of the circle. Put the pieces together as shown in (see Fig. 12.38). Notice that the shape looks like a parallelogram. Assume the edges made up of curves are straight (the more pieces used, the straighter the long side appears). What is the length of the "parallelogram"? What is its height? What is its area? Because the "parallelogram" was made from a circle, what is the area of the circle?

Solution: length = (pi)r. Height = r. Area = (pi)r^2.

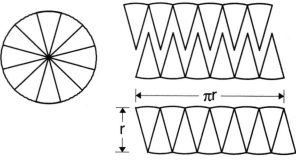

FIG 12.38.

12.47. The Golden Ratio is $\frac{1 + \sqrt{5}}{2}$ or 1.618034. A segment divided into two parts where the ratio of the entire segment length is to the longer segment as the longer segment is to the shorter is divided satisfies the requirements for being a Golden Ratio. The Fibonacci sequence (1, 1, 2, 3, 5, 8, 13, 21, 34, 55, 89, 144, 233, 377, 610,... where each new term is defined by adding the two preceding terms) can be used to provide approximations that approach the Golden Ratio. Provide at least 4 decimal equivalents from different adjacent number pairs in the Fibonacci sequence. Describe a conclusion about adjacent pairs of Fibonacci numbers and the Golden Ratio.

Index

People, Knowledge and Technology:

What Have We Learnt So Far?